Women of the Press in Nineteenth-Century Britain

Women of the Press in Nineteenth-Century Britain

Barbara Onslow

First published in Great Britain 2000 by
MACMILLAN PRESS LTD
Houndmills, Basingstoke, Hampshire RG21 6XS and London
Companies and representatives throughout the world

A catalogue record for this book is available from the British Library.

ISBN 0–333–68378–1

First published in the United States of America 2000 by
ST. MARTIN'S PRESS, LLC,
Scholarly and Reference Division,
175 Fifth Avenue, New York, N.Y. 10010

ISBN 0–312–23602–6

Library of Congress Cataloging-in-Publication Data
Onslow, Barbara, 1937–
    Women of the press in nineteenth-century Britain / Barbara Onslow.
        p.   cm.
    Includes bibliographical references and index.
    ISBN 0–312–23602–6
    1. Women in journalism—Great Britain—History—19th century. 2. Women
journalists—Great Britain—Biography. I. Title.

PN5124.W58 O59 2000
070.4'082'0941—dc21

00–033333

This book is printed on paper suitable for recycling and made from fully managed and sustained forest sources.

10   9   8   7   6   5   4   3   2   1
09   08   07   06   05   04   03   02   01   00

Printed and bound in Great Britain by
Antony Rowe Ltd, Chippenham, Wiltshire

In memory of my parents
Raymond and Eleanor (Helen) McGrath

Contents

Acknowledgments

Firstly, I am grateful to the following for permission to quote from manuscripts in their possession: the Mistress and Fellows, Girton College, Cambridge, for extracts from the Bodichon, Davies and Parkes Papers, the Principal and Fellows of Somerville College, Oxford, for quotations from the Somerville papers and Reading Borough Libraries for extracts from the Mitford Collection. My gratitude goes beyond mere formal acknowledgement. Kate Perry at Girton and staff at the Reading local history centre were enormously helpful on a personal level. At the Bodley I was granted generous access to the stacks, and staff in Oxford and at the reserve at Newland Park did all in their power to make my hours there fruitful and comfortable – and to make sure I escaped through the labyrinth at closing time! The library staff at my own University, in particular those managing the Publishers' Archive, Special Collections, Periodicals and Inter-Library Loans, deserve a special mention for their support. The staff at Colindale, too, made the treks down the Tube well worthwhile. Librarians and archivists, despite the heavy pressure under which they are all working today, assisted cheerfully and, from my point of view, to great effect.

My thanks are also due to kind colleagues in the UK and the United States who ploughed through drafts of chapters and whose valuable comments, suggestions and corrections were made with such generosity and encouragement. In particular I must mention Patrick Leary, especially, for his stimulating correspondence on editorship and networking, Kay Boardman, Dennis Butts, Loraine Fletcher and Geoff Harvey. I hope it is obvious from my references how greatly I am indebted to individual scholars in my work on particular writers and themes, especially those who shared their unpublished work and ideas, among them Robert Patten (the vexed question of what editors do), Andrea Bloomfield (Clementina Black), and Bernie Lightman (science popularizers). Sally Mitchell not only shared her discoveries on Cobbe but provided me with her own transcripts of letters.

To those working in this field it goes without saying that no one attempting a book such as this could but owe a huge debt to pioneers of periodical scholarship, some of whose work is cited in my bibliography, but I say it again for the benefit of any general readers coming fresh to this subject. Some of my ideas for various chapters were explored in papers to conferences and I should like to mention how helpful I found the ensuing discussions, and how valuable – indeed essential – conferences such as those of the *Research Society for Victorian Periodicals* are for anyone working in this inter-disciplinary field. The Internet will I believe now be regularly occurring in 'Acknowledgements' and deservedly. The kindness of those many subscribers to the Victoria list with whom I corresponded privately is impressive. This was brought vividly home to me when explaining how I use email to an accountant friend, ignorant of the arcane workings of academia and whose own use of the internet is for business. 'That is wonderful! The sharing of knowledge –' he exclaimed, 'a true Renaissance community of scholars.' To all you nineteenth-century members of that 'Renaissance community' out there – thank you. I should like also to thank my own head of department who has done his best to arrange such alleviation of my normal workload as he could to enable me to complete the manuscript.

Finally, it is usual I know, to thank fulsomely one's devoted spouse for boring chores like typing and checking manuscripts, and to accept full personal responsibility for any errors. In this case, in truth, the author can do neither. The responsibility for errors must be at least partly shouldered by my journalist husband, whose assistance to me has been, in the traditions of his profession, to insist on opening a well-chilled bottle whenever I wilted or faltered at my task. That at least was one hazard few of my subjects had the luck to be faced with.

Preface

Nineteenth-century periodicals are seductive, not to say addictive. Which of us looking for a reference has not been sidetracked by a report of some man's last minutes before ascending the scaffold? Or, seeking a review by Meynell, been tempted to copy out a recipe for Pigeons *à la Marquise*?[1] Paused in *London Illustrated* before a children's fancy-dress party, or wasted time solving a 150-year-old conundrum? To those of a certain age an advertisement for patent custard powder or boot polish carries childhood memories of products still going strong several decades later. Partly this book was fuelled by my addiction to such ephemera. But other factors are to blame.

Many readers will have discovered the delights of periodicals via a serial novel. It was in *Household Words* that years ago, researching Mrs Gaskell, I first lit upon Dickens's journalism, and was struck by the impact that periodical publishing must have had upon Victorian novelists as well as their serial-reading public. Over subsequent years of teaching nineteenth-century literature I became increasingly attracted to the journalism which offers insights into nineteenth-century culture difficult to obtain in any other way, and which indeed was part of its formation. Finally, having begun my own postgraduate career as a newspaper journalist, I was intrigued by the notion of nineteenth-century women ploughing the same furrow.

The germ of this book lay in a happy coincidence of a change of job giving at last some time for research, the arrival of my computer allowing me to collect and access data, and the RSVP Manchester Conference, bringing me into contact with academics distant in space, but close in interests. At that time I was working on the links between Victorian women's fiction and their periodical writing. It was the realization that the book I wanted did not exist that finally determined the direction of my project. There have been studies of individuals like Geraldine Jewsbury, Margaret Oliphant, Barbara Bodichon and Emilia Dilke, useful but specialized. More general works on the subject did not quite fit my bill. Alison Adburgham's *Women in Print* concentrates on the eighteenth century, indeed suggesting that by the 1830s women's energy and enthusiasm for journalism had died out. Laurel Brake's *Subjugated Knowledges*, while dealing with gender as an issue, concentrates largely on male journalists. Margaret Beetham's *A Magazine of*

Her Own? focuses on women's papers. I sought fruitlessly for an overview of women and nineteenth-century journalism, a map of how they fitted in to what I presumed a very masculine world. The die was cast. I should have to write it myself.

Modern scholarship, notably the Wellesley project, has made great strides in identifying anonymous contributors. Their personalities, however, often remain shadowy. In bringing some of these pioneers back into the spotlight I hope others will be encouraged to make them the focus of their own studies, and that this overview of the female contribution to nineteenth-century journalism may illuminate work in other fields. My approach is broadly historical and mildly feminist. Virginia Crawford contrasting the attitudes of nineteenth-century English and French feminists suggested that in England women worked to alter the law in practical ways; whereas in France they aimed to change the idea, the view of women.[2] Like those Englishwomen's, mine too has been a pragmatic rather than theoretical project, filling in some of those blank spaces on the map.

The structuring of chapters was not easy. Few women worked for only one title; many undertook different kinds of periodical work. There is a fluidity between genres which makes absolute categorization both difficult and misleading. One may confidently assert that Mrs Humphry's *Truth* 'Letters' and, say, Eliza Linton's *Saturday* 'Girl of the Period' series and George Eliot's *Westminster* essays are all different species. But where along a spectrum would one place Mrs Humphry's 'Letters', Florence Fenwick-Miller's *Illustrated London News* columns and 'The Wares of Autolycus' writings or, come to that, Mrs Oliphant's 'Looker-on'? They share some distinctive features. Yet in terms of genre some 'Autolycus' pieces might usefully be compared with earlier *Saturday* essays, and Meynell's criticism be discussed alongside George Eliot's. Sometimes it was easy to place a writer firmly in particular chapters. With others I had to make pragmatic decisions on grounds of available material and space; Christian Johnstone, one of the century's earliest women newspaper editors, appears in the chapter on editors, not newspaper journalists, even though she undoubtedly wrote much copy. She could indeed equally have joined the reviewers.

Further, I offer in advance an apology and an explanation. Naturally I tried, in dealing with the several hundred women on whom I collected details, to avoid misidentification and misattribution, but I cannot claim certainty. Apart from practices of anonymity and pseudonymity, the variable use of maiden and married names, and family kinship of writers perpetuating names across and down the generations, are all confusing for the researcher. If their contemporaries so frequently muddled A B E (Amelia Blandford Edwards) and her cousin M B E (Matilda Betham-Edwards) it is perhaps not surprising if I too have mistaken others. I should welcome corrections.

Next, some matters of terminology. Readers should note certain words like 'reporter' or 'editor' which today refer to either sex in the earlier nineteenth century often implied a man. So *The Morning Chronicle* of 2 January 1850, pleased at the success of *Eliza Cook's Journal*, queried her use of 'editor'. '[W]e observe that the lady disclaims the feminine when referring to herself officially.' I should also explain that terms such as 'conservative', 'radical', 'activist' and 'feminist' are used here in their looser nineteenth-century sense. Social historians will be aware of the myriad nuances with which their historical contexts endowed these words, but non-specialist readers may need warning that a stance on one issue did not necessarily indicate a 'parallel' stance on another. Women advocating women's employment opportunities or property rights, could yet oppose suffrage. Over time, too, some modified their views. It is salutary to find Janet Courtney, who once assisted with the *Anti-Suffrage Review*, writing admiringly of women's trades unionists and remarking that had Millicent Garrett been younger when women were enfranchised she would have been 'in her right place as the first woman in the Cabinet'.[3] I hope this book fairly reflects this multiplicity of viewpoint.

1
Introduction

Some nineteenth-century women sought social and political change through activism, social work, public speaking, or fighting for a rôle in professions like medicine. Others chose to influence by writing. One of the most effective channels for their views was the newspaper and periodical press. Yet outside the cohort of specialist scholars women's collective contribution to journalism has largely gone unregarded. Much has been written, in studies of individual periodicals and the press in general, about male journalists. It seems timely to assess women's involvement in this press. Of course many names of these women will be familiar to scholars specializing in nineteenth century feminism, female novelists or periodical reviewing, but more general readers, familiar with, say Florence Nightingale, are often unaware of the work of Harriet Martineau, Geraldine Jewsbury and Margaret Oliphant, let alone Eliza Linton, or Anna Maria Hall.

Women's lack of visibility is not surprising since early studies of the press concentrated primarily upon influential journals, publishers and editors. Newspapers were often linked with party political support and their editors were unlikely to emerge from the disenfranchised. Financing and managing the press required funds and skills few men, with all their educational advantages, could summon. Women, with limited access to finance and little encouragement to engage in business, found it difficult to enter the realms of publishing and editing at national and provincial daily newspaper level. Thus male editorial predominance in the high-profile sectors of the press has clouded women's editorial work elsewhere. So a seminal early study of journalistic history whose very aim was to concentrate on the individual rather than the enterprise virtually ignores the involvement of women. T H S Escott subtitled his book (1911) 'A Study of Personal Forces' but significantly entitled it *Masters of English Journalism*.[1] The personal forces to him were largely those who founded influential papers and those who dictated their policies. Harriet Martineau, 'the she-Radical', merits less than five lines, yet her achievement was such that she was lobbied to support political causes and approached to edit a political journal. Martineau, too, is the only woman journalist to be accorded a chapter entry in Joseph Hatton's sketches of London's 'pens and papers of the day'[2] though a thin scattering of names occurs in lists of contributors. Even in the accounts of individual journals a major female contributor can mysteriously disappear. One of the most prolific writers of fiction for *Fraser's* between 1836 and 1850, Selina Bunbury, is simply not mentioned in its history.[3]

Until recently in the realms of literary reviewing where women – major producers of novels – were clearly an important force, George Eliot apart, their work had little attention from academics. In the 1980s Nigel Cross found standard surveys virtually excluding them from the 'non-imaginative categories', with writers like Eliot and Oliphant 'invariably listed as novelists' – their essays, histories and reviews being considered trivial by comparison.[4] Of course one must select, but the emphasis bore out only too well Dale Spender's summary of the work of female novelists: 'Once acclaimed, but now denied. This is the problem of women writers.'[5] During their lifetimes Harriet Martineau, Anne Mozley, Eliza Linton and Frances Cobbe, for instance, all had periodical work republished in volume form. Women themselves certainly celebrated the work of their predecessors. The period saw a flurry of series like the *Englishwoman's* 'Women Writers of the Century' which included the Jewsbury sisters, Lady Blessington and Caroline Norton. Frances Cobbe reminded her readers how many of the books in a lending library were written by women, instancing then household names like Jewsbury, Martineau and Jameson.[6]

Other factors affect women's visibility. Some women acquiesced in a supportive rôle to their journalist husbands so that their informal but very real contribution is masked. Modern feminist scholarship has rescued from obscurity those writers who advocated female suffrage, but less attention has been paid to those on the other side of the debate. Writers like Margaret Oliphant, Eliza Lynn Linton and Mary Ward are only just beginning to receive their due critical attention; Fanny Kortright is virtually unknown; Flora Shaw known but avoided. Why study women's journalism? Arguably their feelings, particularly on women's rights, are more powerful in their fiction. Perhaps. But often their *opinions* on their society are more explicit in their journalism, and cover a wider frame of reference. Mrs Oliphant uses journalism not fiction to articulate her suspicion of globaliz-ation. On almost every issue, from vivisection to the penal system, from fashion to astronomy, women had their say in the press.[7] If we mine their writings only for opinions on one question – however important – we are getting a very partial intellectual picture. Nor must we forget the centrality of periodicals within the literary market. Our reading of nineteenth-century fiction should be enhanced by an understanding of their operation and a study of reviews. Finally I believe the ways in which women negotiated entry into journalism and the reasons it attracted them, enrich our appreciation of nineteenth-century women's lives.

Early press historians and nineteenth-century pressmen were aware of the existence of women journalists. They were conscious of them as anomolous. 'Miss Mitford, among the earliest of lady journalists' wrote Escott, mentioning her presence at James Perry's dinner-parties. Edward Porritt noting that at the dawn of the nineteenth-century the 'woman journalist was already at work', cited names like Mrs Graham writing for the *Representative* in 1825, Caroline Norton and Hannah More. Leonard Raven-Hill remembered Clotilde Inez Graves, whose career began in the 1880s, as the 'first woman journalist'. The 'first and greatest of women journalists' was Gardiner's tribute to Harriet Martineau at the Jubilee of the *Daily News*.[8] Such identifications depended upon personal knowledge but also upon one's definition of journalist.

As John Gross succinctly put it, 'The main reason why a satisfactory history of journalism will never be written is that journalism itself is such an elastic term.'[9] Even today defining the journalist's rôle is not simple. The editors of *The Sun*, *Country Life* and *Exchange and Mart* may share certain functions but their different aims, objectives and target readerships ensure that their day-to-day work has little in common. Journalism had probably greater divergences in the nineteenth-century. There were distinctions, in self-perception and sometimes practice, between the educated gentleman editor who felt he belonged in the exalted echelons of 'higher journalism' and the commercially-minded penny pressman who emerged from the ranks of hacks and printers. Morley, editor of the *Pall Mall*, was accused of treating a news-paper as 'a medium for circulating leading articles' and lacking 'the journalist's *flair* for news – a coming crisis, an interesting personality, a picturesque event...'.[10] There were similar deviations in the interpret-ation of terms like 'reviewer' or 'sub-editor'. Career patterns were variable, encompassing the regular contributor to a monthly, the full-scale freelance with a portfolio of varying commissions from different journals, and the staff-man, and (rarer) staff-woman.

With women, whose careers were fragmented, definition is even more difficult. Reference books and listings of women writers characterize them differently. Cobbe appears as 'journalist and feminist' and 'philanthropist, writer', Linton as 'novelist, essayist' and 'novelist, journalist', Meynell as 'poet/journalist' and 'poet and essayist', Geraldine Jewsbury as 'novelist, journalist' and merely 'novelist' and so forth. In 1893 Blowitz defined a journalist as 'any man who lives exclusively by regularly writing in a regularly appearing journal; who is a part – not necessarily a fixture, but a normal part – of a regularly organized sheet, and who treats in one or more such sheets, living questions whatever their nature'. For him 'a man who writes exclusively in reviews is not a journalist, or he has ceased to be one'.[11] This definition would not only exclude by its choice of pronoun the subjects of this book, but many nineteenth-century men who operated within the 'higher journalism'. My definition is much broader. I have adopted the more inclusive interpretation of the Society of Women Journalists which admitted that 'a good many' of its Presidents and Vice-Presidents 'can scarcely be called journalists, in the ordinary acceptation of the term .... although all of them have occasionally been contributors to newspapers or magazines....'[12] Among these officers were Mrs Crawford and Mrs Humphry who were clearly journalists. Mrs Meynell, Mrs Craigie ('John Oliver Hobbes') and Mrs Stannard ('John Strange Winter') were undoubtedly better known for work in other genres, yet journalism played a sufficiently important part in their writing lives for it to be as unreasonable to omit them in this overview as it would be to ignore the journalism of male lawyers and politicians in a study of male journalists.

My subject is a vast one, but I hope the individuals serving as exemplars in each chapter will bring into sharper focus the different sections of the panoramic picture. Because of the importance of London, this is predominantly a study of women working for nineteenth-century journals published in England, to a lesser extent elsewhere in Britain. But my subjects were by their nature outward-looking and exploratory so this concentration in no way implies an insular approach, and certainly not an exclusively 'English' one. One of the striking things I discovered was the influence of what one journalist called 'the Irishry'. Frances Cobbe, Flora Shaw, Anna Maria Hall, Charlotte Riddell, Mrs Humphry were among the many born and bred in Ireland. Others were European or American by birth; many were seasoned travellers; many were fascinated by foreign cultures.

Although nineteenth-century periodical material is increasingly available on CD-ROM and via the internet, accessibility is still a problem. Of course the ideal is to go back to the original. Even then it will usually be a bound, possibly rebound, volume shorn of its advertisements and preliminary matter. But for students access even to this can be difficult. I have chosen, therefore, to refer to at least some examples of writing reprinted in modern editions. The somewhat arbitrary demarcation lines of a century are not strictly adhered to. There are references to the later years of the eighteenth century and the opening ones of the twentieth, but a hundred years conveniently allows for the overlapping of different generations. One can have some sense of both constants and change, and this particular hundred years saw change dramatic enough in the press itself, and equally striking cultural shifts. It is something of a constraint upon any tendency towards comfortable generalization to keep meeting small instances that disturb one's complacent judgements.

For example, the social-problem novel of the 1840s so altered the literary landscape that it seems to belong in a real world quite the other side of the watershed from the pastoral idylls of *Our Village*. It comes as something of a shock to find Mary Mitford calling *Mary Barton* a 'charming story', and still herself figuring in 1850 alongside the Howitts and Geraldine Jewsbury in a new weekly.[13] Here we are on the verge of the early women's rights campaigns and Miss Mitford, she of the charming bonnets, violets and brinded cows in Thomson's illustrations, is still publishing. Though amongst her circle of women friends she numbered pioneers like Harriet Martineau and Anna Jameson, she would surely scarcely have anticipated such a radical shift in women's expectations? Her knowledge of Womens' Rights was her sense of filial duty. And yet – one now recalls – her own life and many of the characters in her sketches, exemplified female creativity, resilience and stamina, those very qualities which fed the successes of the Women's Rights movement. The charming bonnets are but the nostalgia of that decade of the New Woman, the 1890s.

With such a time-span how to choose? So many women. So many periodicals. I started with a select few – names one couldn't ignore – and my list grew longer and longer. The final choice was largely governed by the availability of reliable attributions for unsigned work, accessibility of material, and the desire to cover a spread of journalistic genres. Apart from recent work done on women's magazines, the most 'visible' female journalists are largely identified contributors in the quarterlies and more literary monthlies, or those known through their polemical writings in national newspapers and feminist journals. Nevertheless, within these constraints and limited space, I acknowledge women's work in the provincial press, specialist and 'popular' magazines. There are inevitably numerous interesting women, who appear only fleetingly. For quite different reasons Jane Loudon, Camilla Toulmin, Agnes Clerke, Eliza Meteyard, Clotilde Graves, Mrs Humphry, Mrs Cashel Hoey, Florence Marryat, Frances Low, Scottish and Welsh journalists like Mrs Batey of the *Dundee Advertiser* and Sarah Jane Rees, editor of the Welsh women's magazine *Y Frythones*, all deserve attention I cannot give them.

I have drawn upon a range of sources. The nineteenth century was acutely aware of itself as the age of burgeoning literacy and popular literature. Writers, particularly in the second half of the period, had much to say about the processes of writing, newsgathering and the profession of the journalist. By the end of the century the periodical press seems to find its own history an endless source of copy. Looking back from the 1890s journalists like Wemyss Reid describe the dramatic changes over the decades of their own careers. There are articles about the phenomena of periodicals themselves, comparisons between the British and foreign newspaper press, discussions of the relationship between press and parliament, advice to would-be contributors and on careers in journalism, and fictional accounts of the 'Struggle for Fame' to borrow the title of Charlotte Riddell's novel on earning a crust in 'New Grub Street'. Amongst my other contemporary sources are biographies, memoirs, letters and runs of the periodicals themselves. The picture of the conditions in which women journalists operated is a conflicted one, not just because, as one would expect, individual women experienced journalism differently and sectors of the press varied considerably in their organization. Different sources paint different images. Autobiographies structure lives.[14] Journalists' memoirs, can be vague and inaccurate. Editors' letters to authors, as Robert Patten suggests, may be an unreliable guide to proprietorial policies, when editors sheltered behind their publishers in declining work or limiting payment.[15] Recollections may not always be accurate in detail, but do at least reflect later judgement upon experience. At 65, Matilda Betham-Edwards may have mis-remembered seeing her first publication in *Household Words*, but in describing the thrill of Dickens's approbation she betrays her mature astonishment at the good luck her youthful 'audacity' produced.[16]

The novels tend to stress the exhaustion of the work and the betrayal of ideals. Fictional protagonists who turn to Fleet Street as a literary apprenticeship find themselves driven remorselessly down-market by the perceived demands of 'the public' and the over-supply of writers to meet it; those who are ambitious as journalists and strive to be honest and influential, like Lady Colin Campbell's Darrell Blake, are corrupted by the machinations of political hostesses. The same writer may often present her experience in contrasting ways. Eliza Lynn Linton's *Sowing the Wind,* in emphasizing the physical and psychological hardships of journalism, masculinizes the heroine in ways she herself painstakingly resisted in her public and private persona. Charlotte Riddell's novel, *The Rich Husband,* gives a much grimmer picture of the apprentice writer hawking her work round the publishers than years later she gave to Helen Black. Now not only Bentley and Charles Street but even Newby and his nice capable 'woman of business' Miss Springett are remembered kindly. 'Everyone was good to me in those days.' Is she more cautious in an interview? Has time dulled the memory? Or was the reality sensationalized for the demands of fiction?[17]

By the mid-1890s a depressing, superficial Bohemianism taints the image of journalism in women's novels. Mrs Everard Cotes's 'Daughter of Today' is a small-town American girl out for independence, fame and fortune, who sinks to 'stunt girl.'[18] Ella Hepworth Dixon's 'Modern Woman', Mary Erle, ventures into a sleazier Fleet Street than her creator's memoir tells of. Mary's is one where the divorce case of the day filling columns of print 'like some foul miasma ... poisoned every-thing' and the supercilious young editor of a new fashion magazine commissions her on the strength of her social connections to write a society column 'smart, you know and just a wee bit malicious' yet where magazine fiction must be '*banal*, the pretty-pretty, the obvious'. Ella's own experiences in the late 1980s on Yates's *The World* seem much jollier – journalism mingling with dancing and dining-out, 'white tulle skirts and natty little laced-up bodices' for the evening instead of 'inky fingers'. She remembers with amusement how her own 'terribly "knowing"' story was considered by one of her young dancing-partners not quite the sort of thing a girl should read.[19] She dismisses her powerful novel as a rather dismal book.

The image of the journalist which emerges from the fiction of the final decades of the century is multi-faceted. *New Grub Street,* the best-known novel, reveals its depressing, sleazy side. But even writers whose professional experience has been not unsimilar to Gissing's can reflect the tough energy of Fleet Street more sympathetically. When Charlotte

Riddell uses a cynical, 'unbelieving' Fleet Street hack as a listener in the narrative frame of one of her best ghost stories, 'Sandy the Tinker', he represents *trustworthy* scepticism.

The main chapters of this study cover writers in various journalistic genres, reviewers, periodical essayists, correspondents and columnists, functions such as editor and reporter, and work in different sectors of the press. In the final three chapters the emphasis shifts, focusing specifically on women's motives and opportunities for getting involved in journalism, illustrated by several different career patterns from the professional author to those for whom the press was primarily a platform. I have tried to reflect their work on different types of publication: newspapers, national and provincial, magazines with differing target readerships. The questions with which I began my researches, and that are raised in these first two chapters, continually surface throughout the book. What kind of women turned to journalism? How did they get started? To what extent did they support each other? What problems did they face and how did they tackle them? How far did they professionalize? To what extent was their work concentrated in the 'quality' market and did women restrict themselves to 'ladylike' subjects? How successfully did they harness the power of the press? Was there a 'Woman's Voice'? There are other books which deal in much more detail with such developments as technological advances, the commodification of the press and the professionalization of journalism, and with such issues as the links between journalism and book-publishing, editorial independence and anonymity.[20] Still, given the broad scope of my theme it may be useful for the general reader to have a brief introduction to these topics by way of scene-setting. The outline in these opening chapters has an emphasis on how women's participation in the press was affected by them.

The century was a dynamic and exciting period in terms of experimentation both editorial and technical, an age which saw the establishment of the newspaper press and the profession of the journalist as we understand it today, but also saw its own unique flowering of the literary quarterly and monthly. Walter Houghton persuasively suggests that the great prose writers of the age were, like Arnold, not writers of books, but of periodical literature.[21] The excitement of newspaper journalism is encapsulated by J M Robertson Scott when he wrote of Stead that his conception of the journalist 'kindled a fire in the hearts of a few young men (and a smaller company of women with, at that time, limited access to education and no votes) who, if they lacked the endowments of the *Pall Mall* editor, had some of his fervour and conviction. They were minded to enter Journalism as some entered the Church.'[22]

It was quite acceptable for men to be working in other professions concurrently with being effective journalists.[23] For women this cut two ways. Editors were accustomed to the correspondent journalist delivering or having copy collected but few women could benefit from another professional specialism. On the other hand, those who wanted to work from home, or only sporadically, benefited. The energetic could piece together a viable portfolio just as men like Escott and George Saunders did. Ethel Lloyd helped her sister with her column for the *Globe*, wrote regular fashion and society articles for the *Telegraph*, whilst being a staff member of the *Lady's Pictorial*.[24] The openness of journalism could be a mixed blessing. It needed no apprenticeship. Men with no 'previous newspaper drudgery', the smart MP, successful barrister or popular novelist 'may slip into an editorship or be made a principal leader writer in preference to men of long standing in the office, who perhaps have to teach him his duties and correct his blunders'. These drudges easily obtained work as young and eager novices, but often denied promotion, found it a trade easier to enter than abandon. 'The traditions and infirmities of Grub Street [of the eighteenth century] are not extinct.'[25] Equally the rise in social status of journalists made it more respectable, thus more appealing to women yet co-incidentally made it harder for them to compete from that 'women's sphere' beyond gentlemen's clubland.[26]

It was a period of both technological change within the press and of the development of mass readership.[27] Fox Bourne, the nineteenth-century press historian, looking back at the turn of the century discerned four stages roughly corresponding to each quarter-century (though the latter two overlap): Press Persecution, Press Liberation, Press Cheapening and Press Widening (by which he understood the development of niche markets and innovatory journals). Or as Hulda Friederichs put it: in the early 1870s 'the extraordinary number and variety of papers offered to-day was not yet thought of'.[28] Fox Bourne's chronology may be rough and ready, and too slickly developmental, but he encapsulates well the nineteenth-century press perception of itself. Changes in taxation, together with improved printing technology, had a marked effect on the commercial prosperity of the press, enabling the publishing of the penny newspaper and many more pages – and ads – for your penny.

In the 1830s new and lively journals sprouted up following reductions in the punitive advertisement tax and stamp duties. In 1832

Christian Johnstone's *Tait's*, was complaining that 'The workings of these great enlighteners, the newspapers, might have been increased a hundredfold, but for the short-sighted policy which has landed them with a tax so heavy as to place them far beyond the purchase-price of the majority.' A year after the easing of the advertisement tax in 1834, *Tait's* lowering its price argued that the significantly increased reading public was not a monied public. The market had changed. The new technology and the logistics of fixed and variable costs relative to circulation figures made price cutting inevitable. It was the day of the 'cheap periodicals' – 'a new era in literature'.[29] Cheap periodicals could reach very high sales. *Household Words*, even at twopence, achieved a circulation of 40 000, but that was somewhat later. The abolition of the stamp duty in 1855, the expanded, more leisured middle-class and what Wilkie Collins called 'The Unknown Public'[30], the newly-literate working-classes, together led to an explosion in periodicals and a new style of fiction publishing. Serialized fiction became a vital weapon in the magazine circulation fight, though it was a two-edged sword. A successful work could trigger a dramatic increase in circulation; a dud one remorseless decline. Still, for fiction writers and editors alike, the serial became essential.

Successful dailies reached not only a wide readership but, equally important for some writers, an influential one. In the early decades of the century sales of tens of thousands were a thing to wonder at. *The Times* in 1817 had a daily circulation of between 6 000 and 7 000 though sensational news could, then as now, have a dramatic impact. (The trial of Queen Caroline in 1820 more than doubled sales.) By 1878 the ordinary circulation of *The Times* was over 60 000; by 1898 Harmsworth's highly successful *Daily Mail* averaged 800 000.[31] Whilst for a period the stamp acts established publication numbers, establishing actual readership is fraught with difficulty. Class and numbers of readers are difficult to calculate. Readership of magazines was likely to be greater than stamp duty figures indicate. Cheaper papers passed from hand to hand; dearer ones were housed in circulating libraries; the spread of reading-rooms and local libraries continued the trend. Expensive bound volumes were kept long after their publication date. Their contents were not ephemeral but might influence readers months – even years – after their original date of issue. Writers potentially had a much wider area of influence than circulation figures alone indicate. On the other hand the sheer diversity of contents in popular magazines means that – serial fiction excepted – we have little evidence as to how much of any paper was read.[32] By the end of the century readers looked to periodicals for something quick and light. '[T]he day of leisurely reading was gone.'[33] Older journalists may have regretted this, but the new generation accepted it as in the nature of things.

From the journalist's point of view the scale of the changes is illustrated by the image of the mid-century editor of a daily newspaper in Eliza Linton's fictionalized editor of the *Morning Chronicle*, Cook, with the options facing Janet Hogarth's husband, W L Courtney, in the 1890s. Linton's fictional version of Cook was at once 'manager, editor, and part proprietor' and his 'grinding at the daily mill' kept his wife and family 'above the pressures of want, if not lifting them into the airy latitudes of luxury'. Courtney apparently refused the *PMG* editorship because with his family commitments 'the *Daily Telegraph* offered a safer background and better pension prospects'.[34] 'Pressures of want' in such circumstances is a nineteenth-century phrase; 'pension prospects' that of the twentieth.

The technological changes which Christian Johnstone remarked were to accelerate at a rate she could never have envisaged. In the early 1880s the *Daily Telegraph* had ten Hoe's machines together turning out an average of 120 000 copies an hour, utilizing a new 'patent roller composition, which did away with frequent 'cleaning up' and boasted a clear image.[35] By 1900 Hoe & Co, whose first small cylinder newspaper press had been constructed in 1833, advertised its latest 'octuple newspaper perfecting press and folder' as the 'Largest Newspaper Machine in the World' capable of producing an eight page paper at the speed of 96 000 copies per hour and even sixteen pages at 48 000. This was double the speed of its machine of seven years earlier. There had also been significant changes in periodical illustration. For the Jubilee even *The Times* 'blossomed out in colour with a supplement – made in Germany' and most dailies were illustrated. Monthlies and weeklies had been illustrated for decades, and even the dailies had for special events inserted large wood-engravings, but as Joseph Pennell, writing in the *Nineteenth Century* pointed out, the printing methods were different. The technical advances in typesetting and speed of printing actually militated against high quality daily newspaper illustration. Monthlies and weeklies were printed on a stop cylinder or flat press. The illustrations for the *Century* went to press three months in advance. Dailies in the 1890s run off rotary presses produced copies at around 20 000 an hour. The monthly therefore needed many presses, operating at a much slower rate, for its production and could easily afford to take one out for experimental purposes. When Pennell had been involved in experimental work on the *Chronicle* the financial risk had been contrastingly high.[36]

The proliferation of direct competitors and the spread of the cheap magazines posed problems for the finances of periodical publishers. The would-be contributor, however, though facing increased competition of her own as more girls rushed into journalism, enjoyed a widening market for her work. Indeed Florence Fenwick-Miller saw Martineau as a pioneer in an almost inevitable process which linked the emergence of such women directly to technological advances.

> The printing-press which multiplies the words of the thinker; the steam-engine, which both feeds the press and rushes off its product, and the electric telegraph, which carries thought around the globe make this an age in which mental force assumes an importance which it never had before in the history of mankind. Mind will be more and more valued and cultivated, and will grow more and more influential; and the condition and status of women must alter accordingly... we can no more prevent it than we can return to hornbooks, or to trial by ordeal....[37]

It is almost a Whig view of progress and enlightenment.

One of the key features of nineteenth-century journalism which Fox Bourne's broad categorization sweeps over is that of anonymous publication. The practice was of great importance to women. The unsigned article both aided and hindered women. It shielded their sex and gave their press personæ the authority accorded to men. Bessie Parkes saw women's journalism flowering as the periodicals flourished. The two demands, that of the magazines for 'short, graphic papers, observation, wit and moderate learning' and that of the women for paid work they could do at home, met. Yet women's identities were hidden. 'If editors were ever known to disclose the dread secrets of their dens' the public would learn of the women 'whose unsigned names are Legion; of their rolls of manuscripts, which are as the sands of the sea.'[38]

Barbara Bodichon claimed that two-thirds of the writers in *Chambers's Edinburgh Journal* (*sic*) were female, and that 'Mrs. Johnson'[39] of Edinburgh was for years the real editor of the *Inverness Courier*, the principal paper in the north of Scotland. In mentioning Christian Johnstone she hints at one of the difficulties in estimating the amount of journalistic work carried out by women *viz.* that they often worked 'behind' men, doing the work but not receiving the credit for it. Mrs Johnstone chose to remain elusive. The practice, however, was a contested one. Charlotte Tonna thought that an editor ought to be willing to be identified, and in a tough, competitive world anonymity, Mrs Baron-Wilson suggested, could mask the drudgery of writing for a living.

> Do people ... ever ask how are supplied the multitudinous works which issue from the press, unheralded by any sign as to the authors of them? The ... sparkling or profound magazine articles; reviews; leading articles; contributions to our excellent cheap literature such as swarm at the railway termini ... The producers of these riches are ... working authors, often possessed of great talents and erudition.

But they lacked the iron constitution and business sense necessary for fame.[40]

This shield was, for all but the most factual reporting, virtually abolished by the 'New Journalism' of the final decades. The journalist was now promoted above her article. The 'New Journalism', a phrase attributed to Matthew Arnold, was characterized by a popularization that evoked the emotions of its readers, and engaged its expanding public in a commercial enterprise that viewed itself as part of a process of democratization.[41] T P O'Connor argued both that the personal side of public men was intrinsic to 'the history and wisdom of a nation', and that the press was a bastion against fraudsters and conmen. Stylistically it was characterized by its emphasis on 'human interest', what O'Connor called its 'more personal tone', and the narrative format of 'the interview'.[42]

The concept of 'New Journalism' was both partially created by and contested by the press.[43] One of its practitioners, Hulda Friederichs, saw Newnes's 'lighter' papers as supplanting the staple reading matter of the newly literate – the 'mawkish serial story' and 'sporting publications with their pernicious influence' for which the 1870 Education Act had created a market which would last 'while the world stands'.[44] Other journalists echoed her welcome to expansion and innovation, despite reservations about its excesses. The *Saturday Review* surveying the growth of the British press as the phenomenon of the last half-century remarked the value of advertising and circulation and capitalization to secure 'early intelligence and brilliant contributors'. 'The marvellous inventions of modern science are all in favour of the moneyed journals.' Yet the new distribution and intelligence-gathering mechanisms the railways and telegraph, produced more pressurized working conditions for correspondents and editors alike.[45] The brash side of 'New Journalism' is seen in *Tit-Bits* with its accompanying sensational modes of advertising – carrying a copy guaranteed £100 insurance in the case of death in a railway accident – and competitions with dramatic prizes. A seven-roomed house was the prize for a short-story competition; £1 000 for a serial produced over 20 000 entries (only to be won by Grant Allen).[46] But it was not all as feather-brained as Arnold claimed. Stead's investigative journalism was as much a part of it as the flamboyant advertisements for *Tit-Bits*. The interviews, gossip column and format innovations like cross-heads were hall-marks of his work, but Stead, with his reforming instincts, used them to more serious effect than Newnes.[47]

Criticism focused upon the deleterious effects of advertising and intrusion of privacy. The veteran Eliza Linton was shocked by some of the journalistic manifestations, strongly objecting to being asked 'to submit yourself to the inquisitorial acumen of a girl young enough to be your granddaughter'.

> The editor of such-and-such a paper [asks] ... you to see a young lady, whom you knew when ... she was a golden-haired child, and to answer her on such topics as she shall see fit to broach. The girl is a good girl, a clever girl, a pretty girl, and one whose literary career you would willingly help. But a certain feeling of self-respect and dignity, as well as regard for the general fitness of things, makes you decline..... you are asked to bare your soul, scarred and seamed and tear-stained as it is with sorrow and experience, to the gaze of a fresh young maid ... With the creation of the interviewer, reticence on the one side is destroyed – on the other, honour goes by the board.

She regretted equally the decline of the scholar editor who knew how to choose his contributors, and the advent of 'young lions ... fatuously credited with literary, scientific, political and artistic omniscience'.[48]

Certain problems seem to have been shared by all female journalists, whether British, mainland European or American, but there were differences dependent upon local political circumstances as well as cultural conditions. The new journalism of America was brassier and more sensational than its English counterparts; it is difficult to imagine the women journalists of London in the 1890s turning themselves into stunt girls. Perhaps because nineteenth-century American society was much less cohesive, and the Civil War itself a great disruption, some early women journalists seem to have been much more adventurous and eccentric than their British counterparts. Yet in other ways they faced the same prejudices that Victorian would-be journalists met.

There are reflections and precursors of Martineau and the Langham Place group in Margaret Fuller, who like early English women journalists was precocious and enjoyed an unusual education from her lawyer and politician father; she could read Latin at six. 'Her vigorous mind struck flint on many of the issues of the day.'[49] Her first *Tribune* article was a two-and-a-half-column front page analysis of Emerson's essays. Ross considered her articles 'choked with detail ... editorial in tone ... her point of view was advanced and her style was always scholarly'. She apparently shocked the *Tribune* readers by writing sympathetically of prostitutes. Again in the 1850s Jenny June and Fanny Fern's 'tears, fashions, recipes and women's problems out ... [in] the open' were just a little more advanced than their English equivalents. The developments in the later decades, however, particularly the 'yellow press' and the stunt girls had no exact British parallels, although American influences affected the 'New Journalism'.

In one sense American journalists were nearer to their English counterparts than those just across the channel. Though the veteran Paris correspondent, Emily Crawford, found Mme Claude Vignon and 'Séverine', both moulded as journalists by political events, inspirational, she thought the profession 'well-nigh closed' to women in France, because of 'the pest of gallantry' and narrow ideas of a Frenchwoman's place in society.[50] British society may have been more open in its views than the French, but its womenfolk who successfully entered journalism were still in many ways atypical. Many of them enjoyed a rather cosmopolitan life. Extensive travel abroad was common, and Mrs Gatty and Miss Yonge were unusual in their relatively limited experience of foreign parts. Their personal domestic lives, too, reveal common factors, a high incidence of spinsterhood or equivocal marital status, legal or informal separation or divorce.

The numbers of women in journalism almost certainly increased over the century, but we have no exact figures. Census returns provide a rough guide, but many freelance women contributors, particularly in the earlier decades, may not be entered as such.[51] Journalism was never an easy option, and by the end of the century when girls found it peculiarly attractive there was a widespread perception among their elders that it was overglamorized and overcrowded. Janet Hogarth and Frances Low, both from a journalistic background, considered the requisite educational level well below that of the new breed of Girton girls. One woman's magazine reader added the attractions of journalism to the standard reasons why even at good rates needlewomen were impossible to find. 'Our girls will rush into journalism, teaching or the stage, three professions already overstocked, and neglect really useful branches of employment, by which they might earn a steady, if not luxurious livelihood.'[52] A decade earlier *The Girl's Own Paper*, remarking journalism's attractions to the young of both sexes, warned that it was overcrowded and 'likely to prove a very precarious enterprise' for any girl needing to earn her own living.[53]

Yet for those who took up the challenge journalism had much to offer, giving opportunities for writers with no talent or inclination for fiction. It provided an arena to debate directly those social and political issues from which women were excluded at all levels of government, a vehicle to promote political and religious beliefs, a channel to educate or influence other women. In the absence of higher education it gave a formal outlet for sustained consideration of their informal studies. It offered, if precariously, a source of earnings from work which could in many instances be done from home, and 'fitted round', albeit with ingenuity, effort and strain, domestic commitments. Those who edited or published even engaged in business. Collectively these women made a distinct contribution to the development of journalism in the nineteenth century, so influencing their culture and society. One can trace through their work and the divergence of female streams of thought on the 'Sex' question, the struggle for women's rights to education, employment, property and the vote. Norton, Blessington, Howitt, Martineau, Lynn Linton, Oliphant, Bodichon, Cobbe – their names interconnect and part company as the decades roll on. One can read in their critical debates ideas that helped to shape literary genres and public responses to the arts. Whether editing a religious paper or writing an etiquette column women shared in that dynamic interaction of press and reader which was such an important factor in the shaping of their society. Their work should not be underestimated.

2
Obstacles and Opportunities

Money, or rather the lack of it, was a major reason why women entered journalism. Some sought personal independence but, like the widowed Mrs Oliphant, others were perforce the family providers. 'Labouring night and day at literary work, all her anxiety was to be clear of debt'.[1] This tribute by one of the Countess of Blessington's servants could apply to many other women in this book, paying off debts, keeping themselves and ineffectual male dependants by the point of their pens. Mary Mitford supported her parents when her father's gambling ruined the family. Mrs Humphry Ward developed her own journalism when her husband failed as a leader writer. A common thread in the lives of female contributors to *Fraser's Magazine* in its early years was the need to support themselves and dependants.[2] In different ways journalism helped Harriet Martineau, Isabella Fyvie Mayo and Charlotte Riddell following the collapse of family businesses.

Journalism could potentially offer considerably better pay and more freedom than the alternatives. At her peak Lady Blessington lived very well off her writing. Periodical work might be precarious and tough, but then so might governessing. Even an educated, accomplished girl like Mary Novello, in a select position with considerate employers, found it exhausting. 'The noise and fatigue' of looking after five young children proved too much for her health. (Well it might!)[3] Magazine articles continually deplored the plight of governesses. *Eliza Cook's Journal* quoted advertisements demanding paragons for twelve guineas a year and less. Conditions were no better abroad. 'Engagements made in England through agencies often prove terrible failures.' Employment opportunities expanded but so did the potential labour force. By the final decade lady clerks were fighting for jobs at 10s a week and Post Office applicants complained of impossible odds in the competitive examination.[4] Journalism in comparison, though demanding, was seen by some women as a form of liberation. The youthful Bessie Parkes may have been shocked to discover Mary Howitt still 'slaving' to make a living after thirty years. Why were not the founders of cheap penny magazines more generous to one of their 'most efficient coadjutors'? But Mary Howitt had viewed matters otherwise. 'Self-sacrifice' to help one's family had seemed emancipation.[5] In different terms at the *fin-de-siècle* an experienced woman freelance expressed her sense of independence. 'I do my work when and how I like, the sole condition being that my copy shall be good, and punctually delivered. When I see the tyranny to which governesses and nurses are obliged to submit, I count it a great gain that in journalism the woman is entirely her own mistress as regards the ordering of her life.'[6]

Of course women faced problems, directly or indirectly, because of their sex. Isabella Fyvie could not even afford to buy papers to see if her early articles appeared.[7] A woman like Harriet Martineau actually able to invest money in Chapman's *Westminster* was an anomaly. When Bessie Parkes's journal faced much more modest problems, though her father too had assisted Chapman financially, she and her friends were reduced to offers by female well-wishers of free contributions.[8] Editorship of the most influential sectors of the press was virtually barred to women. Even in the provinces a newspaper editor participated in public life and was 'invariably an active centre in all the political movements of his party.'[9] When occasionally the opportunity arose a woman might well refuse for reasons hard to understand today. Harriet Martineau pondered over the qualities she would need to edit a new economics journal 'undertaking a man's duty, I must brave a man's fate', yet eventually refused the offer because of her brother's disapproval.[10] Mrs Ireland writing of Geraldine Jewsbury's ambition to become a 'journalist, to move in the world of letters as a man, a good comrade, "one of the craft"' expressed the conventional view that constitutional weakness placed limits on women's employment. Delicate health and lack of 'staying qualities' were a major handicap for 'Journalism is rather a stern occupation'. Successful practitioners like Mrs Linton, Mrs Crawford and Mrs Oliphant did indeed at times experience the exhaustion and strain of the 'drudgery demanded of a professional literary woman'.[11]

Women adopted various strategies for dealing with their anomolous position in journalism. One was the deliberate cultivation of the traditional female virtues of delicacy, modesty and reticence. Anna Maria Hall made a particular point in Lady Blessington's favour that 'she never wrote a line that might not be placed on the book-shelves of any English lady'. Her taste was 'womanly and refined; I say "womanly" because she had a perfectly feminine appreciation of whatever was delicate and beautiful'.[12] Harriet Martineau thought it 'delightful' to see Mrs Somerville 'always well-dressed and thoroughly womanly in her conversation and manners'. Advocating reform was by no means synonymous with 'unfeminine' behaviour. The manner of both Emily Shirreff and her sister, Maria Grey, impressed Mary Cowden Clarke as a 'living instance' of the 'peculiar modesty and unpretendingness' of particularly gifted women.[13] In their autobiographies women were on the whole more self-effacing than men. Edith Simcox never published her somewhat ironically termed *Autobiography of a Shirtmaker*, probably because of the intense emotions it expressed.[14] Mrs Oliphant thought family loyalty demanded reticence since the most creditable things in one's life might reflect badly on other members of the family. Eliza Linton told Layard she dared not publish because she knew too much. Her solution – an autobiographical novel in which the sexes are reversed – was unorthodox to say the least. Self-deprecatory comments on their sex creep even into articles written to encourage other women by women who were themselves achieving success. Mary Billington thought 'a true journalistic instinct a rare enough attribute in a man, and in a woman remarkable'.[15]

Other social factors were major inhibitors. One problem was, as still today, the necessity of combining domestic responsibilities with the demands of working to tight deadlines. Men often took up journalism as an adjunct to another career in law or politics, but these two 'lives' could be kept apart. Women's other life could not so easily be compartmentalized. The all-pervasive demands of running a household and the family's social life constantly intruded. Edith Simcox makes the point well when she writes of the brilliant self-taught mathematician, Mrs. Somerville 'When she was over forty she taught herself to stop in the middle of a calculation to receive morning callers, and to take it up where she had left off when they had gone'. But she also had, according to Harriet Martineau, exceptional powers of blocking out distraction. Martineau herself found the 'dissipation of mind caused by interruption' more fatiguing than hours of uninterrupted concentration.[16] The absence of 'a room of one's own' echoes down the decades, yet women writers still sought to locate themselves at the heart of the household. Mary Howitt laments her 'greatest want' in 'not having a little working-room to myself, obliged to write in the dining-room, exposed to continual interruptions.' The 'bright side' however is her ability to bear them better than either husband or daughter. 'It would drive them mad; the poor mother of a family learns to be patient; that is one comfort'.[17]

Women journalists stressed the compatibility of home-making and professional rôles. Articles promoting successful independently-minded women subtly domesticate that image. Mary Billington having defended Rachel Beer's record as editor of a Sunday newspaper closes her pen portrait with Mrs Beer the society hostess, opening her drawing-rooms to charitable societies and up-and-coming 'musical artists'.[18] Emily Crawford, one of the most remarkable journalists of her time, well schooled in the rigours of her profession, was clear that 'A press life need not disqualify a woman for home life' though she urged the necessity of a good housekeeper and sending the children to school. Her model of Mrs Frederika Macdonald managing her charming house 'enlivened by three well-brought-up and highly educated children' *without* the assistance of a housekeeper, and still managing 'a good deal of press work' counteracts that of Chicago-based Mrs Margaret Sullivan, who was childless. But significantly it is Mrs Sullivan who is 'the most busy press woman I know'. Mrs Macdonald's journalism does not extend to the gruelling demands of daily paper work.[19] Late 1890s woman could no more 'have it all' than her counterpart a century later. In their memoirs women highlighted their own commitment to domestic duties. Isabella Fyvie Mayo praised 'household work' along with agriculture as lying at the 'very root of human living'. 'When the world shall in time grow quite sane, these two avocations will take precedence of all others'.[20] Mary Cowden Clarke reflecting on a long life in which writing and editing had been continuous activities deliberately included evidence of her skill at broiling a mutton chop and making her husband's dress waistcoats to demonstrate that 'a woman who adopts literary work as her profession need not either neglect or be deficient in the more usually feminine accomplishments of cookery and needlework.'[21]

Such protestations are not unnatural given the prejudice against the professional woman. A career was often perceived as at odds with a woman's 'true' mission in life and her chances of happiness. Lady Blessington's male biographer considered her professional ambitions 'the intellectual species of coquetry' and saw her pursuit of them as precluding her from 'all that is calculated to make a woman happy', the 'wear and tear of literary life' being ultimately destructive. Alice Meynell, no admirer of Martineau's writing, yet noted the double standards that operated to her detriment. 'You are not to be considered a woman of masculine understanding for nothing. Harriet Martineau paid for the distinction.'[22]

Assuming a male persona was a subterfuge women other than Martineau found useful. Maria Jewsbury, Miss Rigby, Mrs Oliphant, and Mrs Busk all adopted it on occasion. Norma Clarke suggests that for this reason the press provided a more effective veil than fiction behind which women could express their suffering.[23] There were other practical advantages. The 'male voice' proved convenient in business transactions, particularly early approaches to editors. Long before she took the name 'George Eliot', Chapman writing on her behalf to the *Edinburgh* with samples of her published work and suggestions for articles, referred to her as a man. Isabella Mayo thought 'Edward Garrett' the pseudonym Strahan bestowed in her guise of 'an old City merchant' for the series of papers he commissioned, 'a very convenient screen in the event of failure'.[24]

The newspaper office could be a particularly hostile environment, even at the end of the century. Recalling T P O'Connor's advice to aspirant journalists to get a foot in the door as 'office-boy' if need be, Charlotte O'Conor Eccles ruefully noted the much greater difficulty women had in finding any such a foothold. 'Where a man finds one obstacle, we find a dozen.'[25] Eliza Linton's journalist, Jane Osborn, in *Sowing the Wind* rejoicing in the secret power her masculine persona as newspaper leader-writer bestowed, adopting masculine traits, using slang and delighting in being referred to as 'Mr John', was choosing stratagems to which at least some real-life women resorted. Clotilde Graves even wore men's clothes.

To English eyes the 'forward' American woman journalist of myth appeared shockingly liberated. Certainly some like 'Polly Pry' (Leonel Campbell) or Mabel Craft had the kind of adventures Englishwomen would only meet abroad.[26] But many New World women journalists seem to have faced problems similar to those of their British sisters. Laura Searing who wrote for the *New York Times* apparently adopted the pseudonym Howard Glyndon for its masculine sound. Helen M Winslow, a founder of the New England Woman's Press Association in 1885, complained there was little welcome for women in newspaper offices. Elizabeth Banks was told sternly by her city editor 'You will never be able to do big things in journalism ... you're all woman and no journalist'. In America as in England women were often channelled into covering social events and women's issues.[27]

Restricted mobility was another limitation. Young Eliza Linton and Marian Evans were unusual in being allowed to go to the capital to try their fortunes. Male journalists like Stead moved from the provinces to London in order to carve their careers, and a series of relocations as they jumped from paper to paper was commonplace.[28] Such a course was comparatively rare for women of the same class. On marriage women were expected to move with their husbands. Yet fortuitously some found family circumstances an asset. Travel, in the wake of husbands and relatives, to foreign parts occasionally offered opportunities to write upon matters of great political moment. In this way did Miss Wreford unexpectedly become in 1859 the first woman foreign correspondent of *The Times* when her brother Henry, their correspondent in Rome, fell ill most inconveniently from its manager's point of view in the early stages of the Italian war. More usually experience of foreign countries provided less dramatic openings for reviewing, translation, or topographical essays such as Mary Cowden Clarke's adventurous trip to Genoa in 1860 which furnished material for an *Atlantic Monthly* essay and *Athenæum* reviews of Italian productions of Shakespeare.[29] Many women published only a handful of such articles, but some became effectively foreign correspondents.

   As journalism professionalized women's lack of formal education and restricted participation in public life became more significant, though not insuperable, obstacles. By the eighties Joseph Hatton saw 'the writer for the press' belonging to the best clubs and entertaining 'the greatest in the land.' 'The Potts of Dickens would be as hard to find in the country today as the Shandon of Thackeray in London.'[30] Journalists, especially on the more serious papers, were often high-achieving university men. The fictional Jane Osborn spoke for many women in bewailing her lack of social contact in the world of public affairs. '[T]hat's what we women want so much – that varied knowledge got by men – the knowledge you pick up among each other at clubs, and lectures, and in studios and places. You have such different friends – one is an artist, another an engineer, another a chemist ... you can keep yourselves informed on the last things in art, science, and politics.'[31] The *Athenæum* of that decade (1860s) carried vacancies for experienced reporters, assistant editors, sub-editors. 'Oxford or Cambridge Honours – man of Liberal principles will – *cæteris paribus* – be preferred' was not atypical, amid the neighbouring offers of services from educated young men boasting extensive practice in verbatim reporting or sub-editing. It was an *Athenæum* advertisement, seen by chance, that attracted Edwin Arnold from his academic posts in Bombay to leader-writing for the *Daily Telegraph*. He claimed to find his classical education of immense value even 'in the commonest work of a cheap press'.[32] A classical education, let alone a University one, was precisely what so many women were denied.

Some were relatively privileged; others took the trouble to educate themselves. At Hans Place, though Mary Mitford found the enthusiastic attention of her English teacher exhausting, the school fed her love of literature and the theatre. Harriet Martineau enjoyed a 'somewhat desultory' yet 'what would then have been called a "boy's education"'[33] learning Latin and relishing her two years at a co-ed school. Bessie Parkes's youthful reading was eclectic – Charlotte Smith, Scott, *Shirley* 'written by a *woman* I am sure', 'beautiful lucid Mill', Burke and Hare's trial, 'more atrocious than anything I *ever* read.' But she enjoyed an unusually enlightened education: 'It was not in the least like a "school for young ladies."' One of her schoolmasters even gave classes on optics, hydrostatics and astronomy.[34] Such experiences were untypical. A governess like Mrs Gibson or a school like Rosamund Vincy's was much more likely. Eliza Linton's education was unusual in a different way. 'I never went to school; I never had a governess nor master; so that everything I do know I have taught myself, with the time-losing result of having a dunce for my schoolmaster.' Paradoxically, despite approving extended work opportunities for women, she believed that apart from an elite few, girls suffered from the strains of Higher Education.[35] These 'Girton Girls' like Linton's protégée, Beatrice Harraden, and Rachel Cook appeared only in the final decades. A small number of the earlier generations had like Barbara Bodichon and Emilia Dilke benefited from institutions like the Bedford Square Ladies' College or art schools, but these did not of course provide the male social networks.[36] Eliza Linton's own higher education had been within the walls of the British Library, which afforded a mental lifeline for many others. Maria Rye, researching there in the early sixties, was delighted to discover several women employed in deciphering ancient manuscripts. Twenty years on Clementina Black found it a wonderful source of intellectual stimulation providing valuable contacts as well as literary resources.[37]

There was one respect in which girls' traditional education could be useful, that of foreign languages, and many women journalists developed this facility throughout their lives. Matilda Betham-Edwards considered French, German, Spanish and Italian 'the obligatory equipments of a literary calling' and claimed herself '[i]n odd moments' to have mastered sufficient Latin and Greek to read Tacitus and Plato in the original. Lady Dilke knew Italian, and could read with ease Latin, German and French, and 'by taking pains...[could] make out the essentials' of books in Greek, Spanish, Portugese, Dutch and Provençal. In the last month of her life she 'was improving her Swedish and attacking Welsh'.[38] Alice Werner, apart from knowing French and Dutch, was a scholar of Swahili and Bantu and taught at the School of Oriental and African Studies. Edith Simcox, in addition to excellent French and German, could read Plato in the original and had a working knowledge of Dutch. Mary Howitt translated from German, Swedish and Danish.

Plato and Danish alone, however, were insufficient. How did young, often reticent, women break into journalism? A handful engineered a start in the family newspaper business. Without such connections however, periodicals and local papers themselves often provided the most accessible opening, especially in the provinces. Not through their advertisements. Even at the end of the century when 'New' women were positively encouraged to take up a career neither press advertisements, nor for that matter employment registers, were a fruitful source of jour-nalistic jobs. Any editor rash enough to advertise for a lady journalist would be overwhelmed by inexperienced hopefuls.[39] It was cold-calling – by post or in person. Arnold Bennett's insistence that despite the atmos-phere of 'mystery, aloofness, and sovereignty' which editors cultivated, pertinacity and a business-like approach would eventually secure an interview, was probably good advice for the young freelance confident of her bright ideas. When Elizabeth Banks approached London editors, 'I had a sort of triumphal progress from one office to another. Not a single editor refused to see me … and one of them accepted a subject right off.'[40] But she had the novelty value of being an experienced *American* journalist. For the relative newcomer it was not so easy. Traipsing the streets in the rain to arrive tired, hungry, muddy and dishevelled at a cobwebbed office up a 'flight of stairs, steep dark, and silent' only to find entrance to the editor's room guarded by an unsavoury receptionist[41] – Sara Duncan's fictional image of the frustration and degradation when visiting editors in person echoes Charlotte O'Conor Eccles for whom Fleet Street 'was my *via dolorosa'*. 'The mysterious little alleys and side-streets seemed cut-throat sort of places, where provincial young ladies might be robbed and murdered. The dark stairs leading to eminently respectable editorial sanctums looked dirty and bewildering; I went in terror of the men who bobbed suddenly out the gloom and asked me what my business was.'[42] No wonder most aspirants preferred the rela-tive security of the postal service.

Journals visited *you*. They came into the house. They carried their publishers' addresses. You might study them in the privacy of your room; you may even have felt a sense of relationship with the editor. The 'Notes to Correspondents' provided a kind of 'basic training' in their replies to readers who submitted work. Naturally not everyone approved of the encouragement thus given to the 'domestic author' who had better stick to writing in ladies' albums and epitaphs for pet dogs. One journalist particularly deplored the 'female of the genus' whose "eye in fine frenzy rolling" does not see the pot boil over, or drop easily from octave rhymes to the bathos of weekly accounts'.[43] He cannot have had in mind the Mary Mitfords managing the household accounts alongside the essays and plays.

Charlotte Yonge's brief responses in *The Monthly Packet* 'Very pretty but for younger readers than ours' or 'Thanks for your much improved verses' were on the contrary positively encouraging. When Mary Ward submitted her early fiction to the *Packet* Miss Yonge, rejecting it, even took the trouble to explain her reasons, too much romantic interest for that paper.[44] Religious magazines were important because in so many respectable homes they were the most readily accessible. Periodicals provided a window on the world, both in overt discussion of women's work, and in fiction. Isabella Fyvie Mayo was inspired to apply to Maria Rye's office by a *Family Herald* story of a landlady's daughter substituting for a sick young man who earned his living by law-writing. '[I]t was a hint that some women could do things as well as some men if only they made the attempt.'[45]

Girls sometimes used extraordinary subterfuges either to prevent parents from knowing of their plans, or because they feared failure in taking so bold a step. Harriet Martineau, though encouraged by her brother 'as a new pursuit' to send a piece to the *Monthly Repository*, told no one but carried the 'expensive packet', containing her article under the masculine signature 'Discipulus', to the post-office herself. She later recounted the thrill of hearing him single out passages for praise without knowing its authorship.[46] Eliza Lynn's ploy was particularly ingenious. When she was fifteen she wrote to the publisher of *Bentley's Miscellany*, then edited by Dickens, expressing her desire to contribute. 'I know not if you will think my *sex* a disadvantage or not.' He was asked to reply by sending a newspaper Liberal or Whiggish if the answer were 'Yes', Tory if 'No' – 'do not *write* to Miss Lynn, a newspaper from an anonymous hand will pass off as from one of her friends – but a letter – I shall be undone – *lost for ever.*'[47] Bentley duly sent a Whig paper, though the story preceded by an effusive letter was apparently not accepted. Even girls from enlightened backgrounds were often wary of telling their families of their plans. Mary Novello as a

17-year-old engaged girl, wanting to contribute to the family income, and with only her sister as 'confidante', sent an article under the initials M.H. to Hone's *Table Book*. Only afterwards did she enjoy her 'happiest triumph' when she showed it in print to her fiancé.[48]

The development of juvenile papers stimulated ambitious girls to write poetry, fiction and essays. Amelia Blandford Edwards was first published in a penny weekly when she was only seven. Isabella Fyvie was encouraged by a distant connection, a student of King's College, who read her school essay. As a 13-year-old she wrote for advice to Jean Ingelow of *Youth's Magazine* and received two detailed letters. Jean Ingelow apparently received so many letters from young hopefuls that she ran a series of 'Hints on Composition' which Isabella at least found 'most suggestive and instructive' and *Youth's* eventually printed her work.[49]

Young girls often produced their own magazines and such ventures sometimes led to greater things. For the Gatty children who kept up theirs throughout much of the 1860s it was a form of apprenticeship to their mother's *Aunt Judy's*. Charlotte Yonge was 'critic and referee' for the quarterly *Barnacle,* to which 'the goslings' a circle of young cousins and friends, including for a time Mary Ward, contributed. The venture folded only as the main contributors graduated to the *Packet*. Charlotte also printed hints to budding fiction writers in an issue of the *Packet* (July 1861) which co-incidentally carried an early Juliana Gatty story. Christabel Coleridge was not, however, correct in saying that when the society of 'goslings' was founded in 1859 'Magazine competitions were not [then] invented'.[50] *The Englishwoman's Domestic Magazine* had been running such essay competitions very successfully for some years. Christabel was probably thinking of the kind of magazine considered suitable for young women in pious households. By the 1880s competitions were appearing in journals like *Girl's Own Paper*. In Arnold Bennett's *Woman* essay competitions were restricted to women and readers actively encouraged to submit short 'smartly written' pieces for publication at 1 guinea per 800 words.[51] This accorded with his view that the 'time-honoured' 'proper' way to enter journalism was as an outside contributor who by 'dint of a thousand refusals' learnt to write what was saleable, although another strategy he thought practical was the editor's secretary route.[52]

Braving a 'thousand refusals' was a lonely, dispiriting process. Women needed mechanisms for mutual support. Bessie Parkes and Barbara Bodichon, attempting to get poetry and articles into their provincial papers, enclosed each other's work with their own. Bessie even copied out one of Barbara's to send on. They exchanged progress reports, advice and encouragement. Bessie thought 'there are rather too many ! and ? in your style of writing for a *public paper* where they always deal with things so cooly. Moreover they never write in *paragraphs*, at least not in *small paragraphs*...' But before the letter was finished Feeny's note accepting one of Barbara's essays arrived and Bessie hastened to pass on the good news – 'admirably conceived' and 'expressed in beautiful and simple language'.[53] Letters were one of women's mechanisms for fruitful contacts substituting for the university and clubland networks men enjoyed. Her voluminous correspondence enabled Mary Mitford in her Berkshire village to discuss personal and professional issues as well as exchange literary and social gossip with a wide circle of acquaintance embracing Elizabeth Browning, the S C Halls, Felicia Hemans, Henry Chorley, Harriet Martineau, the Hoflands, and the painter Heydon. Men often acted as professional confidants. Miss Mitford used Sir William Elford as a sounding-board for her plans and problems, as Mary Braddon and Eliza Linton in different ways used their writer-patrons Bulwer-Lytton and Landor.

Some male publishers and editors offered women valuable patronage, either individually as the Blackwoods for Mrs Oliphant, or more broadly like the influential W T Stead, famed for encouraging journalists like Flora Shaw, Hulda Friederichs and Alice Werner. Earlier in the century John Murray's home-cum-publishing-house at 50 Albemarle St provided his protegées, including Mary Somerville and Elizabeth Rigby, with generous hospitality and literary contacts, and Dickens appears to have been a particularly helpful editor to young writers, as Mrs Mayo among others recalled.[54] Established women journalists too could be useful patrons. Eliza Linton, savage in print, was kindly in person. Mrs Annie Hector first met her through Adelaide Procter in their *Household Words* days. When her husband became paralysed and she needed to write again, Mrs Linton urged George Bentley to give her work. She seemed equally generous with her time to struggling young writers patiently pouring 'over a crabbed manuscript, word by word, suggesting, correcting, improving, advising'.[55]

Family connections encouraged authors like Mary Arnold and Anne Mozley in the same way that painting families supported young women artists.[56] The Low family is a striking example. Both Frances and Florence were journalists as were their more famous brothers, Sidney and Maurice. Matilda Betham-Edwards and Amelia Blandford Edwards, her older cousin and 'boon companion', were actually unusual in never discussing each others' 'literary work or business'.[57]

The Jewsbury and Clerke sisters were a more common model. Marital patterns of authority and visibility may have varied, and the cultural ideal of husband as bread-winner be deeply entrenched, yet husband/wife teams like the Ellises, Howitts, Halls, Beetons and Meynells, appear to have operated to mutual advantage. Families assisted daughters and nieces as well as sons and nephews. Anna Howitt studying art in Germany benefited from her parents' friendships. Chorley, editor of *The Ladies' Companion* asked her to write a descriptive sketch of the Oberammergau passion play. From this sprang further work for the *Athenæum* and *Household Words*, and the resultant book was generously reviewed by another friend, Mrs S C Hall. Mary Howitt thought such contacts essential. 'Everything in the literary world is done by favour and connections.'[58]

Religious denominations provided women with natural social and intellectual networks linking private and public spheres. One thinks of the Unitarians, or Anglicans like the Yonges and Mozleys. Supporters of women's suffrage and other early feminist movements created new systems of mutual support, though often originating within the family circle.[59] The Winkworth sisters recalled Mrs Gaskell's household as a centre for meeting female activists like Anna Jameson and Adelaide Procter. Emily Davies remembered meeting Anthony Trollope, RH Hutton and William Allingham at breakfast and evening parties given by Langham Place women. Louisa Hubbard was apparently in contact with 'perhaps every woman of any mark who was working in the same direction as herself.'[60] Organizations like the Society for Promoting the Employment of Women and later the various suffrage leagues provided more formalized channels for contact.

Older feminists influenced the younger generation. Anna Jameson, an advocate of new employment opportunities for women became, in Geraldine Macpherson's phrase, a 'tower of strength to the girl-editor and writers'[61] of the early ventures at Langham Place. From Italy she wrote encouraging Bessie on the launch of *Waverley* and giving detailed advice on improving her 'critical department'.[62] Long before contacts could be established through organizations, female authors possessed valuable informal support systems, passing information down the generations. Anna Jameson had, for example, been advised on the importance of holding on to her copyright by Maria Edgeworth[63]. Geraldine Jewsbury was encouraged by the example of her much older sister, Maria, a leading *Athenæum* writer of the 1820s, and indirectly by the example of Lady Morgan. Encouragement did not imply unconditional support. Women critics could be severe on their sisters when maintaining their critical criteria. George Eliot, though personally supportive of Bessie Parkes and Barbara Bodichon would not relax her standards over their journal, just as Emilia Dilke, who trained as an artist and exhibited in her youth, was stringent in assessing the work of other women and grew unsympathetic towards 'ladies' exhibitions'.[64]

These different networks overlapped. There were interlocking circles of close friends, co-religionists, fellow activists and literary acquaintances. The Howitts for instance had connections through the Society of Friends, the Carter Halls, the Leigh Smiths, the Pre-Raphaelites and through their publishing ventures. There was one literary network, almost entirely controlled by women, since it was subsumed by their social duties as ladies. Ella Hepworth Dixon recalled the 'celebrated Fridays' of Millicent, Duchess of Sutherland where 'wits, poets and journalists' were entertained in the grandeur of Stafford House. 'The only Englishwoman of the last century who was bold enough to hold a "salon"'.[65] Here she was wrong. There was a model for social networking for women well established in the fashionable aristocratic salons of pre-Victorian England. Lady Blessington's in the early 1820s was the haunt of dukes, politicians including Canning, Castlereagh, Grey, Palmerston and Russell, attracting fashionable writers of the day like Thomas Moore and Henry Luttrell. When, years later, she re-established it with Count D'Orsay, despite their dubious social position, they were a magnet for politicians, English and French, and literary figures of the older and newer generations – Landor, Forster and Dickens among them . Indeed 'les salons de Gore House' were open 'à toutes les illustrations de l'art et de la science'.[66]

They were imitated by those of far lower social pretensions. The Carter Halls had known Lady Blessington mainly through their publishing ventures, particularly the annuals. Shared charitable efforts[67] and probably their Irish ancestry cemented the women's relationship. Mrs Samuel Carter Hall's circle included besides her own friends such as Mary Howitt, Letitia Landon and Jean Ingelow, acquaintances of her husband, best known as editor of the *Art Union Monthly Journal*. In London she ran what was virtually a salon, to which were invited 'a most wonderful collection of people' – 'they were fond of every kind of lion and wonder, great and small' – according to a scathing Margaret Oliphant. But it was at their parties in Surrey or town that she met the Howitts whom she liked, the American journalist 'Grace Greenwood' whom she didn't, and Rosa Bonheur, the French painter then at the height of her fame. The Howitts when visiting the Alaric Watts went to one of the Hall's evening parties 'in their queer old house' (The Rosary, Brompton) 'to meet over tea, biscuits, and weak negus various literary lights' one of whom, Letitia Landon, later featured them in *Romance and Reality*.[68] The young Isabella Fyvie, one of the young women whose writing career Mrs Hall assisted with introductions and recommenda- tions, had flattering memories of their receptions in the Boltons, with its dainty china, carved furniture and fine paintings, a kind and amusing hostess, and often 'exceptionally good singing'. Jane Loudon's receptions were so informal that impecunious 'lady artists and literary women' could turn up in 'walking costume' instead of the usual elabo- rate 'toilette'.[69] Such social opportunities went some way to replace those which the universities and clubs offered to young men.

A rather more intellectual female 'salon' collected around George Eliot, whose 'spiritual daughters' included Barbara Bodichon, Bessie Parkes, and, half a generation younger, Francis Pattison (Lady Dilke) and Edith Simcox all of whom were to engage in journalism. By the turn of the century women could be members of dining-clubs. Following her *Story of a Modern Woman*, Hepworth Dixon, along with five other female authors of the year's most successful novels, was invited to join The Vagabonds. She took the chair at a Lyceum club dinner, addressing a public audience of writers and editors for the first time, and in 1910 was joint founder of The New Toys which numbered Sidney Low, William Heinemann, W B Yeats, Mrs H G Wells and May Sinclair amongst its early members.[70] Mrs Humphry valued women's clubs for providing professional single women like journalists, lectur- ers, reviewers and milliners with often their sole 'companionship', and Charlotte O'Conor Eccles later wished she had joined the Writers' Club as soon as she arrived in London, and saved herself much fruitless effort. Through their clubs these women gained professional and social contacts.[71] The formation of professional journalists' associations even- tually created more formal and open networks. Mrs. Linton was among those who joined the Society of Authors in its early days and having been elected to its Council in 1896, when women were first eligible, took great pride in her place of honour at its annual dinner in 1897. The Institute of Journalists, founded in 1890, admitted women from the start, and Catherine Drew and Grace Stuart from the London branch were the only two female delegates at the first International Conference of the Press. The Institute's 'great experiment' in 'universal suffrage', however, had not been universally welcomed. Moreover, though it interpreted the term 'journalist' liberally, members needed to have been habitually practising as journalists for two years to be eligible. By 1895 there were over 60 female members and associates.[72] The founding of the Society of Women Journalists, in 1893, less exclusive in its professional demands, reflects the difficulties women still found in getting full-time employment. Membership was open to women engaged in journalism either as writers or artists in black and white. The initial criteria by 1901 seemed 'somewhat drastic, shutting out ... useful members merely because they have not been working regularly on the staff of a paper, although they may have done work of the highest excellence at stated periods'. At the same time the rules were changed to allow distinguished women *writers* rather than *journalists* to be vice-presidents. By this time the Society was organizing lectures, had rooms with facilities for writing and tea, offered legal assistance for members seeking unpaid fees and through its employment register occasionally helped members obtain for instance holiday relief work or an opening on 'an agricultural paper.'[73]

The accusations of dilettantism levelled at earlier generations of 'lady authors' did not recede as journalism professionalized. Some women always took their work seriously, even if it were not their only source of income, nor their only responsibility. Professional issues in terms of their duties as writers or editors, and of fair financial returns for their work mattered. Harriet Martineau, for instance, was actively involved in the campaign for international copyright, addressing the US Senate and House of Representative in 1837, and despite ill-health offering assistance to the proposed Society of British Authors in 1843. Victor Bonham-Carter thought hers 'by far the most helpful and far-seeing' of the many responses to the 'Proposed Prospectus'.[74]

But there was a widespread anxiety about the amateurism of women and the reasons for it. In 1862 Frances Cobbe viewed writing as an established area of work for women. 'There is little need to talk of literature as a field for woman's future work. She is ploughing it in all directions already. The one thing is to do it thoroughly....' Yet she feared not all treated it with proper professionalism and prepared themselves seriously. For some 'quickness' was a substitute for 'patience' and tact a cover for 'a defect of study'.[75] Twenty-five years later Edith Simcox was still arguing that if women undertook literary or other intellectual work 'it is for the interest of the community that they shall be taught and required to do it as well as their natural faculties will allow'.[76] At the end of the century Stead's concern was that female members of staff expected to be treated more gently. A 'lady must not be scolded when she does wrong ... a lady ought not to stay up late or go about late ... Ladies with such notions had better stay at home in their drawing-rooms and boudoirs. The great rough real workaday world is no place for them.'[77] Arnold Bennett's guide for women journalists took them sternly to task for unreliability and castigated almost the entire sex for slipshod literary style, Jane Austen and Alice Meynell being the honourable exceptions. 'Lack of restraint' and 'gush' were particularly feminine characteristics. All these inadequacies, however, arose not from their sex. Bennett blamed 'lack of training', seemingly without recognizing that an *education* equivalent to their brothers' would have not only enabled them to pass the 'most ordinary tests of spelling, grammar and punctuation' of which they were so ignorant but equipped them for many other public duties.[78]

But if inadequate training encouraged an unbusinesslike approach what sort of training should women seek? For most of the century this was largely of the informal variety gained piecemeal by Isabella Mayo. Geraldine Jewsbury living 'without any professional judgement and advice to guide me' was grateful for criticism passed on by Jane Carlyle. 'If my sister had lived she would have said all these things, and given me the "drilling" necessary and taken all the dilettantism out of me.' A rather tougher version of the same discipline seems to be exactly what Stead advocated in the nineties. 'Vigorous admonition' was what women needed 'more than anything else' because 'while all human beings need it, men get it and women often do not'. Much of a man's success in life was attributable to the 'jacketings' of his 'prentice days'.[79] This of course assumed one had acquired an apprenticeship in the first place. By this time not everyone was convinced that beginning 'on the lower rungs of the ladder' and working 'up to the top' was the most appropriate route for male journalists either. The London School of Journalism founded by David Anderson of the *Telegraph* already offered a year's course covering 'paragraphs, reviewing, shorthand, interviewing, special and war correspondence, preparing telegrams, leaders, art and dramatic criticism, sub-leaders, sub-editing, and the writing of stories and magazine articles'. Women pupils could 'read individually' with him. But however effective the course may have been it was not nationally, let alone internationally, agreed and de Blowitz for one thought that as journalism grew ever more influential the lack of a systematic programme of professional training was positively dangerous. With 'no body of doctrine, no series of fixed rules, apparently no possible method of instruction' the profession attracted opinionated men to whom discipline was anathema and who therefore reported events purely according to their fancy.[80]

Whilst there was a general agreement that journalists needed wide interests, curiosity, good physique, stamina and persistence, on those qualities which might be acquired there was less certainty. Haranguing women over spelling only encouraged some to think that the sole reason for rejection of their work.[81] Even over the value of shorthand there was no consensus. Stead advised learning it and keeping up one's speed. Others like Charles Cooper thought it not essential even for parliamentary reporting. Mrs Crawford thought it useful for the press and indispensable for secretaries, but otherwise rejoiced that 'its day in the other departments of newspaper work is declining'. She considered *verbatim* reporting only valuable for law reporting in sensational cases and advised girls to spend their time learning typewriting instead. 'More type-writers and fewer pianos!'[82] Although apparently typewriting machines were not common for 'reportorial purposes' in the United States, it was so vital a piece of equipment for American Elizabeth Banks that when forced to sell hers to finance a journalistic project in London she immediately replaced it with another on the instalment plan.[83] Stead recommended typing if the absolute essential – writing 'a neat, legible hand' – was beyond you, and Isabella Mayo's experience of editors' reaction to her own handwriting of 'uniform "colour"' with sufficient character to make it 'less fatiguing to read' confirmed the value of a 'good hand'.[84]

Even in the era of the typewriter newspaper reporting was undoubtedly problematic for a young girl. As the *GOP* put it 'It is not an occupation which tends to the development of feminine graces.'[85] Did women then restrict themselves to 'ladylike' topics and concentrate upon the 'quality' market? There was certainly a notion of the 'lady' and 'ladylike' or 'womanly' behaviour to which many subscribed, but it was an unstable concept. Women journalists did write on subjects particularly relevant to the somewhat restricted lives of many of their women readers: reviewing (novels, biographies, art exhibitions); travel writing; articles on fashion, domestic, social and educational issues. Partly these reflected editorial emphases and the demands of the market-place. After all there was a large female readership. But some men also covered such topics, even ones like 'domestic servants' where they might be supposed to have less direct experience than women, and journalists like Harriet Martineau and Frances Cobbe ranged much further afield. Others in harnessing their personal experiences for articles arguing feminist issues inevitably trespassed on the domains of politics and economics. Several women specialized in the traditional male preserves of science or theology. Mrs. Somerville's 'short, scientific article' for the *Quarterly* predated Elizabeth Rigby's appearance as female contributor in the 1830s.

By the 1860s Frances Power Cobbe saw a shift in how women of creative genius expressed themselves. Male artists welcomed this move from 'Angelical' prettiness but many other men found the display of female strength distasteful. As Cobbe put it, 'There is a feeling (tacit or expressed) "Yes, it is very clever, but somehow it is not quite feminine".' She blamed the 'old error that clipping and fettering ... was the sole method of making a woman ... that, as the Chinese make a lady's foot, so we should make a lady's mind' Cobbe's suggestion that the 'feminine mind' was a construction, or rather distortion, has its parallel in the question of the 'woman's voice' – a subject of debate in the nineteenth century as today. Some men clearly thought there was such a thing. Editors and publishers of women's magazines commodified it. Lockhart inviting Elizabeth Rigby to contribute to the *Quarterly* spelt it out. He 'had long felt and regretted the want of that knowledge of women and their concerns, which men can never attain, for the handling of numberless questions most interesting and most important to society.' His sense of the woman's viewpoint was probably some distance from Cobbe's claim that a 'woman naturally admires power, force, grandeur'.[86]

To one twentieth-century feminist critic Victorian female intellectuals may speak in unison offering 'both the resistance to, and the compliance with, the hegemony of a male-dominated middle-class culture'.[87] To others, women writers are constrained by the permitted limits of male editorial control. The situation seems to me even more complex and fluid than either of these positions suggests. Women writers were quite capable of subversion in their conformity; male editors of receiving challenges to their own orthodoxy. There was a multiplicity of women's voices, varying in their rhetoric and utterances, but which together demanded and made space for 'that knowledge of women and their concerns' which they shared.[88] However constrained they may appear from our twentieth-century vantage-point, nineteenth-century women themselves believed the developing press *did* provide a new platform.

Some sought deliberately to harness the power of the press. They recognized the value of newspapers if not to propagate new ideas, at least to promulgate them much more widely. As Bessie Parkes wrote in defending yet another article on the need for professional training for women 'It has all been said over and over again in the last twenty years. But that is no reason why it should not be reiterated.... An idea may ... obtain great hold over a select class of minds, long before it penetrates familiarly into the columns of newspapers, and becomes really incorporated with our national thought....how are the active merchants and masters of factories ....to be convinced of the benefits of certain changes, unless they are presented to them in the newspaper which they read on the railway ...?'[89] It is a moot point whether the small circulation magazines consistently arguing a coherent case for increased employment opportunities, married women's property rights, women's suffrage, rights in divorce proceedings etc. served those causes better than the more fractured, less radical but much more widely-read surfacings in popular journals like the *Englishwoman's Domestic Magazine*. When its article explaining marriage settlements referred to the Divorce Courts in such spirited terms as the following it probably stirred more uneasy ripples than it purported to calm: '....the power on the part of the wife to say, "I will take my settlement, and live with you no longer" has often been the one and only argument that made her life with some brutal tyrant by any means endurable.'[90] Florence Fenwick-Miller spoke for many others in calling the press

the pulpits from which our modern preachers are most widely and effectively heard ... For every hundred persons who listen to the priest, the journalist ... speaks to a thousand; and while the words of the one are often heard merely as a formality, those of the other... may effectively influence the thoughts and consciences and actions of thousands in the near future. Shallow, indeed, would be the mind which undervalued the power of the journalist, or under-rated the seriousness of his vocation.[91]

3
A Fifth Estate

Women journalists 'have the honour of their sex and the reputation of one half of the human race, more in their keeping than any other women of equal numbers. For the newspaper is the educator of the public, and the people who write in newspapers have the best opportunities of creating public opinion.' Stead's encouraging words express a major reason why women seeking influence looked to newspaper journalism.[1] As Frances Cobbe, describing with hindsight its attractions, enthused

> Journalism is ... a delightful profession, full of interest, and promise of ever-extending usefulness.... To be in touch with the most striking events of the whole world, and enjoy the privilege of giving your opinion on them to 50 000 or 100 000 readers within a few hours, this struck me, when I first recognized that such was my business as a leader-writer as something for which many prophets and preachers of old would have given a house full of silver and gold. And I was to be *paid* for accepting it.[2]

Later she doubted the effectiveness of 'literary influence', and there were moments when she realized what comforts she had relinquished.[3] Returning to visit the family estate she confided to Mary Somerville 'Sometimes it comes over me there in the stately old rooms & beautiful parlours that I was born a gentlewoman & have rather had a downfall in becoming a hack scribbler to a halfpenny newspaper! But the scribbler is happier than ever the idle lady was (as if indeed I ever was idle) & my regrets always end in a laugh.'[4] One senses the attraction as much as the frustration. It was certainly possible to make a living from newspaper journalism. Cobbe found it 'much more remunerative than

36

writing for the best monthly or quarterly periodicals' even if she avoided reviews which had the 'double labour of reading and writing' for the same money. For those women prepared to accept its 'unyieldingly hard conditions' Emily Crawford considered the financial rewards 'handsome' and even greater the non-monetary one, living a life among interesting people and close to 'the pomps and pageantries of the great world ... the celebrities of the day.'[5]

National newspaper journalism was at once the most exciting and discouraging arena for women journalists. Relatively few made a significant impact upon it. Those who did needed all the qualities the would-be female journalist was so often exhorted to acquire. In their careers and work as leader writers, columnists and specialist correspondents one sees exhibited staying power, commitment, adaptability and independence. Some of these women were icons in their own century. The names of Martineau, Norton and Cobbe were constantly quoted for their success as writers and influencers. The *Christian World Magazine* saw Martineau as undertaking 'public ministry'. Catherine Drew cited the 'brilliant examples' of Harriet Martineau, Frances Cobbe, and Mrs Norton for their 'reviews of scientific, philosophical, and literary books' and sociological essays in the leading papers of their day. Fox-Bourne regarded Harriet Martineau as one of the few women to find 'congenial employment in regular newspaper writing'. Frances Low's gloomy view of journalism at the dawn of the twentieth century saw a decline from the standards of Martineau, Cobbe and Lynn Linton 'fifty years ago' when 'women journalists were picked members of their sex, possessing scholarship and culture' and 'a high sense of responsibility'.[6] But by then there was general unease at the proliferation of papers and pressmen, and the pursuit of speed at all costs.

Journalism was an open profession, but a masculine one. As Hatton put it 'The Bar, the Church, the Laboratory, the Barracks; no matter where the pen has tried its earliest flights, the press has no prejudices.'[7] There were few women whose experience matched any of these professions. Almost half a century after Eliza Linton's pioneering staff job on a national newspaper Charlotte O'Conor Eccles complained of the difficulties encountered by an experienced newspaperwoman. 'One is horribly handicapped in being a woman. A man meets other men at his club; he can be out and about at all hours; he can insist without being thought bold and forward; he is not presumed to be capable of undertaking only a limited class of subjects, but is set to anything.'[8] Mary Billington's account of 'lady journalists', endorsing this, admits – or boasts – that she was herself unusual in being assigned major events like state visits. Most women's work on the press consisted of fashion 'chronicling', the more routine society functions, weddings and bazaars, those philanthropic social issues which women had taken up, and domestic topics. For 'the "rough and tumble" work of outside reporting the ordinary proprietor will continue to prefer a man'.[9] One 'Wares of Autolycus' article reckoned that it took six months hard work just to survive 'I wouldn't call it living' on £2 a week and that female journalists were having to 'exist and keep up appearances on £4 a week'. This was about the rate for reporting or sub-editing on a small country weekly.[10]

As women's demand for paid employment expanded so the attraction of journalism, fuelled by its perceived glamour and the articles about it, seems to have increased disproportionately. A mid-1870s edition of Louisa Hubbard's *Year-book of Women's Work* gives no mention of newspaper work except to remark in the section under 'Reporter, Shorthand Writer' that those connected with a newspaper get 'a stated salary'.[11] By the 1890s such directories might have a whole entry on 'Journalist'. The prerequisites – sound physical health, a quick mind, good memory, accurate observation, sound general education, with rapid shorthand and an interest in current affairs for reporters – were ones that many bright young girls must have considered they possessed. Warnings that the life was hard and exacting and the profession precarious clearly did little to dampen enthusiasm, since there were frequent complaints that the profession was over-crowded. If only the starry-eyed individualists in the universities knew of the 'desperate struggle to make both ends meet', the 'trials of the interviewer, and the endless subterfuges of the society reporter' they wouldn't want to be journalists cried Janet Hogarth. The 'really successful women-journalists' judged by masculine standards could be 'counted on the fingers of one hand. … If a woman cannot do night work, and regular night work, the prizes of Fleet Street are not for her.'[12] Emily Crawford agreed that for the major dailies night work was the norm, and partly because the hours were not regular, very taxing – 'got through in a state approaching to brain-fever.' One needed 'great reserves of nervous force', vitality and staying-power to cope.[13]

It was, as we have seen, tough for men too, its openness, encouraging bright, but untrained, youngsters into an expanded profession having as its corollary the trapped 'jaded proficients' of the rank and file. A Press Fund was set up in 1878 to assist journalists who through ill-health were unable to carry on their profession. For those hanging on the fringe the nature of the work could be intrusive – the very antithesis of the gentleman leader-writer or university-educated editor. Allingham recalled visiting Cheyne Row as Carlyle lay dying. 'Newspaper reporters or penny-a-liners used to ring at the street-door nearly all through the night, but at last bulletins pinned up abated the nuisance'.[14]

The combined effects of the new technologies, the reduction and abolition of taxes, increased advertising, and falling paper and telegraphy prices encouraged the launch of new titles and allowed for the expansion of individual titles and increased staffing.[15] Some of these innovations also changed the nature of journalists' work. With the telegraph 'no longer can there be a tranquil life either for foreign Correspondent or English editor.... the Correspondent becomes the slave of the remorseless wire. He must fill the maw of the voracious cormorant somehow....'[16]

By the late 1870s the facilities for parliamentary reporters were a far cry from the cramped space Dickens had known. Apart from the writing-room where verbatim reporters on a shift basis transcribed leading speeches on to 'flimsy' for the waiting messengers and telegraph boys, there were a cloakroom and lavatories, a news-room with magazines and weeklies, a smoking-room and a refreshment-room, where the hungry pressmen might find a 'fine round of beef on the side-board'.[17] The work itself might well have been ideally suited to women's capabilities, but the ambience was decidedly masculine, very like a gentlemen's club. Indeed a decade later when 'A Journalist of the Old School' defended the Serjeant at Arms for refusing to the Reporters' Gallery a *Daily Chronicle* journalist who had lampooned MPs he used precisely that terminology, arguing that the privilege of access was 'understood' in the same way as it would be to any respectable club.[18] It would be many years before women had access to the Press Gallery. Women who hoped that by acquiring shorthand and typing they were equipping themselves to become reporters or correspondents might have been surprised to know that even in the early eighties 'many [male] journalists' dictated their work to short-hand writers. Hatton said of the 'several men' who tried to use a typewriter only one managed to master it, and he was originally a printer. Eliza Linton, too, claimed never to have used one, but kept fine pens, scrupulously wiped, and carried round with her a squat glass inkstand, full of ink, protected in an old glove.[19]

The newspaper office varied both over time and according to the importance of the title. To the outsider the image of the newspaper office was perhaps always a retreat 'amid cigarette smoke and the rumour of continual event' where clever people write what they like, and others between intervals of brilliant repartee with the writers, correct proofs with cabbalistic signs and lightning speed, against a background of hovering errand-boys and the basement roar of steam-driven machines.[20] On the verge of the eighties a *Blackwood's* contributor looked back to 'the old system' when offices were in backstreets that seemed to typify the '*incognito* that was guarded by the writers'. The printing machinery was in the basement and above ground 'everything showed a sublime disregard of appearance'. The editorial *sanctum* might be roomy but it would be begrimed by gas smoke, with piles of manuscripts and papers against the 'ink-splashed skirting-boards'. Ancient offices with 'rickety floors' and perpetual babel on the staircases are contrasted with Modern, epitomized by the *Times's* spacious airy rooms for each department, including advertising, a well-lighted library like a London club housing the paper's files, and telegraph room where world news telegraphs could be almost simultaneously transmitted to the neighbouring compositor.[21] The gist of the changes was no doubt captured, but generalizations are inevitably sweeping, illustrations probably untypical, and personal reminiscence tinged with a touch of romanticism.

When Eliza Lynn ventured into the editor's sanctum of the *Morning Chronicle* in the late 1840s the approach was via a 'narrow, dingy court' up 'the still narrower and still dingier stairs to a room whence I could not see the street for the dirt which made the windows as opaque as ground glass'.[22] Printing House Square round about the same time may have been, compared with the splendid new offices of the 1870s 'a simple concern conducted as a wholesale manufacturing business'. But it had its own counting-house, if no separate advertising department, and on separate floors the editorial department, the compositors and printing machinery, and the dispatch department.[23] Harriet Martineau finds a morning paper's offices at mid-century decidedly civilized. It is relatively quiet, even at ten in the evening because Parliament is not sitting. The stream of short-hand reporters in strict rota dashing back from the Gallery to transcribe their notes on to slips is absent. Instead the music critic and a journalist abridging law reports work peacefully by a tea-table. Alongside the piles of correspondence and proof-sheets the editor's desk is adorned with new books for review, resplendent in their gilded bindings. Four speaking-tubes connect him immediately to the different departments. Everything is very efficient. The advertisement department houses the repeat ads already set in type. One of the suite of editorial rooms even accommodates the 'gentleman' who sleeps there, roused at five every morning to catch important despatches that will just make the press in time for the seven o'clock mail train. Efficient and, excepting perhaps only that 'pleasant-looking tea-service', uniformly masculine.[24] If newspaper offices themselves seemed generally masculine in atmosphere, then the social life of Fleet Street was even more so. In the sixties WE Adams as a starry-eyed ideal-ist on Annie Besant's and Bradlaugh's *National Reformer*, was disillu-sioned. When work was done the 'more or less muzzy and muddled' hacks disported themselves drinking and arguing, first in the tavern and when that closed, into the early hours in a 'night house'. It was 'calculated to take the heart out of a young and ardent propagandist'.[25]

The atmosphere on provincial papers was somewhat different. Women, particularly those with family connections, did find opportu-nities for work in the provincial press. In the early decades, even before Christian Johnstone's Scottish paper, a woman is reputed to have done 'a considerable amount of work' for the *Sheffield Register*, and in 1838 Fanny Kortright joined the staff of another provincial paper. Much later in the century came two editors' daughters, Emily Hawkes Marshall of the Darlington *Northern Echo* and EM Tait of the Rugby *Advertiser*.[26] Opportunities varied within the United Kingdom, however, and in England were relatively good compared with those in Wales.[27] But provincial papers ran on very small staffing levels. As Lucy Brown summed it up, though the dailies in large cities might operate more like the London papers – in 1868 the *Manchester Guardian* for instance had seven reporters – 'the weekly local paper was likely to be run by a man and a boy, as part of a jobbing printer's establishment'.[28] In the late 1880s a contemporary press historian knew of provincial editors who were even then their own 'leader writers, critics, reporters'; when needs must, turning printer or errand-boy.[29] Rural transport might have scarcely moved on since Dickens's early reporting days. AG Gardiner as a junior reporter on the *Chelmsford Chronicle* spent most of his time out of the office racing through the perilous country lanes in a dog-cart from petty session to church festival.[30]

In some ways too the characteristics of the successful presswoman remained constant. The manifold qualities of the 'general practitioner' as spelt out by Catherine Drew – 'quick to observe, keen to appreciate, cautious to accept statements' a sense of proportion, adaptability and voracious knowledge – were almost exactly those of Eliza Lynn decades earlier.[31] 'She was, indeed, the first of women journalists' wrote Helen Black of the ten years during which Eliza Linton virtually gave up fiction and devoted herself to journalism.[32] Mrs Linton herself claimed that the 'first three women who ever wrote for the press at all were Mrs. Grote, the Hon. Mrs. Norton, and myself'. It depends how you define the 'press' and as Layard noted, there was also Miss Martineau. Eliza Linton was, however, the first *staff* (i.e. salaried) woman on a national newspaper and found it 'up-hill work'.[33] She joined the *Morning Chronicle* when it had only recently been taken over by the Peelites, who placed John Douglas Cook in the editorial chair. She would be part of an impressive team, including Thackeray tempted in October 1848 with 'an awful bribe' of five guineas an article to 'blaze away in the *Chronicle* again'. The paper at the time was energetically managed, issuing several editions a day, to catch late news items, and printing the sort of social articles at which Dickens was so effective, one of the most notable being the long series, devised by Henry Mayhew, on the conditions of the poor in the manufacturing towns, rural areas and London.[34]

Young Eliza Lynn needed some courage to face Cook in his den and persuade him to give her a chance to be a journalist. The inquisition was spiced with laughter and oaths before she was given a three-and-a-half hour deadline and set to work with an annotated Blue Book to produce a leader on a Parliamentary Commission into the effects of the truck system on miners. 'To my great joy and supreme good luck, I seized the spirit of my instructions, and wrote a rattling, vigorous kind of paper' which secured her the job averaging over 20 guineas a month from 1848–51.[35]

I worked hard for very moderate pay ... My work was my pleasure, and to do well was its own reward. I had that appetite for work which is the essential of success on a newspaper; and I was to be relied on at a pinch as well for the day's steady routine. I filled the office of handyman about the paper – was now sent down to describe a fête; now given a pile of books to review; sometimes set to do the work of the theatrical critic when this gentleman was away; and given certain social leaders to write – but never political......Twice I got the paper into trouble because of my unsound political economy, and the trail of the socialistic serpent, which made itself too visible for even.....(what)....was one of our then most advanced Liberal journals.[36]

Eliza's enthusiastic radicalism was not the only cause of her exclusion from political issues. The paper had its male leader writers like

Abraham Hayward, with access to the clubs and fashionable dinner-parties.[37]

Leader-writing was a civilized occupation. 'The editor used to send me a little note in the morning with the House of Commons discussions or the Blue Books. I wrote my leader; and at four P.M. the printer's devil came to fetch the "copy" for the next morning's edition' she told Mrs Tweedie years later, adding 'Things are not done in this dignified and sheltered manner nowadays.'[38] Yet it was not all sheltered and dignified. She was still operating in a man's world.

Cook could be a fearsome figure, with a fiery temper. He was, she told Escott, 'A Napoleon among editors, indeed, but, mercy on us! what a temper. Has he not sworn at me? Yes, and actually hit me, if he thought I had not carried out properly any of his commands in the smallest detail.' The *Chronicle* rumour was that he once placed 'an offending printer on the fire'.[39] Something of her own sense of inferiority bred from the conditions of her sex seeps into the remarks of her fictional editor to his sub regarding women,

> Their worst faults are looseness and partiality; and their most annoying, the uncertainty of their work and their want of reliable power.... Then they are so desperately touchy!.... If you ... rap their knuckles as you would a man's, they fire up and stand upon their dignity as 'ladies' ... the creatures want the cream of both states – the independence and money-getting power of men, and the conventional respect of drawing-room ladies.[40]

This view so uncannily anticipates Stead and Bennett that it may come from Cook himself. Eliza became highly organized, cultivating efficiency and punctuality, virtues which led to her pride in Dickens' comment that she was 'good for anything, and thoroughly reliable'.[41] In Paris in the early 1850s as correspondent for the *Leader* and free-lancing for the *Chronicle* she found things financially precarious and was glad of the £5 fees for her *Household Words* contributions. Here she had the support of Frazer Corkran, Paris correspondent to the *Morning Herald*, who helped her get newspaper stories and welcomed her to his home despite the notoriety of her 'shocking book' *Realities*.[42] Mrs Lynn Linton in her old age, the age of the New Journalism, protested at the school of 'young lions' who boggled over Dante but were at home 'when they note who talks to whom, ... and who are not to be trusted in interviews'. The 'questing hound, his nose to the ground, sniffing the scent', was 'more than a trifle offensive'.[43] Her own reputation had been founded on a different style of controversy, in an older school of journalism. Yet Mrs Linton was undoubtedly the archetypal 'all-round-journalist' and with her 'Jezebel *à la mode*' articles was an early contributor to Yates's *World*. The difference was that she saw herself as expressing serious views.

Give me 'the real solid pleasure of work – a man's work – work that influences the world – work that is power! To sit behind the scenes and pull the strings – to know what one says as "We" in the *Comet* is taken among thinking men as a new gospel' cried Jane Osborn of the pull of leader-writing.[44] In Eliza's days on the *Chronicle* and Martineau's early years on the *News* there was leisure to give serious consideration to the matter of a leader. From the 1860s onwards, with the advent of technological change in communications and the printing process, the conditions under which leader-writers worked altered. Material coming through from 'continental wires in the editorial room' increased the pressure. Some clearly thought these conditions 'stimulating' to the well-equipped journalist; others thought it impossible to deal intelligently with complex situations on the basis of inadequate information on some 'startling piece of news'.[45] Fanny Green thought few women intellectually equipped to be leader-writers. Her account of women journalists, though mentioning Frances Cobbe and Eliza Orme, gives only Martineau's 'valuable and successful' leader-writing as an exceptional female achievement.[46] By then daily leader writers were well-paid. *Times* staff had minimum retainers of £1 000 a year, though they were not permitted to write for any other periodical, and the London dailies' retainers were between £500 and £1 000.[47] Harriet Martineau's achievements were both an inspiration to her women contemporaries and a touchstone of what 'a woman can do' for the generations that followed. Women as disparate as Eliza Linton and Mary Mitford admired her. Miss Mitford, though disagreeing with her theories thought her a great honour to both her sex and country.[48] Between 1852 and 1866 the 'she-Radical' produced over sixteen hundred leaders for the *Daily News*.[49] Her writings, appearing almost daily during the 1850s, significantly contributed to the formation of the paper's style and success. She made her mark precisely because she dealt with masculine subjects. 'I wonder', thought Florence Fenwick-Miller, 'how many of the men who have presumed to say that women are "incapable of understanding politics", or of "sympathizing in great causes", received a large part of their political education, and of rousing stimulus to public-spirited action, from those journalistic writings by Harriet Martineau?'[50] Yet within a couple of years of her engagement with the

News Harriet was so seriously ill that it was thought she had little time to live let alone write. Her work was done almost literally from the invalid's couch. Action in the style of that 'true journalistic aptness' which had enabled her to take to the *Daily News* advance information on the sailing of the fleet to the Baltic during the Crimean war was not the kind of journalism she would ever undertake again. 'It is pleasant', wrote George Eliot in 1856 'to think that Harriet Martineau can make so much of her last days. Her energy and her habit of useful work are admirable.' Just when she might have rested on her laurels and cared for her 'always precarious health', she turned instead 'to her fourth career'.[51]

Harriet had fortunately long since acquired the technique of writing rapidly, like letters, with little need to amend or correct. From The Knoll, her Ambleside retreat, with its study-cum-dining-room lined with bookcases, sunny drawing-room and porch embowered in summer with clematis, honeysuckle and passion flowers, she poured out her trenchant leaders. Occasionally the drama associated with daily paper work broke the peace of Ambleside. A telegram from Florence Nightingale 'Agitate! agitate' for Lord de Grey in place of Sir G. Cornewall Lewis' alerts her to the imminent death of the War Minister. The leader is written in time to catch the coach and duly appear in the *News*. Lord de Grey is appointed. Of course she could not claim it was cause and effect, but she did feel that journalism afforded scope to influence practical affairs. '[S]he repeatedly, in her letters, speaks of her journalism as the most delightful work of her life, and that which she believed had been perhaps the most useful of all her efforts.'[52] Her journalistic methodology was to take some tract, society report or speech, or an article from another paper and rework the material as a peg for her own views.[53] She frequently revisited causes and issues she espoused several times. To take a less well-known topic than her views on the American Civil War or women's rights she returned on several occasions to crime, punishment and prison. In 1853 for example she addressed the subject of reformatories and juvenile delinquency in four separate *Daily News* leaders. It turned up again in more leisurely style in the prestigious quarterly the *Edinburgh Review,* 'Our Convict System' appearing in January 1863, and 'Female Convicts' in 1865. Typical of her robust but humane attitude was her *Daily News* leader of September 22, 1864 objecting to the export of criminals to Australia. Martineau believed in the duty of prisoners to earn their keep as much as she believed in the duty of society to manage the punishment and reformation of its own offenders. '[W]e cannot shift the charge of our criminals upon anybody else.' Hard labour, but 'the real thing and not the sham' – was a discipline from which even female convicts could benefit *if* the right kind of work, '[u]seful, necessary, self-supporting public works' could be found.

She made her point with sharp turns of phrase. On opposition to copyright: 'supported as it was by a public, who not only liked to have books excessively cheap, but was possessed of some grand notion of ideas being free as air, of intellect being above barter for money' (3 March 1853). On occasion she used shock tactics, lulling the reader into a false complacency: 'It is fearful that child murder should exist in England to the extent it does, and has done since the lowest working-class became acquainted with the use of arsenic. It is shocking that so many children should die by the neglect of working mothers, and the administration of narcotics'. Then she introduces her real point. Some people may think it 'more fearful and more shocking' that far more infants die from lack of a suitable milk supply. (17 September 1864) Though her work was conducted far from the capital, Martineau's polemicizing of the writings of others was symptomatic of the way in which the periodical press afforded women a kind of vibrant debating chamber.

Frances Cobbe came to the *Echo* when the popularization of newspapers was well under way. She started with the *Echo*'s launch and stayed for seven years. The *Echo* was a four-page paper until in January 1869 it announced a doubling in size to include just about everything 'editorial articles ... Foreign intelligence ... authentic and exclusive political information ... News from the provinces, received daily' sport, crime, theatrical and musical 'gossip', 'shipping intelligence' and so on. The increase in size, though naturally this had not been trumpeted, also allowed for whole pages of 'advertorial'. Prior to this the back page was largely small ads, with the centre pages devoted to summaries from the morning papers, 'This Evening's News' carrying timed Reuters' reports, city news, 'Sporting Intelligence' (i.e. mainly racing) and crime. The latter included vivid accounts of punishments – 'more dangerous prisoners' were 'enabled' to witness the flogging of three garotters when two men yelled for mercy but nineteen-year-old Solomon Robinson 'bore his thrashing with a surprising amount of fortitude and endurance' (6 January 1869). The *Echo* leaders filled most of its front page. This was the context in which Cobbe's work appeared. The leaders had to catch the eye and make an impact. Hers were usually the second leaders, varying in length from one-and-a-quarter columns to almost two columns. She summed up her work as on 'all manner of subjects, politics excepted' but she preferred those with 'some ethical interest' or 'an opening for a little fun!'. When Arthur Arnold offered her the opportunity late in 1868 to work on a halfpenny paper she had experience as foreign correspondent of the *Daily News,* had recently been on the staff of a short-lived journal and written for various periodicals. The arrangement was that she should go 'three mornings a week at ten o'clock' to the Catherine Street office to write a leading article 'on some social subject' chosen after due consultation with the editor, together with any 'Notes' that were required. She had the privilege of a private room for her own use and if her claim is true she repaid the privilege by never once failing to turn up. 'Sometimes it was hard work for me; I had a cold … or the snow lay thick and cabs from South Kensington were not to be had.' By turning up regardless on time and fulfilling her tasks she 'proved, I hope, once for all, that a woman may be relied on as a journalist no less than a man'. Her following remark 'I do not think, indeed, that very many masculine journalists could make the same boast of regularity' suggests, however, that she recognized women had to be *more* efficient than men if their deficiencies were not to be attributed solely to their sex.[54]

Arthur Arnold got considerably more than mere reliability. At her best, fuelled by some social horror or injustice, and with the bit between her teeth, Cobbe wrote with a vigour and fresh turn of phrase that even today strikes home. Partly this stems from her literary style, mixing straightforward reportage with telling comparisons, challenging questions, eye-catching openings and sting-in-the-tail conclusions; partly from checking out her sources in person.[55] Reports of coroners' inquests provided ample material for leaders. The account in her autobiography of visiting in Drury Lane the 'filthy coffee-house, frequented by unwashed customers' where a middle-aged former governess, daughter of a country rector, had been found literally 'Starved to Death' is a harrowing tale, with its poignant and ironic finale of burial in 'some family vault'. But Frances Cobbe, even early on, was equally able to shock *Echo* readers with a tale of starvation amongst the labouring classes. The facts of 'Starved to Death!' (30 January 1869) in summary were perhaps alas, not unusual. Catherine Spence, her husband and child lived in one room in a six-roomed house in the Isle of Dogs, where all the families were on parish relief 'a sort of "chapel-of-ease" of the workhouse'. Spence was unemployed. They paid a shilling a week and their furniture was a bed, a box and a chair. The last blanket had been pawned. Spence applied to the workhouse Guardians and was ordered to the stone-yard to collect meat, tea and sugar. He never arrived. A fortnight later Catherine and the baby were lying 'dead on the wretched bed without bed-clothes, and two days later the husband was raving mad, in confinement at the workhouse'. Cobbe structures her tale with an introduction on responses to tragedy during the Reign of Terror when Frenchmen who wept at theatrical tragedies next morning 'shouted with glee' as the tumbrils trundled to the guillotine. 'He who has a taste for tragedy here, in London, need not trouble himself to pay for a stall at any of the theatres.' He should go to a coroner's inquest. Having told the story starkly she assumes the reader's shocked response, and desire for a scapegoat. 'But it is by no means clear "Who should we hang?" The neighbours were themselves starving.' The only alternative for the Guardians was to offer hard, useless and ill-paid tasks like stone-breaking. She proffers a constructive suggestion – employment in public works. But it is in her conclusion 'it seems a trifling detail, but to us it is hardly short of appalling' that Cobbe hits her readers hardest, picking up on that curious reference to the house as 'chapel-of-ease' and making an ironic juxtaposition with the first leader 'Prayer Book Reform'. 'On the box beside her dying bed, – her bed of slow starvation' lay a gift 'of some charitable visitor. Was it a little nourishing broth or tea, or perhaps warm wrapping of some sort? No, it was nothing of the kind, – something of "higher value", as the donor would probably have told her. It was a tract – a tract on the subject of the "Goodness of God!"'√

Cobbe handled serious religious issues and religiosity as effectively as she dealt with both social evils and social mannerisms. 'Lent in Belgravia' and 'Sunday Best' deal as lightly with the trappings of religious observance as 'Girls and "Drawing Rooms"' deals with the excesses of the social 'Season'.[56] Even in the early days she handled confidently a range of topics. In March 1869, for instance, her leaders included beggars, girls' education, 'Moral of the Boat Race', 'Elopement', 'Sentiment of Lamartine' as well as the religious questions. 'Sunday Best' followed a more serious discussion objecting to the introduction of the confessional into the Church of England, and a day or two later came 'Swallowing Camels' (15 March) an essay on social and moral hypocrisy, straining at gnats and swallowing camels. 'To witness a small transgressor inspires us with noble moral indignation.... But give us a good large, unmistakeable vice to devour, and our appetite rises generously with the occasion.' Indeed she probably found as she said some initial difficulty in keeping her ideas within the straightjacket of a newspaper column. She felt herself chopped into little pieces by the subs on the *Echo*, *News* and *Examiner* but the constrictions of space helped to produce some of her liveliest and hard-hitting writing.[57]

By the end of the century the numbers of women working for newspapers had increased. Some like the foreign correspondents, Flora Shaw and Emily Crawford, had already made their mark. Others like Mary Billington, who worked for the *Echo* and later the *Graphic*, hoped to. By 1896 there were over two hundred members of the Society of Women Journalists, and Mary Billington estimated that 'a very large proportion' of Writers' Club members were solely engaged in newspaper work. But the picture is still a mixed one. The message to aspiring women journalists was ambivalent. Fanny Green suggested that there were lots of opportunities but pointed out that few women had gained a substantial footing in journalism. Salaries were equal to those of men for those women who did 'good work'. Men could get a start as short-hand reporters, but few papers employed women in that capacity. They could of course be 'unattached reporters' but 'lining' – even at the more inflated rate of twopence a line – clearly had its risks. The most promising fields still seemed to be 'social and political questions of special interest to their own sex' although Green also mentioned 'descriptive' writing, i.e. the lively sketch of an event or situation, as an area in which women had made their mark.[58] Mary Billington, despite her own success, thought journalism a career 'very far from being a generally suitable one for women'. She was writing particularly from the point of view of the 'correspondent', doing work that nowadays is often done by a team of reporters, though 'correspondent' still appears under bylines. The use of the term 'reporter' in the nineteenth century was much more restrictive. It almost always referred specifically to the verbatim shorthand reporter, and though a few women attempted to earn a living at it Mary Billington thought it a field 'alike very limited and very overcrowded', even if not going quite as far as the writer who in 1891 considered 'reporting' inappropriate for an 'unprotected girl'.[59] There seems general agreement that a correspondent's working day could be gruelling. Flora Shaw often wrote during the night. Mary Billington wondered if many women could stand a day such as she often had 'when we were in Portsmouth Dockyard at nine in the morning, inspected the ship, saw the various receptions and addresses presented on board, attended the Queen's Birthday review ... came up to town in the special train, and had three columns of material to write on arrival'. Emily Crawford recalled the Shah's visit to France with festivities 'of surpassing splendour' finishing with a garden-party at Versailles and a *soirée* lasting till midnight, and not a moment free to write. A snatch of sleep in the carriage home was insufficient to relieve her fatigue. She went to bed arranging to be woken at two so she could write her column refreshed.[60]

The necessity of sometimes having to switch one's plans at a moment's notice was a hazard for newspaper journalists of both sexes, but women had the added problem of their dress. For Frances Cobbe it may not have been too great an obstacle. She was once amused to be offered the pick of her *ensembles* by a fashionable dressmaker for the honest account she gave of the lady's workrooms. Naturally she never took up the *douceur*. In any case she wore simple clothes made by her maid.[61] Women correspondents, however, usually had to attend social functions, and perforce dress appropriately. Emily Crawford's coverage of the Shah's day in Paris involved two changes of dress and two 'complicated' hair-dressings. There were journalists who had to maintain themselves 'and keep up appearances' on £4 a week. One at least thought she would have done better financially to have settled for the much castigated 'toilet column' or 'Decoration by correspondence' rather than interviewing or special article writing.[62] It was with an irony born of experience that Charlotte O'Conor Eccles in one of her fashion articles took to task the French journalist M Jollivet who pitied the poor woman condemned to dress on a pittance of £240 a year. While consenting to strike off the 'odd £40' 'self-respect forbids the revelation' of how much less her own annual budget was. 'I have heard and read, however, of persons who strike off the £200, and – pray whisper it in the very smallest type – present a good appearance on the forty.'[63]

In some ways 'New Journalism' assisted women as Bennett implied when pointing out that among 'morning papers, the most attractive to the outside contributor' was the *Mail* which did 'not ask itself on receiving an unsolicited contribution: "Is it our custom to publish things of this kind?" No, it scorns precedent and is always anxious for novelty.'[64]

Structural changes in the industry however did not particularly benefit women. Reporting the establishment of a Women's Press Agency, with Catherine Drew as editor, to syndicate articles by women journalists on 'subjects which may be supposed to interest women', the *Englishwoman's Review* noted that the press agency system had been entirely in the hands of men. 'Even articles by women pass from the hands of the writers to become the exclusive property of their employers, who re-issue them to daily and weekly journals. Profits made, if any, go to the agency, and no woman can receive any share of them.'[65]

Susan Carpenter was the first woman to work for the PA and many of her assignments there seem to reinforce women's complaints about being channelled into more frivolous 'women's interests'. Her entry in journalism followed her series of letters in the *Lady* exposing the reality of prospects for educated women in Australia. With the PA she seems to have spent much time chasing from coiffeur to Court dressmaker to get details of the *ensembles* to be worn at Court occasions.[66]

The advent of the electric telegraph system was bound to have some effect upon the work of the foreign correspondent. When the *Times* established its wires from Berlin and Vienna (via Brussels) in the sixties old hands had to adapt more leisured letters to the speed and new technique of telegraph transmission. It was partly his skill at this that endeared de Blowitz to the paper. By the nineties, when he was Paris correspondent, his salary was £3 200 per year.[67] Women who worked as foreign correspondents entered a stressful world. No wonder Drew demarcated women like Mrs Crawford and Miss Shaw from the normal run of female journalists.

Emily Crawford's apprenticeship was more stressful than most. 'Battles, barricades, bombardments were so familiar as to cease to frighten. The noise of cannonading lulled to sleep at night' but she thought it good training. 'One was deconventionalized and thrown back on first principles.' When *Truth*, the highly successful weekly mixture of exposés, political and financial comment and society gossip, published its history in 1913, one of the handful of 'literary staff' (as opposed to proprietors and editors) mentioned by name was Emily Crawford 'the veteran Paris correspondent' and one of its two journalists who had been contributing since the seventies.[68] Her 'Letter from Paris' appeared in every issue from 1877 to 1915 wittily reflecting her understanding of the French nation and appreciation of its art and culture. As the wife of the *Daily News* Paris correspondent, she had long lived in France and was on friendly terms with 'Victor Hugo, Gambetta, Clemenceau, and every one else of note in France, male or female, during two generations'. Fox Bourne considered the paper 'exceptionally fortunate' in securing the services of a contributor whose experience, 'facile pen', 'sound judgment and keen sense of humour', enabled her to describe the details of political and social life with remarkable precision and truthfulness.[69] To a contemporary journalist *Truth* appeared 'Bitter, personal, brilliant, chatty, impudent, sometimes reckless, always amusing, *Truth* is liked and feared'.[70] But Emily Crawford was perfectly able to write in more serious and radical vein. On the death of her husband in 1885 she succeeded him as *Daily*

News correspondent sending weekly her 'chronicle and exposition of French politics'[71] until 1907. The 'queen of journalists' as Fanny Green called her, was mentioned favourably by almost every chronicler of presswomen of the time. As a correspondent she was both versatile and professional. For the debate of May 25, 1871 she received special permission to sit on the front row of the *large grille* at Versailles and it is said she sat listening from seven in the morning until midnight, unable to take any notes, returning to Paris to write up the account of the defeat of the Government, to catch the early mail to England. Mrs Crawford found the work of foreign correspondent taxing. It was highly competitive and one never let up. Writing at night against the clock one had neither time to 'prune and polish' nor the opportunity to check one's proofs. Even with weeklies the carefully prepared article might be overtaken by 'some thunderingly big event … I had at once to turn round to hunt this hare'.[72]

Emily Crawford's brief included as much social pageantry as politics, but there were female foreign correspondents who like some of their male counterparts took up a partisan stance on foreign issues, even occasionally becoming embroiled in political events. Lady Florence Dixie who reported on the Zulu war became a prominent advocate of Zulu independence. Jessie Meriton White, who was Italian correspondent for the *Daily News* and *Nation*, acted as a field nurse during Garibaldi's campaigns, married one of his officers and was an ardent supporter of his cause.

When Janet Hogarth characterized the girl graduates hankering after journalism as ignorant of the work, 'But they have heard of the lady who swayed South African politics', her readers would have needed no further identification.[73] She was thinking of Flora Shaw. Flora Shaw was, according to the *Westminster Gazette*, one of those 'women writers whose style is marked by judgement and argumentative strength sometimes supposed to be specially male characteristics'.[74] Her political views may not endear her to modern radical feminist critics. Contemporary feminists saw things rather differently. The *Englishwoman's Review* referring to the recent volume publication of her *Letters from South Africa*, and her Australian dispatches currently running in the *Times*, rejoiced in repeating an anecdote told by financier and politician, Lord Cromer (Sir E Baring). He once expressed surprise that having expounded to a journalist upon some 'financial matter of great public importance, but tedious and complex in its details', to find in print not some 'loose … generalization' but 'an exposition of the case … at once lucid, detailed, and absolutely correct'. The journalist in question was Miss Shaw, whom he concluded was probably better informed on colonial affairs than 'almost any other London journalist, and than any other lady in England except the Queen'.[75]

Her career as a foreign correspondent began when in 1886 she accompanied friends on a long visit to Gibraltar. Something of her approach is revealed in her tactics for her first important interview. Through Meredith she had an introduction to Stead, then editor of the *Pall Mall Gazette* who invited her to submit any letters she thought worthwhile. It was here on one of her explorations she chanced upon the exiled Zebehr, whom Gordon had wished to have as his successor in the Sudan. Week after week with the interpreter between them she sat in the dilapidated cottage that was Zebehr's prison, taking down his version of his life, and as a kind of trust grew between them, facing him with the hostile English view and noting his responses to the accusations. She handled her material scrupulously enough for Stead, whose paper had bitterly attacked Zebehr as a slaver, to publish her account. By the end of her tour she was established as a journalist, the *PMG* and others having taken her articles on the protection rackets of European traders in Morocco and the indifference to the situation of the great Powers. By the time she went to Egypt in 1888 she was the accredited correspondent of both the *Manchester Guardian* and the *PMG*. Here she met Moberly Bell of the *Times* and Sir E Baring who as administrator in Egypt was anxious to get over to the British press his perception of the Egyptian situation. The mutual arrangement whereby politician and journalist helped each other was a staple of foreign correspondence work. Flora was an advocate of British emigration to the colonies and later broadly sympathetic to Rhodes's imperial policy. Yet she researched her topics thoroughly, using available Blue Books, press articles and available documents and seems to have tried to get opposing views on complex situations. On one occasion after an exhaustive interview with a Colonial Office official she boldly asked him to recommend someone who held an opposite opinion. Despite differing with CP Scott politically and with Stead journalistically she was apparently objective enough to enjoy successful working relationships with both papers. The *Guardian* sent her as its representative to the Brussels Conference of 1889, the only woman correspondent present. When she eventually joined the *Times* she was spiritually at home though as a woman she could not make the kind of straightforward application a man would. Harcourt Kitchin for instance simply wrote speculatively to Bell and having completed the application form received by return a hand-written letter inviting him for interview. Partly because of his modest demands he was immediately offered a job, though Bell's arrangements for his reception were chaotic.[76] With Flora, despite telling her if she were a man she would be 'Colonial Editor of the *Times* to-morrow', Bell had to be more circumspect. He gave her a regular assignment but her identity was kept under wraps. John Walter had, he believed, 'a horror of females doing anything ... when he heard [the article he admired] was by a *Miss* Shaw it nearly killed him, but he had the generosity and honesty to say that it was "highly creditable" to her, much as if she was a self-educated Kaffir.'[77] Eventually the proprietor was sufficiently mollified and she got her departmental appointment.

If Mrs Crawford faced bullets with calmness, Miss Shaw faced a Select Committee inquiry into the Jameson raid with equal equanimity, She answered questions from the likes of Labouchere and Harcourt on the coded telegrams sent under her name fluently, skilfully, rapidly and with an apparent openness that concealed as much as it revealed. Her explanations have been described as 'ingenious rather than complete'. Campbell-Bannerman in the Commons considered her unaware of the implications of the messages she sent to Rhodes and her actions the result of a lady journalist's 'zeal and excited temperament'. This attitude may have been as naive as it is patronizing, but Flora could exploit it to protect Bell and the *Times* from any accusation of collusion with Rhodes. Her handling of the Committee was so tactically sophisticated[78] it is no wonder she inspired the Girton girls.

Emily Crawford had little doubt that the lively and fashionable descriptive writing of her day was something for which women had a particular talent. The one thing no editor wanted was a 'dryasdust' writer and she thought few women writers had ever been that. Looking at press accounts of state occasions of the past she found many of them lifeless and wondered why the female novelists of the time had not been seized upon by the national press. Sala's report on the Prince of Wales's wedding was a 'masterpiece' but even so she would have liked a sketch from 'say, the vivid, rattling pen of Miss Braddon. She had written several books in 1863. But it did not occur to any one in the neighbourhood of Fleet Street to tell her off for brilliant sketch work at the Royal wedding.'[79]

There was a general view that women journalists made the best interviewers, though one writer attributed this to the unscrupulous methods they used to ensnare their victims, a view to which Emily Faithfull's experience in America gave the lie. Elizabeth Banks thought women tactful, adroit, 'quicker, and more apt at observing' and was

impressed by the young English journalist who 'sized her up' wonder-
fully well, never took a note and turned out entertaining copy.[80] By the
early 1890s Hulda Friederichs had a high reputation as a woman interviewer.[81] Stead made systematic use of the interview and as his 'Chief
Interviewer' on the *Pall Mall Gazette* she was sent to conduct the major
ones. Her career exemplifies the precariousness of journalism even for
those with staff positions. She recalled 'vividly ... the anxious period'
when Newnes was besieged by businessmen and politicians advising
him that the *Westminster* in maintaining its political stance 'was steer-
ing straight for ruin'. It survived. She had not been so lucky on the *Pall
Mall Gazette* in 1892 when she had been one of the young editorial
team who left en masse following Yates Thompson's sale of the paper
to Astor. She had been among those who 'left the dear, tumble-down
old office in Northumberland Street on Friday at the usual time' to be
greeted the next morning by 'the bill of the morning paper' using 'the
fattest type' 'decorating the wall of the news-room in good journalistic
fashion' with the screaming headline 'Sudden Sale of the *Pall Mall
Gazette*'.

> It seemed so impossible, so like a poor joke, that ... our *P.M.G.*
> should, or even could, have been sold, so absolutely and entirely
> had we felt it to belong to us ... the paper was our pride and glory ...
> in the service of which there was great joy and much fun. And
> behind all the pleasure, the excitement and the fun there was the
> feeling that ... it was at the same time bent on grave missions ...
> that its sympathies were as wide as the world ... What did it all
> mean?

What it meant, the editor told them, was unless something dramatic
happened they would be walking out. What particularly upset the staff,
apart from the cavalier manner in which they had been treated was
'that it had been done with no care that its politics and social outlook
should be as they had been'. Hulda soldiered through the remaining
weeks of her contract with the rest 'as people work for some one near
and dear on the eve of a departure after which, humanly speaking,
there will be no return'. The loyal staff had their reward in the end for
the editor took them with him to Newnes's new *Gazette*.[82]

There were a number of American women like Annie Wakeman in
London as correspondents for American dailies, but they were not the
subject of Mary Billington's contempt when she rejoiced that 'English
lady journalists' had not descended to 'the vulgar sensationalism and

semi-detective business' of some 'American reporteresses'. '[H]appily our editorial methods and our own instincts as gentlewomen do not lead us to try being barmaids, or going out with costermongers'[83] to get copy. In fact British editors were only too delighted to get as many such articles as they could. When Elizabeth Banks 'a red-haired, freckle-faced girl from Wisconsin'[84] turned up they couldn't get enough of her 'stunts'. She was used to late hours and discomfort from her early days as a society reporter in America, and was enterprising in her ideas and approaches. She once boldly sent on to a second editor a rejected manuscript scribbled with blue-pencilled 'excellents' and 'not-so-goods' by the first. (It was accepted!) In London her articles on going undercover as a domestic servant, a West End flower-girl or strawberry picker caused a furore. She came to regret her original bright idea, becoming a victim of her own success. One editor told her she was introducing 'a bright, new attractive kind of journalism into London and ... Americanizing' the papers. If she carried on she could easily earn £1 500 a year. She was offered three times regular rates to go up in a balloon or work in a sweatshop but was unable to persuade editors to consider more conventional articles, or to take her on at a modest salary of £3 or £4 pounds a week.[85] Back in her homeland in the wake of Nellie Bly 'stunt girls' were risking 'their lives and reputations in order to crash the papers' by posing as 'beggars, balloonists, street women, servants, steel workers, lunatics, shop girls and Salvation Army lassies'. When she returned Banks reluctantly turned to 'Yellow Journalism' to make a decent income and was offered some assignments she refused as 'indecent'.[86] Interestingly she thought the absence of co-education in England would make it almost impossible for men and women reporters to work together in that field. The English reporteress was saved by her schooling.

One of the legacies of Britain's 'New Journalism' to our modern press was the rise of the columnist. Most of the newspaper columnists also contributed to magazines, the women columnists in particular to women's journals. There was in content and style some overlap. But the spectrum of individual columns was a broad one. The political change to the *PMG* which Hulda and her colleagues had feared came about. The new editor too was of a different cut. Harry Cust belonged to that cultured aristocratic social set who called themselves the 'Souls'. Once when every other paper's bills advertised a murder Cust's *PMG* ran with 'Art Notes. Special'.[87] Cust may not have much cared for 'female influence in the office'; his wife claimed never to have entered either the new or old *Pall Mall* buildings. But he clearly did not object to women contributors. Mrs Cust did 'a certain amount of [unpaid] reviewing' and it was under Cust's regime the 'Wares of Autolycus' column opened in May 1893 continuing under Straight to the end of 1898. All the contributors were female journalists. It appeared most days of the week, allowing scope for female and domestic interests, but not exclusive to them, Female aesthetes were prominent as contributors but a whiff of feminist feeling perfumed Autolycus' basket.

Although the column was anonymous the *Academy* gave some names away – Elizabeth Pennell was the 'enthusiastic gastronome'. Mrs Dew-Smith clearly wrote the gardening column and Miss Fleming was 'the satirist of her sex'. Among other contributors were Violet Hunt, Rosamund Marriott Watson, Katherine Tynan, E Nesbit and most famous of all, Alice Meynell. EV Lucas recalled her columns, 'In the midst of the riot of news and comment, rumours and sensation, turmoil and restlessness that make up an evening paper, came this silver rivulet, cool, limpid and peaceful.'[88] Meynell's pieces for 'Autolycus' were originally the Wednesday and later the Friday columns. They might be impressionist sketches or speculations on colours or clouds, gaining stylistically by the relative speed at which they must be written. Often they were literary critical, often too they were reworked for other journals.[89]

The 'Autolycus' articles in general however were constructed in the style of a gossip or social column, though slanted to various interests – food, fashion, décor, social news. It might open with a description of Saturday night at the Opera and 'Church parade' on Sunday, dropping a few society names ('Woman's Ways', 29 May 1893). The emphasis though is on social commentary. 'Fewer prayer books were seen than was the case in olden times'. The fashion paragraphs remarked what didn't suit (prune velvet bow 'which didn't quite accord with the gown') as well as what did. Sandwiched between Church parade and the gowns at a 'very select dance in Paris' one suddenly meets a recommendation of shop-window dressing as career for impecunious gentlewomen. Then there is a spirited objection to women being expelled from the Royal Geographical Society, an issue taken up again the following month when the Chicago women's conference was reported. Olla Podrida's column follows items on furnishings and fashion with a (no doubt heartfelt) plea for a woman's restaurant in the Fleet Street/Strand areas (12 June 1893).

A typical week in June that year offered 'Behind the Scenes with the Ladies' papers', fashion, social commentary including Fourth of June celebrations at Eton, the Fine Art Society's exhibition and New

Journalism interviewing, description of the manufactury of lace, décor, flowers etc. for Princess May's wedding, and a chat column including serious discussion of attitudes to women's ageing. The aesthetic quality of Autolycus' wares removed the feature from the ghetto of the gossip and society columnists.

In a similar way to the Autolycus 'Glass of Fashion' Florence Fenwick-Miller's *Illustrated London News* columns had a serious as well as frivolous side. Her initial piece (March 6 1886) spelt out her intention. She would treat of 'matters specially interesting to ladies, as they arise in the great world week by week'. The traditional 'woman's sphere' may have been 'Society, Dress, Domesticity and Charity' but 'To that is now added Culture, Thought and Public Welfare.' She kept her promise. Paragraphs on women's higher education jostle against Royal engagements, charity events against observations making feminist points. At a Mansion House children's fancy-dress ball, where little Miss Fenwick-Miller is garbed as a Doctor of Science, the 'young ladies' were noticeably more efficient in organizing the children than the male stewards. She dislikes female forms of address like 'Mrs Chairman' 'a sort of mermaid or centaur-like designation'. Middlesex magistrates are rebuked for an unwarrantedly harsh sentence, a male correspondent from enquiring of her about 'stays for men'(5 February 1887). Her accounts of social events are spiced with tart asides and personal opinion. Attending a Drawing-Room tea (an afternoon reception at which ladies after the Queen's Drawing Room show off their gowns to assembled admirers) gives her an excuse simultaneously for a description of fashion and a sardonic view of the process. When 'one has paid as much money for a single dress as would keep a poor family in comfort for a year … and … had that costly robe … spread out, passing through the Throne-room, for but some sixty or ninety seconds – well, perhaps it does seem as if it would be wasteful to go straight home in it' (28 May 1887).

Although the society column flourished in the 1880s and 1890s, with many of its most successful practitioners contributing to both newspapers and journals, it was not an invention of that period. Soon after the *Daily News* was launched Lady Blessington was asked to contribute social gossip – 'sayings, doings, memoirs, or movements in the fashionable world' on a confidential basis. She asked £800 a year and eventually agreed to a rate of £500 pa for the half-year with £400 pa 'for a year certain'. In the event she decided not to renew after the first six months, and was paid the £250.[90] 'Society journalism' expanded during the 1870s and was by no means exclusively the province of women. It was arguably a man, Edmund Yates, who in making '"gossip" essential reading' created a niche for the aristocratic lady columnist. He wrote gossip, edited it, and made it a central component of his own *The World: A Journal for Men and Women* (founded 1874). His notion of 'gossip' was far broader than receptions and *soirées*; it embraced the political and financial – the stuff of Stead's investigative journalism, yet it was always entertaining. Where a journal like *Belgravia* in the 1860s constructed its aura of High Society through the imaginative efforts of professional writers, the papers of the 1890s, like the annuals of the 1830s, turned to society ladies themselves, though now the mission was to supply snippets of 'gossip'. Lady Greville, daughter of the fourth Duke of Montrose, was one of Edmund Yates's 'discoveries'. One of the more professional society journalists she contributed to the *World* and provided the *Graphic's* 'Place aux Dames' column. Mrs Humphry, who came to be known as 'Madge' of *Truth*, for her 'bright and breezy letters' was probably the doyenne of social columnists and was reputed to earn £500 pa for her *Truth* weekly letters.[91]

All the papers seemed to have social columns, even that class of women's magazines aimed at a 'lower social status' than 'women of education and breeding'. They attracted criticism on several counts – triviality, intrusion, vulgarity, and hidden advertising. Evelyn March-Phillipps laid the blame for the excessive number of weddings chronicled and the dreary lines of pictures of court ladies 'decked in trains and plumes' firmly at the door of the advertisers. TP O'Connor defended gossip – 'between slander, scandal, and personal and pleasant detail, there is a wide gulf. Why should not the public be told of how the party of Mrs Smith went off; of how Mrs Robinson looked; of the dress Miss Jones wore? These are things which deeply interest a large number of people'. Yet he agreed with those who feared that British journalism was going the way of America. Others claimed the columnists eroded the pay of *bona fide* journalist. Of the 'dilettante scribbler' of the 'fair sex' plentifully endowed with 'this world's goods' writing reports of entertainments a writer in *Atalanta* asks 'Does she ... ever stop to think that the few guineas which she merely looks upon as a little extra fund for special luxuries and amusements represent to many the staple income on which they are to depend for absolute maintenance?' Frances Low felt so strongly about the adverse impact upon the 'legitimate' woman journalist of the well-to-do woman happy to write for poor pay for the sake of a free ticket to some society 'do' or to see her name in print that she advocated some form of trades unionism.

She certainly did not recommend 'society journalism' for the beginner, since most papers already had their upper-class correspondents eager to publicize their friends' events, and in any case it required an expensive wardrobe.[92] The staff reporter on a morning paper had always contended with late hours but the advent of an increase in society reporting with its late nights created additional problems for unchaperoned women and indeed their editors. For educated middle-class girls at the flimsy end of journalism the conflict between being a good reporter and remaining a lady was a real one. Despite the formidable challenges women did make their mark on the newspaper press. Florence Fenwick-Miller and Emily Crawford like the 'Wares of Autolycus' contributors wrote with a 'light hand' yet gave more solid fare than a permanent diet of 'frivolity and fashion'. Correspondents like Flora Shaw and Jessie White dealt with key foreign issues of the day. Leader writers like Harriet Martineau and Frances Cobbe wrote forcefully and effectively on subjects they cared about. Their views were quite individual but they stemmed from a woman's experience; the perspective was inevitably female. Matters important to women were aired. To that extent they provided a different voice. Unlike the 'Gentlemen of the Press' they had no formal access to the halls of government – no suffrage, no place in the Press Gallery. But they had some influence. Outside the corridors of power was a Fifth Estate.

4
At our Library Table: Reviewers and Critics

In the wake of a growing reading public came the authors and publishers anxious to satisfy its perceived needs. Alongside flourished the Reviews, the pages of publishers' advertisements in papers like the *Athenæum,* and the critics whose trawls through new books claimed to guide readers to gems amongst the chaff. Some more ambitiously sought to improve public taste to appreciate the literature of the past and of other nations. Women played a prominent, though often obscured, rôle in this process of popularization and education.

Women have been critics almost as long as they have been novelists, but Eliot and Woolf excepted, until very recently received little attention. Patrick Parrinder's *Authors and Authority,* acknowledging the existence of these female reviewers, notes the relative inaccessibility of their work.[1] Perhaps male critics were more inclined to write critical books, reprint essays in volume form, and in their memoirs strip the cover of anonymity from their periodical work. Certainly as literary criticism became embedded in wider public concerns, the rise of the 'sages' established a hegemony which marginalized female critics whose public access to the intellectual milieu of these 'Men of Letters' was difficult.[2] Even in the 1870s John Morley significantly entitled his series of critical monographs *English Men of Letters.* This image was reinforced in the academic canon of the present century. John Gross' 1991 edition of *The Rise and Fall of the Man of Letters* still credits, though generously, only one nineteenth-century woman journalist, predictably George Eliot.[3] But 'image' is not all. Influence can be pervasive without being apparent. As Maria Jewsbury put it, 'Power is power; and the power of disseminating opinions is not much less valuable than that of holding a levee or opening parliament.'[4]

The practice of anonymity encouraged women to write by affording them a shield – and, should they so choose, a masculine cloak for their views – yet paradoxically veiled their contribution from later scholars. Recently, however, women's reviewing has begun to attract the attention it deserves, their individual and collective influence begun to be recognized. In their critical capacity, Dale Trela remarks, they 'gradually rewrote the rules, gradually altered the consciousness of their age.'[5] Elizabeth Eastlake and Emilia Dilke in their rejection of Ruskin's ideas on art, and Edith Simcox in proposing a theory of autobiography, made significant and original contributions to criticism. Geraldine Jewsbury and Margaret Oliphant helped shape the direction of the realist novel. Despite problems of attribution, our existing evidence indicates that female reviewers found considerable scope for affecting public perceptions of literature and art, and since many were also essayists, some opportunity for addressing wider concerns. Mrs Mary Margaret Busk flooded *Blackwood's* and the *Foreign Quarterly* with her proposals.[6] For twenty years Hannah Lawrance contributed to the *British Quarterly* on history, literature, women's issues, as well as reviewing exhibitions and works like the *Life of Charlotte Brontë*, *Modern Painters* and *Idylls of the King*. Mrs Oliphant supplied *Blackwood's* with fiction, essays and reviews in almost every field except science and politics. The summary of Isabella Mayo's journalism in Blain's *Feminist Companion* (1990) 'reviews, articles on history and travel, and biographical essays for a variety of magazines' could serve equally for many other women. Chapter 5 considers these other genres. Here in foregrounding women's reviewing, I hope to indicate something of the scale of their critical influence and the distinction of their contribution.

The *Edinburgh Review* and its Tory rival the *Quarterly*, founded in the first decade of the century, dominated public discussion of cultural and social issues in the early years. With the appearance in 1817 of *Blackwood's Edinburgh Magazine*, the forceful, sparklingly cheeky rival to the staid Whiggish *Edinburgh,* there were already signs that critical debates might be as easily handled by a monthly with its inbuilt advantage of covering 'new' books before that epithet ceased to have any meaning. By 1820 Mary Mitford thought Magazines had 'all the best writing... – the best criticism, the best essays – the best fun' and she relished *Blackwood's* new blood 'with its audacious impudence' against the *Edinburgh* 'grown sober & elderly & gray haired – it walks with a stick and wears spectacles.'[7] Two major weeklies devoting substantial space to literature, the *Spectator* and *Athenæum*, were founded in 1828. The *Athenæum*'s reputation actually depended upon reviews rather than original writing. By mid-century the three weeklies – (the newcomer *Saturday Review*, absorbing 'the brains and capital' of its ancestor the *Morning Chronicle*, arrived in 1855) – bid fair to rival the quarterlies and monthlies in critical influence.[8]

Book reviews were a motley crew; some mere summaries padded out with extracts. At the other end of the scale James Mill characterized the *Edinburgh* and *Quarterly* as 'publishing dissertations' under the guise of reviewing books.[9] Constraints of space varied enormously. In the *Quarterly* Lady Eastlake might have 32 pages (A5 equivalent) whilst in the *Athenæum* Miss Jewsbury would be lucky to get two (A4). Almost from its outset the *Athenæum* professed to eschew editorial political stances, recruited specialist reviewers and rejected the model of review-as-peg-for-opinion. Even so, one of Charles Dilke's liveliest writers Lady Morgan manipulated her criticism to argue for democratic reforms.[10] The boundaries between review, biography and critical essay became particularly fluid in commentaries on the work of dead authors.

In the leisured monthlies composite reviews contextualized critiques of individual works, elaborating some underlying theme. This might be cultural (perhaps French or American fiction) or subject-based (travel books, new biographies, manuals on bee-keeping), aesthetic, like Mrs Oliphant's 'Sensation Novels', or topical, like Elizabeth Rigby's notorious article which opened with 'A remarkable novel is a great event for English society'. By discussing the 1847 Report of the Governesses' Benevolent Institution it proceeded to link *Vanity Fair* and *Jane Eyre* to the Governess question. Obituary tributes apart, assessments of an author's work and critical reputation often followed publication of an autobiography or memoir. Whilst convention encouraged politeness in the wake of a recent death, reviewers were not necessarily bound by the same form when dealing with biography. Mrs Linton's ostensible review in *Temple Bar* of Cross's *Life of George Eliot* is a brilliant, savage attack on Eliot's moral character and literary achievement. As the century wore on, the Queen's Jubilee and approaching millennium sparked off sweeping retrospectives like Mrs Oliphant's 1887 'The Literature of the Last Fifty Years' mining her own long career with *Blackwood's*. Beyond the old-established quarterlies and dominant weeklies many papers carried regular literary columns. Here, at the most modest level, were the 'Notices' of new books which within a paragraph or so summarized theme or plot and commented on calibre and style. By the turn of the century Frances Low indicated a widening gap between 'review' and 'notice' when she advised that though reviewing was of all its branches 'the prize of the journalistic profession' it required either an established literary reputation or close acquaintance with an editor. 'Book notices in inferior journals' were she warned paid at 'sweating prices' and a 'disastrous' introduction to 'quality reviewing'.[11]

One might expect daily newspapers to be the most up-to-date with the latest books. This was not always so. Nor was speed an improvement. By the 1890s a publisher could send out 'an important work ... in two large octavo volumes' one evening, and a daily publish 'what purports to be a criticism' the following morning. In earlier decades when Parliament was sitting the *Times* had little spare space, and most reviews were worked off during recesses. 'That a book was old was no obstacle, that it was new small recommendation.' Its predominate subjects were biography, memoirs and travel. Novels appeared sparsely during the first half century and though from the early 1820s it regarded the visual and performing arts as newsworthy, coverage was in the hands of men.

The official *Times* history gives the rare female critics short shrift. Caroline Norton and Lady Barker are introduced by the admission that some 'reviewers of fiction were not of the first order'. One might reasonably argue that Norton's standing on the *Times* was exaggerated. But to summarize her work: 'She wrote very charming letters to Delane on lace-edged paper, but her contributions to the paper were not many. The novels of her cousin, Sheridan Le Fanu, were her preserve' seems gratuitously insulting, even accepting her dilatoriness over a review of Froude's history. Of poor Lady Barker, other than discovering she retained her title after marrying Frederick Napier Broome, we learn only that 'it was her misfortune to be given *The New Republic*, which left her bewildered'.[12]

In fact in the later decades the *Times* used several women critics including Emily Gerard and Mary Ward. (It was rumoured the latter was dropped from the panel on grounds of her bias against women writers.)[13] Among other newspaper reviewers were Eliza Linton for the *Morning Chronicle* in the late 1840s/early 1850s; Rachel Cook for the *Manchester Guardian* in the early 1870s; Amelia Blandford Edwards on music, drama, and art for the *Morning Post* and Miss Dyer on art for the *Daily News*. Women also contributed significantly to the columns of the *Pall Mall Gazette*, where Alice Meynell's style and moral aestheticism established a distinct critical voice.

By the end of the century the dilemmas of the woman critic were sufficiently ubiquitous to figure in fiction. Sara Duncan contrasts the intellectual literary critic, Janet Cardiff, with Elvira, would-be Bohemian journalist and flashy exhibition reviewer.[14] Ella Hepworth-

Dixon ironically juxtaposes the 'female journalist' in 'a waterproof and a pince-nez' with her youthful heroine facing Grub Street pressures at her first Press View. 'She must find ... some phrase which might encourage the fair artist to go on painting editors' portraits.'[15]

Throughout the century debates on the purpose of criticism and complaints of superficiality and corruption in reviewing practice continually surfaced. Bagehot described reviewers as purveying literature like snacks. The ever-bustling Victorian readers snapped it up 'like sandwiches on a railway journey'. By the 1890s Charlotte Yonge was grumbling that 'a real review – not a mere notice' was seldom seen and Eliza Linton was attacking reading public and new generations of authors and critics alike. 'We can read nothing that takes time or trouble. Our science is got by reviews ... boiled down to their bare bones.' Only 'three or four men in the kingdom' were capable of reviewing 'a really deep and learned book'.[16] Already in the 1860s Grote saw contemporary newspaper reviewing in decline with little real discussion: 'each reviewer has pretty much the impression that with his own readers he has the last word ....' George Eliot privately made similar points. A sensible *Athenæum* review was 'quite a white crow' and the 'rarest thing' in newspaper reviews, whilst weeklies and monthlies offered a 'miserable hodge-podge of conceited incompetence.'[17] In this context RH Hutton argued for modesty in the claims of criticism: 'It is not the great judicial function that it affects to be.' Though the critic should help readers without sufficient 'time or culture' to appreciate 'works of power and genius', he also had a duty to 'the emphemeral productions of a busy generation. .... Unless he can enter into the wants of his generation, he has no business to pretend to direct its thoughts....'[18] Margaret Oliphant at the start of her own critical career thought the transitory quality of reviewing bore something of the orator's arts, 'of their very nature fugitive and ephemeral' but with 'innumerable advantages – immediate influence, instant superiority, a dazzling and unlaborious reputation'. The position of writers like 'Christopher North' and Sidney Smith (whose memoir she was reviewing) was of speakers, addressing the public 'out of a natural pulpit'. Oliphant and Hutton, even in stressing its fleeting nature, locate reviewing at the centre of contemporary cultural power; powerful not in an Arnoldian sense of critical legislation, but more dynamically. The reviewer's persona rather than judgement affects his public; the public's wants receive respect.[19] Whilst literature never quite became the monster of Carlyle's prediction 'one boundless self-devouring review',[20] reviews constituted a significant influence upon literature. Mrs Busk attributed the comparative extravagance of the fantastical in German irony in part at least to the English writers' 'fear of Reviewers before their eyes ... [whereby they are] sobered and fettered to boot'.[21] Despite certain authors' protestations that they never read them reviews carried weight through their potential effect on sales. Some writers even found criticism helpful. Charlotte Yonge thought it 'a great mistake' that George Eliot was protected from unfavourable reviews, 'they teach one much'.[22]

Looked at from another perspective reviewing provided a welcome supplement to literary earnings though, work for the stately quarterlies excepted, it was wearisome because of the sheer weight of reading, even had one perfected the art of skimming as Geraldine Jewsbury surely had. That voracious reader, Mary Mitford 'obliged to read every word' of an Epic Poem in two volumes concluded that 'No Poem should be longer than one can comfortably read at once'. Mary Ward complained she could just manage three or four volumes a week.[23] Despite this such writers as Lady Morgan, Margaret Oliphant, Geraldine Jewsbury, Mary Ward, Frances Cashel Hoey, Elizabeth Gaskell and George Eliot participated, sometimes vigorously, in the reviewing business. The resultant interplay of their own fiction with their critical assessments of fellow novelists and contemporary literary trends, created an animated cultural arena in which writing was practised, promoted and debated.

The policy of anonymity, dominant for a significant period, complicated these debates particularly over contentious gender issues. As argument raged round the identity and sex of 'Currer Bell' and 'George Eliot' reviewers speculated – often wrongly – on the masculine or feminine qualities evinced by the text.[24] Female reviewers 'protected their own identities sometimes more effectively than their subjects'. Thackeray seems not to have discovered that it was Miss Jewsbury who savaged his daughter's novel, nor Mary Braddon that it was Mrs Oliphant who attacked her character and work. The writer of the *Saturday Review* article 'Authoresses' went so far as to claim that since no one expected women to be capable of 'balanced and cold criticism' a woman critic 'has to judge and write as a man'.[25] Titles of composite critical columns, 'Our Library Table' (*Athenæum*) and 'The Old Saloon' (*Blackwood's*) suggest a distinctly male space. Mrs Oliphant's introductory description of *Maga*'s library, smelling of freshly bound books, firelight flickering on portraits of founding fathers, reinforced this impression. The masculine stances she assumed teasingly exploited it.

Long after other monthlies, in the wake of the *Fortnightly*, had dropped it, *Maga* defended anonymity on grounds of giving 'unknowns' a fair chance and preventing established writers from resting on their laurels.[26] One suspects Mrs Oliphant enjoyed the authoritative – and masculine – tone which the 'We' of the narrative voice lent to her critical judgements. She claimed anonymity liberated the reviewer from embarrassment. The man who could write of his friend's work 'with absolute impartiality... and sign his name ... must be braver and better than common men'. Though recognizing potential danger in the power to influence minds 'under his mask' she used its cover to dismiss what she deemed 'unworthy and decadent with mocking and stinging irony'. Some decades earlier Mrs Busk too developed a range of reviewing personæ to shield her personality, on one occasion specifically to avoid distressing friends.[27]

But in unscrupulous hands the system was open to abuse. There were continual complaints of the puffing of books, and worse. *Fraser's* and the *Athenæum* battled hard in the 1830s to stop publishers like Bentley and Colburn puffing their own books but dubious promotional practices never entirely disappeared. In 1843 Hood warned Hannah Lawrance against Colburn's policy on his *New Monthly*.[28] Mrs Linton, dismissing rumours that reviewers were actually paid for favourable notices, recorded a lady author's attempt to use her social position to influence an editor. For herself she claimed she neither sought nor gave personal favours. 'I was notoriously beyond fear or favour.'[29] Still, novels were commodities, and she had urged Bentley to send her own second novel to periodicals where she enjoyed friendly contacts. Nor was she alone in covering the work of 'known friends'. Geraldine Jewsbury, despite telling Bentley for whom she acted as reader that the *Athenæum* assigned books quite impartially, noticed sympathetically seven of her close colleague John Jeaffreson's. Mrs Oliphant even reviewed a book she had actually edited, 'Geddie' Macpherson's memoir of Anna Jameson, though the circumstances were unusual in that Mrs Macpherson had recently died.[30]

'Free and frank' reviewing did not just promise freedom from puffery; it also facilitated that savagery which, so the disgruntled author of *The 'Athenæum' Exposed*, complained, in the hands of 'a literary garrotter' brought ruin to the aspiring author.[31] Frances Cobbe thought the 'severe review' so cruel she shunned the 'office' of birching 'juvenile offenders' and hanging 'anarchists' on behalf of the literary community.[32] Female pens were as sharp as the male. Even George

Eliot, tolerant in her fiction, could be acidic as a critic. Lord Brougham was severely berated for his slovenly style. Like the kings and emperors who turned to 'making locks and sealing-wax' in idle moments she supposed him, on relinquishing the chancellorship, to have taken 'to what we may call literary lock and poker-making ... writing third-rate biographies in the style of a literary hack!'[33] Geraldine Jewsbury could be scathing. 'This novel has a narrow escape from being exciting; as it is, it is merely incoherent and confused.' '*A Troubled Stream* resembles the old Minerva Press novels ... a very foolish story, narrated in the style of a boarding-school girl.'[34] Mrs Oliphant tartly noted that after 350 pages of Charles Wood's adulatory memoir of his mother 'we are as little acquainted with her as we were at the beginning...'.[35] Linton's assessment of George Eliot's powers – 'the most magnificent kind of Papin's digester' – as she diminished them further by faint praise, exemplified her forceful irony. 'The chameleon-like quality of her mind, and her marvellous power of assimilation, made George Eliot able to profit by outside advantages as those of a more original and independent nature cannot.'[36]

Victorian spite was equally upsetting to critics. Mrs Oliphant diplomatically advised dealing with 'foolish, bitter, and useless remarks' about *Maga* in Macaulay's *Life and Letters* by a review 'in a loftier and more generous spirit' with one dignified but pointed reference to this lapse of taste. Mrs Linton however took such umbrage at Forster's life of her patron Landor that Dickens would not publish the review he commissioned. In the one that *was* printed in the *North British* she felt Forster's jealousy fully justified her 'taking the skin' off that 'harbitrary gent' of the cabman's rank'.[37]

The stereotypical Victorian female critic of myth, Mrs Grundy on the warpath, poisoned darts primed for the throw, is now justly a contested figure, but she had some basis in truth. Lady Eastlake did indeed complain 'Jane Eyre is throughout the personification of an unregenerate and undisciplined spirit', her 'auto-biography' 'pre-eminently an anti-Christian composition'. Mrs Oliphant did indeed write of Jude's relations with Arabella that 'nothing so coarsely indecent ... has ever been put in English print', although it is sometimes forgotten that she added 'that is to say, from the hands of a Master', and that *Jude* suffered similar attacks from other quarters. Miss Jewsbury did indeed lambast Rhoda Broughton's *Cometh Up as a Flower* as 'ignorant of all that women either are or ought to be'. Miss Broughton's reference to 'old Jewsbury's pen dipped in vinegar and gall' and her fictional portrait of her as Miss Grimstone tomahawking novels for *Porch* are too good to miss.[38] But such narrow selective quotation tells a partial story. The Eastlake and Oliphant remarks are extracted from lengthy reviews, and though these snippets express genuinely-held attitudes the breadth of their work reveals far more sensitive critical minds. Their criticism was as much grounded in morality as in aesthetics; they felt responsible to the readers of their relatively conservative periodicals. It is salutary to recall how widely shared was their dislike of anything smacking of 'coarseness'. The *Athenæum* was scathing in its suspicions of Felicia Skene's motive in portraying the evils of prostitution in *Hidden Depths*. Eliza Lynn's fiction came under fire from Dickens for its sexuality. George Eliot fully endorsed Chapman's serious reservations about the tone of a 'warmly and vividly depicted' love scene in Lynn's *Realities*. *Adam Bede* in turn suffered for its 'perilous voluptuousness'. Eliot who herself would express powerful sexual feelings yet drew back from such exposure in Lynn's work. Mrs Oliphant judged hereditary insanity an unsuitable main theme for fiction, and was almost as offended by the railings against providence of Geraldine Jewsbury's *Constance Herbert* as Lady Eastlake by Jane's recalcitrance.[39]

Women critics welcomed honesty in fiction, but one woman's honest expression of emotion sometimes seemed to another gratuitously self-indulgent once it appeared in cold print to be judged for her readership. This whole question of good taste and what was fit matter for the novel-reading public was fraught.[40]

These attacks on transgressing the bounds of decency ostensibly appeal to a universal standard, but the variations in responses suggest that this was never monolithic but always fragile. In the notices of the *Athenæum* can be traced the fluctuating boundaries of the acceptable as succeeding generations of novelists and critics alike, explored new freedoms. 'Notices' served a distinctly practical purpose. As Emily Davies advised a contributor to *Victoria* 'People see a book advertised, and wonder whether it would be worth while to order it in their Book Society, or to send to Mudie for it. They ask one. What is it about? Is it worth reading? Is it trustworthy, as far as it goes? Is it beyond the comprehension of ordinary readers?' Her reference to Mudie's reminds us that Victorian readers sought recommendations for their library subscriptions rather than purchases. By the 1880s '[B]orrowing books instead of buying them has become ... ingrained in our habits'.[41] Davies' suggested model was a shorter version of *Westminster*'s 'Contemporary Literature' column, but for fiction the sheer sweep of the *Athenæum*'s coverage made it the most comprehensive source of advice. To call it the mirror of its age is no exaggeration if one seeks in its glass a reflection of Victorian middle-England. Its women contributors were more numerous by the 1880s but always influential. Even Catherine de Mattos, most prolific of the substantial group of female contributors in the final decades, didn't match Jewsbury's estimated 2300 reviews between 1850 and 1880.

De Mattos covered almost all the Broughton novels of her period.[42] Her response to *Dear Faustina* reflects how far public opinion shifted over the thirty years since Miss Jewsbury's disgust at the slang, sensuality and self-indulgent sentimentality of *Cometh Up As A Flower*. *Faustina* now seemed straining to keep pace with current fashions in 'emancipated woman'. Whereas in the 1860s Broughton wrote 'with discrimination and daring' of the kind of girl she knew, establishing 'a convention ... [she] handled with ability and abundant conviction' she was out of her depth with the 1890s variety.[43] Yet the early work of both Jewsbury sisters, Geraldine's for Douglas Jerrold and Maria's for the *Athenæum*, was overtly feminist, in many ways ahead of its time.[44] Maria, encouraged to write by Alaric Watts editor of the *Manchester Courier*, began reviewing for Dilke's paper in 1830. Under her cloak of anonymity she set out to undermine the ideology of subordination which demarcated feminine 'heart' from dominant masculine 'head'.[45] Her attack on Anna Jameson's portrayal of female sovereigns as unfit to rule because of moral deficiencies would have its echoes sixty years later in the 'Wild Women' debate between Mona Caird and Eliza Linton. Maria died young, but her sister worked long enough to find her strict standards of reticence on female sexuality out of kilter with public taste. Geraldine's most sustained critical commitment was to the *Athenæum*. Many notices were admittedly brief. She not uncommonly reviewed five novels in the space of a page. The Christmas and juvenile reviews were even slighter, one such spanning twenty stories and annuals within two pages. Modern readers no less than her contemporaries probably enjoy Jewsbury's witty 'tomahawking' of dreary fiction as they do her amusing letters. In her reviews the waspishness is however contextualized by moral and aesthetic judgements. Before acidly remarking the luck of a hero and heroine to live 'in the limits of a novel with a guardian angel in the shape of the author ...' she has already established inadequacies of character and plot.[46] She observes improvements in a writer's technique, marking the merits of books she condemns – well-written sections, good descriptions, effectively-drawn characters – just as she notes faults in those she admires.[47] Her assessments can be shrewd. She detects Eliza Linton's bitterness in *Grasp Your Nettle* 'as though all the world ... were one vast nettle, ugly, contemptible ... to be .... trampled on', tellingly contrasting her treatment of foolish characters with Jane Austen's.[48] Dismissive incidental remarks succinctly suggest failures of style and structure. Her favourite way of dealing with the meretricious was to summarize the plot and give away the ending. She avoided revealing the *dénouement* when she approved, urging readers to get Mrs Riddell's *George Geith*, themselves – despite one deplorable element. 'Why are novelists so fond of bigamy? and why do they always treat it as a misfortune, and never ... as a crime?' But it was powerfully written, with a hero capable of winning the reader's respect. Miss Jewsbury sought pyschological realism. When she found it her sympathies were broad. The 'severest stickler for wifely duty will find no fault' with the unhappy wife in Lemon's *Falkner Lyle* who leaves her blackguard husband because 'her conduct secures the reader's sympathy'.[49] Her professional standards led her to put the readers' interests before advertisers'. Ward Lock's prominent advertisement promoting Miss Braddon's *The Lady's Mile*, on 5 May 1866, and a full-page displaying some thirty fulsome press endorsements on 26 May did not temper her subsequent criticism. In resigning 'her sceptre over the realm of the sensational novel' and aspiring 'to become a preceptor in the didactic school of manners and morals' the author like her readers 'seems to find the exchange a little dull'. Monika Fryckstedt detects a rare failure by Jewsbury to recognize the novel's social satire, but she did in fact see the symbolism of the Mile. She thought it heavy-handed, sardonically noting authorial lack of moral courage in the heroines' safe return from their gallop, neither having bolted from her 'glittering responsibilities'. Given Geraldine Jewsbury's moral standpoint and preference for the realist text it comes as no surprise to find her urging Bentley to take some of Margaret Oliphant's fiction because 'she is *really* the best story writer going *after George Eliot*'.[50]

As a critic Oliphant enjoyed an even more powerful platform than the *Athenæum* afforded, too powerful for male novelists like Hardy and James.[51] As *Blackwood's* main literary reviewer from June 1854 to almost the end of her life she responded to every keynote of the passing decades. In 1857 she was discussing contemporary portrayals of London 'Society' in the novels of Thackeray and Mrs Gore. She lived long enough to argue that the 'New Woman' was a creation of the Press and cast a sceptical eye over the *Yellow Book* and the *Second Mrs Tanqueray*. Her scope, covering fiction, biography, history, poetry, reference works, art and theatre, was impressive.[52]

Her criticism is grounded in the view that art is vital to the spiritual health of the nation, and should emanate directly from the society it serves. Hence her insistence on addressing the social context in which art flourishes, whether the question is the patronage of painters or the popularity of the sensation novel. The commodification of painting was destructive to the artist's integrity, the sensation novel particularly dangerous because so fatally easy to imitate.

Dale Kramer has convincingly argued the case for Oliphant as a major power in the shift of Victorian concepts of tragedy from the classical to the social. She virtually formulated the idea of 'domestic tragedy'. She certainly crystallized it.[53] She found Hamlet so tragic a figure because he perfectly exemplified disillusionment, 'that disenchantment .... about the bitterest pang of which the soul is capable'. In her identification with his personal angst she strikes a surprisingly modern note, reading his vacillation not as weakness but as a passionate struggle 'against the inertness of despair'. This reading underlies her savage critique of Irving's unsubtle rendering; he had studied *scenes*, but not pyschology.[54]

If neo-classicism, in literature as in art, appeared to her alien to Britain, she was equally suspicious of the Gothic and fantastic. Like Jewsbury she admired socially realistic, psychologically truthful fiction, in which evil had no charms. *The Woman in White*, which scored highly on the first two counts, but whose brilliant Fosco failed disastrously on the third, was written by a master. In the less skillful hands of imitators this new fashion would corrupt the novel. (She correctly predicted it would lead to the rise of the detective/crime fiction genre.)

The grotesque in literature and painting repelled her because it falsified reality.[55] Hardy's resolution of the 'great insoluble question' of the children's fate in *Jude* was in the 'regions of pure farce ... too grotesque to be amusing'. But her main objections to *Jude* paralleled her attack on the shock factor of Grant Allen's and Muriel Dowie's novels which, supplanting ideals of love and fidelity by 'the Sexquestion', undermined marriage and social decency. The sub-text of *The Anti-Marriage League*, written the year before her death, is her ironic self-awareness that for her the woman's 'emancipation' she had – albeit with some trepidation – welcomed in *Jane Eyre*, had gone too far.[56] Yet she still confessed to a soft spot for 'Madame Sarah Grand' whose *Ideala* she had admired.

In the sexual politics of contentious fiction from Brontë to Grand as the restraints on the 'unacceptable' loosened Jane Eyre became the touchstone. Elizabeth Rigby's assumption that 'Currer Bell' shielded a man was shared by reviewers of both sexes. In their motivation and acknowledgement of the novel's spellbinding *power* her slashes anticipate Mrs Oliphant on Collins's Fosco. *Jane Eyre* is dangerous precisely because 'half our lady readers are enchanted' with Rochester, 'captious and Turk-like' though he be. Jane's vicissitudes are 'not unmixed with plunder from Minerva-lane' but the book cannot be dismissed as mere library fodder. The 'stamp of truth' in Jane's 'suppressed feeling' and suffering is what makes her 'heathen' pride so subversive. The conclusion on authorship was grounded in expectations of a realist novel where social conduct matched characters' sex and status. Currer Bell's ignorance of kitchen etiquette and ladies' fashions determined his sex.[57] But the argument was primarily moral.

By 1855 Mrs Oliphant could remark upon the blindness of not seeing behind 'incorrect costume and errors in dress .... the new generation nailing its colours to its mast .... this furious love-making was but a wild declaration of the "Rights of Woman" in a new aspect'. But it was exactly these ground-breaking modes of expressing female sensuality and independence that were at the root of Elizabeth Rigby's fears. Oliphant's praise of *Jane Eyre*, 'one of the most remarkable works of modern fiction', was itself tempered by its impact. 'The most alarming revolution of modern times' followed its 'invasion'. It dashed the romantic ideal of 'chivalrous true love', even influencing the concept of courtship in *North and South*, at a time when women's fiction 'summarily discussed and settled' 'vexed questions of social morality'.[58] In the mid-1860s Miss Jewsbury discovered at least one author still reproducing Jane, if differing in her 'angelic temper', and a decade later Mrs Oliphant contrasted Anne Thackeray's *Miss Angel* with the 'Jane Eyres of recent fiction', 'fascinated and enslaved' by critical, brutal 'bear-lovers'. By the 1880s, with the sensation novel well-entrenched and the New Woman on the threshold, she could urge readers to renew their acquaintance with that original 'powerful spell' of Lucy Snowe and Jane passionately expressing 'that yearning of the woman towards the man.'[59]

As monthly publication facilitated exchanges between reviewers, women acquired access to a dynamic critical forum. Sensation fiction gave rise to the most vigorous debates on new directions within fiction. Female critics, many of whom as novelists had a vested interest in tendencies of public taste, took a leading rôle in an argument whose antecedents were ultimately early Romance-versus-Novel discussions by writers like Clara Reeve and Scott.[60] What originated as defining of genres developed into a critical privileging of the classic realist text

over escapist forms, setting standards against which popular fiction
from 'Silver Fork' to 'Sensation' was judged wanting. Archetypal
romance characters, picturesque Corsican bandits and glamorized
highwaymen, were not, Eliot pointed out in *Adam Bede*, as frequent in
life as vulgar labourers. This notion of 'realistic' permeating Eliot's
fiction was anticipated in her attack on the evangelical school, characterized as swapping the 'silver fork's' epaulettes and opera boxes for
'cambric bands' and pulpits. 'The real drama of Evangelicalism .... lies
among the middle and lower classes.' Where were the pictures of religious life among English industrial classes to compare with Mrs Stowe's
of the negroes'?[61]

Charlotte Brontë in *Shirley* and Dickens in *Oliver Twist* sought to dis-
abuse readers of romantic expectation, yet *Jane Eyre* was the precursor
of the staple bigamy-novel and Margaret Oliphant classed Dickens as
'sensationalist'. The sensation debate was complex. Unlike the gothic,
the best sensation exemplars combined the thrill of the forbidden with
the conviction of the realist text. As Pykett argues, in the hands of
Ellen Wood and Mary Braddon it re-worked gothic and melodrama to
problematize women's position in the traditional family.[62] Opponents
attacked the sensational on artistic grounds – commodification of literature – and moral grounds – destabilization of moral norms. Specific
manifestations offering subversive patterns of 'unfeminine' behaviour
posed additional dangers.

Near the century's end Adeline Sergeant speculated that *East Lynne*
owed its extraordinary popularity to mid-century reaction against
'inane and impossible goodness'. By then Mrs Oliphant had reluctantly
accepted Mrs Wood's success. Thirty years earlier, identifying the
attraction of 'the Magdalen' she clearly hoped this 'dangerous and
foolish work.... false, both to Art and Nature' would be but a 'momen-
tary celebrity'. In real life *East Lynne*'s 'flames of vice' were no
purification ordeal. More fundamentally, the novel foretold the
dangers of emulating a master like Collins in 'making the worse appear
the better cause'.[63] She was certainly not alone. Criticism was widespread. Ironically *St James's*, founded by Braddon's lover, carried articles identifying sensation literature's links to stage melodrama and
contemporary French fiction, and deploring its effect upon 'young
ladies'.[64] When, with Braddon in her sights, Mrs Oliphant returned to
the fray, she believed her fears, that 'literary excitement' from serial
'Story-tellers' threatened fictional art, fully justified. She accused sensation novelists of corrupting literature and youthful readers. An infuri-

ated Braddon, stirred into action, used her position as editor of *Belgravia* to orchestrate a vigorous defence of her genre.[65]

If it seems surprising that Geraldine Jewsbury recommended Bentley to publish Mrs Wood we should remember she never condemned popular fiction *per se* but only its absurdities. Gothic novels were one thing but a Gothic novel which made *photography* its lietmotif was alas! another. (*Unconventional: a Novel* Thomas Sutton B.A.) Equally contemptible were inept copycat plots. We sense weariness in her notice of *Nelly Deane: A Story of Everyday Life*: 'We hope that every-day life is conducted on more rational principles and 'The style is even more absurd than the story; if that be possible' frame her resumé of yet another tale of innocent second wife's wedding-day marred by re-emergence of first wife (7 January 1865).

Inevitably Miss Jewsbury and Mrs Oliphant wrote from their standpoint within the fiction business. The critical aims of George Eliot and her protegée Edith Simcox were primarily intellectual. Eliot's 'German Wit', credited as the most influential introduction of Heine to the English-speaking world, incorporated a philosophical discussion of distinctions between humour and wit. A short notice of a school textbook of *Antigone* in the *Leader* argues for the universality of that tragedy's 'dramatic collision' of two valid principles and the ensuing moral conflict.[66] Her 'Belles Lettres' for the *Westminster* might notice almost thirty books but she still afforded space for a careful analysis of the chosen few. Although as Pinney suggests one is aware she empathizes with the human authors behind the texts, the specifics upon which she focuses broaden into aesthetic, ethical or political issues. Thus her sympathy with Frederika Bremer's ideals shines through her attack on the 'rank' growth of sentimentality in *Hertha* and is vocalized in her view that 'Women have not to prove that they can be emotional, and rhapsodic, and spiritualistic; every one believes that already. They have to prove that they are capable of accurate thought, severe study, and continuous self-command.' More tolerant than Mrs Oliphant, she found no problem with the theme of *Constance Herbert*, but criticized Jewsbury for 'nullifying' its insistent moral principle of renunciation by undermining the value of the sacrifices. The formal point is similar to Miss Jewsbury's own a decade later when taking Mrs Craik to task in *Christian's Mistake* for failing to trust 'her heroine to the strength of her cord' and growing 'afraid of her own [excellent] text'. Eliot, however, expounds in detail the ethical issue at stake.[67] Her intellectual interests, particularly her attraction to positivism, influenced directly younger critics like Edith Simcox and Emilia Dilke.

Edith, the most passionate of these 'spiritual daughters', was arguably also Eliot's most perceptive contemporary reviewer. Her *Academy* review of *Middlemarch*, 'a profound psychological study', claiming it as a fictional landmark because its action stems from the 'inner life' still bears studying today.[68] Though better-known for her activism, she believed 'Books *have* an influence'. Her erudite, well-argued, witty essays articulated her own theories and served to promote that influence 'on the side of truth and righteousness'. Gordon Haight noted forty years ago her 'fine critical intelligence', and a recent appreciation shows how her reviews 'exemplify her feminism, her concern with economic issues, and her extensive research and erudition.'[69] Even a discussion of *Groundwork of Economics* with its 'literary eccentricities' – no index and 659 pages leaving 'the great problems of political and social economy as they were' – provides Edith with an opening for her own theory on why protective tariffs are not necessarily efficacious even when circumstances appear to justify them.[70]

Her subject range was quite astonishing; she moved as easily from economics to ethics, or history to science, as between the literatures of Britain and Germany. This frame of reference served her well in the spacious arenas of the *Fortnightly* or *Saint Paul's* when dealing with Morris's views on art, politics and morality; or ranging over physiognomy, the Dutch school, Hogarth, Frith, and Callot to explain Darwin's disappointment at finding art of little use for his theories of expression. Her incisive commentary was ideally suited to *The Academy*, whose critics were typically Oxford dons. Like its art reviewers, Emilia Dilke and Amelia Blandford Edwards, her erudition admitted her to the fold.

Elizabeth Hasell, another notable scholarly critic of that time, was an effective popularizer of classics.[71] Despite her formidable range – she 'read with equal facility Hebrew, Latin and Greek' – she knew how to engage the interest and emotions of less learned readers. She empathizes with the accessibility of Talfourd's *Ion* (noting an anachronism with 'if that matters') against the language of Swinburne's *Erechtheus* where, despite real echoes of a 'very grand strain', readers 'must think in Greek while listening to English'. Her critical review of Tennyson's *Queen Mary* is located within a discussion of the demands imposed by historical subjects upon a dramatist. She scrutinizes his task and flawed achievement within a frame of reference drawing on Shakespeare, Schiller and Victor Hugo. Yet rather than dismiss *Queen Mary* with the irony she bestows *en passant* upon Macaulay (apt to caricature 'people who had not the good fortune to be Whigs'), she gives generous space to extracts so well-chosen she almost tempts one to read it. An essay like 'Elegies' sweeps from David's lament for Jonathan, through Greek fragments, *Adonais*, *Lycidas* and Petrarch, comparing a Jesuit Latin elegy for Ferdinand's empress with Thomas More's for Elizabeth of York and Byron's for Princess Charlotte. She distinguishes stylistically between the formal lament and expressions of private grief, remarking that Tennyson's 'wise and thoughtful' *Ode to Wellington* would yet never become the 'household possession' that is Wolfe's on Sir John at Corunna.[72]

Such women excelled at broadening public horizons by making foreign literature accessible. At polar ends of the century Mrs Busk and Mrs Ward educated readers' appreciation of European literature as they expended prodigious efforts to keep their families financially afloat. Facility in translation enabled many women to develop writing careers. Mrs Busk, a prolific periodical reviewer/translator in the first half of the century, wrote for *Blackwood's, Foreign Quarterly* and the *Athenæum*. Her longer essays on French, German, Spanish and Italian literature often included substantial passages of original translation. Sarah Austin, one of Dilke's Continental foreign correspondents, was a mainstay of the *Athenæum*'s coverage of German literature in a team of foreign book reviewers which included Louisa Costello and Lady Morgan. Julia Kavanagh reviewed French literature and history for the same paper at the mid-century. George Eliot, whose early journalism was translation from the German, knew enough Greek to refer incidentally to the inadequacy of a version of *Antigone*. Edith Simcox's facility in German even tempted her to consider compiling a German dictionary.[73] In the later decades, apart from Mary Ward, we find Catherine Phillimore on Italian literature in *Macmillan's*, the Hamburg-born Helen Zimmern on German for the *Examiner*, Emily Gerard on French and German literature for *Blackwood's*, and Alice Werner, a specialist in African languages, covering foreign books for Stead's *Review of Reviews*.

In art criticism languages proved equally valuable. Emilia Dilke's knowledge of French enabled her to criticize translations. Part of her acclaimed book on Claude originally appeared in a French journal, and she considered writing her study of the eighteenth century in French.[74] Lady Eastlake reviewed and translated German books. Her long critical career is almost as impressive as Mrs Oliphant's. She began in the early 1840s. She was 80 when in 1889 she reviewed amongst works on Venetian history Mrs Oliphant's *Makers of Venice*. Her first *Quarterly* 'dissertation' about books on Russian travels appropriately followed from the success of her own book of letters based on her Baltic journeys. Travel was a subject to which she always returned with enthusiasm. She reviewed histories and wrote a masterly series of three articles on books for children, notably rejecting the overtly didactic and anticipating Dickens's championing of fairy tales. In her art criticism she opposed Ruskin, explicity in her *Quarterly* essay on *Modern Painters* providing, with Lady Dilke, an alternative to his dominant voice on aesthetics.

Lady Dilke, the former Francis Pattison,[75] was one of the century's most distinguished art historians. Although her involvement in social reform led to articles on such labour issues as trades unionism, her writing career was deliberately grounded in her chosen specialization. She would never, like Elizabeth Eastlake in her preface to *Five Great Painters* (1883), have suggested that her thoughts on art were those of another.[76] Despite the miseries of her first union to the formidable Oxford scholar, Mark Pattison, she gained intellectually from that 'tutorial-marriage', though it put paid to the artistic career on which she had tentatively embarked. It was Pattison who urged her to make herself '*the* authority' on some subject, eschewing hack-work however well-paid. Having successfully studied with Ruskin art history was a natural choice, though her early journalism for the *Saturday Review* was equally motivated by her desire for some financial independence. She was soon writing for the *Westminster*; became the *Academy*'s art editor and, by the 1880s was also working for the *Magazine of Art* and the *Athenæum*.[77] When reviewing the French Salons she undertook rigorous research and many studies and her scholarly criticism was underpinned by her theoretical stance. From her own 'strictly professional point of view' 'technical execution' was 'the capital question'. Her insistence that 'All representation is by symbol' emerges in her reviews.[78] 'Given the keynote [of a Millais painting] .... everything is right. As regards the apparently reckless handling, we must bear in mind that the science of representation is a science of symbols .... each man has to adapt or invent symbols' appropriate to what he would represent. In contrast to Millais' 'splendid realism' is 'the intellectual power' of Whistler, conceiving his sitter's *mental* attitude and 'selecting the key of colour and the lines of composition' to enforce that.[79]

She fell under the spell of Comte's philosophy, and the *Westminster* with space for extended essays like 'The Use of Looking at Pictures' or 'Art and Morality'[80] offered scope to develop her theory of art influenced by positivism. The independence of mind which encouraged her when a student to study anatomy and dissection and draw from the nude now led her to oppose her erstwhile mentor Ruskin. The 'sauciest of girls' at Kensington was indeed to contradict if not 'everything' he ever said about 'Art and History and Social Science' certainly the fundamental basis of his 'social art history'. Through her reviews one may trace the complex route whereby she came to discard both Ruskin's methodology and Pater's version of æstheticism in favour of an 'art for art's sake' position which nevertheless recognized the dependence of artistic production 'upon social and historical conditions'.[81]

Eastlake and Dilke were probably the most influential of the female writers on art. Amongst earlier contributors were the art historian Anna Jameson whose biographical series on painters appeared in the *Penny Magazine*,[82] and Mary Merrifield on art and fashion for *Sharpes's* and Hall's *Art Journal*, to which Marryat's sister also contributed on the decorative arts. In 1904 Frances Low complained that music and art criticism was 'for some extraordinary reason almost wholly in the hands of men'.[83] Amongst the turn-of-century exceptions in art, apart from women who like Mrs Jack Johnson of *Gentlewoman* provided art coverage for niche periodicals, were Lady Colin Campbell of the *World* and the versatile Pearl Craigie and Elizabeth Pennell. Mrs Pennell's sharp phrases conjure visual images in both condemnation and praise. The wearisome sensationalism of the *Salons* is encapsulated in 'The purple dot has dwindled into a nuisance, and M. Eliot, its chief apostle begins to bore' whereas Whistler's 'idealized dandy *Comte Robert de Montesquiou-Fézensac* has the simplicity of Rembrandt's *Syndics* or Velasquez's *Philip* – no superfluous upholstery to inform or explain. The man himself, standing upon his legs within the frame ... painted with a brush dipped in light and air ... a type for all time.'[84]

Literature and art were the most common fields for women reviewers but there were other specialisms. Hannah Lawrance covered historical and antiquarian books for the *Athenæum* and Mary Ward theology for the *Times* and other journals. Harriet Martineau focused on the subjects which engaged her as a leader writer: history, economics, and contemporary politics. Given men's superior educational opportunities one is struck less by women's limitations than by the breadth of their subject range and the assurance of their opinions. Thus Mary Ward having broadly supported a critique of Newman's essay on miracles, adds a postcript of her own: 'yet – as one thinks over the whole matter – what one seems to see is that miracle will keep its place in religion till the religious temper itself has supplied the alternative. Nothing religious is ever destroyed, but only supplanted.'[85] The first of Harriet Martineau's 47 *Daily News* reviews, in its succinct summary of William Rathbone Greg's views throughout the great Reform Bill debate, demonstrates beautifully the claim of Mrs Johnstone's *Tait's* that 'there is something in the female mind which peculiarly fits it for elucidating, in a familiar manner, the intricacies of political economy'.[86] Given Martineau's radicalism it is strikingly balanced. She locates the author in the political context of the *Edinburgh*, where his *Essays* first appeared, assessing his abilities and con-servative influence. Despite such 'ordinary whig traits' as 'condescending explanations of trite matters' and 'a curious obtuse complacency' he is honest and consistent. Once the battle was half over, he neither rushed 'to the head of the column, with valorous flourishings' nor took 'credit for reforming, when all chance of retarding reform' was gone. Within his own class and economic field 'he is eminent for clearness and .... earnestness and good feeling'.[87]

Fiction reviewing itself encouraged the discussion of social questions. Responses to Stowe's novels provide a case in point, appropriately since Emily Crawford later accounted for the 'stupendous consequences' of the literary hit *Uncle Tom's Cabin* by its excellence as *journalism*. Mrs Stowe 'aimed as if she were doing a leading article for an imme-diate effect, and she produced it.'[88] Its theme was widely debated, spilling over into gossip and readers' correspondence columns.[89] Whereas Eliot's welcome of *Dred*, a book of 'uncontrollable power', avoided discussion of its political problems which belong to quite other than 'polite literature'[90] Martineau exploited the *Times* review in her leader on the Kansas crisis, 'Ignorance of *The Times* on America' (24 September 1856) to renew her attack on the rival paper's 'absurd-ities' over America. The reviewer's stance that the North 'poured their negroes into the Middle States' 'exhibits an ignorance, geographical and historical, which is perfectly astonishing ... The South has to deal only with the slaves she chooses to purchase and rear.'[91]

Martineau elided the genres of review and leader as others transmuted reviews into essays on broader subjects and, since debates on literature and the arts took place as much between magazine covers as within University cloisters, reviewing afforded women space for argument and exposition across a spectrum of issues. The equally flexible essay provided an alternative platform.

5
Something to Say – a Living to Earn: Periodical Contributors

Reviewers needed a track record or influential introduction to gain entrée to a journal. Editors were scarcely in the habit of inviting the unknown public to submit reviews, certainly not to journals which paid their contributors or professed to scholarly standards. In terms of access, however, the essay genre enjoyed some of the supposed advantages of that 'female' branch of literature, the novel. Like fiction, it could draw upon all manner of personal experiences and, like fiction, it provided space for women's discourse. One would think it held considerable attractions for educated women with no talent for fiction or who found that market over-supplied, but the very sporadic and opportunist nature of the work made it equally attractive to men. There were plenty of retired military men who had travelled widely, and university educated clergymen, lawyers and other professionals who fancied themselves in print or sought to supplement their income. Some became major periodical writers, some, like the engineer Robert Patterson who could make 'even the currency question interesting', became full-time journalists. In some ways the increasing professionalization of journalism militated against women.[1]

Other chapters concentrate on the feminist, religious and women's press. Here the main focus is women's working practices as 'regular' general periodical writers, though I have not ruthlessly excluded general interest articles that happened to be published in ladies' magazines. Limited space precludes any detailed critique of their essays, but in highlighting individuals and a major debate which women orchestrated, I hope to suggest why I believe their work deserves attention.

What was the scale of women's contribution to this press? This is difficult to assess even by some simple numerical yardstick, partly because so much work is unattributable, partly because of the problem of deciding the basis for comparison as *Household Words* illustrates. Of some 390 identifiable contributors the vast majority had only occasional pieces published. The 'regulars' numbered thirty-five. Does the proportion of women in the total – approximately ninety – or in the core, provide the better guide to their participation? And, if the latter, how does one weigh length of association against numbers of items?

Eliza Linton was clearly a core writer with sixty items spanning the periodical's nine years of existence. But then – Harriet Martineau contributed over forty, though all within five years, Harriet Parr thirty in little more, and Mrs Gaskell fewer but over the paper's life. Against a staff member like Henry Morley's 300 plus these counts look modest, but more typical 'regulars' like Dudley Costello (40), Blanchard Jerrold (20) and Sidney Blanchard (20) suggest that all four women are rightly bracketed with them.[2] Such quantifications, moreover, do not distinguish between journalistic and literary contributions. Eliza Linton's score certainly includes several short stories. Harriet Parr's were mainly fiction and verse, Elizabeth Gaskell's largely fiction, although the boundaries between 'sketch' and 'tale' were themselves blurred. Generalizations are therefore dangerous to make, and such as are attempted here should be understood to carry this caveat.

Broadly speaking named women periodical writers are outnumbered by men. Even when anonymity is breached, assuming the *Wellesley Index* entries to be fairly representative of the literary monthlies and quarterlies, the picture is similar. Only 11 women from over 11 500 identified writers have more than 50 entries, Mrs Oliphant heading the list by the astonishing margin of two-and-a-half times the total of her runner-up.[3] Women certainly contributed to less prestigious papers – particularly the vast religious, women's and cheap 'family' press. Scanning runs of journals, one's eye is caught by once popular, almost-forgotten names like Mrs T K Hervey and Miss Pardoe, and others less familiar and less frequent. Who was Maria Norris whose 'A Few Words on Geology' earned her a by-line in *The Ladies' Cabinet* in 1852? Or Mrs White who surfaced in ladies' papers about the same time? We may never know the extent of women's work in these areas. Most of the essayists discussed here belonged to the relatively high-profile elite who established a niche in the periodical press. How did they do it? Mary Mitford spelt out to Frances Trollope the difficulties facing the aspirant. Having warned that her first book will have to be given away to make her reputation, she cautions 'I would not advise you to offer any article to periodical publications until your book be published – you can then send them as the writings of the authoress of so & so & will meet with a degree of attention very different from that commanded by an unknown name – in point of fact I rather think recommendations to Magazines [?do] harm ...'.[4] Still hopefuls *did* use others as emissaries, with variable outcomes. Several women invited by Dickens to contribute to *Household Words* tried to assist others. Mary Howitt actually edited her daughter Anna's sketches of life in Munich before submitting them. Mrs Gaskell, whom Dickens had entreated in fulsome terms to write for him, sent various pieces by Mrs Jenkin and others, some of which he published. When, however, Geraldine Jewsbury included papers by another hand in a packet she was gently rebuked. They were 'not adapted to the purposes of *Household Words*'.[5] Probably success depended upon the relationship of editor and would-be patron as well as upon the quality of the work. On Sala's recommendation *Belgravia* accepted a sketch by the then unknown Helen Mathers and her career was launched. In this case, however, *Belgravia*'s editor, Mary Braddon, knew him as a seasoned journalist and former editor, well capable of spotting promising newcomers.[6]

From the mid-century some enterprising ladies' papers encouraged reader participation more positively than by using unpaid offerings as space-fillers. Maria Rye, a successful contestant in an *Englishwoman's Domestic Magazine* essay competition, soon became Beeton's 'talented contributor' writing regularly for the paper. Apart from articles raising women's issues *EDM* published her various historical series including the ambitious (and incomplete) *Domestic History of England* which ran over 24 issues from May 1861. When feminist activism superseded her journalism she turned her skills to PR, issuing press releases on her work. She was in many respects fortunate in her introduction to journalism, earning sufficient income from Beeton to support herself until, in 1867, she was awarded a state pension for services to female emigration.[7]

For others the entrée was less smooth. Harriet Martineau's initiation was not untypical, though her eventual fame undoubtedly was. She contributed regularly without payment to the evangelical *Monthly Repository* until the failure of her late father's business forced his daughters to earn their daily bread. For Harriet governessing was out of the question. To quote her Victorian biographer, Florence Fenwick-Miller 'pupils could not easily be found who would say their lessons into an ear-trumpet'.[8] It was endless fancy-work or literature. Since she could no longer afford to write for nothing her editor managed to find

£15 a year for as much work as she 'thought proper'. Mary Mitford, after her father's bankruptcy, seems to sense the grind ahead which her parents' dependency imposed. She describes her early magazine writing:

> I work as hard as a lawyer's clerk & besides the natural loathing of pen & ink which that sort of drudgery cannot fail to inspire I have not really at present scarcely a moment to spare even to the violets and primroses. You would laugh if you saw me puzzling over my prose ... I ponder over every phrase – disjoint every sentence...[9]

Even when one was well established with regular commissions the need to constantly replenish one's purse and the paper could seem relentless. Alice Meynell in the 1890s producing her 'Wares of Autolycus' columns to firm deadlines reveals a tangled burden of domestic worries and nagging journalist conscience. 'If I can think of a P.M.G. column I need not hurry, for I am more or less wanted here. The nurse is very good but the two smaller children are wild' and 'I must turn again to adding up those 1600 words. Once the *Pall Mall* is off my mind I can face the rest [other editorial and journalistic commitments] serenely. But before I find a subject for the "Autolycus" I do feel uneasy.'[10]

Meynell's brief, elegant essays, where arresting phrases and swift turns of argument illuminate what is praised and just save the sharpness of criticism from sinking into malice,[11] were in format scarcely recognizable as belonging to the same genre as Lady Eastlake's. Though the dominant forms of the essay varied over the century there was never just one format. By the 1880s the mini-theses were outclassed in their influence by the snappier, breezier articles of the New Journalism era. (In their brevity at least, despite their mannered style, Alice Meynell's *PMG* essays were of their time.) But the format of such extensive pieces as Lady Eastlake's essay on photography was as much 'of the periodical' as 'of the period.' Back in the 1860s *Saturday* essays, whether Anne Mozley's on manners or Eliza Linton's satirical *Girl of the Period*, had to make their point briefly. Tailoring one's style to types of periodical had long been the key to journalistic success. Arnold Bennett's advice urging detailed study of titles may have been especially relevant once the New Journalism had made its mark, but generally speaking his reasoning held good throughout the century: 'Each paper has its own public, its own policy, its own tone, its own physiognomy, its own preferences, its own prejudices.'[12] Dickens continually stressed the distinct editorial policy of *Household Words* to staff and contributors. The intention behind his reiterating to Henry Morley the 'indispensable necessity of varying the manner of narration' and investing it with 'some fanciful attraction' or 'new air' was continually echoed. Hannah Lawrance's suggestion for articles drawing on seventeenth- and eighteenth-century primary sources was thought 'very suitable' 'but of course the manner of its execution is important'.[13]

Diversity of readership and style had its corresponding advantage in the scope offered for all manner of subjects and treatments. Personalized accounts of topical or unusual events, philosophical disquisitions, travel sketches, biographies, reminiscence, whatever one's passion – history, botany or astronomy, some periodical would welcome it. Clearly women were at a major disadvantage in terms of credentials as qualified scientists, lawyers or clerics, but magazines also sought popularizers and interpreters of science, history, economics and in this capacity women proved themselves just as able and effective as men. Many had more limited opportunities for the 'interesting experience', exotic travel or unusual job which aspiring male journalists depended upon, but in one respect women had useful rôle models. The female novelists were admitted to possess, even praised for, their narrative skill, powers of observation and attention to social detail. In fiction these 'strengths', whether viewed as an innate gift or a compensatory strategy, may have been devalued by being regarded as 'feminine',[14] but for making knowledge accessible to the masses they were assets. Harriet Martineau's writings on economics provide an obvious instance, and, though declining to write tales for *Household Words* because she felt she had left story-telling behind her, she applied narrative techniques to some of her articles for it. Narrative forms became a widespread mechanism for popularization, one of the most striking instances being its application to science. The story was ideal when writing for children. Mrs Gatty and other women drew on such models as the parable and fairy tale.[15] In fact Victorian scientific popularizers experimented with a spectrum of styles in addressing adult readers too. The lively monthlies of the 1860s encouraged this development and the prolific journalist Richard Proctor, for instance, experimented with fictive formats in some of his more speculative astronomy articles for *Cornhill*. The general periodical, needing to attract readers by entertainment as well as information, allowed for a blurring of fictional and non-fictional genres in other ways. Just as in the quarterlies, the book review might turn into a disquisition or in a juvenile magazine the article on insects or botany metamorphose into an adventure, so in 'polite literature' reminiscence might dissolve into fiction rather than solidify into an essay. The sketch in particular lent itself to fictionalization. As Mrs Gaskell discovered with *Cranford* it was sometimes difficult to separate fact from fiction.

By the late 1860s Anne Mozley saw 'lighter periodical literature' as offering 'Clever Women', by which she meant not the exceptionally gifted, but the ordinary intelligent 'domestic type of woman', an outlet for her education and talents. '[W]herever there is definiteness of aim, independence of thought, and freshness and accuracy of style – something to say, and the power of saying it attractively – a woman may find in these days employment for her pen.' She thought woman's 'didactic turn' especially appropriate for periodical literature designed for children, the poor and 'that vast mass of uncritical readers [requiring] … a literature adapted to an immature taste or judgment … [those] who have no taste for the delicacies of criticism, and by whom the leaders of public opinion are neither appreciated nor understood'. In performing this useful popularizing function through their 'unpretentious form of authorship' such women also advanced the arguments for female education within the family circle. 'Ever so modest a cheque from a publisher, or from the editor of a Society's periodical' coming as 'a cheerful family event' was a 'marvellous reconciler to woman's work'.[16] Two decades earlier Eliza Meteyard, with that 'look of abstraction in her clever but singular face' scribbling her juvenile stories or practical articles for *Sharpes's* and *Eliza Cook's Magazine* to support her brothers, had inspired Mary Howitt to a similar conclusion.[17] Anne Mozley herself in editing *Magazine for the Young* and writing on dress, social manners, domestic and other women's issues seems to exemplify her 'Clever Woman', though with contributions to reviews like *Bentleys Quarterly*, *British Quarterly*, the *Saturday Review* and *Blackwood's* she was certainly operating at the classier end of the 'light literature' market. Her *Saturday* essays are characterized by her singular reflective point of view on social experiences and sensations and by the aphoristic quality and quirks of argument which enliven the moral element. Pieces like 'Hugger-mugger', 'Shirking' and 'Scenes' merge the philosophical, psychological and social for a popular audience yet in their brevity meet the needs of the livelier format of 1860s journalism.[18]

By the end of the century, when aspirants were overwhelmed with advice, Arnold Bennett went so far as to categorize the periodical market for freelance articles. Of his three classes of magazines, the 'purely popular' (e.g. *Strand*, *Pearson's*, *Windsor*, *Lady's Realm*), the 'high-class general' (*Blackwood's, Macmillan's, Cornhill*) and 'the reviews' (*Nineteenth Century, Fortnightly, Westminster*) he advised the beginner to try the second 'since the first demands names of renown, and the third either expert knowledge, scholarship, or high technique'.[19]

How much might one earn by periodical journalism? There is no simple answer except that payment was – as indeed it still is for free-lances today – extremely variable. It was not even a question of change over the decades. It depended upon the paper; it depended upon the type of contribution; it depended upon the reputation and negotiating powers of the writer; it depended upon the general profitability of pub-lishing and the level of competition at the time.

Mary Mitford, working on Dramatic Sketches for *Baldwin's Magazine* in 1821 thought the pay 'well up' and 'extremely advantageous' to herself at fifteen guineas a sheet. A few years later she was getting ten guineas a sheet from the *Monthly*. She knew her value, protesting in no uncertain terms to Cyrus Redding over payment for material solicited by the *Metropolitan*. In accepting the commission she had informed Mr Valpy 'that I never received less than 6 guineas an article prose or verse, short or long'.[20] The 1830s, with its flurry of new papers, tended to put up prices and it was said that Colburn's *New Monthly* was paying as much as 20 guineas the sheet, but as Patrick Leary has illustrated with *Fraser's*, individual payments could vary considerably and Thackeray was able to negotiate an increase on his 12s. 6d. a page (£10 a sheet) for the early *Yellowplush Papers*.[21]

At mid-century Mrs Gaskell was so astonished by the 20 pounds Dickens gave for her first contribution to *Household Words* that she reflected she must be 'swindling' the proprietors.[22] But she was excep-tionally generously paid. Despite a 'going rate' the magazine's pay-ments varied. In January 1853 Louisa Costello, an established author, received £4. 14s. 6d for her seven-and-a-half column article on domes-tic life in France, whilst George Dodd's seven columns on the indus-tries of Bermondsey that same month earned £3. 13s. 6d. The untried Anna Howitt, was at the lower end of the scale of pay, and generally below the stated rate of a guinea for a two-column page. Dickens's sub-editor Wills pared payments down if he got the chance.[23] Her remuner-ation sometimes yo-yoed dramatically within a short period – three guineas for eight-and-a-quarter columns (1 March, 1851), £3. 15s. for eight columns (29 March, 1851), three pounds for six columns in April, £2. 12s 6d for the six-and-three-quarter columns of the last of her 'Bits of Life in Munich' (7 June), the same amount for 6 columns of the first of 'A Chapter of Models' (21 June) and £3. 10s for eight-and-a-quarter in August.[24]

By the end of the century, with the tendency to shorter essays and a wider market for brief features in the newspaper press there was a move towards payment by wordage or even 'per article' rather than pages. 'Sheets' with their implication of essays running to 16 pages upwards had faded from the calculations. What remained constant was potential variation from the norm and the theoretical possibility of riches. Helena Swanwick, a contributor to *The Woman's World*, was rumoured to have earned an 'enormous sum' for 'The Evolution of Economics' commissioned by Wilde. Alice Meynell asking what the *Pall Mall* will pay for her brief articles reflected 'I shall not growl at £1.10s.; but £2 would make me very happy'. In 1891 Fanny Green quoted 'articles' in the *Spectator* and *Saturday* as paying three to five guineas, and by the end of the century career guides were giving guideline rates of one to two guineas a page for the monthly and quarterly journals. *Illustrated London News* paid two guineas a thousand words, the *Strand* three guineas a thousand words and 'very liberal terms for specially suitable matter'.[25]

Journalists dependent upon their work for a living were not only concerned with variations in remuneration rates; cash flow was equally important. The freelance contributor was, as today, vulnerable to dilatory payers, and magazines folding before paying their writers. Even successful magazines like *Fraser's* could hang on to material for months before publication, on which payment depended. When a paper folded the situation was more precarious as a fraught Mary Mitford complained. 'Mr Thelwall's magazine has stopped, and he has not paid me a farthing. He says, indeed, that … [the treasurer] when he recovers will pay me; but that he has advanced 700l, for the concern, and cannot lose more. Now I have nothing at all to do with his losses. He applied to me, and I shall always consider him as bound in honour to pay me.' She was even more aggrieved because Thelwall had proved the 'most fidgetty and troublesome' of editors, sending back articles and holding seasonal ones until it was too late to send them to another magazine that year.[26]

Women contributors, perhaps more than most men, were particularly sensitive to the response they received from editors. Supportive criticism from those they respected was welcomed as endorsing and improving their efforts. It was not necessarily the case that women editors were more helpful. Ella Hepworth Dixon claimed to find them more 'stiff and uncompromising' than men. But this was clearly not universal. The régime of *Sylvia's Journal* under Miss Graham in the early 1880s was so informal that, with no office boy or commissionaire to placate, EE Nesbit once walked straight in to meet the editor and young assistants correcting late copy.[27]

In their letters and memoirs women express appreciation of high editorial standards, clearly considered as contributing to their own literary success. Mary Mitford endorsing Talfourd's view that a magazine was 'like a steamboat & must come to the hour in spite of wind & tide' was disgusted at Colburn's engaging the ineffectual poet Campbell to edit the *New Monthly*. She exploded: 'To be sure they are to have the Lectures for makeweights – but for anything else they had better engaged the Dalai Lama. ...' A firm hand on the tiller seems to have been approved rather than otherwise, provided its owner supported rather than crushed the crew. Anna Maria Hall liked Lady Blessington for the 'importance she attached to every little attention' paid to her editorial requests. Isabella Fyvie Mayo admired Dr Guthrie for reining in his contributors gently, praising generously what he approved and caring 'for the significance of every line printed' in contrast to editors of the cheap illustrated papers who 'take literature by the yard'. Alice Meynell was so shocked by the implication of editorial weakness in a 'too ghastly' interview in *Sylvia's Journal* that quoted her as boasting the *National Observer* 'take[s] anything I like to send' that she wrote to Henley disclaiming it.[28] There are, Eliza Linton thought, 'editors and editors' and though long experience gave her sympathy with them when their 'young lions' roared 'fitly' and out of tune or landed them with costly libel actions, she disliked editorial bullies and 'dumb dogs' whose silence was the only clue to their approval. 'Others again, give you heartening words of encouragement when you fail, and the reward of commendation when you do well ... These are the best editors. They get by far the most out of their staff ...'.[29] She recognized the relationship as the two-way process, evident in Dickens's correspondence giving his reasons for rejection or instructions for improvement, and in Mary Braddon's soothing letters to a querulous Lytton.

Experienced writers were likely to have had considerable contact with different editorial styles since even writers with good connections to a prestigious journal, like Mrs Oliphant and Lady Eastlake, whether for financial necessity or prestige, usually wrote for several others. In the few years of frantic journalism before she established herself as a popular novelist Mrs Humphry Ward published in *Macmillan's*, *Pall Mall Gazette*, *Quarterly*, *Saturday* and *Fortnightly* reviews as well as newspapers. At about the same time Alice Meynell was writing fairly regu-larly for *The Spectator, Saturday, The World, Scots Observer, Tablet, Magazine of Art,* and *Art Journal*.[30] Of all Victorian women journalists Mrs Linton's contributions list is the most astonishing for length and for variety. At various times she contributed regularly to Dickens's magazines, the *Saturday* and *Universal Reviews* and *Queen.* The roll-call of titles in which she appeared sounds like a history of periodical pub-lishing in the second half of the century: *Ainsworths, Athenæum, Chambers', New Monthly, Cornhill, Fortnightly, Fraser's, Macmillan's, Saint Paul's, Temple Bar, National, New British, Nineteenth Century,* and then the unexpected – *English Republic, London Society, Good Words, Watch Tower, Tinsley's Magazine.* As journalists go there was much more of the chameleon about Eliza Linton than George Eliot. Sometimes placing work required determination. Geraldine Jewsbury mentions an article written for one paper 'rejected with ignominious disdain' being revised and sent via Carlyle's good offices to *Fraser's* where it was again turned down, before being taken 'in hand' a year later, again rewritten, this time successfully for Jerrold.[31]

Yet money was certainly not the only motivation. Miss Jewsbury wrote excitedly to Jane Carlyle after Jerrold printed an essay of hers 'the first attempt I ever made to say anything practically. I feel a real want just now to indite essays... Whether he will behave like a brick and pay me, I cannot speculate, but as I am like the ghost in "Hamlet" and "want a hearing", I am content either way.'[32] With her notorious 'Girl of the Period' essays Eliza Linton established her name and made something of a speciality of satirizing the 'fast girl'. Yet there is a ring of sincerity below the rhetoric. She later main-tained they were honestly motivated: 'I had something to say, and I said it with what literary force and moral vigour I possessed, indif-ferent to personal consequences.'[33]

For some 'definiteness of aim, independence of thought', wanting 'a hearing', having 'something to say' was a spur every bit as powerful as a pressing bill. Mrs Oliphant, Lady Eastlake, Mrs Linton may have played to different galleries, but their paper-platforms were their route to cultural influence. For other women like Agnes Clerke and Amelia Blandford Edwards periodicals provided one outlet for their scholar-ship. For Mary Mitford and Louisa Stuart Costello, financial mainstays of their families, periodical writing significantly impacted upon the direction of their careers, in Mitford's case quite startlingly. She belonged to the generation which produced women as various in their literary talents as Christian Johnstone, Mary Somerville and Sydney

Morgan; Louisa Stuart to that of fellow Irishwoman Anna Maria Hall, Mary Howitt, and Maria Jewsbury. Usually it was feckless husbands or brothers female writers supported, but in Miss Mitford's case it was her beloved father, who gambled and spent his way through his wife's fortune and his daughter's lottery win, necessitating the move to Three Mile Cross, a straggling Berkshire village on which Mary based the sketches which secured her astonishing international fame. No doubt she would have preferred not to be *obliged* by necessity to write for profit. She told Elizabeth Barrett Browning she was never without 'pecuniary care' pressing on her thoughts last thing at night; waking every morning 'with a dreary sense of pain and pressure'. Perhaps, too, there was a touch of maidenly reticence in the protest that writing was not a healthy occupation. Only her parents' needs 'reconciled me to the perpetual labour, the feverish anxieties and miserable notoriety of such a career.'[34] Although she was no stranger to hardship the essays which made her famous and encouraged a new prose sub-genre, the regional rural sketch, also bestowed on her a rather unfair reputation for romanticization. By the time she wrote the first *Our Village* series for the *Lady's Magazine* she was already the family breadwinner, writing poetry, criticism and 'dramatic sketches' for magazines. The descriptive sketch was tailor-made for the burgeoning periodical market. Like the 'tale' it was short and self-contained; presented within a 'series' it tempted readers with the promise of 'more to come' rather as the serialized novel would do later, yet was more flexible since it could appear sporadically. If a new series proved popular the writer would be encouraged to continue; if it failed the experiment could be cut off abruptly. Throughout 1823 *Our Village* sketches appeared regularly, lifting the sales from 250 to 2000 a month, and chaining Miss Mitford to her desk eight to twelve hours a day.[35] In volume form it was an instant success.

Readers of *Our Village* who actually visited Three Mile Cross were usually, like Charlotte Yonge, Anne Ritchie (and modern-day tourists) disappointed 'to see how small and narrow it was, after what those rose-coloured spectacles had shown'. Samuel Carter Hall thought "Sunny Berkshire" was a very Arcadia' which Mary Mitford's 'feeling and fancy had magnified into the perfection of a rural retreat – *rus in urbe*,' whilst her home in reality was 'a small and somewhat dismal cottage with a poor bit of garden'.[36] In fact Our Village as rural idyll is as much a construct of later Victorian readings and volume illustrations as it is hers. In the insipid context of the *Lady's Magazine* aiming to provide amusement and instruction for the 'fair sex' Mary Mitford's character sketches appeared, not so much sentimental, as earthy and realistic. One reviewer tempered praise by admonishing the author not 'to clothe her ideas in the phraseology of the dog-kennel and the kitchen',[37] for *Our Village* cheerfully embraced an admixture of the classes – genial farmers, daughters of dukes, milkmaids, inn-keepers, seamstresses, and Tom Cordery, rat-catcher and erstwhile poacher. Though Mitford grows lyrical about wild flowers and the sky, and her narrator's attitude is as determinedly optimistic as that she herself adopted in the face of perpetual financial worry, the hardships of rural life remain embedded, if occluded, in the text. She rebutted accusations of sentimentality but she had to meet readers' expectations, distancing them from the immediacy of human misery by consoling, occasionally ironic, conclusions and shifts of focus. The tale of 'Tom Cordery', transported from collapsing hovel to sheltered workhouse, opens and closes like an elegy; the irony of his death carrying in its echoes of *King Lear* a fatalistic, Hardyesque note. 'He used to foretell that it would kill him, and assuredly it did so. Never could the typhus fever have found out that wild hill side, or have lurked under that broken roof.... Alas, poor Tom! warmth, and snugness, and comfort, whole windows, and an entire ceiling, were the death of him. Alas, poor Tom!'[38] Mitford's informal narrative style permits continual shifts of subject and tone. Before she reaches the sudden glory of the bank of violets, symbol of Utopian innocence, the narrator's walk in 'Violeting' takes her from children playing by a pond to the silent building bereft of flowers, the Workhouse; from colourful bean-setters to derelict farmhouse – romantic at a distance, but – 'crumbling to decay under a careless landlord and ruined tenant'. The vitality of the bean-setting vignette is tempered, 'What work bean-setting is! ... Only think of stooping for six, eight, ten hours a day, drilling holes in the earth with a little stick, and then dropping the beans in one by one.'[39]

Significantly Mrs Hoare, one of her many imitators, pleased her mentor with the 'unmistakeable truth' of her 'painful' images of the Irish famine.[40] 'Country Pictures' with its ideal, 'a little village far in the country', that Mary Mitford never quite achieved since Three Mile Cross even then was perilously near Reading, echoes a poignant letter written after her move. Far from an idyll with 'a spire, a pump, a green, a winding street' which was Anne Ritchie's 'preconceived village in the air'[41] we get 'a small neighbourhood, not of fine mansions finely peopled, but of cottages and cottage-like houses, 'messuages or tenements' as a friend of mine calls such ignoble and nondescript dwellings ... a little world of our own, close-packed and insulated like ants in an ant-hill ...'.[42] It draws on the painful honesty of her letter to Elford. 'The Cross is not a borough, thank Heaven, either rotten or independent ... Our residence is a Cottage ... no not a Cottage, it does not deserve the name – a Messuage or Tenement such as a little farmer... might retire to ...'. She first crossed out 'Tenement' before substituting the messuage phrase. Such echoing is not surprising since she asked Elford to lend her letters back so she could recapture phrases which 'written in the first freshness of feeling & with perfect ease and unrestraint, are more effervescent and sparkling as well as more just than anything I am likely to write now with the fear of the Public before my eyes'.[43]

Writing of a period before the full impact of industrialization was felt, but its rumblings could be heard, Mitford's rural themes touched a sensitive pulse. She disliked creeping urbanization, was wary of constant change and robust in her criticism of Enclosures.[44] The long-established English ideal of countryside as spiritual retreat, given a new impetus by the developing awareness of the adverse effects of industrialization, contributed to her continued popularity. By 1855 shortly after her death, when Mrs Oliphant gave a complimentary review of Anna Maria Hall's *Irish Sketches* comparing them to 'Miss Mitford's beautiful *English* sketches', there were already major shifts in literary taste.[45] Miss Mitford herself anticipated the classic realist novelists in seeing the fictional potential of one new field:

> To the novelist, indeed, an English provincial town offers ground almost untrodden; and the bold man who shall first adventure from the tempting regions of high life, or low life, or Irish life, or life abroad, or life in olden times, ... will ... find his reward ... But when will such an adventurer arise? ... Who will have the courage to make a hero of an attorney? or to throw the halo of imagination around the head of a country brewer?

It needed 'a grand literary reform'.[46]

Periodical journalism had a rather less dramatic impact upon Louisa Costello, but the availability of additional income from this source, and her brother Dudley's switch from a military to journalistic world must have influenced the direction of her working life. Her writings appeared in such magazines as *Household Words, Fraser's, Athenæum, Bentley's Miscellany, Literary Gazette, New Monthly* and *Ladies' Companion*. On the family's move from Ireland to Paris after the death of her father when she was only 15, she supported her mother and brother by working as a governess and miniature painter. The profits from her painting put her brother, Dudley, through Sandhurst[47] and she continued to assist him subsequently. Some of the cheques from Dickens for her articles were made payable to Dudley. When he retired on half-pay they co-operated in copying French illuminated manuscripts. Louisa's *Specimens of the Early Poetry of France* (1835) illustrated by these illuminations, established her own reputation as a writer; from then on she concentrated on authorship. This 'highly-accomplished woman' as Elizabeth Barrett called her[48] carried her scholarship lightly. She drew on her intimate knowledge of France and its history for *Household Words*, and on personal observation, gossipy excerpts from original documents, histories, and interviews with the locals for her series of 'Sketches of Legendary Cities' covering places like Bath and Monmouth for *Bentley's*. 'We saw that the *Penny Magazine* had not been unread by our guide' she remarks of the 'venerable peasant' who took them to the druid Buckstone.[49]

Another *Bentley's* contributor, Katherine Thomson, adopted the persona of 'A Middle-aged Man' to bring to life artists, writers and others in the context of their once fashionable society, the 'Departed Great', as if from the recollections of a *gentleman* who knew them. The effect, notably in the case of the tragedy of Letitia Landon, is of vivid historical fiction. The scandal surrounding Landon is skilfully filtered through the romantic 'memory' of a man. 'Think of her! When do I not think of her?' 'It was an intoxicating career, to all appearance, but, like other intoxications it had its collapse. *She was not happy!*' Thomson's descriptive powers here are the equal of Mitford's. There is an extraordinarily evocative image of the vigil of Victoria's coronation – 'London, one great, though free Bedlam' where waiters needed 'strait-jackets' and hairdressers came like ghosts at midnight.[50] Although Thomson is now forgotten this fictionalization of the 'sketch' was as ingenious as *Our Village*.

To some extent chance played a part in determining that Mitford would be immortalized and Hall's, Costello's and Thomson's sketches forgotten. The cultural power of essays in magazines had much to do with what caught the mood of the time. By the 1890s when Anne Ritchie's Preface and Hugh Thomson's line-drawings fixed readers' idea of *Our Village* for generations to come, Alice Meynell could not understand what all the fuss was about. She seized upon the very 'passage of word-painting' praised by Lady Ritchie to demonstrate that 'Miss Mitford misses everything ... even the dog of whom she prattles so much ...' 'It is a wonder that anyone ever thought the sincerity of Miss Mitford in "Our Village" to be a matter of significance to literature.'[51] Mary Mitford's *Our Village* like Eliza Linton's *Girl of the Period* had caught the public imagination on the wing. Contributing consistently over decades to one of the long-lived quarterlies or monthlies guaranteed a very different kind of press influence, one Elizabeth Eastlake in the *Quarterly* and Margaret Oliphant in *Blackwood's* enjoyed. Lady Eastlake's writing career spanned the gap between the worlds of Mitford and Meynell. It was nurtured by the selfsame Lockhart who helped launch that cheeky *Blackwood's* which so delighted young Mary Mitford and to which Margaret Oliphant later devoted so much energy. Alice Meynell's first book of essays was published in the year of Elizabeth Eastlake's death. It was Lockhart, now editor of *The Quarterly*, who invited her to contribute, approving 'Signora Estonia's' first effort as cleverly extending a review of Russian travel books, and doing his journal credit. It was Lockhart who encouraged her to write rather than draw. When he died she felt she lost both friend and mentor. 'My whole poor literary life is connected with him, and indeed was formed by him.'[52] Lockhart had seen her as providing the *Quarterly* with papers addressing 'social subjects' appealing to women readers, and indeed she did so, covering women travellers, the arts and occasionally social problems such as pauperism. All that she treats, even more 'frivolous' subjects like the review-essay on costume (1847), written under the thin disguise of a male persona, is approached as worthy of serious consideration. Her article on 'Lady Travellers' had noted women's talent for detailed social observation, and her own essays reveal her sense of the social significance of her topics. Her discussion of the amassing of the collections of the Louvre from the fourteenth century to her own day demonstrates her thesis that 'It is not only the main stream of public affairs which reflects the character of the age ... the annals of a jewel will be found identical with those of an empire'.[53]

Her discussion of the 'new and mysterious art' of photography in exploring its relationship to 'art' also acknowledged its impact upon the populace. If with hindsight her dismissal of the technique as having reached its limits, its artistic effects 'falling off' in line with the technical improvements, seems misguided, her remarks upon the social value of the medium were prophetic. She saw it as a socially unifying force. In little more than fifteen years it 'has become a household word and a household want; is used alike by art and science, love, business, and justice; is found in the most sumptuous saloon, and in the dingiest attic'. Its practice brought together enthusiasts 'in a kind of republic' where tradesman, royal prince, innkeeper and artist were brothers. And if photographic portraits, those 'facial maps', were not art yet they provided 'landmarks and measurements for loving eyes' for the masses, not just the elite, and provided the new colourists with better pay than the inferior miniaturists whom they supplanted.[54] She was still writing in her eighties. When she died in 1893 not only were the miniaturists superseded, but photographs had crept into periodical illustration.

Mrs Oliphant could not match Lady Eastlake in longevity, but in length of service to *Blackwood's* she equalled that association with the *Quarterly*; in terms of productivity she surpassed it. *Maga's* obituary paying tribute to her versatility, claimed for her 'the proud title of the most accomplished periodical writer of her day' arguing that despite her many books 'it was nevertheless in periodical writing – the medium she loved best – that she attained perhaps her highest felicity of style'.[55] Her work, often hastily written, is uneven in quality, but at its best offers a perceptive view of society in which superficially conformist views are undermined by a vein of irony.

Not unnaturally Mrs Oliphant matured as a writer herself. In her biography of Pugin she remarked that fiction was for youth, but biography,' this art of portraiture, little studied, but much practised', supplanted it for the middle-aged. These biographical essays, often developed from a book review, focus upon personality, in Pugin's case upon personal struggles and ultimate tragedy. It was after this essay that she wrote 'I begin to think biography is my forte!'[56] In discussing the visual arts she identifies with a diffident British public unsure of its 'own taste or judgment' yet loving 'beauty in its way'. Her commentaries reveal her concerns about the effects of commerce and industrialization upon art, and reflect Victorian initiatives which aimed to open the world of art to the masses, which she wholeheartedly approved.[57] Her London sketches, covering art exhibitions and the theatre in the context of London at leisure, and switching perspective from panoramic to close-up, have a lively sense of ambience. Their portrayal of the fashionable crowds in Rotten Row or Burlington House echo her fictional treatment of the endless whirl of the London social season. Yet the image of London is an affectionate one; 'Art in May' is a virtual panegyric to England in spring.[58] Over the decades she adapted to changing journalistic styles and towards the end of her career began the 'Looker-on' *causeries*, which Charlotte Yonge considered to be some of her very best journalism.[59]

These discursive commentaries, adopting a male persona as narrator, are extensions of her earlier London essays, ranging much more widely in their coverage of topical events. 'The Looker-On' might begin with a discussion of the curious ramifications of the August break following the 'Season', debate the degeneration in morals and manners of Society, deplore the 'daughters who revolt, and demand latch-keys, and go to music-halls of an evening' along with 'Sex-literature' and *The Heavenly Twins*, (discussed but never named) delight in the honours given 'nominally to the American fleet' but really to an American author, visit the galleries and compare the French and English parliaments.[60]

Margaret Oliphant was not alone in covering art exhibitions from a relatively amateur point of view. Writers on their travels seized the opportunity for a topical periodical article. Mary Ward wrote on the new Rijks Museum for *Macmillan's*, though she would have been better advised to see art through Emilia Pattison's eyes than her own husband's – despite his *Times* art post he had limited artistic horizons. Coverage of the 1878 Paris Exhibition by Matilda Betham-Edwards, who travelled extensively in France, discussed its social aspects, good and bad – the encouragement given to working-class visitors by arrangements for free entry, on the one hand; the incessant noise of Parisian traffic on the other.[61] Through the 1870s and 1880s, Matilda's intimate knowledge of France and its people crossed the Channel surfacing in articles in *Fraser's*, *Macmillan's* and elsewhere. There were others who, following in Lady Eastlake's literary footsteps, transmuted their journeys into articles. Essays by the Scottish traveller Constance Gordon-Cumming on the Far East and America appeared in the 1880–90s in *Blackwood's, Cornhill, London Quarterly, Macmillan's* etc.

A capacity for great industry as well as high intellectual abilities was a quality common to many of the specialist contributors. One of the most outstanding of these, Amelia Blandford Edwards, contributor to the *Times* and *Morning Post* and who wrote over 100 articles on Egyptology for the *Academy* alone, turned to the subject for which she is now remembered only after she was a published novelist. Equally, according to her cousin Matilda, she might as easily have turned musician, rather as Emilia Dilke and Elizabeth Eastlake once thought of art. Her career began as a church organist, and some of her earliest writing, 'musical stories' for *Chambers'*, reflected this alternative talent. Self-taught, she took up Egyptology with the same thoroughness with which she had once practised at the piano.[62]

Mrs Oliphant's image of the woman historian in the British Museum, with her poke bonnet, umbrella, india-rubber overshoes, and packet of sandwiches, is more literally true to the earnest lady researcher than perhaps she realized.[63] Some self-taught women substituted for the formal higher education denied to them, a passionate interest in researching a subject, and like Eliza Linton, made the British Library their University College. Not all *Household Words* articles accorded its readers the compliment of the thorough research using primary sources that went into Hannah Lawrence's pieces on pre-steam travel or the autobiography (1705) of the bookseller, John Dunton. Miss Lawrence's efforts, however, must have gone at least as much into obeying Dickens's injunction as to the importance of 'the manner of execution' for her account of Dunton offers an insight into seventeenth-century courtship practices as much as into the bookselling and printing trades. 'Flying Coaches' captures a real sense of the feverish excitement with which Oxford greeted the first flying coach to make Oxford to London in a day. Maria Rye's historical essays for the *EDM* drew on an even more impressive range of primary sources, original documents, coins, portraits, manuscripts, even legal evidence since her father and brothers were solicitors.[64]

The scientific journalist, Agnes Clerke, popularizer of astronomy, was equally scholarly in her approach, making a point of using primary sources in her historical works and taking up opportunities to gain practical observational experience. Yet she was curiously nearer to the Egyptologist and Art Historians than to most of the female writers on science. Partly this was to do with her audience for, as Lightman has put it, she was not just 'a mediator between the scientific experts and the uniformed public but also stood as an interpreter of the larger meaning of recent astronomical discoveries to the professional astronomers themselves'.[65] Like Eastlake, Dilke and Blandford-Edwards her ideas were aimed at fellow experts. It was also the case that, unlike the Mrs Gattys and Mrs Lankesters, who were undeniably well-informed and, certainly in Mrs Gatty's case, contributed to scientific knowledge, she chose to adopt the predominantly masculine style of scientific writing. She eschewed the charms of story-telling narrative in favour of the 'impersonal, objective point of view'.[66] Significantly, as far as periodicals were concerned, she published in the most serious of 'general' as opposed to specialist journals, the *Edinburgh*. As a woman she stepped outside her sphere, was attacked by certain members of the scientific establishment and, more subtly, sidelined as a highly admirable *historian* of astronomy.[67]

Magazines offered a platform for articles on serious social issues which journalists of the calibre of Harriet Martineau and Frances Power Cobbe could exploit. Among Martineau's articles for the *Edinburgh* in the late 1850s and 1860s are ones discussing the slave trade and convict system, topics which recurred in her newspaper leaders. Being deaf herself, she passed on practical advice to fellow-sufferers in *Tait's* in 1834. One of her papers on disabilities for *Household Words*, 'Deaf Mutes', argued for special school training for totally deaf children but education at home for the partially deaf who 'should be least exposed to isolation and forlornness'.[68] Frances Cobbe made something of a speciality of philosophical and religious speculation. She even once delighted in the excuse, on the pretext of reviewing a 'capital' French book on the subject, to write an article on the Devil, which she offered to send to Mary Somerville 'if you will not be shocked'.[69] But interspersed with such essays are her attacks on vivisection and witty, hard-hitting, informative articles raising issues of women's rights and questioning conventional and legal assumptions about marriage. In particular, those in *Fraser's* in the 1860s with titles like 'What Shall We Do With Our Old Maids?', and her later exposure of domestic violence in the *Contemporary* attracted wide attention to many of the causes espoused by women activists.[70]

The press provided an arena for the debate over Woman's Rights extending it from law court, Parliament and public meeting into the home. For every man or woman who studied the arguments over issues like the extension of the suffrage, access to the professions or legal rights in pamphlets and books dedicated to the subject, there were many more who read a summary or picked up snippets from their newspapers. Kensington ladies who would never have subscribed to the feminist press might see the *Englishwoman's Journal* reviewed in *The Court Suburb*. Women who confined themselves to the pages of magazines designed especially for them might still find in the *Englishwoman's Domestic Magazine* 'Silkworm' (Matilda Browne) taking issue with Eliza Linton's attack on the modern girl, blaming Linton's *Magasin des Mauvaises Idées* itself for any lack of respect accorded modern women. 'Whenever a couple of columns are required to be "filled-up", ... then the services of the "bilious contributor" are called in, and the Englishwoman ... is torn to pieces ...'.[71]

These debates were themselves commodified by the press, and Eliza Linton, the consummate journalist, with her rhetoric, her vivid if distorted encapsulations, and her slogans – 'Girl of the Period', 'Shrieking Sisterhood' and 'Wild Woman' – played a major part in this process.

She had joined the *Saturday Review* in 1866 as a columnist at a painful time in her personal life (see Chapter 10) when her conflicting senses of wifely obligation and professional independence were at their most tortured. Her periodical writing like her fiction, powered by strong emotion, carried autobiographical overtones. Personal feelings surfaced as easily in a quiet sketch for *Belgravia* as in her attack on George Eliot or fulminations against wild women.[72] The 'Girl of the Period' essay, appearing in March 1868, was a sensation. In vivid terms it castigated the modern girl as a 'creature who dyes her hair and paints her face, as the first articles of her religion'[73] and who had supplanted the ideal of English womanhood. Though Linton's satire was aimed at extravagant dress, decadent manners and girls who married for money, its tone and elevation of the 'simple' girl of the past with her 'pretty bashful modesties' aroused the ire of women's rights' activists. 'The Girl of the Period' catchphrase was picked up by the press as a buzzword to be exploited. There were caricatures, farces, even a journal and almanacs.[74] The attack was both debated and reworked. In her *Court Suburb Magazine* Fanny Aiken-Kortright, on the conservative side of the suffrage debate, blamed men. If 'the famous portrait' really *were* a realistic likeness her *Father* must be a 'selfish, indolent, cowardly fellow' shirking family responsibilities. 'Let the Man of the Times be ... manly enough to show his real ... feeling on the subject' and 'the Girl of the Period' would soon 'fill her proper place, in the music hall, or the tap-room'.[75]

  Like Margaret Oliphant Linton helped establish women as professional journalists, yet figures today as conservative anti-feminist. She was radical in her youth, taking Miss Martineau rather than 'literary fossils' like Miss Pardoe as her model;[76] praising Wollstonecraft's *Vindication* because 'We have the same fight to fight that she had'.[77] As Mrs Oliphant approved of education for women, whilst maintaining the importance of maternal responsibilities, and distrusting the power of the law to right women's wrongs, so Mrs Linton's feminism was always tempered. But over the decades Mrs Oliphant modified her opinions; they cannot be accurately gauged solely from anti-suffrage remarks in early essays[78] but should be read against, for instance 'The Grievances of Women' (1880). By then she was unsurprised that 'all hot-headed and high-spirited women' resented a situation in which the 'occupations of mother and housekeeper' were regarded as 'bearing no comparison with that of the "bread-winner".[79]

  Mrs Linton had always held to an idealized image of woman's rôle of wife and mother, whilst arguing for legal reforms to give justice to married women. In *Household Words* she simultaneously supported Caroline Norton's fight for a wife's property rights and qualified her own support for women's emancipation arguing that though women undoubtedly suffered 'grave legal and social wrongs' they would not be righted by 'making them commanders in the navy or judges on the bench'.[80] Unlike Mrs Oliphant, however, she never wavered publicly from this stance. If anything with the passage of time she hardened her attitude, even claiming that her early 'ardent and enthusiastic' espousal of emancipation had been mistaken and doubting the value of higher education for women.[81] To some extent the vehemence of her public utterances belonged to the anti-suffrage persona she found so marketable, if uncomfortable. Yet one suspects that when she copied out from Coleridge's *Table Talk* 'We are none of us tolerant in what concerns us deeply ...' it was because it held some significance for her.[82] The 'Girl of the Period' was followed by the 'Shrieking Sisterhood'. The Suffrage movement of the 1890s brought Mrs Linton back into the fray at her most vigorous, castigating her opponents as 'political firebrands and moral insurgents' 'Wild Women', insisting that for women 'The cradle lies across the door of the polling-booth, and bars the way to the senate'.[83] The furore surrounding Mona Caird's attacks on the inbuilt inequities of marriage[84] resonates here too. The *Nineteenth Century* encouraged this female dispute. Mrs Linton's three articles during 1891 and March 1892 were followed in April by Clara Collett's statistically-based paper demonstrating the need of women to be self-sufficient; the following month by Caird's 'Defence' of the 'Wild Women', a direct challenge to Linton, demonstrating her illogicality with some stirring metaphors of her own – 'Her arguments, when formidable, mutually and relentlessly devour each other....'. For Caird Mrs Linton's argument came down simply to 'the time-honoured quarrel between yesterday and to-day, between reaction and progress ...'.[85] There was probably an element of this. It is tempting to speculate on where Maria Jewsbury would have stood over the 'Shrieking Sisterhood' of the 1870s had she been spared her untimely death and lived as long as Mrs Linton. To read the 'Wild Women' battle between Mrs Lynn Linton and Mrs Caird against Eliza Lynn's articles for *Household Words* on the 'Rights and Wrongs of Women' (1854) before Mona Alison was even born, is to recognize something of the complexity of press debates. There were undoubtedly differences in understanding of 'Woman's Rights' between the generations; perhaps even greater differences between the New Woman's confident manifestation of her independence and the young 'insurgents' of half a century before, who may have 'despised all that was old and proved in favour of all that was new and untried' but possessed the innocence of those with 'the eggshell' still resting 'in our curly heads'.[86] There were other factors that had to do with the personalities of the combatants. The elderly former radical was grown shriller in her castigation of those who did not match her 'old English' ideal of Womanhood which the 'Girl of the Period' supplanted in the 1860s.

Women writers of the time had no difficulty in connecting the generations of Revolting Daughters and seeing them as constructed images. Mrs Oliphant said categorically that 'The "New Woman" ... is a creation of the Press ... but her importance to the newspapers cannot be gainsaid ... She was started some thirty years ago – or is it more? – as the Girl of the Period ...'.[87] Sarah Grand in the 1890s could still exploit the terminology of the 1870s, transforming the 'Shrieking Sisterhood' to 'Bawling Brotherhood', and echoing Mrs Oliphant saw the New Woman as 'Gorgon' with the faults of both sexes and charms of neither as but 'the finest work of the imagination which the newspapers have yet produced'.[88]

However manufactured and packaged, the cultural importance of such press debates is indicated as much by those who stood aloof as by those who were involved. In reflecting that she had enough to do with the immediate business of any conscientious author 'whether novelist or otherwise' attending to 'subject-matter and sentences', and the 'Woman's Suffrage question, with many another of abstract justice' did not attract her, Matilda Betham-Edwards implicitly acknowledges that her 1890s readers assume the suffrage issue *would* have done.[89] The mass reading public now looked to the press for its ideas – cultural, philosophical, ethical and political. Periodicals rarely paid as well as daily newspapers, but most women found them more accessible and the debating arena they afforded a more expansive one.

6
In the Editor's Chair

'There is no paper now in existence which can be to me what the *Echo* is. I have given it its character, its existence, its circulation. It is myself.' Thus Stead on his editorship of the *Northern Echo*, though time proved him wrong in thinking he had 'more power and more influence here than on almost any other paper'.[1] Other journals were to give more scope. But he expressed here one reason why journalists sought to be editors. Launching a new magazine could be thrilling. Sala describes with gusto selecting 'a very strong staff', choosing a name, designing the frontispiece, and inventing a Dr Johnson 'quotation' as *Temple Bar's* motto. There was a further motive. Editorship could impart status, intellectual influence *and* financial stability in the form of fixed payment with potential 'extras'. Sala recalled Maxwell's invitation to edit this rival to *Cornhill* as bringing 'not only a handsome salary as editor, but remuneration at the rate of thirty shillings or two pounds a page for my contributions'.[2]

Thackeray's dramatic pay rise from £1000 to £2000 as editor of *Cornhill Magazine* was exceptional, but even his son-in-law Leslie Stephen's much lower editorial income of £500 enabled him to reduce his journalism and 'set about a book'.[3] On the *Times* in the 1840s bonuses raised Delane's salary steadily; he once received an *increase* of £200. When in 1880, on the strength of his first in Greats and imminent call to the Bar, Buckle was recommended as its potential editor his initial salary was 'decidedly higher' than in any of 'the regular professions'.[4] By the 1890s the editor of a London daily earned between £1000 and £5000.

Few women editors made the national daily league, though when working for sound publishers they received proper salaries. Despite Fanny Green's assertion that women journalists in the 1890s were paid equally with men, as editor of the ill-fated *Mirror* Mrs Mary Howarth's £50 a month was lower than the average for male newspaper editors a decade earlier.[5] Many factors influenced editorial salaries: the type of periodical, its success, the proprietor's financial health, the level of competition in the industry, and with the annuals and, later, the monthlies in the 1860s, the pulling-power of a celebrity name. One cannot extrapolate too much from a few examples, but the figures quoted suggest the financial attractions of editorship.

In the heyday of the annuals rewards could be high, though there were risks. Samuel Carter Hall was ruined by his editorial agreement with *The Amulet* when it folded after eleven years;[6] the Countess of Blessington spent more than her remuneration lavishly entertaining the literary lions whom she courted for contributions. But Mary Howitt's modest £100 pa in the later 1830s compares well with Stead's initial £150 editing the *Echo* in 1871.[7] Financial success for women editors was frequently linked to full or part ownership, although in husband and wife joint ventures women's fees, where they existed, often disappeared into the 'family' coffers. Isabella Beeton seems never to have expected direct monetary reward for her substantial contribution to Sam's publishing ventures.[8] Gissing's sardonic portraits of the embittered Yule pipe-dreaming of the 'joy of sitting in that dictatorial chair!', calculating money-chasing Milvain who gains that comfortable berth, and the energetic publisher Jedwood planning 'a score of untried ventures' on the back of his novelist wife's earnings were not pure fiction.[9]

The title 'editor' covered vast differences in salary, prestige and responsibilities; from the individual who, backed by a compliant financier-cum-publisher, organizes – even writes – the contents, to the Fleet Street editor in his 'sanctum' with fine galleried library, supervising a large staff of outside contributors, inside writers and sub-editors.[10] Over the century changes in technology, communications and distribution affected editors' jobs as well as reporters'. The work became more complex and professional, though small scale publications were edited 'from home' even late in the century. Since work on dailies and weeklies was inevitably office-based compared with the monthlies, women with heavy domestic calls on their time would find the strain of their tight deadlines prohibitive. Even weekly number publication of one's own work, with none of the complications of external contributors, was 'rather an anxious task, as we had to work to time'.[11] Editing a literary quarterly, however, was an interesting if exhausting adjunct to one's real profession, and it possessed at mid-century the social status achieved by most daily newspaper editors only two or three decades later.[12] As a friend counselled John Lockhart before he took on the *Quarterly*, editing such a journal 'is the office of a scholar and a gentleman, but that of a newspaper is not'. Joanne Shattock's comparison of the *Quarterly* and the *Edinburgh* shows that editorial powers of policy-making could differ markedly between similar periodicals[13] while the more arduous technical side, sub-editing manuscripts and proof-correcting, remained constant. For daily newspapers Russell's encapsulation of editorship as papers, piles of proofs and a mass of letters is probably as neat as any. Here hours were unsocial. Delane's routine at the *Times* was 10pm till 5am, and that after two hours dealing with correspondence; his successor Chenery, even when ill, stayed until three to check proofs.[14] Men like Delane and CP Scott of the *Manchester Guardian* prided themselves on their detailed control of leading articles and checking the text of the paper. The ambitious hero–editor of Lady Colin Campbell's novel *Darrell Blake* seems scarcely exaggerated. 'After working the greater part of the night at the *Tribune* office, going over everything', tossing out leaders and rewriting other pieces, he was up at seven o'clock in the 'little study at the back of the house in Onslow Crescent'.[15]

The reality of editorship was not just cash, power and glory. One needed, unlike the ever-wavering Campbell of *the New Monthly,* to be decisive.[16] Those who did not merely lend their name but were genuinely involved in the everyday tasks found it time-consuming, sometimes wearisome. Ella Hepworth Dixon saw it as a mixture of 'unutterable boredom', 'delirious excitement', struggling to suffer fools gladly and the delight of 'pouncing on the right man or woman for one's purpose'.[17] The meticulous way in which Dickens sub-edited contributions and conveyed to Wills precise editorial instructions was a major contribution to the success of *Household Words*.[18] By the end of the century the woman editor of *Queen* was in her office three or four days a week, shirking 'none of the dull routine business of "making-up", proof reading, or attending to correspondence.'[19]

A modern critical view might judge editorial success in terms of its intentions – intellectual and commercial – and its negotiation with different groups – publishers, contributors, readers – in society. Contemporary publishers only survived if their journals' 'success' included profitability, but often their motives were not wholly commercial. A publisher like Strahan would probably have agreed with John Morley that success was 'the increase of influence'.[20] The women whose work is described here were motivated to varying degrees both by the prospect of financial success and of influencing public opinion or taste. Women's efforts in the religious and feminist press and the niche markets of women's and children's magazines are dealt with in more detail in Chapters 7 and 9. Inevitably there are cases of overlap. Emily Faithfull might well have preferred any discussion of the *Victoria Magazine* to be located with general periodicals; but her involvement with the Langham Place group makes its placing in Chapter 9 more convenient.

Women advising on editorship as a career set formidable standards. Mary Billington giving Miss Low of the *Queen* the 'first place' among contemporary women editors attributes to her the qualities of 'knowing everyone of social or literary importance', understanding what her public wanted, recognizing and encouraging new talent.[21] Fanny Green thought the ideal editor had 'all the literary qualities of a successful writer, together with a fineness of tact and knowledge of men and things that would bring him to the front in any profession'.[22] Her comparison with other professions is scarcely calculated to encourage youthful female readers. For what other professions were girls well-equipped to glitter in? The only 'open calling' which Bennett could instance to compare to journalism was medicine.[23]

Whatever the ideal requirements of successful editorship, achieving it at all depended on factors which were the reverse of women's usual condition. Their education was all too often inadequate, political sophistication was discouraged and their personal expectations and ambitions modest. In such circumstances it is perhaps more surprising that so many, rather than so few, reached the editorial chair. Family connections aside, the most likely route was via success as a novelist. By the late 1880s there were complaints that smart barristers and MPs, or popular novelists, anyone with influence, intellect or 'a name' could 'slip into an editorship' in preference to experienced newspaper men.[24] Set against the disheartening battles to secure reasonable terms from publishers, running a magazine must often have appeared to novelists an attractive alternative. Charlotte Riddell, who had experienced the murkier side of commerce and Grub Street, was briefly co-proprietor and editor of *St James's* in the wake of her best-seller *George Geith*, and in 1879 launched her own sixpenny 'literary and domestic' magazine *Home*. Lady Ritchie's mobilization of Margaret Oliphant and Dinah Mulock to help 'a less successful literary woman' with contributions as a 'present' when Mrs Riddell was in 'rather a miserable position' suggests financial rather than ideological motives.[25] Yet financing and editing was fraught with risks. Even in 1891 when Henrietta Stannard launched *Golden Gates*, the first penny weekly ever 'exclusively owned, edited and published by a popular novelist', the usually optimistic Helen Black saw 'such enterprises' as 'treacherous and adventuresome'. It lasted three years. No wonder the worldly-wise American journalist Elizabeth Banks looked to a millionaire to finance her dream of editing a London magazine. Unfortunately he died before he could bring her hopes to fruition.[26]

A complex mix of causes barred aspiring women from editorship in the most influential sectors of the press. The much respected and talented Margaret Oliphant, despite continuing efforts, never acquired a stable editorial income. Quite why is uncertain. Critics have speculated that the reason was as much her habit of changing publishers and hankering after the higher-level journals as her sex. Her letter to Blackwood when editing the Foreign Classics Series suggests her confidence in her editorial abilities, and awareness of both organizational logistics and marketing. At moments the coveted position seemed within her grasp. In the early 1880s she had hopes of both Longmans and Macmillan. She was so sure of getting *Fraser's* that she even commissioned articles for the revamped magazine. Then when Macmillan toyed with the idea of a weekly she set out her editorial plans to Craik for a society paper, possibly under the Queen's patronage, with a 'creaming of the foreign press' and 'Spectator' style sketches but no iniquitous gossip. None of these hopes was realized.[27] As Beetham argues, the position of women editors was always anomalous, even when like Christian Johnstone, Mary Howitt and Eliza Cook they made notable contributions to the press.[28]

It was usually men who were proprietors, held the purse-strings and exercised control. Whilst some were content to give their editors a long rein, others could be a considerable irritant. The best, said Hulda Friederichs, were 'like the constitutional monarch who reigns but does not rule, unless in a great crisis'.[29] This monarch was rarely female. If a woman held such a position a male relative usually took the editorial reins. Inheritance occasionally gave women vested financial interest in journals, and there are instances of women taking vigorous action to protect their position. When Clarissa Murray, widow of James former chief reporter of the *Times*, inherited shares she took legal action over what she considered excessive printing charges. Decades later Clara Sibley, strong-willed granddaughter of the first John Walter, similarly engaged in legal disputes over loss of profits. In her long-drawn out efforts to gain access to the accounts she even attempted selling shares to Harmsworth.[30]

Financial stability apart, a periodical would not last long without locating its space in the market. Gimmicks, publicity, big names – might aid a successful launch. John Maxwell's flamboyancy assisted *Belgravia*'s birth, celebrated by dinner at the Langham and advertised on railway hoardings, but without the market for Braddon's fiction and the editorial talent which engaged her readers it is unlikely it would have lasted so long. For all her impressive list of influential, rich subscribers Lady Randolph Churchill's exclusive quarterly *Anglo-Saxon Review* appealed to too narrow a sector to be sustainable.[31]

A dispute between editor and proprietor could cut off a promising editorial reign at a stroke. Partnerships foundered over incompatible attitudes. Dickens almost immediately lost the editorship of his new *Daily News* following disagreements over his rôle. Stead's anticipated problems with Thompson affected his salary negotiations as assistant on the *Pall Mall Gazette*, and he parted company with Newnes barely three months after launching the *Review of Reviews*. Hood left the *New Monthly* because Colburn would not allow him full editorial control, and his own *Hood's Magazine* hit serious trouble when his financial backer proved a crook.[32] Women editors were just as vulnerable; with less financial clout, more so. Some were nevertheless throughout the century prepared to take a stand on principle. Caroline Norton had a major dispute with Bell, proprietor of the *Court Magazine* when he insisted contributions be provided 'gratis'.[33] Jean Ingelow 'not approving altogether of the way' in which the publisher managed *Youth's Magazine* soon resigned her editorship.[34] Lady Florence Dixie turned down £150 000 to set up a women's paper because of a disagreement over policy – her financier wanted it restricted to *his* perception of women's affairs.[35] The beginning of the twentieth century provided a dramatic instance of proprietorial power when Harmsworth, having lost £100 000 on his ill-fated launch of the *Daily Mirror*, the 'First Daily Newspaper for Gentlewomen', packed editor Mrs Howarth off to the *Daily Mail*. His new man at the helm, Fyfe, dismissed the all-female editorial staff, later describing the event ambiguously as 'An horrid experience, like drowning kittens'.[36]

Other reasons, more to do with their sex than editorial stance or professional failure, explain why some women had comparatively short periods in office. Titles within family businesses tended to pass to sons, or to the management of men by marriage, unless the heiress's family considered her match imprudent. Typically when Alexander Mackay died in 1845, the man appointed manager of his *Belfast Newsletter* eventually acquired the paper partly 'by purchase' and partly by marrying Mary Mackay.[37] If marriage could curtail a career, bohemian attitudes were equally inhibiting. Linda Hughes suggests a mixture of reasons why Rosamund Marriott Watson abruptly resigned from *Sylvia's Journal* which was holding its advertisers and was well, if not widely, reviewed. Her editorial stance as 'female aesthete' sat uneasily in a journal addressing women; the *Yellow Book* already met the aesthetes' market and her abandonment of husband and child for her lover made her position untenable.[38] Long-lasting editors like Mary Braddon (10 years), Ellen Wood, (20 years) and Charlotte Yonge (40 years) either had a controlling share or established strong links with the publisher. Even where journals were run for ideological reasons rather than profit, as the early history of the *English Woman's Journal* shows, this did not guarantee an editor long tenure.

Almost all editors face two perennial, seemingly paradoxical problems – finding enough publishable material at a price they are prepared to pay and dealing with the flood of unsolicited manuscripts. Obtaining high-class contributors was always a challenge, as Dickens well knew. In 1863 Emily Davies, first editor of the *Victoria Magazine*, faced major difficulties in obtaining the crucial serial. Despite useful literary connections she tried in vain to tempt 'names' like George Eliot, Trollope, Kingsley and Tom Hughes. All declined. They were fully engaged, had 'nothing to hand' or were pledged to another publisher. Trollope's brother eventually obliged.[39] A network of tried and trusted writers, preferably including a famous 'name', and dependable for copy suited to the title, was essential. The first editor of *Sharpe's*, inundated with manuscripts, but anxious not to alienate readers whose hopeful contributions had been declined, spelt out the dilemma at some length. Rejected manuscripts were not necessarily without merit nor even inappropriate, but 'in common fairness' regulars could not be 'elbowed aside by casual contributions'. In the time-honoured phrase, 'to prevent the risk of disappointment' readers should note that 'we do not solicit contributions from the writing public generally'.[40] The appeal to readers' sense of 'fairness' does not mask the desire for an efficient system of collecting copy.

Possession of a marketable name, and energy to write as well as edit, were valuable assets. On the combination of his own comic genius and the generosity of friends depended the quality of *Hood's* early issues. Mrs Hall's 'terms' were 'the mere pleasure of helping' the author of *The Song of the Shirt*.[41] Other ideal qualities were a nose for potential writers buried in the 'slush pile' and the knack of developing as well as editing their work. Dickens's immense success with *Household Words* and *All The Year Round* depended on all these. Additionally he had a powerful sense of the aims of his journals and understood the particular require-ments of serialization. But even good contributors could let one down. This was particularly troublesome with serialized novels, whether a commissioned work turned out a flop, as Dickens suffered with Lever's *A Day's Ride*, or as Strahan found with *Good Words*, writers could not meet his requirements or failed to deliver at all.[42] One solution was for the 'editor' to write most of the material herself. 'Margaret Blount' of an obscure magazine, *Saturday Night*, explained to Isabella Fyvie that it was purely a vehicle for her own writing, and though she admired Miss Fyvie's poetry she could not afford to pay contributors. Running a magazine was tough, 'The cost and risk are heavy ... The profit may be nothing'. The magazine soon changed hands.[43]

Women editors who moved beyond the literary and domestic spheres into the political faced specific discrimination. In Washington for a period during the 1870s[44] some women gained access to the Press Gallery; the British Parliament was more resistant. Not until the end of the century did women hold influential managerial positions on national newspapers. The situation in the provinces was somewhat different. Over the decades provincial newspapers underwent dramatic changes though at any one time there remained huge variations in management and organization. By the 1860s daily papers in the cities employed highly competent editors and journalists, and many had London correspondents who exploited the possibilities of post and telegraph,[45] whilst local weeklies operated much more modestly. In some ways the division between 'trade' – the running of newspapers especially the provincial – and gentlemanly pursuits – the editing of quality quarterlies – lingered on well into the century. Women who owned and edited newspapers generally did so as part of a family trade. In the provinces local papers had often been founded or were re-established on a political ticket, like George Eliot's Will Ladislaw in *Middlemarch*. Proprietors were often staunch party supporters, and such political affiliations made it less likely that women would be actively engaged in their management. Nevertheless some old-established titles were family concerns, originally linked to a general printing business. In this climate a widow might very well take over the running just as she might manage the draper's shop or the inn which she inherited. It was the family livelihood. Equally when a firm flourished the propri-etor might become a person of considerable note in neighbourhood.

By the 1880s journalism was not 'only a power of the State outside Parliament, but in the House of Commons itself'. Directors and proprietors of both national and provincial papers sat as Members.[46]

In her ironic fictional account of how the ambitious journalist Darrell Blake makes his way, via a judicious marriage and dash of Irish brilliance, to a Fleet Street editorship and thence into politics, Lady Colin Campbell, herself a journalist, gives an incisive image of the relationship between a newspaper and its community. 'An editor of a large provincial paper may be an important local personage, but an editor who is son-in-law to the proprietor of the paper is considerably more so.' The world she sketches is dangerously limiting for women. Although the *Middlesborough Herald* is 'Liberal ... with strong leanings towards Radicalism' the Tidmarshes who own it are 'intensely Conservative in their own lives'. Pretty Miss Tidmarsh, in her patriarchal provincial society has little scope outside the domestic sphere. Marriage to Blake for whom 'it was not part of his creed that women were possessed of brains' is not destined to improve matters. Once installed in the editorial sanctum of the *Herald* 'akin in glory to an official residence in Downing Street' Blake is offered a national daily. The clever society women he meets in London have both too little scope for their energies, and too much political influence. The combination is corrosive.[47]

But the dynastic principle enabled some women to retain financial control, even active editorial management, until they chose to pass on the reins of power. Mrs Knox, widow of the founder of the *Irish Times*, kept the paper only until she could sell it on. When Mrs William Frederic Tillotson became, jointly with her late husband's partner, manager/proprietor of the *Bolton Evening News* and its weekly paper series she maintained the link for several years until her son could take over.[48] Other women were more than caretakers. Janet Harrison, proprietor of the *Marylebone Mercury*, was its chief writer. The *Cambridge Chronicle*, started in 1744, was acquired a little over a century later by Charles Wharton Naylor, who added to its title *University Journal, Isle of Ely Herald and Huntingdonshire Gazette*. On his death in 1878 his widow managed it, and having expanded its influence eventually left it to her daughter Miss AT Naylor as sole proprietor.

The *Reading Mercury*, founded 1723, exemplifies both early printing links and patterns of family inheritance. It was remarkable for the involvement of women in its ownership and management, notably Anna Maria Smart, who ran the paper extremely successfully from 1762 until 1809 when she died aged 72. According to her own paper she 'settled her accounts on the eve of her decease'. The business was left to her daughters Marianne Cowslade, whose husband had been Mrs Smart's partner, and Elizabeth le Noir, married to a French emigré. The sisters ran it together for a couple of years when they were joined by a male Cowslade.[49] Marianne, however, continued to edit the paper, to which her sister contributed features such as a 'Common-Place Book' intended for the 'fair sex'. Editorship eventually passed to Marianne's son and with her death (1830) direct female influence seems to have faded, though the title continued to thrive under the Cowslades. A facsimile of the first edition was reproduced as a supplement in 1882, copies being presented to the Queen and Prince of Wales.[50]

Mrs Christian Johnstone, perhaps the most influential woman editor of her time, is best known for her work with *Tait*'s. But prior to that she edited from 1817–24 the *Inverness Courier* a weekly journal 'which has claims to a special notice' according to a nineteenth-century press historian. It was launched to rival the established *Journal*, run by a local landowner 'much opposed to the authorities in town and county'. The *Courier* was founded partly to repel the *Journal*'s attacks and partly to provide the Northern Highlands – it covered the counties of Inverness, Ross, Sutherland and Caithness, Nairn and Moray – with 'a moderately Liberal and useful paper'. It clearly met a need in the district, rapidly acquiring a 'very considerable circulation' and with it 'a large share of advertisements'.[51] Even so, the income from Mrs Johnstone's cookery manual was needed to help finance the press. Although nominally edited by John Johnstone, her second husband, it was well known that the real work was done by his wife, and it was she who gave the *Courier* its distinctive literary tone. In preserving the fiction of masculine control provincial Britain was little different from the more conservative American states, where in 1842 the Boston *Transcript* tried to keep secret the sex of Cornelia Walter, its new editor who avoided the office, working from her drawing-room.[52]

Right at the other end of the century Hulda Friederichs' career illustrates the growing professionalization of journalism. She achieved her position as editor of a Newnes paper only after a thorough training as interviewer and a successful stint as section manager on his *Westminster Budget*, an illustrated sixpenny weekly developed alongside the *Westminster Gazette*. When its editor Charles Morley left, Newnes 'accustomed as he was to enormous circulations and large profits' decided to close it. Miss Friederichs, tactfully attributing the *Budget*'s decline to the 'enormous' increase of sixpenny illustrated weeklies in the eighties, thought it 'a pity to kill a paper which at that time had an extremely interesting, if not large' international circulation. Her own involvement intensified her attachment to it and her 'mild objection to the execution of a living paper', as she put it, resulted in the offer of the editorship. Although she had a formidable reputation as a journalist her account of Newnes's offer reflects the modesty which so many women felt appropriate to their sex. The idea of editing had, she says, 'never occurred' to her. She had 'little time and less ambition to take over additional responsibility'. She thought Newnes's offer ('Well, if you like to play with it for six months, and see what you can make of it, do so by all means') a joke, though not apparently an offensive one. She merely countered 'that executioners had no right to harrow the feelings of the relations of the condemned'. But Newnes meant it. She gave up some of her work on the daily to edit the *Budget* for nine years, well into the twentieth century.

Although it had been a woman who launched the first Sunday paper back in the eighteenth century, Mrs Rachel Beer's assumption of the editor's chair at the *Sunday Times* in 1893, when her husband purchased it, was immediately read as a signal that amalgamation with his *Observer* would rapidly follow. Clearly her husband's finance was a crucial factor in enabling Rachel Beer to fill this post for four years[53] but the retrospective account by a later editor seems unduly misogynistic. 'This wealthy, slapdash newcomer' having worked first as assistant editor on the *Observer*, then, according to Fleet Street gossip, editor, 'her ambition still unsatisfied', bought the rival *Sunday Times* and to the amusement of journalists proceeded to edit them both. These implications of amateurism and unseemly ambition are at odds with contemporary views. She became a member of both the Institute of Journalists and Society of Women Journalists. Mary Billington claimed that Mrs Beer collected a 'strong and capable staff' on the *Sunday Times*, took an independent political line on occasion and increased the paper's circulation. She aimed to offer a broader imperial perspective than contemporary penny papers gave, allowing more space to 'Colonial and Indian matters' and rather less to cultural and social topics. Her own leader column 'The World's Work' exemplified this concept. Unlike male editors whose wives entertained for them, she was herself perforce the hostess at her fine house in Mayfair. Here too she received each Saturday page proofs brought from the Portugal Street office for her approval.[54]

Women found more scope in other press sectors. Though she has filtered down to us as a somewhat shadowy figure, perhaps because of

her unusual marital position, Christian Johnstone's professionalism resulted in quality journals, and she was highly regarded by
contemporaries. When she became joint proprietor with Tait in 1834
she was already working on his magazine and the Johnstones' firm was
printing it. The merger with her own *Johnstone's Edinburgh Magazine*
gave her a proprietorial interest. Mary Howitt, meeting her at Tait's
'amazingly entertaining' tripe supper during their visit to 'that intellectual centre' of Edinburgh in 1835 thought her only a major contributor; in fact Christian Johnstone made the editorial decisions and
selected the contents. She reviewed the work of almost all the new
women writers of the 1830s and 1840s; Linton, Martineau, Mitford and
the Howitts wrote for her; and *Tait's* was distinguished by its singular
patronage of self-taught and artisan contributors.[55]

Tait's met with Mary Howitt's approval because of its articles on
serious, important issues. Her recommendation of it to her family
implies a middle-class audience, but its lowered price and format aimed
at the literate artisan. Mrs Johnstone's proprietorial influence was more
pervasive than merely overseeing contents. *Tait's* took on the larger
double-column format of *Johnstone's*. Her experience of running journals priced in pennies must have influenced the decision to drop the
price from half-a-crown to a shilling. *Johnstone's* claimed a Scottish circulation of 5000 in four months, and shortly before the two magazines
merged, she argued in *Tait's* that cheap monthlies were inevitable.
Expensive ones were losing circulation to the penny weeklies, and in
growing more dependent on the circulating libraries relied increasingly
upon 'flash' articles. *Tait's* was not prepared to abandon its 'higher
purpose' to furnish frivolous reading for libraries. Mr Tait's solid tripe
supper in contrast to the banquet where the Howitts met *Blackwood's*
'Christopher North' was apposite.[56]

While Christian Johnstone was using her influence to endorse liberal
principles and encourage serious writing, the popularity of the illustrated annual, those 'butterflies of literature' as Letitia Landon called
them, provided quite different opportunities. The proliferation of journals offered women space for fiction, articles and poetry, but only
rarely a route to an editorial chair; whereas many female contributors
to the annuals enjoyed a spell editing one. Annuals were not primarily
literary productions. Their main focus was the elegant engravings.
Poetry and brief essays accompanied them. Many were edited by
women, but men didn't despise the considerable financial induce-
ments they offered. Lady Blessington's biographer, writing as the

annuals were withering from the landscape, remarked that publishers relied upon aristocratic connections to lend lustre to their publications, but also needed 'sparkling gems of genius'. Popular writers employed as editors were 'largely paid in general; some for their name alone, and others for their services'.[57]

It was possible to be a working editor even by the domestic hearth. From her beloved Berkshire village Mary Mitford sent out a stream of correspondence, soliciting material for *Finden's Tableaux* from writers – including Elizabeth Barrett; fuming over the disastrous effects of Mr Tilt's cavalier behaviour in not sending her proofsheets; explaining forcefully to the publisher why a particular order of contents should be followed and who should get complimentary copies. 'The Minstrel of Provence' was such 'a stirring poem' and likely to be so popular that it should 'be placed just in that part of the Volume where people looking over a book with a view to purchase are likely to open'. Sending a copy to the *Morning Chronicle* 'with Miss Mitford's compts [sic] to John Eashope' would 'be of great advantage to the book'. When a contributor let her down at the last minute she cajoled her 'second string' to produce a minimum of forty or fifty lines on the plate of 'a Georgian selling two beautiful girls for a Turkish harem'. The fee was £5 and a copy of the work but 'the real advantage' was the choice company which offered 'the very best possible introduction to authorship'.[58]

The market the annuals met is characterized by George Eliot's choice of one of the best known, the *Keepsake* as Ned Plymdale's bait for wooing Rosamund Vincy.[59] Though not directed exclusively towards them, women were recognizably important consumers. The editor of the *Drawing-Room Album* for 1835 dedicated his work to the 'Intelligent and Intellectual' Ladies of Great Britain. It was designed as a presentation album, many pages printed on coloured paper – yellow, lilac, pink, and shades of blue and green – with blank pages for the recipient's own water-colours and drawings. Competition led to elaborate bindings in silk, morocco and velvet, engravings of work by the most fashionable artists, and high payments to well-known authors. 'Chaffy, frivolous, and unsatisfactory species of publication … only valuable as works of art' they may have been but even Mary Howitt who so characterized them, herself stooped to the task, unlike Sir Walter Scott who received an invitation to edit the *Keepsake* when professionally secure enough to refuse it as 'not to be thought of' (though he was rumoured to have accepted £500 for a single contribution).[60] By the time Charles Heath, engraver and a major publisher of annuals, died in 1848, his business had long since failed and there had been a sea-change in literary taste.[61] The mid-century *Mrs Ellis's Morning Call*, in its scarlet binding heavily embossed in gold, may have looked like a butterfly, but its editor's more solemn intent is evident in articles on female emigration or advocating moral and domestic training for girls. The annuals like the silver-fork novels lost their glitter, but a small though significant legacy was that women had been visible as editors.

Probably the most successful annual editor was Lady Blessington who edited *Gems of Beauty* (1835–40) and Heath's *Book of Beauty* (from 1834) and *Keepsake* (from 1841). Her responsibilities were far more arduous than Mary Howitt was to find them. Apart from her own contributions (nine out of 23 in 1834) she selected illustrations, corresponded with engravers, artists and contributors, suffering 'all the turmoil of contentions with publishers'.[62] She recruited for the *Book of Beauty* (under her ægis) fashionable titled society – the Viscounts Castlereagh, Morpeth, and Powerscourt, Lord Wellesley, the Marchioness of Hastings, Lord Leigh, Lord John Manners, Lady Emmeline Stuart-Wortley and Lady Stepney. But she also used her salon and literary connections to commission others of greater literary stature – D'Israeli, Grace Aguilar, Barry Cornwall, Lytton and Landor. Nor were all her titled contributors mere fly-by-nights. Lady Emmeline had edited the *Keepsake* in 1840 and thirteen years later was contributing to the *Ladies' Cabinet*. Anna Maria Hall produced Irish sketches and Lady Blessington reciprocated with material for the Halls' journals. Though well-paid for *Heath's Annual* and others, Lady Blessington spent so much energy and money on the round of entertaining to secure contributors and literary influence that her earnings were finally insufficient. Gore House and its contents were auctioned in a dramatic sale shortly before her death.[63] Like Miss Mitford's, her journalism had partly been necessitated by the financial demands made by dependants. She also used her patronage to find employment for impoverished female relatives like Louisa Fairlie who contributed and briefly edited the *Keepsake* and Marguerite Power who worked as her assistant and eventually edited it for several years.

Annuals allowed some scope for innovation. Louisa Henrietta Sheridan attempted something original and controversial in launching her comic annual designed for women. The first issue of the *Comic Offering* (1830) was entirely her own work. She was editor, writer and illustrator. Despite her assertion that a '*female*' editor best recognized the 'strict boundaries of delicacy and taste', there was contemporary unease at the notion of a woman editing a humorous book. She must have dispelled such anxieties since very proper ladies like Agnes Strickland and Miss Mitford contributed to later issues. Only ill-health forced her retirement in 1835.[64]

Mary Howitt blamed the annuals as much as the 'wretched, degraded state of criticism' for the parlous state of literature in 1830. Her reason for taking on work she despised is partially explained by her excuse for William's accepting the *Winter Wreath* – it kept a 'young author alive in the mind of the public', attracted 'the favourable notice of reviewers', and brought in 'a little cash'. In any case, surrounded as they were in 1829 by new friends all busy editing annuals, the habit must have been catching.[65] A decade later Mary took on the *Drawing Room Scrap-Book* following Letitia Landon's fateful marriage, years later admitting 'I was not proud of the work'. Its very appearance suggests a possession to admire rather than a book to read – gilt-edged, the entire binding heavily embossed with gold borders and classical motifs, its mock leather spine emblazoned *Album des Salons*. Nevertheless within the constraints of a genre she found unsympathetic she struggled to maintain literary standards. Unlike Lady Blessington neither LEL nor Mary had a genuine editorial rôle; they had solely to provide text for engravings selected by the publisher. Mary's first volume included the fashionable oriental genre – 'Interior of a Moorish Palace', 'The Odalique' [sic] – one or two portraits, something more homely – a Newcastle streetscape. Eight LEL poems were to hand and Letitia's portrait was supported by William's appreciation and Mary's 'L'Envoi'. It is clear from the way in which her Preface and the appreciation deal movingly and honestly with the 'mysterious circumstances' and 'tragic horror' of Landon's death that Mary's emotions were engaged in taking on this work 'as it were, from the very hands of the dead'.[66] That, perhaps as much as monetary reward, motivated her. If LEL found difficulty in moving poetically from Dowlutabad to the Caves of Elephants, Mary was scarcely going to find it easy writing to 'themes of chivalry and romance, feudal pageants and Eastern splendour'.[67] She managed a poem in a day, sometimes adapting suitable German ones, sometimes twisting her subjects so that a camel train provided an excuse for a poem on Homer's childhood ('Smyrna'), struggling to reconcile artistic integrity with writing to order. The new editor's poetic strain had, after all, in Mrs Johnstone's phrase, hitherto been pitched more to the 'cottage hearth',[68] but she edited two further *Scrap-Books* before Sarah Stickney took over.

This level of practical experience was however scarcely adequate preparation for co-editing 'our *own Howitt's Journal'*. Mary was 'quite unprepared' for 'the amount of labour and painstaking'. Their initial optimism – 'It is the very time for us to establish our paper'[69] – was misplaced. Political sympathizers enthused over their plans for a high-class magazine aimed at working men. The volume format, bound in fine green cloth and elegantly gilded, was as attractive as an annual; but it was too expensive a production and too earnest in its educational aims for their target market. Years later Mary quoted a friend's 'shrewd, pithy letter' – 'Men engaged in a death-struggle for bread will pay for amusement when they will not for instruction. ... If you were able and willing to fill the journal with fun, it would pay.'[70]

Anna Maria Hall's literary career was founded in the heyday of the annuals. When the Howitts first met them both Halls were engaged on these publications, Mrs Hall's being the *Juvenile Forget-Me-Not*. This interest in children's literature would be reflected in her future editorial policies.[71] Irritating though he must have been personally – even Mrs Mayo referred to his unfortunate egotism of manner – and others like Mrs Oliphant were distinctly more scathing – Samuel Carter Hall's publishing involvement, influence as editor of the *Art Journal*[72] and delight in entertaining were probably on balance helpful to his wife's career. She contributed to his publications and acquired useful contacts for her own editorial ventures.

Her Irish tales had brought her into some literary prominence; she had even featured in Maclise's literary ladies in *Fraser's*[73] and by 1852 when she edited *Sharpe's* had acquired a useful reputation, good contacts and knowledge of the mundane side of editorship. *Sharpe's* proprietors regarded it 'simply as property' giving its succession of editors free rein.[74] Mrs Hall seems to have relished editorial power, and during her short period in office put her stamp on the paper, whilst maintaining its stance as ideal family reading. Her first preface enthusiastically emphasized its astonishing value at only one shilling, promising even better things 'inasmuch as her resources will be increased, and her plans more thoroughly developed during the year that approaches'. She revealed a clear sense of what she considered an attractive magazine. The 'Contributors forming the "Staff" of the Magazine, are among the best and most popular authors of the day... in addition to what is brilliant and amusing, there is much solid and useful information, hallowed by *religious* but not *sectarian* principle'. This last point was important. *Sharpe's* was a general magazine, not backed by any church group, but Mrs Hall targeted its 'family' market, drawing parents' attention to 'the fact that she watches every page with minute care, so that nothing can creep in that may not be read aloud in the domestic circle'. Subscribers were told she never made up the table of contents, or cut the leaves of the latest number, without surprise 'at the small price charged for a magazine combining so much artistic and literary attraction – every page of which is liberally paid for'.[75] She was clearly very much a working editor. Samuel Hall knew the Fraserians and his wife presumably noted *Fraser's* successful strategies of projecting its contributors as a coterie of eminent literary figures and drawing on contributions from diplomats, medics, lawyers, architects etc.[76] At any rate, the Halls' assiduous cultivation of literary society bore fruit.

Her own contributions included the serial *Helen Lyndsey*, destined to be unfinished. Mrs Hall supported other working women, encouraging female writers and publishing serious articles addressing social and educational issues. 'The Female Industrial Schools of Cork' described good practice; Mrs Merrifield, who had written for Hall's *Art Journal*, commended practical simplicity in children's dress, arguing powerfully against tight-lacing.[77] The regular unsigned 'Books and their Authors' bears Anna Maria's touch.[78] Its format was brief reviews of fiction, poetry, travel, informational and children's books, touching on topical issues and slipping in literary gossip. She interspersed commentary on professional questions like the Anglo-American copyright agreement and Fox Talbot's resignation of his patent. One article proclaimed an 'unprecedented movement on the part of the WOMEN OF ENGLAND' viz. the response to the slave-trade following publication of *Uncle Tom's Cabin*. The novel itself gets little space, but its anti-slavery stance is supported by lengthy extracts from a letter by Frederika Bremer[79] whose forthcoming *Homes of the New World* had already been praised. Readers get a sense of *entrée* to a writers' coterie – the reviewer corresponds with Bremer and is privy to the book's progress. 'Part of the M.S. is now in the hands of Mrs. Howitt, who has undertaken the translation.'[80] The impression of being a publishing 'insider' is reinforced by snippets: Amelia Opie 'still living and enjoying life' in Norwich, William Howitt 'off to Australia with his sons to visit the "diggings"' and write a book, John Payne, the US consul at Tunis – 'not generally known ... [that he] was author of *Home, Sweet Home*'.[81] A review of Jerdan's memoirs is personalized by a lament for 'Billy Maginn' whose 'grass-grown unrecorded grave' was hard to discover. 'We desire to see a little slab to his memory.'[82] Her literary column thus anticipated the later *causeries*, also foreshadowed by 'Silkworm' in Beeton's magazine.[83] Mrs Hall's construct, however, is neither 'Silkworm's' feminine world nor the masculine one of Yates's Lounger in clubland, but a literary society, to which like her own At Homes, both sexes had equal access.

The way in which she used her 'salon' to identify and promote contributors is well-illustrated by the emergence in *Sharpe's* of Margaret Oliphant. *Adam Graeme* is generously reviewed and intimacy inferred by an arch reference to the author's recent marriage. Shortly afterwards 'Annie Orme' 'Communicated by the Author of "Margaret Maitland", &c, &c.' appears; later volume publication of *Katie Stewart* gets a puff. Had Mrs Hall continued as editor she may well have created a distinctive magazine, but she evidently had a major disagreement with the new proprietor after Virtue sold it, since when she left she took the 'unprecedented step' of refusing to finish *Helen Lyndsey*. The publisher was forced to placate readers faced with an 'abrupt and unceremonious breaking off' with a new tale.[84]

A decade later she embarked on another short-lived editorial venture with Maxwell's *St James's Magazine*, launched, like *Cornhill*, *Saint Paul's*, *Temple Bar*, and *Belgravia*, during the fad for capitalizing on a fashionable corner of London to market a new periodical. Friends warned the Halls of Maxwell's capriciousness, but only after the contract had been signed.[85] Mrs Hall again set her mark on the paper. *St James's* aimed to 'Promote the Interests of Home, the Refinements of Life, and the Amusement and Information of all Classes'.[86] The note of 'Refinement' was struck by the first leading article on the Court of St. James's. *Can Right Be Wrong?*, considered her best novel, was the opening serial. There were articles on astronomy, travel, literature and science; fiction and poetry by Thomas Hood the younger, Diana Craik, and Adelaide Procter. Social questions were addressed; philanthropic enterprises described. Leisured women's interests were met by hints for lady equestrians or on the servant problem.[87] She introduced a children's column. The overall tone was optimistic, recalling Mrs Mayo's comment that Mrs Hall 'hated anything gloomy'.[88]

Her first prefaces stress her success in commissioning 'eminent and popular Authors'.[89] Apart from old friends she drew on former *Sharpe's* writers like Mrs Merrifield and Robert Hunt, FRS (who wrote popular articles on geology). A later preface recalled her 'distinguished writers' – alongside Trollope, Mrs Wood and Mrs Craik, the academics, doctors, clergy and military officers whose strings of letters adorned the

Contents. Neither she nor Mary Howitt enjoyed lengthy editorial tenure, but through their extensive social and literary networks they influenced aspiring younger women, passing on their experience, and Mrs Hall trained one of the most effective female periodical editors of the century – Mary Braddon.

Belgravia was successful on all counts: commercially, as a promotional vehicle for Braddon's fiction, and as an outlet for her views on society. She was acutely aware of her readership, a shrewd negotiator, and adept at marshalling her contributors. This overt marketing of her sensation fiction may partly explain why *Belgravia* has attracted relatively little scholarly attention. Whilst in terms of literary stars the Chatto and Windus years are the more glittering,[90] it was Mary Braddon who established *Belgravia* as a lively successful magazine. She apologized for the 'snobbery' of the title as 'the best bait for the shillings of Brixton and Bow', and Wolff is no doubt right in describing its intention as making 'lower middle-class readers think they were entering the world of high fashion'.[91] Yet she also set out to attract, amuse, inform and occasionally challenge, more educated readers with a shrewd mix of fiction, verse, social satire and topical essays. Braddon's editorship no less than her fiction placed *Belgravia* amongst the most commercially successful of Maxwell's stable, with a circulation reaching 18 000 in 1868 and averaging around 15 000.[92].

It was a tough market. Emily Faithfull in founding the *Victoria Magazine* some three years earlier visualized 'a first-class magazine of *Fraser* or *Macmillan* type'[93] but though robust enough to survive until 1880, in circulation and influence it was scarcely a competitor of either. *Belgravia*, however, despite not aiming at that intellectual level, genuinely competed against those mainstream periodicals launched by book publishers – *Tinsley's*, *Longman's*, *Cornhill*. Protracted exposure to the mundane essentials of editing during her apprenticeship under Mrs Hall paid off.

Maxwell twice disappointed her hopes of sole editorship[94] but her letters to Lytton suggest she had been seriously considering the problems of editorship for some time. Acquiring contributors 'of *his* standing' would be one.[95] In the case of fiction she solved it by writing much of it herself, a strategy Mrs Wood later emulated. She had not set out with this in mind but was driven by market forces. Initially she hoped for a novel by Trollope, but hearing the high price *Cornhill* was supposed to have paid for *The Claverings* decided to produce 'a strong sensation novel' because 'strong measures' extracted the shillings from the public. She understood how a magazine serial should tantalize its readers; the 'slow torture' of unfolding drama eked out over the months instead of 'one lump of excitement & delight'.[96]

Early in her writing career she saw herself as a professional, choosing to be painted with the tools of her trade in Frith's portrait of her.[97] Professionalism embraced understanding market forces. She once admitted to Lytton divided fictional aims; she wanted to be both 'artistic and please *you*' and 'sensational' and please Mudie, whose lending library was dominant in the book trade. Lytton would have understood her dilemma; he had faced similar conflict with Bentley.[98] In *Belgravia* she managed to serve both masters – the god of art and Mammon. Her main weapons were irony and the opportunities afforded by the periodical format – the sequence of items, the titles, the clever juxtaposition of genres and discourses. Though Victorian critics often assumed the readership of sensation fiction to be young women it was more catholic. A *Punch* cartoon of 1868 implied it crossed class and gender, and Charles Wood claimed *East Lynne* transcended racial culture too.[99] Kate Flint's view that Braddon's fiction assumed not a passive reader but an interpreter responsive to the allusions which suffuse the texts[100] applies equally to *Belgravia*. The phrase 'Shillings of Brixton and Bow' acknowledges 'periodical' as ultimately 'commodity' and posits *Belgravia*'s reader as ignorant outsider eager to be initiated into fashionable society. Yet its contents assume a reader who, though revelling in sensation fiction, recognizes classical allusions, engages in cultural debate and will consider a serious argument. The comedy of the society sketches which purport to educate the Pooters of an earlier generation paradoxically depends upon a constructed cynical reader who already shares this world. Braddon may have commodified her art but she retained the ability to destabilize comfortable, conventional assumptions.[101] It was a delicate balancing act.

Readers capable of navigating between discourses of discussion, comic anecdote, social irony, and fictionalized horror could also exercise power. The worst readership crisis occurred in 1868 when *Birds of Prey* was overrunning the allotted space. Braddon announced that it would eventually have a separate sequel, but the serial would cease, making way for work already commissioned. Her sanguine assumption that this tactic would satisfy 'the wishes of readers' was misplaced. Subscribers flexed their muscles, claiming the sequel as part of *Birds of Prey* and demanding it within the magazine. It duly appeared. 'The satisfaction of the greater number must always be the Editor's object' despite the 'loss and embarrassment' which extra pages and printing would cause. Had she been working for an outside proprietor she might not have survived as editor. As it was, Maxwell increased the size for two issues. It must have been an alarming as well as costly lesson in reader power, though Braddon put the best gloss on the situation by claiming that *Belgravia* now offered more 'printed matter' than any other monthly and quoting 'the critical opinion – "Briskest of all the Magazines is *Belgravia*"'.[102]

Her overall editorial strategy for *Belgravia* drew on the models provided by Sala's *Temple Bar* and Mrs Hall's *St. James's* but *Belgravia*'s tone was quite distinctive. The ebullient Sala, known as 'king of journalists', established a style which would survive later changes of management.[103] His prospectus promised a 'domestic romance' 'fair' reviews, essays social, biographical, philosophical, and topical. 'As for politics, there will not be any' though it would 'inculcate thoroughly English sentiments: respect for authority, attachment to the church, and loyalty to the Queen'.[104] *Belgravia* similarly eschewed politics, but Sala's 'thoroughly English sentiments' were part of those very social structures *Belgravia* mocked, and the wholesome family tone of *St James's* was replaced by the exotic and slightly *risqué*. *Belgravia* hooked its readers by a policy of serials including three-part novellas and feature series. Although her own fiction was the backbone of her magazine Mary had learnt from Mrs Hall the value of a powerful contributors list.

Despite the modest level of 'solid cash' paid to contributors she attracted talented writers and by 1872 had enough fiction for two or three years.[105] She depended on a nucleus of journalists and specialist writers with an existing track-record, figures like Walter Besant, THS Escott, Sheridan Le Fanu and the young WS Gilbert, drawing on Maxwell's connections, and the interlocking networks of *Temple Bar*, *St James's*, and *Dublin University Magazine* contributors. This reliable core helped sustain *Belgravia*, even during her protracted illness. Sala, whom she considered brilliant in 'his own peculiar style',[106] was one of her most prolific writers. Although she played no major part in promoting the careers of other women writers two of her fiction contributors later edited or helped found other journals: Florence Marryat (*London Society* 1872–6) and Mrs Cashel Hoey (*World* in 1874).

Belgravia was not overtly concerned with reform but shocking subjects like pit casualties or madness were addressed, albeit in palatable style. 'High Society' was treated ambivalently; its inadequate social round and marriage market were mocked.[107] The piquant juxtaposition of different genres and modes alerted readers to textual ironies.

Juxtaposing Sala's serious, though startling, essay 'On Little Martyrs' (Vol 5, May), offering provocative views on familiar notions of saint-hood, with an illustrated love lyric, 'Saint May', drew attention to the implicit eroticism of the Victorian beauty in church and questioned the motive of churchgoing. Our modern tabloid headline technique was anticipated by sensational titles like 'On Shooting People Down', which promised something thrilling without revealing whether it was fiction, report, or argument. A scientific series, 'Sensationalism in Science', linked itself overtly to the defence of sensation fiction on which *Belgravia* was engaged, and which helped reshape the critical debate surrounding the sensation novel.[108] *Belgravia*'s entertainment was curiously thought-provoking.

The Court Suburb Magazine (1868–70) was another publication aiming to cash in on its London connection. Its founder, Fanny Aikin-Kortright, is scarcely known today but in her time achieved consider-able fame with her first novel *Anne Sherwood* and her writings against the Women's Rights movement.[109] Her long career began in provincial journalism at the age of seventeen with a staff job writing leaders. This training and substantial experience of producing periodical serial fiction presumably encouraged her to compete in the frenetic market of the sixpenny monthlies. The 'Court Suburb' in question was Kensington and Kortright targeted a distinct market, presenting her journal to the denizens of that district as a kind of localized *Temple Bar*, *St James's* or – if more respectable – *Belgravia*. *Court Suburb* readers, like those sought sixteen years earlier by Mrs Hall, a writer she much admired, were assured on the 'essential point' that the editor spared no pains to exclude anything that might prevent her journal's 'safe admis-sion to the family circle'. The shillings of Brixton and Bow are no longer encouraged to buy into socially distant Belgravia; rather the aspiring middle class of 1860s suburbia is encouraged to rejoice in the prestige of its own milieu, and for half the price.

Court Suburb announced itself as 'for Objects of Suburban Interest and General Literature'. Its green cover with engraved pillared wrought iron gate and its motto 'Appealing by an old familiar name/Unto the very heart of memory' connoted historic associations and emotional ties. In her introduction the editor, disclaiming any attempt to meet some pressing need of the day or replace 'good existing periodicals', flatters her readers of Kensington 'daily rising into increased impor-tance' by drawing attention to its 'many interesting localities' and 'illustrious men and women' she proposes to feature.[110] Popular topo-graphical articles – Holland House, Kensington Palace, Campden Hill,

'Chelsea Junior' and Earl's Court appeared in the first two volumes – emphasized the neighbourhood's royal and historic links, and she ran a short series by John Clifford on 'Wild Plants of our Suburbs'. *Court Suburb* was published locally in the High Street and its early advertisements indicate as clearly as the editorial address the middle-class consumers at which it aimed. As well as inside cover ads it carried a supplement 'Advertiser' and smaller slipped pages using coloured paper or printed in two or three colours. They included insurance companies, manufacturers' advertisements for knife polish, silversmith's soap and the like, but the main emphasis was on local services – Saunders's Select Library, a tea, wine, spirit and beer merchant, Dr Wallich's photographic studio, Mr Braine, organist and music teacher, Mr Wheatley teacher of dancing and deportment. Although her outside contributors list was not impressive, 'names' such as S C Hall and Isabella Fyvie occasionally surface. Like Mrs Wood's better known *Argosy* the editor's own writing dominated and *Court Suburb* served to promote her fiction, but through articles and book reviews Kortright also ensured that her magazine reflected her conservative stance on the Woman Question.

She had obviously publicized her journal widely since 'Opinions of the Press', selectively quoting in the manner of modern theatre placards, drew not only from *London News, Morning Star, The Field* and *Court Journal* ('.... promises to hold its own among other works of a similar class'), but local journals and foreign newspapers. One speculates that she happily gave extensive coverage to the Canadian *Daily British Whig* (fulsome praise of its 'fair editress known in Canada as the author of *Waiting for the Verdict'*) but struggled to find the least damaging phrase from *Public Opinion* ('As magazines go, not bad').

The publicity value and money-making potential of a journal which published and promoted one's own fiction, evident in *Belgravia*'s success, had not escaped Mary Braddon's rival in the sensation stakes either. In 1867 Mrs Henry Wood purchased the *Argosy* from Alexander Strahan, the energetic, enterprising publisher of a string of periodicals, who had established it less than two years earlier. *Argosy*'s first editor was also a woman, Isa Craig, a fellow Scot, not without journalistic experience having spent four years on the staff of the *Scotsman*. But though she secured contributions from her friend Christina Rossetti for the new magazine her interests lay in active social work rather than in journalism. She had after all left the *Scotsman* to become assistant secretary of the National Association for the Promotion of Social Science in London. Her reign did not last long, and in fact Strahan found most of the contributors, including Jean Ingelow and Amelia Blandford Edwards. As Isabella Fyvie discovered, he would switch material submitted to one title to another deemed more suitable. The furore caused by Reade's sensational *Griffith Gaunt* in *Argosy*, and the aftermath, led to the disposal of the title only eighteen months after Strahan claimed he would 'stand or fall by its success'.[111] Mrs Wood, who had a shrewd business sense and awareness of her commercial potential,[112] purchased it, raised the price from sixpence to a shilling and – ironically in the circumstances – relaunched it to rival *Belgravia*. It depended for its market upon Ellen Wood's reputation as a sensation novelist. Major serials were attributed as 'by the Author of *East Lynne*' but she wrote a mass of additional material anonymously, leaving enough after her death in 1887 to fill many future issues.

Ellen Wood, like Mary Braddon and Margaret Oliphant, was a prodigious worker, but to modern eyes seems at first sight a much less likely candidate for success as an editor. Partly as a result of a curvature of the spine, she was something of a recluse living 'to a great extent in the retirement of her study',[113] lacking those social networks most editors eagerly sought. She edited from the confines of her home. At one time her semi-invalid status forced her to write from a reclining chair. But she had assets. She was unusual in being able to maintain distinct barriers between the writing and domestic areas of her house. Despite ill-health she had stamina and self-discipline, and organized the routine of her household to suit her preferred working pattern. She usually breakfasted alone, working in her study from eight until one, occasionally all day, stopping briefly for a light lunch. Her son's idyll of domestic harmony – 'Her household was perfectly ruled; the most complete order and system reigned ... It was the rarest thing for any servant to leave her' is somewhat exaggerated. The artist Henrietta Ward, herself dependent on a good domestic staff, was surprised by the 'nice' but 'hopelessly prosaic' Mrs Wood's conversational topic – 'her servants' shortcomings'. Yet Ellen Wood *did* enjoy a well-ordered household, and additionally avoided the problems of editorial staff, never even, according to her son, employing a secretary. Instead she had Charles himself. He was a contributor, partner in *Argosy*'s management, and its effectual publisher until 1871, becoming editor after his mother's death. He even brought back the proofs from the office for her to correct in relative comfort. She was perhaps lucky that her small circle of friends should include supportive, experienced women like Mrs Hall and Mrs Howitt.[114] Outside the family *Argosy* had relatively few contributors – among them Hesba Stretton, Julia Kavanagh, Alice King and Isabella Fyvie Mayo, one of Mrs Hall's protegées. Her illness seems however to have helped her dealings with contributors. Isabella Mayo thought her a just and kind editor whose suffering gave her 'ready comprehension of difficult and trying circumstances'.[115]

Argosy was the type of journal you would find in a provincial private lending library.[116] It offered fiction, travel articles, poetry and occasional historical biographies or uplifting accounts of missionary endeavours. It carried neither reviews nor serious political, scientific or philosophical articles. It met, like *Belgravia*, with the contempt of those taking the high moral or intellectual ground.[117] Edith Simcox, who reviewed regularly for the intellectual *Academy* once scathingly dismissed *Argosy*'s readers as not the sort of people likely to read *The Academy;* although by 1883 *Argosy* was advertising itself boldly across two *Academy* columns, and where *Blackwood*'s and others advertised their contents, *Argosy* relied merely on Mrs Wood's name, 'Sixpence Monthly' and large type. Despite its sensation fiction, however, *Argosy* had none of the raciness of *Belgravia*, and its more serious content, like Alice King's 1880 biography of Alice Procter, was circumscribed by its conventional attitudes to domesticity.[118]

Sarah Doudney's elegy for Mrs Wood herself emphasizes 'Firm friend, sweet mother, true and loving wife' not her professional achievements, and Charles reinforces Doudney's image of a 'hidden life' of homely spirituality, presenting his mother to devoted readers as a real-life 'Angel in the House', 'eminently' domesticated and whose 'whole life was one long, silent sermon'.[119]

Paradoxically Ellen Wood's habits of reticence and silence remarked by contemporaries were shared by another woman from whom as professional writer she could scarcely have been further apart – Alice Meynell. She who was mistress of the precision of language and wittily berated the author of *Dene Hollow* for her slipshod construction[120] co-edited the elegant *Merry England* from the centre of a domestic chaos which Mrs Wood would surely have found unbearable. In less than two years Mrs Meynell had run through nine cooks, five housemaids and three nurses, and 'the pencilling mamma', to use Meredith's phrase, worked with the children playing at scrap-books or editing newspapers under her table.[121] It was perhaps an understatement for her son to describe her as not an 'office-woman'; she was always bored by routine administrative work.[122] But the desperate tone that greeted the Meynell children as their parents worked on the *Weekly Register*

was absent when they were immersed in the 'pleasant and not too bur-
densome task' of editing their own monthly *Merry England*.[123]
(Founded in 1883; they ran it for 12 years.)

As with other married co-editors – Ellises, Howitts, Beetons – it is not
always easy to distinguish the separate editorial contributions but just
as one can reasonably attribute some of the changes in the format and
contents of *The Englishwoman's Domestic Magazine* to Isabella Beeton,
the aesthete's lightness of touch is clearly discernable in *Merry England*.
Alice Meynell certainly had the power to commission articles since she
asked Mary Cowden Clarke for a paper on English cookery in
Shakespeare's time and 'much approved' the result.[124]

Merry England sought to rejuvenate the civilizing social aims of the
'Young England' movement; the first issue's opening article by
Saintsbury linked Disraeli's political ideas to the 'vast Romantic revival,
which influenced literature and religion so vitally'.[125] The emphasis on
delight and charm which the magazine sought to evoke was linked to
that mythic Elizabethan England conjured by the title. The periodical
was physically elegant with relatively short items, well spaced text and
generous margins. Though later it would be known for its discovery of
the poet Francis Thompson, and would attract such writers as Patmore,
Belloc, and Katherine Tynan, initially the Meynells wrote much
material themselves, and Alice's sister Lady Butler provided some illustrations. Other features within the first volume emphasized those
aspects of style, culture and manners which though not specifically
'feminine' might appeal to women readers and to which Meynell so
frequently returned in her essays. A series on 'Bogeys of Provincial Life'
covered topics like 'Scandal' by Eliza Lynn Linton and Meynell's own
essay on inelegance in dress. Mrs Meynell's association of beauty and
decorum with ethics emerges in her own articles and in those of
others; her distinctive blend of aestheticism and morality is pervasive,
Belgravia and *Argosy* targeted the leisure market; they made money by
entertaining. *Tait's* and the *Victoria Magazine*, like *Merry England*, had
higher aims. They were not overtly propagandist and competed in the
general market, but their female proprietors sought high literary standards and their strong social convictions influenced their publications.
Tait's had aimed at the first-rank of periodicals, today critically canon-
ized by inclusion in the *Wellesley Index*. There were many lesser known
specialist publications targeting niche markets which might appear
ideally suited to the talents of women journalists. Here too matters
were not that straightforward.

7
A Niche in the Market

Editing an influential literary periodical was for the very ambitious, but one effect of the expansion of the industry was the publication of papers aimed at specific readerships, the 'consumer groups' of today[1]. These niche magazines servicing cultural and other interests offered women journalists other, if more modest, opportunities. Shared enthusiasms, acquired knowledge and commitment compensated somewhat for women's limited access to formal education, clubland networks and funding. They could target segments, particularly the feminine branches, of the leisure market. So Jane Loudon edited the *Ladies' Magazine of Gardening* in 1842, and Mme de la Blanchardière the lavishly-illustrated *The Needle, A Magazine of Ornamental Work* (1852–5). The end of the century saw a further fragmentation of the consumer market and proliferation of titles. In this climate Mrs Comyns turned her specialist knowledge and 'newspaper instinct' to account with *Feathered World*, designed to appeal to women with the 'pretty hobby' of an aviary. Under her editorship it became the recognized journal for cage-bird fanciers, including professional breeders.[2]

Her family connection with music publishing – she was born a Novello – was, however, the crucial factor in Mary Cowden Clarke's editorship of the *Musical Times* between 1853–6. Brought up in a talented family within a lively literary circle where Mary Lamb taught her Latin and she knew Keats and Leigh Hunt, by 1853 she was already an experienced periodical writer with knowledge of the popular market.[3] Her musical credentials included the translation of theoretical works for Novello. As editor she contributed in Altick's words 'an interminable series of space-filling literary quotations called "Music among the Poets"', a blanket term eventually stretched to encompass bird-song and rushing winds. But she also commissioned other work including several articles by Leigh Hunt, although her magazine's chief claim to fame – as a test case in the campaign against 'taxes on knowledge' – was initiated by the menfolk of her family.[4] The politics of publishing remained largely in male hands.

For most of the period too, journals aimed at trades, professions, and sporting interests were virtually unassailable masculine enclaves. In the 1890s we find Honor Morton, a trained nurse who as a journalist special-ized in her own profession, but then nursing was a 'female' calling. By far and away the most prominent sectors to which women had access were religious magazines and those for women and children. These are not discrete categories. Some women's magazines were deeply spiritual in tone; many juvenile periodicals had a religious thrust.[5] While ladies' fashion and the later domestic magazines targeted the consumer, as increasing reliance upon advertising indicated, at the other end of the spectrum some religious magazines were never intended to run at a profit. But the distinction between commercial venture and labour of love was frequently blurred. Printing, publishing and periodical writing were increasingly seen as money-making activities, albeit risky ones. Just as with national newspapers and the great quarterlies, profit and political motives blended in complex and fluctuating ways, so moral guidance and religious instruction were tainted with commerce. Since the religious press as a whole was notoriously mean in paying authors[6] one might classify it as a genre in which people participated from conviction rather than financial need. On the other hand Jasper Milvain's cynical advice to his sisters to make a speciality of Sunday-school prize-books because they sell 'like hot cakes. And there's so deuced little enterprise in the business'[7] reminds us that many women *did* try to make a living in the 'religious' marketplace, as did several publishers. To that extent it is a somewhat arbitrary division that has led me to cover women's involve-ment in this broadly defined religious press mainly in Chapter 9. There is, however, also an argument for considering together those curious groups specifically isolated by gender and age – 'women' and 'children' – for in consumer terms they were both located firmly within the domes-tic, as opposed to public, sphere.

Editing and writing for children's magazines was not of course women's prerogative; even journals designed specifically for girls might well have a male editor. Early in his career Sir Douglas Straight, barris-ter, judge and eventually editor of the *Pall Mall Gazette*, wrote stories for *Aunt Judy's* at a few shillings apiece and Charles Peters edited the *Girl's Own Paper* for 28 years until Flora Klickman, co-founder of the *Windsor Magazine*, took over.[8] But all these magazines opened up opportunities for women writers and some women did become editors. The Gatty and Sale-Barker mother-daughter teams had associations with their magazines stretching over decades, and Charlotte Yonge's editorship of the *Monthly Packet* for almost forty years was one of the longest on any Victorian periodical.[9]

Compared with women's magazines' swifter move away from the conduct book mode, juvenile periodicals clung to their mission to inculcate moral and religious values or to educate and inform, sometimes both. Yet as the century wore on there is an increasing emphasis on entertainment, even if still allied to instruction. As early as the launch of the frivolous annuals, juvenile versions had been successfully marketed, and the competitive publishing market of the 1860s affected the style of girls' papers. Publishers were not slow to note a burgeoning new market sector amongst middle-class adolescents.[10] Yet innovative high-class children's periodicals like *Good Words for the Young* and *Aunt Judy's Magazine*, highly praised by contemporary reviewers, were not guaranteed commercial success. *Aunt Judy's* profited its long-suffering publishers in only one of its nineteen years' existence.[11] Its appeal was somewhat exclusive and its articles made considerable intellectual demands upon its young readers. RH Hutton urged 'benevolent aunts and uncles' who have injudiciously bought such admirable literature to '*keep* it *themselves,* and try to enjoy it ... *Good Words for the Young* and *Aunt Judy's* are really capital magazines for the old; but for the young they are too luxurious, elaborate and refined.'[12] Still, *Aunt Judy's* gathered a loyal band of readers, and editing it was a labour of love for Margaret Gatty and her daughters.

The introduction to the first volume was addressed as much to parents as to children. Though stories would be the staple commodity 'Parents need not fear an overflowing of mere amusement' with natural history articles, talks about new books and the innovation of the 'emblem or allegorical picture, typifying some moral truth'. Volumes were issued as 'Christmas' or 'May Day' rather than numbered 'to adapt them the better for presents, prizes or birthday gifts'. The reviews sometimes carried postscripts for parents. They might safely include Andersen's stories 'in the libraries of the young'. 'The above hints' will probably make 'parents and guardians' aware that they must not look to *Alice's Adventures* 'for knowledge in disguise'. The 'unusual merit of the illustrations and beauty of format' make a French children's magazine 'an acquisition even to a drawing-room table.'[13]

Mrs Gatty's most distinctive contributions were the Emblems and the natural history articles which spilled over into *Aunt Judy's* from her passion for the seaweeds and zoophytes she collected. Family members provided music and fiction. Almost all Juliana Ewing's writings first appeared in the magazine which offered fiction of the quality of Andersen's fairy-stories and Carroll's *Bruno's Revenge*.

Early in her career Juliana had tried her hand at mystery fiction and been published in *London Society* but she soon discarded that kind of literature as giving her no satisfaction. This rejection of anything sensational in the age of 'sensation' may have been a factor in *Aunt Judy's* lack of commercial success. By 1868 the editor was appealing to adult readers for personal recommendations to increase sales. The 'Letterbox' of the American *St Nicholas* conducted by Mrs Mary Mapes Dodge showed that it followed in the wake of young travellers; *Aunt Judy's* too had evidence of a far-flung readership. This welcome 'from across both oceans' was unfortunately insufficient in itself, though the editor

> grudges no labour, and the publishers grudge no expense, either in adequate payment of contributors, or the tasteful issue of the publication ... [T]he absence of 'sensational' tales – the endeavour to instruct in virtue, without drawing loathsome pictures of vice ... restricts her circulation to the judicious and the domestic.

The bare existence *Aunt Judy's* enjoyed seemed inadequate reward for this investment.[14]

Despite its small circulation one of the magazine's undoubted successes was the involvement of readers through the correspondence columns and in fund-raising for cots at the Hospital for Sick Children. Lists of children contributing pocket-money or giving toys and flowers, alongside progress reports on the young beneficiaries, became regular features. The letter column gradually came to take on an exchange-and-mart function with writers offering story-books for a 'Persian or Russian' kitten, seeking new 'staff' – must be more than twelve – for a manuscript magazine, or over-eighteens 'well advanced in painting' for a drawing club, begging postage stamps for the craze of making 'stamp snakes' for bazaars, or discussing how best to kill moths for a collection. These letters were so important that after Mrs Gatty's death, when the stream of correspondence dried up, readers were reassured that 'Aunt Judy' lived on and urged to continue writing to her.

Over the years some of the readers' 'hints for improvement' which Mrs Gatty had invited bore fruit. By 1874 when Juliana and Horatia became joint editors the Puzzles, which proved popular in rival periodicals, were established as a permanent feature, and there were other adjustments. But even with a new publisher in 1881 *Aunt Judy's* never fully took on board the livelier style and format which affected periodicals generally in the final decades of the century. Rigid editorial attitudes must have been partly responsible. Mrs Gatty's promise to her patrons ('We never mean to purchase popularity by sinking our claim to permanence') found its echo in Juliana's complaints to Bell when he finally gave up the unequal struggle. The 'certain tone of high mindedness and refinement' which she found somewhat lacking in contemporary youth was intrinsic to the character of *Aunt Judy's* which was now looking dated.[15]

Charlotte Yonge eventually faced the same shift in public taste. By the 1880s, as Christabel Coleridge who took over the *Packet* recognized, the conditions of the book trade were rapidly altering. '[C]heap magazines sprang up in every direction; the old *negative* principle of excluding from a magazine, intended for young women, everything that could be thought less than perfectly suitable for them became more and more difficult to carry out, and perhaps some things were excluded which it would have been well to admit.'[16] LT Meade's *Atalanta,* launched in autumn 1887, which she edited solely or in collaboration until the autumn of 1894, aimed at broadly the same agegroup and was a child of the new era. It was managed professionally and operated at an intellectually high level, drawing on writers like Millicent Fawcett and Mrs Oliphant, carrying serials by fashionable novelists like Stevenson and promoting careers for girls, even offering a Scholarship. Salmon thought it rivalled the best American journals and was 'almost aristocratic'. But to produce it LT Meade spent each afternoon until 7 pm at the paper's office, fitting her novels and family round it, a working pattern far removed from that of Charlotte Yonge. (See Chapter 9.)[17]

St Nicholas, that pretty little thing which Mrs Oliphant once thought might be her model for a new children's magazine, was perhaps the archetypal 'American' children's paper, with its wide range of writers and illustrators and its various 'Departments' including 'For Very Little People' (in large type) and 'The Riddle-box' a mélange of acrostics, enigmas, rebus, letter and word puzzles, some quite fiendishly intricate.[18] Frances Hodges Burnett's *Sara Crewe* rubbed shoulders with Elizabeth Pennell on Christmas Pantomime illustrated by Joseph Pennell's photographs. Yet 'the guiding genius of *St Nicholas'* could still appreciate the elderly Mary Cowden Clarke's children's play based on the fairy characters of *A Midsummer Night's Dream*. In contrast, though Horatia had sole editorship from 1876, she was so reliant upon

Juliana's writing that she closed *Aunt Judy's* on her sister's death.[19] *St Nicholas*, like *Aunt Judy's*, *could* claim his share of readers whose parents before them had taken 'you' but he had more readily adapted himself to changing tastes.

Mrs Lucy Sale-Barker's *Little Wide-Awake* launched in 1875 following on the heels of Cassell's *Little Folks* (1871) was geared to a younger age-group and its publishers, Routledge, made illustrations a major selling feature, with ME Edwards and Kate Greenaway amongst the many artists.[20] The competitions suggest a readership of between six and fourteen, though some tales were intended for younger children. Over the years there were changes in format but the 1882 new series is fairly typical – a fourpenny monthly magazine containing eight colour pages. Its early sub-title 'A Monthly Magazine for Good Children' suggests a high-minded tone and there is certainly a moral element in stories where obedient children are rewarded and foolhardy ones warned about venturing too far out to sea, and in educational features encouraging healthy, useful pastimes. Mrs Sale-Barker, though, like Mrs Gatty envisaged a two-way relationship with her readers. The magazine's title was her son's pet name, and when planning the magazine she asked him and other children what kind of stories should go in. Ones about children, dogs and other animals, not giants and fairies, she was told.[21] The 'real life' stories about children reflected an upper middle-class world where uncles were generals or rectors living in large country houses, and mamma's old nurse, now married, might invite one to stay in a delightful farm near the New Forest.[22] Judging by the winners of the essay, drawing and handiwork competitions the readership mirrored this image. Addresses told of vicarages, rectories, large houses, even the occasional castle. Reader participation seems, however, not to have been high. Even prizes of a guinea and half a guinea[23] tempted only small numbers to make pincushions and house-wifes, illuminate proverbs, and write essays on Procrastination or Endurance. The same families featured repeatedly in the prizewinners' lists.

Despite her long editorship Mrs Sale-Barker never seems to have engendered the rapport with her readers which *Aunt Judy*'s enjoyed. When eventually in 1885 the competitions were dropped because of falling numbers of entrants she made a determined effort to emulate the success of the cots at a hospital for children opened near her home in Sydenham. Young readers were urged to fill in cards as they saved pocket-money to support the 'Wide-Awake Cot' and promised that their names would be printed in future issues.

Think of the little children living, or scarcely living, in miserable crowded homes, many of them brought to this hospital in a starving state, many deformed and helpless; think of these same children happy, clean, well-cared for, and well-fed, & with the best surgical and medical aid to restore them to health and strength.[24]

Funding the cot needed £25 per annum which, given the generosity of the money prizes, would not seem an unreasonable expectation, but the editor faced an uphill task. Much of the following issue's 'Editor's Corner' was devoted to stories of the hospital and a convoluted explanation as to why no contributors' names appeared: as they went to press no cards had yet been returned – she did not expect, indeed, they would be full for a month or so – cards only issued ten days earlier – earnestly trusts readers will energetically work at filling them. Her confident assertion 'Indeed I am very sure you will' proved over-optimistic. Though the March issue published ten names raising a total of £1.19s.3$^{1}/_{2}$d Miss Lilian and Master Maurice Sale-Barker were responsible for five shillings of that and a Miss Barker credited with a further ten shillings. The editor's family recurred in the roll of honour over the months, though it is pleasant to note that the Fullers who had carried off a plethora of prizes – Beata Jane's drawing and handicraft alone collected at least four – donated some of their winnings to charity. The *Wide-Awake* Cot never captured the imagination in the way *Aunt Judy's* did. Perhaps a small hospital in Sydenham seemed too local. Perhaps the idea was now old-hat. In the previous year when Horatia closed her magazine she could boast that their innovatory 'special' cot, re-dedicated in memory of her mother and sister, had spawned another 51 in Great Ormond Street alone. Mrs Sale-Barker's own verse and tales were not of Gatty calibre but her magazine survived her, lasting until almost the end of the century.

Jasper Milvain's advice to his sisters to earn £100 a year between them writing for children 'good, coarse, marketable stuff for the world's vulgar' rather than go 'governessing' may have been cynical; it was also practical. Despite Gissing's obvious antipathy to hack-work, the sensitive Dora is allowed a genuine concern for readers, and discovers such enjoyment in writing that she continues her stories for *The English Girl* even after marriage.[25] For women like Dora, Grub Street could enhance their intellectual life and give a measure of independence.

By this time children's columns flourished everywhere. Earlier adult periodicals sporadically flirted with the idea. When *Sharpe's* was launched in the mid-1840s it experimented briefly with 'Reading for the Young' – poems and moral tales. In the 1850s Elizabeth O'Hara and Hannah Clay wrote a 'Children's Corner' in the *Ladies' Cabinet*. Mrs Hall's *St James's* 'For the Young of the Household: In Cozy Nook' featured stories and educational articles. Despite a moralistic tendency her standard of fiction was high. Her contributors included Mary Howitt, Frederika Bremer and Mrs Lankester whose 'Eyes and No Eyes' provides an interesting example of science writing for children. Delicately illustrated and using story format, it conveys the thrill of viewing an insect, and drops of water and blood through a microscope.

By the 1880s and 1890s most ladies' papers had their children's column. Lucie H Armstrong ran a Children's Page in the *Englishwoman*, Mrs Jack Johnson as 'Levana' the 'Children's Salon' in *Gentlewoman*. Competitions and charitable works lived on, though not everyone gave them unqualified approval. Evelyn March-Phillipps was happy enough about the 'Children's Salon's endowment of two cots at the Victoria hospital, less so about columns which encouraged precocious self-publicity by printing a child's portrait alongside its 'feeble literary efforts' or pandered to young egos by publishing 'absurdly trivial letters'.[26]

One might think that if women sought editorial roles in the expanding periodical press, magazines for women would provide the appropriate seat of female power, but as several factors limiting female editorships of literary journals equally obtained here, the man at the helm remained the dominating figure. Looking back from the early years of the twentieth century when women's magazines formed a significant consumer sector, Mary Hargrave saw their eighteenth-century prototypes as virtual conduct manuals:

> [O]ne is struck by the extreme anxiety of the editors to form and regulate the morals of the weaker sex. Their note is always didactic. They are ever inculcating the Virtue and Modesty proper to 'the' sex; ever lecturing, reprimanding, exhorting.[27]

Recent scholarship has argued that Victorian women's magazines created their own control mechanisms. Echoes of the conduct books which so irritated Mary Hargrave lingered on. Women were admonished and advised according to male criteria for feminine behaviour. Even the editorial personæ of periodicals owned by Sam Beeton, a relatively advanced thinker, can today justifiably be characterized as 'teasing, authoritative and implicitly masculine' despite the editorial functions carried out by Isabella Beeton and Matilda Browne.[28]

Periodicals aimed at women, unless backed by a religious organization, were produced for commercial reasons so that as late as the 1890s
they were at least as likely to be edited by men as by women. New ventures were frequently edited by their proprietors, and men had much
easier access to both finance and business training. In 1857 Elizabeth
Bennett Skillicorn attempted to publish a women's newspaper, which
lasted five months; the *Englishwoman's Review and Home Newspaper*
which superseded it and ran for two years, though edited by a woman,
Sarah Sutton, was published jointly with Isaac Argent. Similarly when
Emily Faithfull set up her *Victoria Magazine*, written, edited and printed
by women, she chose to go into partnership with a man. The financial
problems she had seen in the early struggles with the *EWJ* convinced
her that business experience would be vital to the success of her
journal. (See Chapter 9.)

Even at the end of the century family patronage and proprietorial
control loomed large in helping women achieve editorial positions.
Mary Billington writing fulsomely in *Pearson's Magazine* of the 'very
vivacious' Maud Bennett, a 'born' editor, in charge of Arthur Pearson's
Home Notes and various related cookery and dressmaking magazines,
admits that Miss Bennett had no journalistic training whatsoever,
when her brother-in-law appointed her editor in the 1890s. In compensation she thoroughly 'understood domestic economy',[29] and like
Isabella Beeton tried out her recipes, a task by then usually relegated to
one of the ill-paid army of testers and reporters.

EM Palmegiano's bibliography covering the middle decades lists
more than two dozen women's journals whose editors were women yet
in the 1880s and 1890s women still complained that men controlled,
although they didn't write, ladies' fashion magazines. Women were
considered deficient in business sense and knowledge of finance and
could not master 'the intricacies of the laws of libel' but the *appearance*
of female control was important. The sexes of editorial personae and
actual editors were often confused. In the 1890s the male editors of
Woman, a paper sympathetic to many women's causes, hid behind
female names. Fanny Green's comments on contemporary editors of
women's magazines must have seemed even more dispiriting to ambitious girls than her remarks on women editors generally. In 1891 she
knew of only Frances Low of the *Queen* and 'Miss Temple'[30] of the
Woman's Herald as women editors of 'women's papers', and mentions
five other women's titles with 'a man at their helm' though they had
staff women who did 'useful work in paragraphing and contributing
special letters and articles'.[31]

From the vantage-point of the 1890s women journalists might look back and see changes in their position, but the image was a mixed one. Catherine Drew's perspective, in her address to the Institute of Journalists 1894 Conference, stretched no further than the 1840s, but she observed huge differences. 'Ladies' papers and the interests they served have become a great social and economic power'. She valued the explosion in this sector more favourably than did Evelyn March-Phillips remarking that as recently as 1882 of the 42 periodicals for ladies only six were 'high-class' covering general topics of value to women, the rest being devoted mainly to 'modes and domestic management'. The woman editor now enjoyed major advantages over her predecessors. She could rely on female specialists who adopted professional attitudes to their work. The editress, with crochet needle in the inkstand and knitting needles in her table-drawer, checking the fine detail of every proof herself and spending her evenings testing the quantities of 'cookery receipts', was a thing of the past. Technological advances meant she no longer relied upon imported electro-plates for illustrations. Unfortunately neither woman editor nor her army of female assistants was sharing in the huge profits that marked the consumer magazine of that age. Effectively she was supporting but not benefiting from the 'large fortunes' amassed by 'English manufacturers and proprietors of journals'.[32] The professional woman journalist making a good living by her labours was almost as rare then as fifty years' earlier.

As Drew observed, advances in printing, particularly of illustrations, were crucial in expanding the fashion paper market; but exploiting them required both capital investment and business acumen. The Beetons' *Englishwoman's Domestic Magazine* provides the most striking example. Though when relaunched in 1860 in a larger format it had at 8" × 5" a page size not much greater than, for instance, Margaret and Beatrice de Courcy's *Ladies Cabinet* of two decades earlier, its fashion illustrations showed a marked advance.

Early nineteenth-century women's magazines had echoed their eighteenth-century origins. They addressed themselves to 'Ladies' with an aristocratic overtone, drew heavily on readers' unpaid contributions and relied on a formulaic *mélange* of literature, short articles and fashion columns. There was even continuity of titles. The *Lady's Magazine* and the *Lady's Museum*, both founded in the previous century, survived separately until 1832 when they amalgamated. That same year an early nineteenth-century foundation was relaunched, initially very successfully under Caroline Norton's editorship, as the *Court*

Magazine and Belle Assemblée. For two years Norton, a high profile and comparatively well-paid writer, edited and wrote much of its contents. After her departure it declined, in due course merging with the *Magazine.*

The continuing amalgamations of titles and redefinitions of the ladies' magazines in the first half of the century to meet the developing domestic interests and consumerism of the broad middle-class has been remarked by critics.[33] It was into this fluid market that Margaret de Courcy and Mrs Margaret (Cornwell) Baron-Wilson launched their journals. Running a profitable magazine was no sinecure. An ability to respond to shifts in the market was essential for success. In this the de Courcys' joint editorship was less effective than Mrs Baron-Wilson's energetic direction of the *New Monthly Belle Assemblée*, and its fashion coverage would shortly be outshone by the *EDM*.

The *Cabinet* had barely six-and-a-half by four inches in which to display the intricacies of three or four outfits, plus a descriptive paragraph on each. Since these elaborate garments were designed for specific functions – opera dress, ball dress, morning visiting dress, public promenade dress, carriage dress, walking dress etc. – the information was inadequate as a template for all but the most talented. Technical French terms were employed. Knowledgeable, sophisticated professional dressmakers, able to figure how the 'novel shape ... refer to our print ...' of a green velvet *capote* trimmed with a 'double wreath of flowers formed of the beards of feathers' should be cut, draped, sewn and decorated to achieve the desired effect of a collared mantle, were adequately served. They were told the distinctive features of every gown – cut of sleeve and neckline, fabrics, trimmings.

But the monthly reports of London and Paris fashions, though addressed to 'our fair readers', could be equally complicated. General guidelines ('we predicted the vogue of straw bonnets in ... the Spring, and the event has proved we were right'; a new plaid silk named after a princess is 'showy rather than elegant') would drift into technicalities. The demi-long sleeve forms a 'small *bouffant,* descending from a little above the elbow down two-thirds of the forearm ... [displaying] a white under-sleeve *bouillonnée*, on an embroidered or lace *entre deux'*.[34] One thinks of Hollingford's Miss Rose in *Wives and Daughters* and wonders whether a decade or so of the fashion papers had improved the expertise of a country dressmaker to this extent.

In 1844 the *Cabinet* was relaunched with lavish proprietorial claims both for fashion as possessing 'a pure and operative moral influence' on manners and social behaviour, and for this magazine which, with 'eminent authors', translations of European writers and 'first-rate artists', aimed to raise 'the female mind to its true position'. Competitors had emulated this periodical; subscribers swamped the editorial table in 'congratulatory notices'. With four plates readers certainly got more fashion for their money. But despite brave claims that for the price it had 'no parallel in the history of periodical publication'[35] by 1851, just before the launch of Beeton's magazine, the *Cabinet* still devoted three-quarters of its space to rather old-fashioned formulaic fiction, and at 1s. monthly was expensive. On its second relaunch in 1852 readers learned of a change of editorship.[36]

Mrs (Margaret) Cornwell Baron-Wilson, wife of a wealthy London solicitor, had more sense of the shifting market. Her *New Monthly Belle Assemblée* had begun life with a different name as a penny-halfpenny imitation of the ladies' fashion journal, but under her editorship rapidly metamorphosed into a shilling monthly. She intended the revamped journal for 'the Library-Table of the literary or the Boudoir of the Woman of Taste and Fashion' and was soon able to print glowing press reviews. By the 1840s the magazine was abandoning sentimental stories to embrace the realistic school of domestic fiction. Questions of women's education and managing servants were aired; cultural events announced; practical tips on household management, and readers' correspondence published. Like *The Ladies' Companion*, established in 1849 on very similar lines, it was responsive to the developing middle-class consumer market which the Beetons were to exploit so successfully.[37]

The sense of professionalism which the 'editress' promulgated through her reign no doubt also contributed to the journal's success. It is evident from her early complaint that every school-leaver appeared qualified to write for those very annuals which denied 'admission' to so many known authors, to her heartfelt remarks (supporting the proposed Guild of Literature and Art) on the value of journalism. Her often caustic replies to correspondents submitting unsuitable material reflect her powerful sense of both her readership and the practicalities of magazine publication. Laudatory verses on those 'so near and dear to us partake too strongly of vanity' to be appropriate; an Irish reader's lines on widows are 'too dismal' and also inaccurate; *lengthy* poems will be rejected 'however ably written'. The man who thought women now wanted 'stronger intellectual food' is advised that 'however highly seasoned, the dish he proposed to send would not be digested by our readers'. CJT should not attempt even a 'chaste salute to the Muses' again. Fair readers were invited to judge from sample stanzas of his 'Woman's Love and Woman's Hate' whether WOMAN or the MUSES were 'most' [sic] libelled.[38] Promising contributors were, however, encouraged with practical advice on such matters as length. Though she had reason for pride in her period of editorship, her awareness of the power of market forces was tinged with disillusionment as she describes 'the dull routine of mental toil which is necessary for the body's daily existence; but which day by day consumes the powers which might have been far more nobly employed'. She herself may not have been driven by necessity but she had once entertained literary ambitions; in the 1830s Sala knew her as 'a graceful poetess' as well as 'the editor of some fashion periodical'.[39]

The *Ladies' Treasury*, edited by Mrs Warren, and the Beetons' *Englishwoman's Domestic Magazine* occupied key market positions in the middle decades. Mrs Warren never courted the kind of 'tight-lacing' debate controversy which Sam Beeton was prepared to risk. She established the prevailing tone of middle-class respectability from the outset. Her first issue's engraving of the Queen inspecting her troops on Chobham Common is a paradoxical iconic fusion of national power with the nation's idealization of motherhood. The editorial preface to Volume 1 proclaimed the editor's objective 'to illustrate and uphold "Each dear domestic virtue/Child of home"', a not unusual mission-statement for a magazine of that day, but the *Treasury* was not without its modest innovations. 'Our progressive Lessons in French and German' were apparently 'much approved' by readers. In addition to the now usual instructions for Fancy Work there were similar directions for painting. There is a note of relief in the admission that 'The success of a magazine is, in these days, so singular a proof of intrinsic merit and popular appreciation, that we confess to being a little elated ....'.[40] Small wonder. With the *EDM*, the *NMBA* and the *Ladies' Companion* the market was a competitive one.

The *Companion*'s first editor was Jane Loudon, then a well-known name. At 3d it offered good value. Full page detailed line drawings of fashions appeared regularly if not in every issue. There was fiction and poetry, 'Amusements' for children, a gossip column, and the now obligatory 'Work Basket', though Eliza Acton's recipes were perhaps more useful than instructions for working 'La Frivolité', a fancy form of Parisian tatting. Under Loudon's guidance the *LC* also carried articles on social and cultural topics. Edward Solly introduced his science series 'The Chemistry of Everyday Life' with flattering compliments to the founding editor. This particular commission proved popular enough to be continued under the new editor, Henry Fothergill Chorley, a year later.

The *EDM*'s technical innovations, and low cost – cheap even at the increased price of 6d – brought fashion into readers' homes in a revolutionary way. In the new series every issue carried a coloured fashion plate produced to a high standard, a coloured embroidery pattern, folded to allow for a large scale design, as well as occasional black and white illustrations for fiction or the 'Domestic history of England' articles. The intricate embroidery designs for Berlin woolwork, silks or beading were exquisitely hand-painted – even today to open up a volume and find pages of close print suddenly illumined by brilliant carmine and gold is to feast one's eye. These patterns were aimed at the lady with leisure for fancy-work. Embroidering a 'toilet cushion' (Vol VI NS) in beads – steel, gold, alabaster, grey and crystal were specified – implied both outlay and time to fill. Although Isabella had not much cared for the early patterns she proved right in suspecting they would be popular.[41]

Organizing these changes had been quite an enterprise. The engravings the Beetons wanted were produced in Paris by Jules David. Their trip to Paris to negotiate the contract with Adolphe Goubaud,[42] which resulted in the supply of fashion-plates with accompanying newsletter by Mme Goubaud, coloured embroidery patterns, and an arrangement to furnish readers with full-sized paper patterns for the gowns, involved the Beetons in detailed discussions with agents, editors and pattern-makers. Isabella kept careful accounts of their expenses and costed the patterns.

With a circulation approaching 60 000, and changed regulations which reduced the cost of importing plates, these innovations were financially viable, though the dress patterns, then a novelty in England, were offered as a separately costed service to readers, or occasionally included in a supplement at the increased price of a shilling.[43] While Sarah Freeman is probably right in assessing Isabella's contribution as important in defining the direction of the relaunch, the venture would have been almost impossible for a woman on her own. Isabella was still something of an anomaly in a male office when she took over responsibility for all the fashion, commuting by train to their Strand offices.[44] Her editorial work was now substantial, including the women's pages of Beeton's pioneering weekly newspaper the *Queen* where she managed the work of outside contributors, until Sam, driven perhaps by the financial and organizational pressures of weekly publication, sold it to the owners of the rival *The Ladies' Newspaper*. It is evident also that she helped plan the *Young Englishwoman* – the girls' magazine intended to complement *Boys' Own Magazine* – though she lived to see little more than its launch.[45]

Yet she remains an elusive figure. As Margaret Beetham argues, the changes in the *EDM* were in part responses to changes in the positioning of middle-class women readers in the market-place, and Sam's editorial hand is evident in features like the *Conversazione*.[46] But, given her involvement in the design and management of *EDM*, definitions of Isabella as 'editor'[47] are accurate. She was one of those female editors who drifted into the job through male connections – specifically her energetic, enterprising husband who admired her intelligence and capability and came to rely upon her assistance as much in terms of business efficacy as providing the 'woman's point of view'. Isabella exemplifies the 'reticent woman editor' characterized by Christian Johnstone. There were not even notices of her death in any of the three periodicals she helped to create. Her developing confidence as a journalist[48] was never fully tested; Isabella died of puerperal fever aged 28, and before the fashion for the 'editress' persona of women's magazines had fully established itself. It was left to her successor and friend Matilda Browne to achieve this. By that time Sam had been forced to sell the Beeton name.

As 'Silkworm' Mrs Browne established a stronger persona than Isabella had ever wanted, and arguably pioneered the 'advertorial'.[49] Her chatty 'Spinnings' column written in the first person covered almost every female consumer interest, creating the impression of collusion with her readers and privileged intimacy with the milliners and perfumiers she visited. Prices of goods are given, or a visit to a boot-maker is made only because 'so many ladies' have requested such information. At a dress shop she is 'kindly invited ... to assist at the opening of a large case of Parisian bonnets. Two invitations are not required in such a case ...'.[50] That this engagement with her readers was not altogether illusory seems evident when, during a painful period of illness and bereavement, she shared her experiences with them and benefited from their support. 'Long vigils, constant anxiety, regrets, and mourning, are not very good helps to work such as mine. I feel how deficient in interest must be these Spinnings, spun from a heavy heart, and written a few lines at a time during the watchings by a sick bed'.

Recommending 'Albert Crape' as an economical substitute for the usual mourning crepe she remarked with feeling, 'Death seldom visits a house without inflicting pecuniary as well as personal loss. Economy has to be studied at a moment when much outlay is enforced by the rigorous laws of society.' Her closing words to her faithful readers thanked them for their sympathy. 'My lines have indeed "been cast in pleasant places".'[51] Her career was by no means over. She went on to establish herself as editress of the long-running *Myra's Journal* which claimed to be the first to use 'home-grown' fashion illustrations, thereby discarding the stiff Germanic style.[52]

Women's fashion as an appropriate area of female consumerism was always a contested site. On the one hand fashion copy sold periodicals; on the other encouraging its consumption raised moral and social questions. These lay not just in the high-profile debates on fads like tight-lacing, crinolines and bloomers, but were embedded within the expressions of editorial policy and the fashion columns themselves. The ethical issue as to whether women should devote time and money to following fashion continually surfaces.

The *Cabinet*'s unequivocal claim for the improving moral influence of fashion did not always echo so confidently, but the potential for moral influence was continually acknowledged. Mrs Warren urged the ethical validity of fashion – 'Our Fashions will be of the newest and most elegant, for the days are past when Wisdom was a dowdy' – but this had to be tempered. Some months later she published 'How Far should the Fashions be Followed?' arguing for decorum, taste and commonsense. 'Whatever is false or artificial is as reprehensible in dress as in morals.' The great principle must be 'to develop beauties' not 'to conceal defects', not altogether consoling to those Victorian women who filled the agony columns with their worries.[53] The balance was always tricky. One would expect Alice Meynell to argue for an intrinsic relationship between the moral and the aesthetic. 'When dress is ordered into beautiful and disciplined simplicity, so will be conduct and pleasure',[54] but the flamboyance of the 1890s caused even Mrs Aria to protest in the *Daily Chronicle* about the 'too, too common wearing of jewels. We are slowly but surely overstepping all the bounds of good taste.'[55] In encouraging ladies to economize by embellishing, even making, their own clothes, as Beeton's magazines did, journalists faced another moral issue – their effect upon the legions of poor seamstresses and embroideresses. 'Silkworm' recognized this dilemma when she published a correspondent's plea for the northern Irish *broderie anglaise* and satin-stitch workers, the demand for whose skills had been ruined by 'tatting fever', forcing wages down from two shillings to threepence or fourpence a day. Admitting her own share in depressing the trade, she urged readers on grounds of excellent value as well as virtuous feeling to follow her example by ordering trimming instead of the 'eternal looking-bad-when-washed tatting'.[56] Yet she also supported a society for selling 'Ladies' Work' and ended her 'Spinnings' by publicizing her own new book of crochet patterns *The Polonaise Lace Book*. The relationships between patronage, economy, fashion and morality were complex.

At least the 'clotheswoman' had the field to herself in both Britain and America.[57] Men did not intrude, unless the fictional editor of *The Fan* has some basis in truth.[58] Arnold Bennett certainly thought men capable of such work and reserved his most virulent criticism for women's fashion-writing, 'worse written than even police reports in country newspapers'. In a signed article in one of the 'great London Dailies' he found slipshod writing, bad punctuation, lax use of metaphors and worse horrors, and this from a famed fashion journalist paid 'the wage of a Cabinet Minister'. He protested that in every field of feminine interest women failed to reach even moderate competence because they were inadequately trained and, in such specialized fields, lacked better (masculine) models of writing.[59]

The New Journalism manifested itself in women's magazines by a livelier visual appearance, chatty interviews and snippets of information and sensation. The sector now targeted a more nuanced range of interests from interior design or high fashion to health, education and social issues. Many papers acknowledged that a substantial core of their female readers desired a career or needed to earn a living. *Hearth & Home*, despite adding Sport to Fashion etc., might still describe itself as 'An Illustrated Weekly Journal for Gentlewomen' and advertise Mrs Talbot Coke 'On Engaging Servants'; but the specialist spin-offs from Maud Bennett's *Home Notes* are founded on the premise that the reader, rather than her cook or dressmaker, will be following the instructions. Female readership had at once a broader class base and provided a more fragmented market. A proliferation of titles sought to address it, and advertising assumed increasing importance. Victorian critics deplored the pervasive effects of excessive consumerism, but the phenomenon could not be ignored even if the editor set herself high journalistic standards. Mrs Tomson retained her advertisers during her spell as editor of *Sylvia's Journal*.[60]

Ella Hepworth Dixon acknowledged the key place of fashion and shopping in a woman's magazine. Soon after her success with *The Story of a Modern Woman* where she characterized the work of the harassed editor as 'six months of proof-reading, of interviewing incapable artists, of the thousand worries of a newspaper' she was herself in the editor's chair.[61] *The Englishwoman* was elegantly produced and stylishly illustrated with engravings, drawings and photographs. Work was commissioned from the most fashionable female writers like John Strange Winter, Violet Hunt and Marie Belloc. Columnists of the calibre of Mrs Aria and Mrs Humphry provided the consumer articles 'In Fashionland', 'A Day's Shopping' and 'To Those About to Furnish', 'Society's Doings' were edited by 'Belle' of *The World*. Hepworth Dixon's reign was short-lived, and 'Fashionland' and 'Shopping' lasted only to the end of that first year, barely three months after the change of editorship.

As the relative cheapness of the half-tone process of illustration and increasing advertising resulted in an explosion of women's weeklies[62] and features, some women journalists had mixed feelings about the changes. Mrs Everard Cotes, who had worked as a reporter for the *Washington Post*, fictionalized the conflicting attractions and limitations of being a lady journalist in 1890s London. The young American aspirant is lured into the trap of 'women's interests'. She gets her £2-a-week staff job because the editor-in-chief is reluctantly persuaded that there are essential topics which only a woman could treat. Elvira has proved able to write 'the graphic naked truth' à la Elizabeth Banks but as '... the paper doesn't want a female Zola,' she is tied to 'colonial exhibitions and popular spectacles and country outings for babies of the slums'.[63]

Evelyn March-Phillipps credited much of the 'brightness and life' of her contemporary press to the writing by the 'woman journalist on subjects she understands'. She praised the excellence of advice on interior decoration and cookery, the high quality of articles on dressmaking and housewifery, and the value of responses to practical (as opposed to personal) problems – questions on travel abroad or new employment opportunities. But she expressed a widespread unease when she castigated the journals for some of the adverse effects of consumerism – the dangers of 'untrustworthy puffing' of the products of advertisers on whom 'the paper relies for most of its profit and the even more insidious practice of a journalist's puffing goods for a consideration'. One fashion writer was said to receive the equivalent of £300 in one year in *douceurs*.[64]

Criticism of women's journalism thus focused on the fashion and 'toilet' departments as much as upon the frivolity of the social columns. Judging by the number of warnings to young women, they attracted all manner of would-be journalists. There were reiterated concerns about the meretricious nature of the work, the amateurish atti-tudes and the mechanisms whereby wealthy or well-connected women could infiltrate it at the expense of serious young journalists. As Hepworth Dixon suggests it is only her heroine's *social* connections enabling her to provide titbits that the professional 'lady journalist' who doesn't know *the set* cannot ferret out, that secures the commis-sion of a 'smart' gossip column at a guinea apiece.[65]

Working on the fashion papers may not have been 'quite the same' as being 'really a journalist'.[66] They had their limits for ambitious women. Writers complained of the scarcity of women editors when the bulk of the work on women's papers was supplied by female staff. Still the popularity of fashion and ensuing celebrity of its chroniclers led to a group of such women becoming household names – Mrs Humphry, Mrs Talbot Coke, Mrs Aria. Journalists of the stature of Alice Meynell, Elizabeth Pennell and Emily Crawford were not ashamed to turn their eye and pen to dress. Mrs Humphry who wrote for many years on fashion was sufficiently respected by her colleagues to be elected a president of the Society of Women Journalists. The more frivolous 'feminine' topics had always been tackled in mainstream journals. Anne Mozley, even George Eliot, liked such subjects. But these were scattered articles. It was only as the influence of the 'New Journalism' was felt that regular ladies' columns became widespread in newspapers.[67]

Whilst a journalist like Mrs Humphry wrote within several of the women's sub-genres – society column and etiquette as well as dress – Mrs Aria's name was almost synonymous with fashion. Her articles and answers to correspondents on this topic appeared in *Queen, Lady's Pictorial, Gentlewoman* and *Hearth and Home* and her writings betrayed a strong sense of personality. Robertson Scott recalled her as a witty and generous hostess with a penchant for gossip and Mary Billington cred-ited her with introducing 'personal enthusiasm' into her fashion columns as well as observing the interaction of the stage and the fashion industry.[68] Her style may have lacked the clarity of Mrs Crawford, but her opinions were at least as forthright. 'I personally have a horror of the full skirt [and as] … criticism to be of any value must be entirely personal, my sentiments are of vital importance' she declared. Whether her subject was the overuse of buttons or the wearing of a waistband she pronounced her views with fervour. 'There are buttons, buttons everywhere, and we never stay to think why they are there, or what purpose they serve: total inappositeness [sic] appears to be the principle or want of principle of their distribution.' On yacht-ing dress for Cowes she pontificates 'The white kid band on a slim waist, let me pause to tell you, is extremely elegant. The stout woman should avoid it; but then, in fashion, she should avoid most things, the while I tender her my sincerest condolence, which may or may not prove a comfort.'[69]

But women's magazines, like mainstream publications, claimed to address more serious questions than fashion, etiquette and social gossip. Both the 'Woman's' magazine and page which, viewed as gendered ghettos, have proved controversial in recent times, were often welcomed. Even the critical Miss March-Phillips praised Margaret Bateson, an efficient interviewer for *The Queen*, for 'carrying the burning question of women's position in the labour market, into the minds of many who perhaps would not seek out the information for themselves'.[70] Lockhart's sense that the *Quarterly* needed a woman's 'knowledge of women and their concerns' was, over the century, reflected by the monthlies in that women occupied some space with issues important to them. Articles on education, domestic servants, employment, married women's property rights, suffrage and housing all appeared in mainstream periodicals. Dorothy Beale and Sarah Missing Sewell on girls' education, Maria Grey, Emily Pfeiffer, Clementina Black and Mona Caird on suffrage, trades unionism etc. found a platform in the *Contemporary* and *Fortnightly*, *Macmillan's* and *Fraser's*. Prolific journalists like Linton and Martineau also covered topics like dress, domestic service and education; one begins to wonder if any woman writer of the time failed to comment on at least one of these hardy perennials for the benefit of her sex.

The ladies' papers provided an obvious, if circumscribed, arena for women's views. Essays in early fashion journals meant to inspire and educate women still had a whiff of the 'conduct manual'. Mary Cowden Clarke's series on literary heroines in *The Ladies' Companion* (1851–3) offers female rôle models, and her portraits of Shakespeare's women (1849–50, 1854) for the same periodical encouraged Woman to study herself in 'the mental looking-glass' he offered her in order to improve her capabilities, cultivate her faculties, refine her sentiments, strengthen her judgement.[71] A few years later Maria Rye, so formidable when Miss Fyvie made her 'fruitless application' to the women's law copying office, had begun her career on the *EDM*.[72] Here, however, we are on different ground for writers like Miss Rye, active in the Langham Place Group, discovered journalism as a means to an end rather than an end in itself.

8
Handmaids and Decorators

Some female contributors and editors had press personae; others remained anonymous, but behind them all were the unnamed sub-editors, assistant editors and readers and those whose work was literally mechanical. Periodical literature was a collaborative affair. Some editors were very intrusive; assistants, sub-editors even compositors could rearrange the text.[1] Female ancillaries flit through the pages of letters and memoirs. Stead's 'devoted Miss Hetherington' kept for the *PMG* along with the reference books, the newspaper clippings books, called clag-books, a system continued by the succeeding editor, Cook. Mrs Oliphant writes to Miss Walker that she is immersed in De Quincey for a paper. 'Please do the proof as soon as you possibly can.'[2] Occasionally, as with George Eliot, Mary Braddon and Ella D'Arcy, letters give us more detail. Far more research, however, needs to be done on the part women played in these back-room activities – indeed far more about the work of both sexes. What follows are brief glimpses behind-the-scenes.

In the large daily newspaper offices of the 1850s there were plenty of back-room staff beside the sub-editors and departmental editors. There were the messengers and copy-boys. There were the readers working in pairs, one reading aloud from the manuscript, the other correcting the press. Harriet Martineau estimated between 50 and 60 compositors working through the night and going back to their homes, some way out in the suburbs, to sleep during the day. But these workers were all men.[3] The nature and working conditions of these jobs made it difficult for them to be even considered as open to women. The messengers remained crucial figures in the process of news-gathering for many years. They picked up the copy from Eliza Linton in the 1850s and CP Scott still relied upon them in the 1880s. One remarkable member of the species could run the three miles from Scott's home to the *Guardian* in twenty minutes, and never sober. (Although Scott had a telephone it was apparently often out of order.) Dailies of course needed their proof-readers to work at night and until relatively late in the period conditions could be grim. Readers straining their eyes 'by flaring gaslight' amidst 'intolerable' bustle dealt with 'proofs of every variety of subject, knowing that they would be held primarily respons ible for a mistake that might change the entire meaning of an article'. Even in the 1890s Ella Hepworth Dixon contrasted the 'huge gilt letters' on the newspaper façades with their gloomy office interiors.[4]

Just as the actual functions of editors varied at different periods and from journal to journal so the editorial organization varied[5] and the term 'sub-editor' covered different rôles. Sometimes it seems to have been interchangeable with 'assistant editor', whilst on a London daily at the end of the century the sub-editor might combine the duties of the modern news editor and chief sub, selecting and rejecting copy and correcting the 'vagaries of the telegraphists, and the still more strange antics of the wire'. Larger papers even had specialist sub-editors dealing with sport, financial, foreign news etc. The pace was frenzied.[6] Some newspaper offices were certainly prejudiced against women. Emily Hawkes was refused a post as sub-editor on the *Yorkshire Daily Observer* simply because of her sex. Other proprietors and editors were more accepting. When Hulda Friederichs managed a section of one of Newnes's papers she was left 'entirely free' to choose her subjects and handle them as she thought fit. Even when Newnes did make suggestions she apparently felt confident enough to disagree, and on such occasions claimed she generally got her own way.[7] Hers seems to have been a genuine managerial rôle, whereas other women assistants often enjoyed nebulous powers, apt to evaporate when they tried to exercise them.

Work on monthlies, quarterlies and annuals moved at a slower pace than newspapers, though there were still last-minute rushes before press-day. The work of assistant editors varied, but Mrs Newton-Crosland's duties assisting Marguerite Power on the *Keepsake* – proof-reading, correcting and corresponding with authors – were replicated with variations throughout the century. As assistant to Leitch Ritchie on *Friendship's Offering* she did more, reading manuscripts, and commissioning verse to suit the plates. Like George Eliot on the *Westminster*, she was the unacknowledged editor.[8] On magazines, at least, we know there were women readers, sub-editors and editorial assistants. Janet Hogarth worked as a reader for the *Fortnightly*. Catherine Drew referred to the 'accurate and painstaking' women who were 'not the less journalists because they have to arrange, condense, and often re-write, the work of others'. But how numerous were they? Fanny Green believed them to be relatively rare. She thought it conde-scending to consider sub-editing suitable for women on the grounds of being 'mere easy mechanism and quiet work', yet her view that their comparative scarcity had to do with the prerequisites of the job is double-edged: 'judgment, a sense of proportion, and a business ability and training which are rather rare among women at present.'[9] Even on the reviews and monthlies the duties could be tiresome. Back-room workers had perforce to deal with the general ignorance of contributors about the whole process of production. Overwriting must have been a continuous annoyance. Proof-reading and corrections caused prob-lems. Contributors might assume for instance that textual changes could be made on the proofs. As John Chapman pointed out, the printer charged *him* extra for corrections made at proof-stage.[10] Janet Courtney helping Mrs Humphry Ward with her *Anti-Suffrage Review* complained she once 'reserved a place for her always-too-late leading article. She was in the country. I had to wire to her that it overran. She replied "Reluctant to cut article. Can it not be set again in smaller type?" And that when we were already a day behind time!'[11] '

Reviews, and monthlies, however, particularly earlier in the century had one attraction for women. It was sometimes possible to carry out editorial work from home as George Eliot acting as Chapman's assistant did for the *Westminster*. She corresponded with contributors, cut and rewrote over-lengthy articles, proof-read, watched the competition, and tried to steer the wayward Chapman towards a more consistent and con-sidered editorial policy. Why had he told Martineau that Mill was also going to write for the same issue? 'I have told you all along that he would flatly contradict Martineau and that there was nothing for it but to announce contradiction on our title-page.' She suggested contributors in the light of rival papers. The *British Quarterly* advertised an excellent list. The *Westminster* had no good writer on its staff to deal with subjects like 'Pre-Raphaelitism in Painting and Literature'. What about enlisting David Masson whose work for the *BQ* she admired? She was virtually car-rying out the tasks of editor in the frustrating position of not having actual power, and urged Chapman to appoint an editor when he could afford to pay. She found her proprietor irritating to deal with. She was certainly very annoyed when she complained of his 'great many irons in the fire' for the next number, and his taking on of contingent articles and changing his mind about subjects for contributors. On other occa-sions there was hassle with the printers and incompetence from authors.

She 'was stamping with rage' at one issue which ended up with typo-graphical errors in articles and a misspelling on the title-page, none of which were due to her own 'carelessness'. The printers were running so late that she did not get the 'revise' of several pages, and 'that tiresome Mrs Sinnett pretends to correct her proof' but doesn't.[12]

George Eliot was not alone in her frustration. Lesser creative spirits, male and female, found sub-editing and assistant editing disheartening, though in Mary Braddon's case it was a useful editorial initiation. When Maxwell appointed Mrs Hall editor of his *St James's* he arranged for Mary to work one day a week on the magazine under her supervision, explain-ing that Mrs Hall had been impressed by her potential and he had encouraged her view that she was 'most anxious to profit by her experi-ence and counsel'.[13] Braddon may have chafed at the restricted scope for editorial creativity during this apprenticeship but ultimately as editor of *Belgravia* she benefited. On *St James's* she learnt at first hand the practi-calities and clearly handled a substantial amount of the donkey-work of copy-editing, the 'mechanical part' of the profession as she termed it. Her complaint that she had been doing so much editing for the last year or two that, 'when I am in church, I almost want to edit the Liturgy' covers the period of her *St James's* work and seems to refer as much to her magazine work as to revision of her fiction. To Lytton (whom she had been at pains to assure would enjoy all her influence in getting him a *good* review of his poems and who was less than delighted with the result) she emphasized the constraints under which she operated. She claimed most material for the magazine was obtained for her; finding suitable reviewers was difficult; there were restrictions of length, and the Proprietor used his power to intervene. Real editorial responsibilities would speedily drive her to the madhouse. There was an element of exaggeration in all this since her letters clearly indicate that she was already adept at soothing demanding authors and contributors, a talent she carried with her to her editorial chair.[14] Sala certainly found her as the 'youngest and least experienced of his lady passengers' on *Temple Bar* a talented and determined young woman.[15] Real editorial responsibility was surely exactly what she had in mind.

Mary Braddon was unusual in having the opportunity to convert dreary copy-editing into a full-scale editorial opportunity. Ella D'Arcy worked for a highly innovative and challenging publisher but in career terms her work on the *Yellow Book* led nowhere. She proof-read, pagin-ated, arranged the pictures, and indexed as well as contributing short stories to most issues. She also liaised with editor Harland, for whom she was acting as a kind of business and social secretary, publisher

John Lane and his business manager, Frederic Chapman. Though the *YB* was a quarterly the job had its pressurized moments; Harland was often abroad leaving Ella in charge of preparing everything for the press, but with limited authority. When Lane memorably stopped the forthcoming issue during the Easter holiday, wiring Chapman to suppress the Beardsley drawings just as everything was ready for press, Ella turned up at Bodley Head 'with a light heart' on the Tuesday expecting to see the first copies of the *Book*. Though astonished to discover that the four drawings were suppressed without explanation to her, she hunted out replacement blocks, only to find the next day that cover and title page were also to be changed. She wrote plaintively to Lane that she '*really* liked the new cover ... and the mere idea of there being anything objectionable in it, never for an instant occurred to me.' At this stage she gave up and wired Harland to sort matters out.

The extent of her powers seems to have been either unclear or unsatisfactory to her. Chapman apparently confided very little, and her control over contributions and illustrations was restricted. Once when some of the 'pulls' of pictures sent to her were in her view 'simply atrocious' she enquired hopefully why she hadn't been made Art Editor? She never was. Nor was she paid well. She overstepped her authority when she changed Harland's contents list, removing Ethel Colburn Mayne's story, without sending him the 'revise' before she passed it for press. Her reward was abusive wires and a postcard relieving her of her 'duties as Sub-Editor'. She sarcastically remarked to Lane that the Cromwell Road would be blocked by 'needy females' competing for 'that high-salaried post'. The trouble was, that it probably would have been. It was just wishful thinking to hope an influential Chicago publisher might one day secure her a 'London, Paris or Jerusalem letter for a big Yankee paper' at £500 a year.[16]

Women seem to have done this kind of editorial assisting and sub-editing for little monetary reward. George Eliot received no salary at all though probably something in kind. One of the unsung contributions of women to the nineteenth-century press was editorial support for their husbands. One picks it up almost *en passant* in reading about the men. Rachel Cook, whom George Eliot thought the most beautiful woman she had ever seen, also had a formidable intellect. She was one of the guinea-pig girls at Hitchin, and despite having started studying Latin and Greek only a few months before going up, in the Classical Tripos one of her papers on Aristotle was considered the best submitted, against formidable competition. As the wife of *Manchester Guardian* editor CP Scott she assisted him with the meticulous work he did on the proofs. Sometimes they would do the final work at home, he in his study, she lying on the sofa, with the messenger waiting to take it the three miles from Fallowfield back to the office. Sometimes the Scotts would go together to the office about six, taking a simple supper with them, perhaps not getting back until two in the morning. On long train journeys both would use the time to write, with the results telegraphed back from whichever remote spot was their destination.[17]

By the end of the century other types of press office-work attracted impoverished women. Stead warned of a misconception about secretarial work. 'Don't think that secretaryships grow on every gooseberry bush. There are very few secretaryships, and they are usually given to those who are known and proved to be faithful, and also to have a general acquaintance with the business in which their chief is engaged.' Certainly one woman journalist confirmed that her advertisements in the press for such a post got no replies. Her own reply to one for an amanuensis to a 'literary man' had even more depressing results (though it later provided good copy). She was selected from over two hundred applicants by an employment agency who dispatched her to a dubious young man who offered her a guinea a column for puffing dress-shops and ghost-writing. The agent later admitted a previous applicant had complained he tried to kiss her. Unsurprisingly Miss O'Conor Eccles never received a penny for her work. Freelance writers often employed secretaries but here again, even when pay was forthcoming, it was not particularly lucrative, and working in writers' homes had always had its hazards. Isabella Fyvie once faced an inebriated lady on the staff of a religious publishing house.[18]

The 'advertorial' work that Charlotte O'Conor reluctantly accepted, though despised by many journalists, could in fact pay well. Frances Low reckoned that women prepared to work with the advertising department could make up to £500 a year, and recommended those wanting a good income and not caring for the 'intellectual quality' of their work to enter this 'commercial journalism'. She estimated that as opposed to the handful of women engaged in 'serious' journalism – essay and leader writing, descriptive articles and reviews – there were hundreds of women engaged in 'writing up' the shops, fashions, furnishings and the 'toilette department' in order to boost the profits of the advertising department. Catherine Drew viewed some of this work more positively. There was a 'whole army' of women employed in testing and reporting on new domestic products, recipes and patterns to the benefit of reader and producer alike. 'The manufacturer ... recognizes the importance to the trade of the country of the woman journalist.'[19] By the end of the century some technical jobs were open to women. 'Printing' appeared in the Women's Institute dictionary of employment, though for women the main area of work within the industry was in folding papers and working linotype machines. Emily Faithfull had pioneered printing for women through her all-women Victoria Press back in the 1860s. With proper *early* training women proved well fitted for work as compositors. She discovered that many individual printers had thought of taking on women and some of her first workers trained in their fathers' businesses, one Irish girl having twelve years' experience. One of the problems for women was that compositors served an apprenticeship during which they earned little. Boys began at fourteen. Girls, and their parents, therefore, had to make the decision for them to train early in life and so acquire the essential habits of attention to detail, precision and punctuality. Emily herself took no trainees over eighteen. It was not something to pick up in middle-life. She argued too that experience of printing was vital for readers, who might otherwise quite appropriately be educated women, rather than men.[20]

The influence of the telegraph upon the press was considerable and women were employed as operators soon after the system became the established mode of communication, which coincided with the various campaigns for expanded women's employment opportunities. By 1845 the Electric and International Telegraph Company had some 500 miles of lines operating in England, but by 1859 over 4400, and was charging the *Times* £ 1000 per annum to transmit a contracted amount of correspondence, with additional sums for extra vital communications. Maria Rye who with Isa Craig established the Telegraph School for women, was delighted that virtually the whole of the operation was now carried out by women, who proved so efficient that the company was now 'perfectly satisfied that the girls are not only more teachable, more attentive, and quicker-eyed' than male clerks, but 'more trustworthy, more easily managed, and we may add, sooner satisfied with lower wages'. Although she noted the matter of lower wages, Miss Rye was setting the work against other alternatives for these young women, most of whom were tradesmen's daughters. They paid nothing for their instruction, and after six weeks on average, were proficient enough to earn a wage – from eight to eighteen shillings a week. There was an element of the conveyor belt in achieving the speed of delivery. Two operators sat at each machine, one reading off the punched signals, the other transcribing them. The completed message was passed to another section for registering, and on to another girl for pricing, sealing and addressing ready for the messenger. The 'superintending' clerks, who ensured that messages were accurately transcribed, earned from twenty to thirty shillings. The shifts were long but compared favourably with that of 'the twelve or fourteen hours of the miserable needlewoman or dressmaker'. There is a touch of romance in Miss Rye's description of the bustling office with its 'continual clicking of the needles' as 'in one corner London is holding conversation with Liverpool ... here Temple Bar is discoursing eloquently of deeds and parchment, there Yarmouth is telling about her fish and shipping'.[21] Isabella Mayo's short experience as a trainee however was discouraging. After a dictation speed test she was offered training and promised that her rapid writing, ability to read French and knowledge of 'difficult and uncommon proper names' would ensure swift promotion. Unfortunately, despite a kind welcome, she was overwhelmed by the incessant noise of the machines in the huge room where almost all the women worked. Moreover she felt the work a 'dreadful waste of woman-life ... we might have been all boys or young men, only I suppose we were the cheaper "material"'. She was disturbed, too, to find a 'bright girl, an exceptionally clever manipulator' spending all her time transmitting racing messages for Tattersalls.[22] The Langham Place telegraph school and printing ventures enabled women to learn the new technology but Faithfull's promotion of women printers did more. Her Victoria Printing Press became effectively the 'in-house printer for feminist literature', and she both altered the parameters of the tasks to avoid unnecessary physical strain and paid attention to working conditions.[23]

A note on female illustrators

Though I have neither room nor expertise to discuss the work of periodical illustrators, no book on nineteenth-century women in journalism can quite ignore them. Drawing and painting in watercolours was long considered an appropriate female accomplishment and an established part of a young lady's education, but turning an accomplishment into a profession required motivation, training and commercial opportunity. Family connections and support, the availability of adequate instruction and the resolution of domestic and artistic commitments were important factors in determining a career.[24]

Although the illustrated daily paper was a phenomenon of the final decades illustrations featured in periodicals throughout the century. In the 1830s Louisa Sheridan illustrated as well as wrote for her *Comic Offering* annual. Nor were illustrations confined to expensive publications like the annuals. There were weekly newspapers and twopenny magazines using woodcuts in the 1820s, years before the impact of

The Illustrated London News and the *Penny Magazine*, whose woodcuts of classical buildings and of Raffaelle and Hogarth illuminated the childhood of one contributor to *Saint Paul's*.[25] Throughout the century there were launches of journals like the *Illustrated Times* and the *Pictorial World*. There was even a brief, under-capitalized attempt to provide a Midlands illustrated regional paper which employed at least one woman (Miss Bowers). But the arrival of the *Graphic*, 'fresh' and 'progressive', caused something of a sensation and provided the *ILN* with serious competition.[26] Amongst the illustrators and painters whose work appeared in the *Graphic* were Mary Ellen Edwards, on its staff from the outset, Kate Greenaway, Lady Butler, and in the 1890s Sybil Robinson who worked as a sketcher for Mary Billington's descriptive pieces. From 1870 until her marriage to William Allingham four years' later Helen Paterson combined the jobs of staff illustrator and reporter on the paper, writing a monthly fashion column and covering social events, flower shows and so forth. The darker side of social realism, involving visits to the poorer urban districts, was left to the male illustrators to cover.[27]

At mid-century illustrations were becoming a major selling-point across the middle-class market. The Beetons' *Englishwoman's Domestic Magazine* had been formulated round them, promoting future issues by detailing the illustrated delights to come. Even at a much higher intellectual level the attraction of illustrations was accepted. During the lengthy discussions to ensure the viability of the *English Woman's Journal*, Beeton's *Queen*, decorated as it was with woodcuts, was despised by the early feminists as a low-level journal yet nevertheless acknowledged to be much more amusing than their own.[28] The *Cornhill* set a fashion for other popular monthlies of illustrating its serials and several women artists benefited from this work. Amongst Helen Allingham's magazine commissions was the *Cornhill's* serialization of Hardy's *Far From the Madding Crowd*. The prolific Mary Ellen Edwards, who illustrated *Cornhill's* opening novel, Trollope's *Claverings*, was also commissioned for Mary Braddon's launch serial *Birds of Prey* in *Belgravia*, later becoming chief illustrator for the rival Mrs Wood's *Argosy*,[29] which also employed Mary L Gow. Alexander Strahan cheerfully risked the disapproval of strict Scottish evangelicals, by announcing in the *Bookseller* that the second issue of his new magazine *Good Words* 'would contain the first of a series of "Illustrations of Scripture" by the well-known J.B.' (Mrs Blackburn). Strahan encouraged young artists[30] and amongst other women he commissioned were ME Edwards and Florence Claxton. Pictures became an important feature of children's magazines, and *Aunt Judy's* featured illustrations by Juliana Ewing, the co-editor, ME Edwards and Florence Claxton. Colour pictures were a key attraction of *Little Wide-Awake* which employed a range of illustrators including Charlotte Weekes and Miriam Kerns, while highlighting the work of Kate Greenaway and giving her plum positions.

Thus from the mid-century onwards illustrated papers of all kinds offered women artists new opportunities, though there was plenty of male competition. *Belgravia* drew upon as many as nine different illustrators within the space of four months (March–June 1867) and varied the realistic school of MEE by fantasy and mild eroticism – barebreasted mermaids or mythical ladies in revealing draperies.[31] (Mermaids presumably passed the censorious eye of Mudie.)

By the 1880s illustration was integral to fashion and domestic magazines. Beeton even in the early *EDM* days used some homegrown illustrators like the Claxton sisters for non-fashion work. Now, however, reliance upon German fashion plates was a thing of the past.

> Fashion-illustration is a busy industry, and young artists who exhibit in the Royal Academy do not disdain to fill up their time in this way. Going round to shops, to sketch their new goods, is a trade in itself, and one that is fairly well paid, and though we still see an impossible type of face and figure, the artists do sometimes try to make them a little more lifelike.[32]

In the mid-1870s, although Louisa Hubbard's Year-book did not specifically detail periodical illustration it had a chapter on 'Art Employments', mentioned wood-engraving and wax-etching as suitable for the book and periodical press, and referred readers to other articles on art training and work for women. Four years later Mrs Oliphant arranged for her niece Madge to train as a wood engraver partly because if she needed to work she could do it at home 'with credit and profit'. Within the industry, however, there was growing a view that as far as newspaper work was concerned illustrators needed a proper technical training that was currently not available.[33] Technology was outstripping the capabilities of man- and woman-power.

9
A Press for a Purpose

Journalism offered a platform for those committed to a cause. The possibilities it afforded shaped in different degrees the writing lives of many idealists, leading them into editorial and proprietorial ventures, or shifting their focus from fiction and poetry into more overt polemical writing. The periodical press proved particularly attractive to those with strong religious or feminist views. A discussion of the nineteenth-century feminist and political movements, as of discrete women's issues – education and employment opportunities, legal rights, suffrage – is far beyond the scope of this book. My concern here is much more modest, to illustrate how concern about such issues drew individuals into journalism, and how such women exploited the press for their own purposes.

Women often asserted that 'politics' was the one subject closed to them as journalists. Even the editor of the *Englishwoman's Journal* claimed to eschew it as too great a risk.[1] But this assumed a narrow definition of politics, excluding domestic legislation, the social consequences of economic policies, and the 'Woman' question itself. Moreover religious questions held a central place in Victorian debates. As Mermin suggests the very existence of an established church meant that religious and political questions were inextricably linked. Because religious publishing ventures needed contributors and editors willing to work for next to nothing they offered women literary careers in the guise of a voluntary service acceptable to parents and husbands who would otherwise have disapproved.[2] This respectability factor encouraged dutiful daughters to seek publication when they might never have dared approach a secular journal. Its aura of amateurism never quite deserted this sector of the press. Even at the end of the century Arnold Bennett dismissed the 'vast hordes' of religious papers – there were said

to be several hundreds in London alone – as scarcely worth mentioning in terms of career journalism. Many did not pay contributors anything.[3]

But if the religious press paid badly, it was not to be despised as a
channel of influence. Religious journals were not immune to market
forces; titles surfaced and faded as in other sectors. The clerical editors
of *Sunday Reader* and *Twilight* had very short-lived reigns, but resilient
papers were remarkably successful. *Sunday at Home* (1854) sponsored by
the Religious Tract Society, and therefore non-profit-making, claimed a
circulation of 130 000 in 1865. Religious publisher James Clarke
enjoyed great success with his penny weekly the *Christian World* which
topped 100 000 in 1876 and thirty years after its 1857 launch boasted
500 000.[4] Denominational standpoints as diverse as evangelicalism and
the Oxford Movement offered scope for women like Charlotte Tonna
('Charlotte Elizabeth') and Charlotte Yonge. Their views had, of course,
to accord in broad terms with a particular theological stance, just as
the leader writer was constrained by the party political lines of a newspaper. Many of the feminist writers came from politically active families, and the female editors of religious magazines tended to come from
strongly religious if not clergy family backgrounds. They had grown up
in an atmosphere of worship, devotional reading, and even amidst
doctrinal debate. Felicia Mary Skene, editor of the *Churchman's
Companion* 1862–80, published a memoir of her High Anglican cousin
Alexander Penrose Forbes, Bishop of Brechin, who was censured for
promulgating the doctrine of the real presence. Religious literature,
both from parental encouragement and from its relative accessibility
within the household, formed an important part of their education.
Where women like Eliza Linton and Harriet Martineau eventually
reacted against their upbringing and gave up their faith, others were
able to reconcile female Christian modesty with their desire for self-
expression by channelling it into journalistic missionary endeavour.
Yet it would be wrong to imagine this was inevitably an unthinking
zeal, grounded in supine, filial obedience. These women often
expressed strong personal faith and social views through their writings.
Frances Taylor, the original editor of the Jesuits' *Month*, was the daughter of an Anglican clergyman who converted to Catholicism whilst out
in the Crimea. Her first book was inspired by her experiences of military nursing under Florence Nightingale, but most of her subsequent
work was religious in character, and from 1862 to 1871 she was proprietor and editor of another Catholic magazine, the *Lamp*. Felicia Skene
not only donated the earnings from her fiction to charity but was as

prepared to deal with taboo social evils like prostitution as were the more avowedly polemical *EWJ* writers. Her preface defends her novel *Hidden Depths* (1866) against charges of sensationalism. '[T]he hidden depths, of which it reveals a glimpse, are no fit subject for romance, nor ought they to be opened up to the light of day for the purposes of mere amusement.... [T]hough all did not occur precisely as here narrated, it is nevertheless actual truth which speaks in these records.'[5]

Mary Anne Hearne (Marianne Farningham) who from 1885 edited the *Sunday School Times and Home Educator* for James Clarke, came from a humble background where her limited opportunities rankled. She was raised in a Baptist tradesman's family, where her expected rôle was helping with the housework and looking after her siblings, and where her passion for reading was not encouraged. She later recalled reading in some religious publication a sequence of inspirational essays on poor boys who rose to be 'rich and great', whilst vainly hoping to find one about 'some poor, ignorant girl, who beginning life as handicapped as I, had yet been able by her own efforts and the blessing of God upon them to live a life of usefulness, if not of greatness'. Her eventual prolific work as essayist, hymn writer and editor was her way of reconciling her desire to overcome this 'handicap' with Christian acceptance.[6]

'Charlotte Elizabeth' and Charlotte Yonge are, probably with justice, today the best known nineteenth-century female religious editors. Charlotte Tonna, whose father was a minor canon at Norwich cathedral, developed, like her second husband, ultra-protestant though individualistic views. She was always anti-Catholic, yet supported the Anglo-Jewish press. As editor of the *Christian Lady's Magazine* from 1834 to 1846[7] her stated aim was to allow debate without giving offence. This seemed to her a perilous task for her 'little bark' launched under 'a cloudy sky, and amid turbulent billows'. Abandoning her metaphor she spelt out her dilemma plainly. '[I]t is an undertaking of considerable difficulty to conduct a periodical on conscientious principles, in days when not only is the world breaking loose from all wholesome restraint ... but even those whom God hath chosen are so disunited amongst themselves.'[8]

The magazine was also treading a narrow line between encouraging women readers into the public arena and endorsing their traditional domestic rôle as Christian wives and mothers. Her Introduction and the Preface to Volume I set out her editorial policy. Women had a right to discuss spiritual matters publicly, and 'on leading subjects', she aimed 'to take an estimate of opinions from different quarters'. Aware that 'so many private circumstances must influence the judgement of individuals' and she could not possibly please all her readers, she hoped to avoid 'just umbrage' by putting aside 'momentous theological questions like Church Reform and Unfulfilled Prophecy', best left to 'periodicals of a more masculine stamp'. (Though she would not *necessarily* exclude them.) Particularly welcomed were practical articles on subjects affecting 'Christian ladies' in their domestic relationships. Her journal would not deal exclusively in theology. She had been asked to exclude fiction but clearly sensible of the appeal of narrative, promised instead 'interesting biography'. Social questions presented in fictional form did eventually infiltrate her pages.[9] Her views on editorship were pronounced. She would not shelter from what she saw as her editorial duties, disassociating herself from the 'vexatious' anonymous editorial 'We' claiming a share in 'royal immunity'. (She clearly felt that 'Charlotte Elizabeth' was by now sufficient identification.)

> The doctrine of editorial irresponsibility we hold to be most futile ... To exclude all in which we do not individually concur, were indeed to establish a literary autocracy not endurable in the land of freedom; but we claim, and we fully intend to exercise, the privilege of appending a note of such dissent as is consistent with all humility and love.[10]

Throughout her tenure, which lasted until her death, this level of overt editorial intrusion, and the tension between permitting freedom of expression and avoiding dangerous theological and moral licence, are evident.

In the early days she permitted a debate on geologists' attacks on Biblical literalism. This originated in a letter from an Italian Dominican adopting a Creationist position and defending 'Mosaic narration' against modern European geologists, whom he argued had scarcely examined the world's crust at all. The following issue carried a refutation, drawing parallels between these 'present alarms by pious Christians' and the Inquisition against Galileo. Charlotte was clearly amongst those pious Christians, which is presumably why she published a letter emanating from what she once termed the 'blood-red meteor of Papery'. 'Painful as it is to differ from a correspondent so valuable' she could not conscientiously follow so far. GEM's contentious piece was printed 'hoping that, under the divine blessing, our little pages may be made instrumental in checking a spirit of presumptuous speculation' and offering Father Clement Pietra Santa the right of reply. Though Fr Clement had a level of denominational invective almost Charlotte's equal, he also had a sense of humour and picked up the reference to Galileo with gusto. Invested with an inquisitor's robe 'so terrific did I look ... that I instinctively shrank back from the mirror, and thought I felt my own red-hot pincers at work upon myself'. First let geologists 'accumulate facts and settle their own disputes ... in the name of the rack and the thumbscrew, do not let us have theory pushing out theory, each [briefly] maintaining ... its unquiet pre-eminence.'[11]

Such lively philosophical concerns rarely surfaced again. Charlotte may well have felt somewhat out of her depth. It was after this debate that she announced her intention to avoid momentous theological questions. In future the 'practical' worries, like the 'Unguarded Hours' correspondence were more to the fore. This focused on the dangers of visits to families where children might be instructed in 'games of chance'. The editor reinforced this message. Seemingly innocent pastimes like billiards might encourage skills and tastes which later led their possessors 'into dangerous haunts'. 'The subject is momentous, almost beyond any other, when viewed in all its bearings.' Even boys playing for marbles 'are imbibing the very spirit of gambling, weaving the first web of the snare'. Further correspondence showing even higher levels of anxiety – whips, horses, guns and drums inspiring a love of field sports and military life, fragile playthings exciting a taste for novelty, visiting friends *at all*, 'mawkish' religious books and 'nursery tales' – revealed the editor's tension between her responsibilities to readers and her own opinions. '[A]lthough cordially concurring in the main points [we] rather question whether, even in these reforming days, it would be practicable, or indeed desirable, to put the whole treasury of playthings into Schedule A' she responded.[12] Future disputes centred on such domestic matters as the morality of dancing. Here GEM was again partially responsible. A paper, with editorial commentary, 'On the Use of Music' allaying the anxieties of pious evangelicalism, called forth an enthusiastic reader's letter 'welcoming with delight the promise [they] afforded; anticipating the rescue of all our pleasurable occupations from the obloquy under which they have fallen among religious people'. Amongst such pleasure was dancing. The alarmed but conscientious Charlotte printed this letter together with editorial prayers both to God and GEM that his reply would 'expose' and 'oppose that spirit of worldly compliance, which is, as a deadly canker, eating into the very heart of religion'. The resultant 'On the Use of Dancing' fulfilled her wishes by explaining that the earlier paper exonerated *singing*, but dancing though not intrinsically sinful 'in society as now existing' was *not* a harmless occupation for a religious woman.[13] Even more weighty political issues, such as the slave trade and factory conditions discussed by her journal, had to be defended as suitable fare for ladies.[14]

Through the pious, sometimes hysterical, editorial rhetoric the modern reader can detect Charlotte Tonna's genuine concern to meet duties she believed divinely-inspired: to offer Christian women 'literary entertainment' which was as 'socially instructive' as she could render it. When she objected to something on moral grounds, it was not so much repugnant to her personally, as something she considered herself ethically bound to oppose. To individual respondents she remained courteous in print, continually reiterating her personal responsibility for what she printed. She may have been 'innocent of all the ways of literary leadership' when she took on the post (though she had edited a religious annual) but after almost ten years she knew she had made an impact. She took on with some spirit that 'very able, but somewhat eccentric publication' the *Quarterly Review*, taking its dubbing of her as 'a muslin divine' as a back-handed compliment. She did not enter into theological controversy herself but 'when cambric, lawn, and crape, are all agitated by such extraordinary winds of doctrine, muslin will also flutter in the breeze. Women have souls....'; and in claiming for women 'freedom of speech, at least amongst ourselves' she reminded her clerical critics that women too had died for their Protestant faith. By the time her mortal illness made closing a volume a relief she had established a space for female religious discussion rather than mere exhortation.[15]

If for nothing else Charlotte Yonge would have her footnote in the literary history of her period for sheer longevity as editor of – to give it its full title – *The Monthly Packet of Evening Readings for Younger Members of the English Church*. She was sole editor of 80 volumes from 1851 to 1890 at which point she was reduced to joint editor with her assistant, Christabel R Coleridge, until 1899. She parted with it somewhat reluctantly; it had become so much a part of her life – rather like her even longer Sunday School teaching career which lasted from the age of seven until she was 78.

[T]he *Monthly Packet* has turned me out except as contributor. It has been going down, *Newbury* and *Atalanta* supplant it, and the old friends are nearly all gone, and the young ones call it goody-goody. So the old coachman who has driven it for forty years is called on to retire! They are very civil about it, and want me to be called

Consulting Editor, but that is nonsense, for they don't consult me.... It is property, and no wonder Mr Innes views it as such, and not as a thing *pro ecclesia.*

In 1899 she sounded its death-knell to her cousin: 'I'm afraid the poor old *Monthly Packet* is coming to an end, as Innes's affairs have got into a mess. It has not come out this month, but it may revive at half the price.'

The *Monthly Packet* was not her only editorial venture. She took on two other church papers, the *Monthly Paper of Sunday Teaching* from 1860 to 1875 and *Mothers in Council* from 1890. She was still advising on papers a few months before her death. A letter to Christabel Coleridge on a paper on servant girls for *Mothers in Council* asks 'Does not your paper want something more of practical application.... Would it be possible to bring it more to a point? Suppose I made an addition, if you don't.' She suggested some commentary 'on a rather silly paper in *Macmillan's* which she thought misunderstood the general situation *vis à vis* mistress/servant, if Christabel didn't want to extend her paper. Yet her notion of editorship was somewhat amateurish.

[I]n the old days the *Packet* came out on the day it was ready, and, if more space was required, pages were added to a number. Contributions from popular authors were declined rather than sought for, and no attempt was made to court popularity.[16]

Charlotte Yonge, like Mrs Wood and Mrs Gatty, was a home-based editor; her assistants seem to have been always people congenial to her, like Christabel Coleridge, one of her 'goslings', and Miss Finlaison, her sub-editor, who had settled in Otterbourne. Charlotte's literary and intellectual mentoring, the 'careful guidance in good taste and good feeling' as 'Mother Goose' to the brood of goslings and their manu-script magazine *Barnacle,* were equally the hallmarks of her *Packet* editorship. Christabel Coleridge saw the Mother Goose/gosling rela-tionship as precisely exemplifying that she enjoyed with her numerous readers. The 'goslings' association outlived *Barnacle* by some years. It is the measure of its closeness to her own magazine that Charlotte marked its closure with a Michaelmas Day roast goose dinner at which it was 'solemnly decided that our work was done and we must merge into "Arachne" and her Spiders in the *Monthly Packet'.*

Charlotte Yonge was not totally ignorant of commercial considera-
tions when she took on the *Packet*. At first she was cautious, wondering
how serious Anne Mozley, sister of the publisher, was.

> I have my fears, for I believe a new Mag. is an immense risk, and I
> think it is very doubtful whether the Mozleys would choose to start
> one in opposition to Masters. Besides, who will guard us from the
> universal fate of good Mags. of growing stupid as soon as they get
> into circulation?... I wish anyone could tell us what the cost of start-
> ing a Mag. would be.

She had some awareness of targeting a market, suggesting 'I don't
think I would make our Mag. much of a poor people's concern, more
for young ladies and calves; perhaps started in that way it would not
seem so like an opposition'. Even so the magazine she produced was
marked by the educationalist inspirations of her earnest guidance of
her Sunday School teaching. As 'Mother Goose' she disallowed speculative or frivolous questions which had seemed absorbing to her
young relatives.[17] As a real editor she announced her intentions to the
15 to 25 year-olds – 'young girls, or maidens, or young ladies,
whichever you like to be called' – who comprised her market. The
amusement and instruction would be such as to 'tend to make you
more steadfast and dutiful daughters of our own beloved Catholic
Church in England'. To this end she promised 'Cameos' from history,
fiction, travel articles, biographies, translations and 'extracts from
books which are not likely to come your way, or of which the whole
may not be desirable reading for you'. Her target audience also
included young male schoolteachers, and young readers in the servants' hall.[18] When the magazine was first mooted she had in mind
her historical 'Cameos' and working up her Catechism papers into
'Conversations'. This latter proved so palatable a form – or at least
attractive to parents and guardians – that the 'Conversations' were used
to open numbers 2, 3 and 4, and both 'Cameos' and 'Conversations' ran
for many years.

The strictness of her childhood upbringing, which she appears to
have in retrospect fully approved, informed her emphasis on filial
duty. Her rigorous home education, including maths, Greek and
science, as well as the more usual history, meant she set high standards for the content of the educational material she offered her
readers. She attacked one new young people's periodical for
superficiality, inaccuracies and irrelevancies. It would be better 'not to

decide quite so confidently on the precise age of a piece of coal, or the exact date of the existence of the Mammoth'. Nor had she any time for the 'puerile style' and educational assumptions that thought listing the parts of a table-cloth – 'corners, hem, stitches, patterns, fibres' – suitable material for the young.[19] Although interested in all manner of social issues herself, her views on what was fit to print, rooted as they were in her religious belief, whilst far from being in the Sarah Trimmer[20] league, were cautious. Once she even objected to something Mrs Gatty printed, though she praised her books, and published her work.[21] The *Packet*'s early 'Hints on Reading' were formulated round the advice 'What to read – what to read cautiously – and what to leave unread.' Her concern that literature should be morally uplifting and culturally refining emerges in her wary treatment of Dickens's novels. 'They are very amusing, and there is what is carelessly called "no harm in them", that is to say, no offence against moral principles, and few expressions that might not be read aloud. They are not, however, desirable reading.' They not only lacked overt Christian religious teaching, but 'finding amusement in slang and caricature' did not promote good taste or refinement.[22] She believed that fiction could be morally dangerous. 'I do think people with consciences ought to reflect on the harm they do to morbid imaginations by dwelling on suicide, and I do think that contemplation of sin is not the way to purify the heart.' Given such principles it is scarcely surprising that the *Monthly Packet* could be seen by her assistant editor as the expression of Charlotte Yonge's personality, and the extension of her influence.[23]

The dilemma of reconciling their own activities as writers and their often progressive views on women's education with an acceptance of Christian submissiveness was faced by other women editors in the religious press. Emma Worboise edited the monthly *Christian World Magazine* from its inception in 1866 until shortly before her death in 1887. Arguably as editor she used the journal to promulgate her own ambivalent advocacy of women's increased participation in public affairs, and her more wholehearted support for an extension of women's education and rôle in the labour market.[24] Another title from the Clarke stable, it occupied a half-way house between commerce and religious service. Worboise, one of Clarke's fiction authors and an established contributor to his periodicals, was quite prepared to defend fair pay for work, even in a religious context. '[T]he labourer is worthy of his hire whether he till the soil, or preach the Gospel, or write books or magazine articles.'[25]

By the mid-century evangelicalism increasingly recognized the value of women's activity in religious literature. Periodicals like Fanny Mayne's *True Briton* aimed to protect the working-class from the rampant dangers of the Penny Press, mobilizing the energy of their better-off neighbours to ensure her 'popular magazine ... advocating law and order instead of anarchy and confusion' was distributed where it could do good. She was not alone in wishing to stem the 'torrent of moral poison' which Reynolds and others found profitable; Charles Dickens's *Household Words* sought to displace those same 'penny dreadfuls', those 'Panders to the basest passions of the lowest natures ... whose existence is a national reproach'. But Fanny Mayne's moralizing and exhortation was on a different plane. Notwithstanding that her serialized fiction was of an excellent standard, and works like *Uncle Tom's Cabin* raised serious moral questions, her approach to the working-class was based on the containment of potential social disruption.[26]

Few women engaged in radical political publishing – Eliza Sharples, editor of the *Isis* in 1832, being an exception[27] – but women like Christian Johnstone, Mary Howitt and Eliza Cook did use their journals to promote progressive social ideas.[28] Mrs Johnstone was a professional journalist, and Mary Howitt had cut her editorial teeth on the annuals; but *Eliza Cook's Journal* (1849–54) was Miss Cook's sole periodical venture. Despite her inexperience and the 'many difficulties [which] beset the path of a young Journalist' she rapidly learnt the practicalities of the profession, and was able to boast of her 'extensive circulation' and 'cordial reception' by the public for a 'cheap Serial' devoid of 'unhealthy excitement and mere ephemeral entertainment'. Until her health gave out, and she was forced to discontinue it, her magazine succeeded. Her inspiration was not that of 'a moral "Mrs Trimmer" to the million ... I have a distaste for the fashion so violently adopted of talking to "the people" as though they needed an army of self-sacrificing champions'. Nor, she protested, was she into 'literary gambling' or 'anxious to declare myself a mental Joan of Arc ... against Ignorance or Wrong'. She reverted to metaphor when she explained what she *would* offer 'a plain feast ... wholesome and relish' yet she intended a blend of pleasure and moral profit, for she later claimed that 'amusement' was a 'chief essential' of both periodicals and life, yet 'should ever be blended with a principle and purpose tending to advance Humanity'.[29]

As a 16-page double-column weekly newspaper for a penny-halfpenny *ECJ* provided good entertainment value with stories, travel articles, sketches and poetry. 'Silverpen' was a major contributor of fiction. Poetry was given unusual prominence. She put the case in an early article 'People Who Do Not Like Poetry'. Anticipating Charles Dickens' forceful opposition of Fancy and Utilitarianism, she identified a dislike of poetry with 'the flinty crude mass of "utilitarianism" … standing in upright frozen selfishness, entertaining no speculation, but that depending on a thriving railway … They may be useful and necessary – so may the cholera …' Her own poetry naturally predominated – a major attraction was the reissue of her published work. But her strong views on the 'advancement of humanity' – particularly issues of employment and education – were also aired. The same point would recur in different guises. An anecdote in an article on the poor pay and conditions for governesses is reworked into a romantic story of 'interview day' where the son reading his mother's advertisement for a governess exclaims that such a paragon would be his ideal of a wife, as naturally this perfect governess becomes.[30] A leading article on 'Associative Efforts of Working Men' gives rise to correspondence and notes on a tailor's organization.

Her style was often forceful. On women's education: 'Everything that has yet been urged in favour of the better education of men, may with equal force be urged in favour of the better education of women'. On the intolerable 'London season' hours worked by needlewomen at fashionable dressmakers: despite their relatively comfortable conditions

> there are sufferings as genuine as those of the poorest slop-shirt sewer, from which the workers in satin are as powerless to free themselves as the toilers on twopenny calico … Labour …. bids fair to get more money for fewer hours. The women do not participate in the improvement. They stand alone.

In one of her final papers she returns to 'An Old Question' with an acerbic vigour which later feminists might justly admire.

> No, my lords and gentlemen, in order to have a better sort of women, we must have a better sort of men. You are the leaders, the governors, the critics, and the educators of the world. Do not think to get rid of your responsibilities by alleging that we are the educators of the heart, mind, and conscience of the nation; and in the same voice insisting that we are weak, frivolous, and must in all things be subject to you.[31]

As *Eliza Cook's Journal* noted reading was now a general necessity. '[W]e no more think of going without our book than without our breakfast.'[32] The press offered a tempting platform for presenting women's issues, fighting *for* educational and employment opportunities, better working conditions, and women's suffrage; fighting *against* legal injustices. Virginia Crawford reflected at the *fin de siècle*, 'With us women have devoted their main energies to carrying certain definite reforms by Act of Parliament. They have descended frankly into the political arena and have fought men with their own weapons.'[33] Since they could not carry out the fight within the Parliamentary arena itself they had done so in the political byways of the press.

What they wrote could make waves. Mona Caird's controversial series on marriage, begun in the *Westminster* and transferred to the wider arena of the *Daily Telegraph,* caused the *Times* to remember her as a 'talented novelist, a writer of trenchant essays'[34] and Janet Courtney recalled the women's trade unionist leader Clementina Black as wielding an 'effective pen' on labour issues in the reviews.[35] Black's very first article (in *Longman*'s 1887) demonstrated her journalistic talent in exploiting sensationalism and the advertorial to promote ethical consumerism. She later published in a diverse range of periodicals, the *Fortnightly, National, Temple Bar, Illustrated London News* and *Spectator* among them.[36]

Because issues as apparently disparate as the social acceptability of male drunkenness and the Contagious Diseases Acts of the 1860s were recognized as oppressive to women causes like the temperance and anti-regulation movements attracted support from radical feminists, suffragists and religious conservatives alike. Whilst a raft of women's organizations pushed for political and moral change, activists found the press a valuable channel for sustaining their arguments, and promoting specific causes. Josephine Butler's *The Storm Bell* and *Dawn* pressed the anti-regulationist case.[37] The late 1870s saw the *Women's Suffrage Journal, Journal of the Women's Education Union, Woman's Gazette* and *Shield* all supporting women's political causes. (The *JWEU* was founded jointly by Emily Shirreff and a Mr Bartley and she co-edited it for many years. The *WSJ* published by the Society for Women's Suffrage was edited by Lydia Becker from 1870 to 1890, the *Gazette* by Louisa Hubbard.)[38] At a less overtly political level women writers could use the general press to popularize women's causes. The suffragist Florence Fenwick-Miller wrote as 'Filomena' for provincial journals, and Phebe Lankester exploited her syndicated 'Penelope' in regional papers to promote her ideas on women's employment, emigration and public service.[39]

Nearly thirty years after Eliza Cook launched her journal the *Englishwoman's Review* could claim that it would be difficult for any paper with pretentions to 'breadth of ideas' to keep aloof from the 'great social questions of the educational, industrial and legal position of women'. It attributed much of this progress to the efforts of the 'Women's newspaper', defined as a publication dedicated to covering all events bearing on the subject, required to 'keep on "pegging away" at the risk of being a bore … carried on for principle, not for profit, to further a cause, not to pay a dividend.' The *Review* had long viewed the 'Woman Question' as one that transcended national boundaries and it reported on foreign initiatives. In this record of the varying successes in Europe and America of the Women's Press one senses the encouragement which international connections gave. British women took heart from what was being done by women elsewhere – and indeed by men on their behalf. (*Avenir des Femmes* had a male editor.) The weekly *Woman's Journal* edited by Col Higginson, Julia Ward Howe and Mrs Livermore received particular praise for the extensiveness of its coverage. 'The amount of steady, thorough work … can hardly be over estimated. It takes note of every effort made to improve the condition of women … in suffrage, medical, legal, moral and social questions.'[40] Such connections brought personal support to women's causes in Britain. Frances Cobbe delightedly recalled this trio's visit to her in London. Mrs Livermore addressed a Suffrage meeting like a noble Roman Matron, realizing 'my highest ideal of a woman's public address… her sweet manners and playful humour without a scintilla of bitterness in it … were all delightful'.[41] Even Charlotte Yonge while in France found herself discussing women's rights with her hostess Mrs De Witt, who had been asked to write on the subject for a new *International Magazine*.[42] British writers celebrated all such attempts and successes achieved as part of an international movement, even where – as in France – the advocacy of 'Women's rights' in the press struck them as less 'advanced' in terms of legal reform.[43]

In Britain by the 1890s a small army of women's papers with feminist and social agendas involved the energies of women activists. By then some sought to draw upon the practices of the commercial press.[44] Some early pioneering journals were phased out as long-standing editors retired or died. The *Review* charted the changes. When Louisa Hubbard's *Work and Leisure* 'devoted to the extension of remunerative employments to women, their technical training, and ways of assisting them' finally closed at the end of 1893 readers were advised that the editor had arranged for Miss Janes' *The Threefold Cord* to include brief information of the kind previously covered by *W&L*.[45]

The story of the *Woman's Penny Paper* exemplifies some of the ways in which an activist journal of this period sought to accommodate itself to both various feminist causes and to the mainstream press. It was established by the suffragist Henrietta Müller, who like Emily Faithfull had an interest in printing as a founder member of the Women's Printing Society to which the *WPP* was initially entrusted. By 1890 it had become the *Women's Herald* priding itself on its all-women staff. As its editor 'Miss Temple', Henrietta fought an unsuccessful battle for access to the Reporters' Gallery. The refusal on the grounds that no women reporters were admitted prompted even the somewhat conservative Fanny Green to note that these women were reduced to competing for space in the 'Ladies Gallery' 'like every aspiring female shorthand reporter'.[46] After Henrietta went to India it became the voice of the Suffragist Women's Liberal Association, and increasingly enmeshed in the Temperance movement, being absorbed into the *Woman's Signal* edited by Lady Henry Somerset, an ardent temperance supporter, and feminist Annie Holdsworth, who had worked under Stead on the *Review of Reviews*. Following the transfer to Mrs Florence Fenwick-Miller in the autumn of 1895 the journal took on a new lease of life. The new editor had sound feminist credentials; she was known as a lecturer in the suffragist cause and an active London School Board member, and had unusually retained her maiden name after marriage. More importantly she was a highly experienced journalist. Apart from her *ILN* column and syndicated 'Filomena' letter she was a leader writer for two provincial dailies and edited the colonial monthly *Outward Bound*. This broad base equipped her to bring the best of the New Journalism to the *Signal*. Changes were noted almost immediately and Mary Billington warmly welcomed the revamping. '[S]he is fast raising [it] from the hopeless faddism and "anti-man" partizanship which formerly distinguished it.'[47] She increased the advertising and rewarded readers who recruited new subscribers with 'a nice pack of Christmas cards' or new books, and ran a competition for a new cover design. Despite these editorial innovations her aim was propagandist, not commercial. The 'Free Circulation Fund' she established was intended to get copies into public libraries where *men* would be lured into reading it, and she rejoiced when newspaper editors plundered her *Signal* columns for copy. When she took over as sole proprietor and editor she was already heavily committed elsewhere yet she frequently wrote 'four substantial pieces' each week for the *Signal*. She took no income from the paper, and although by autumn 1897 it was covering its costs, she eventually found the financial burden and physical labour too much and it ceased publication.[48]

Female faddism of a different order characterized the turn-of-the-century *Womanhood*, 'An Illustrated Magazine of Literature, Science, Art, Medicine, Hygiene and the Progress of Women'. Physically it had all the hallmarks of the New Journalism – large format, elegant illustrations and eye-catching headlines asking 'Should Ladies Smoke?' or 'Should Clever Women Marry?'. Helen Woods, writer of the latter, a prize-winning letter, argued that the clever woman properly educated and prepared to devote herself to her family without seeking to have her actions 'emblazoned in print' certainly *should* while the professionals such as doctors and the 'objectionable' type whose 'oratorical glibness' enabled her to make a name as a 'public talker' should *NOT*. The letter was effectively a mini-essay where the writer paradoxically sought a journalistic platform to expound these opinions. With a follow-up article the editor sensed a lively debating subject and invited readers 'including men' to contribute their views in 'Women's Parliament'. This feature title itself indicates something of the ways in which the magazine sought to displace radical reform with a more conservative view of 'Women's Progress' – an opportunity to exchange opinions rather than participate in that other Parliament. Progress was celebrated in the articles that dealt with sport, women's clubs, employment or achievements – Madame Blanch Leigh 'the only woman soap manufacturer in the world and a member of the London Chamber of Commerce of which our Editor [Mrs Ada S Ballin] is also one of the very few female members'.[49]

The editor's particular cause was signalled in the sub-title's reference to Medicine and Hygiene and reflected in the magazine's emphasis on 'health' – columns on women's ailments, articles on infectious diseases, hospital treatment for children etc. and answers to readers' 'Health and Beauty' queries. These questions were often very personal and the private answers supplied for 7s.6d. no doubt answered a need, but like the editor's shopping column which plugged goods, also indicated the commercial basis of the magazine. In this respect, as much as in its conservative stance, it differed from the women's rights papers.

It was from what became known as the Langham Place Group that the most sustained efforts at arguing feminist causes through a dedicated press emerged. Journalists and activists alike differed as to the relative effectiveness of diffusing ideas through the general press or through dedicated publications. Bessie Parkes argued the case for the value of a 'special' publication's 're-iterated effort', its capability to 'sustain ... scattered energy' and act as a 'rallying point' and a central focus for debate that involved the thoughts of many rather than the 'separate thoughts' of individuals.[50] The general press offered the great advantage of wide and influential circulation, and a really able journalist presenting a specific cause might succeed to spectacular effect. In the mid-1860s, drawing upon their extensive connections, the Langham Place women launched a surprisingly successful national press campaign in support of The Ladies' Petition.[51]

The *Englishwoman's Review* itself credited Cobbe's article 'Wife Torture' in the *Contemporary* with being more influential 'than any other statement of facts' in securing for battered wives some legal protection.[52] Arguably it was Harriet Martineau's 'Female Industry' in the *Edinburgh* rather than its inspirations, Barbara Bodichon's 'Women and Work' in the *Waverley Journal* and similar pieces in the *English Woman's Journal* that drew the nation's attention to a major problem.[53] In the early struggles to establish the *EWJ* Bessie Parkes, its founder and co-editor, maintained that a thousand people reading an article *there* was better than 60 000 in *Good Words*, on which Emily Davies, who briefly took over the editorship, tartly commented 'This seems pure delusion'.[54] Yet the *Journal* afforded space to views that might not be published elsewhere, and Bessie persisted in her belief that 'reiterated effort' outweighed individual articles.[55]

Most of the women who were to be engaged in Langham Place publications – *Waverley, English Woman's Journal, Alexandra Magazine, Victoria Magazine* and *Englishwoman's Review* – were activists rather than journalists. Their literary and entrepreneurial talents were inextricably drawn into other kinds of practical measures: the establishment of organizations like the Association for Promoting the Employment of Women, the Female Middle Class Emigration Society, the Married Women's Property Committee, and the Ladies' Sanitary Association, and founding and running institutions like Barbara Bodichon's Portman School, Maria Rye's Law Engrossing Office and the Telegraph School she founded with Isa Craig, Emily Faithfull's Press and Emily Davies' higher education campaign which culminated in the creation of Girton College, Cambridge. Ellen Drewry faced with the financial problems of the *EWJ* thought 'Emily Faithfull with her Printing Press does more good than/all/[sic] the thousand and one things that are

written and said on the subject' ['talk about women'], while Emily
Davies in the throes of editing the struggling *EWJ* considered 'An
inspiring thought, once printed, may kindle somewhere & produce
greater results than twenty printing presses'.[56]

Bessie Rayner Parkes eventually published several volumes of verse
and always intended to become a writer. Apart from her youthful
efforts at poetry she was in 1849 planning a romantic novel[57] and early
on expressed her views on women's potential. Her epistle in imitation
of Pope addressed to her great friend Barbara Leigh Smith (Bodichon)
attacked the poet's strictures on women:

> 'Tis a one sided picture; earth has shown
> We have *some* Brains among our Sex, our own.
>
> You cannot need another word to show it;
> I need but name a Martineau and Howitt.[58]

But both she and Barbara were at the same time trying their hand at
writing articles for the press. (Among their exchanged manuscripts
were abstracts of Mill's preliminary remarks.)

The publishing venture of the *EWJ* was characterized by youthful
enthusiasm, commitment and amateurism. Several of the group had
some experience of writing for periodicals – Isa Craig's spell on the
Scotsman and Maria Rye's association with the *EDM* being among the
more substantive. None had any real knowledge of the business side of
journalism. Emily Davies expressed relief when Bessie's cost-cutting
scheme to get her to oversee a jobbing printer was dropped. 'Bessie told
me, she did not feel up to managing the printing on the spot, when
the Journal began, & if she did not then, certainly I don't now.'[59] In all
their enterprises they had to learn about the practical business side of
things the hard way. Mrs Mayo recalled the law office suffering
financial loss from generating a demand it could not fulfil. 'Capital and
connection, after all, can do nothing without competent labour.'[60]

In one important respect these young women were lucky; they had
access to what seemed substantial funds. When Bessie and Isa's contributions to a little Edinburgh magazine 'professing to be edited by
ladies', *Waverley Journal*, led to the publisher's offer to buy him out,
Barbara was able to place 'a considerable sum of money' in the hands
of George Hastings. He negotiated with the publisher on their behalf,
eventually advising them that the property was not worth it and that
they should set up their own new journal. The group was thus in the

fortunate and unusual position of having at its centre that Victorian anomaly, a woman of property – which she controlled. Barbara was in this respect, as in the circumstances of her birth and upbringing, unusual.[61] Her father settled the same annuity upon each daughter as he did upon his sons. More normal was the situation of Frances Cobbe who reckoned her eldest brother 'as usual with elder sons in our class' drew each year from the family property more than she received over her whole life.[62]

Another key factor in the group's success was their network of valuable contacts. The family backgrounds of both Barbara and Bessie brought them into intellectual and political circles, where social and economic issues were hotly debated. Barbara's father, Benjamin Leigh Smith, the Radical member for Norwich, opened the family home as a meeting-place for abolitionists, and was a member of the council of the anti-Corn Law League. Her girlhood friend Bessie was bred of reformers. Her maternal grandfather was Joseph Priestley. Her father, a solicitor and like Leigh Smith a Unitarian, numbered Mill, Bentham and George Grote amongst his friends. He had radical sympathies and Bessie later remembered how the results of her father's work as secretary to the 1833 commission on municipal reform impinged upon her childish consciousness.[63] Such family connections and the networks they later developed were important both as influences and for the support which experienced writers offered them. In Hastings the Leigh Smiths became close to the Howitt family. Anne Jameson, a friend of Barbara's aunt Julia Smith, welcomed them as 'adopted nieces'. The work of friends of their own generation like Adelaide Procter and Christina Rossetti would appear in the pages of the *Journal*. Their activism brought them into contact with women like Phebe Lankester.

Bessie Parkes' account of the founding of the *EWJ* highlights the close connection between the journal and other Langham Place activities. She also attempted to justify the journal's *raison d'être*. It had no intention of attempting to compete with the 'able monthlies'.

> Such an idea would have been perfectly hopeless and absurd … If it had been wished to start a brilliant and successful magazine, some eminent publishers should have been secured and persuaded to undertake active pecuniary interest and risk; all the best female writers should have been engaged, 'regardless of expense'; *and then –* good-bye to the advocacy of any subject which would have entailed a breath of ridicule…[64]

What her account glosses over – naturally enough – are the differences of view, the battles over policy, and the struggle to keep a fragile ship afloat.

While enthusiasm for a cause gave the group its strength, the amateurism of the editorial control, the varying views of the members as to what should be the specific objectives of the paper, and eventually its precarious financial basis, were all to cause problems. There was a delicate balance to be achieved in interesting but not alienating its readers. George Eliot recommended to Bessie Parkes Lewes's doctrine that a new journal should attract readers by having a 'specialité' but *not*, she counselled, what was implied by the inscription 'Conducted by Women' which she was glad to hear was to be dropped. Similarly Anna Jameson advised getting 'the help and sympathy of good and intelligent men & do not *feminise* your journal too much – if you do – it will break down.' In letters on both the *Waverley* and its successor she encouraged her *protegée* in the venture 'with your *active* mind & strong convictions on certain subjects' whilst explaining her own difference of view on such key issues as divorce. A detailed critique of one number, commenting adversely on an article on Harriet Hosmer which read like 'a puff', cautioned 'that women should not make your journal a vehicle for bepraising each other'; and approving an article on 'Examinations' advised 'you must follow it up – but with good taste & get the men on our side'.[65] The Hosmer piece was by Matilda Hays and by all accounts the early choice of this beautiful charmer as assistant editor did not help. George Eliot had a low estimate of her journalistic ability fearing that she had 'been chosen on the charitable ground that she had nothing else to do in the world'. Although apparently her direct influence on the *Journal* was relatively limited[66] her association caused the editors to be wary of any really challenging articles. '[I]t has got the credit of Bloomerism ... for *nothing*, so to speak' complained Emily Davies. Even five years after its launch she was still fearful of publishing any 'startling manifesto' which might damage the journal's fragile recovery from the reputation Miss Hays had given.[67] Here was the 'Glass House' on top of a mountain of which Bessie's father had warned.

The contents of that first number of the *EWJ* (March 1858) today seem scarcely revolutionary. Apart from book 'Notices' and 'Passing Events' there was poetry, a story by Amelia B Edwards, and the social issues covering teaching as a profession, married women's property and a penitentiary for 'unfortunate women' run by Anglican nuns. Yet favourable reactions in the general press stopped short of approval when any really challenging question was raised. Responding to the *Saturday's* criticism of its stance on women's employment the *Journal* thought it must have in mind 'a settled type of womanhood, which, like the English "milord" in the brain of a French dramatist, is not to be effaced by innumerable examples of its falsity'.[68] Some years later Emily Davies was amused by the *Sunderland Times'* report that the *Englishwoman's* serial had improved and was now 'womanly, motherly, simple and genial'.[69]

The unexpected ferocity of an attack in the *National Review* and the resultant angry response of her usually supportive father must have taken Bessie by surprise. He wrote at length. 'I have anticipated for months past, that you would have the Cat O' Nine Tails on your back ... if you do not heed some fine day you will have a flagellation in the *Times'*. Admitting the article was somewhat unjust, he still felt she had invited the attack, and seems to have sided with the *National* over 'your earlier Nonsense' (Barbara's *Rights of Women*) on women's franchise. Bessie must learn as her mother and grandmother had perforce before her that men would not allow women to 'usurp their natural sexual superiority'. Other material was ill-advised. There were not 80 000 prostitutes in London. 'And why stain your Periodical by a *disgusting* term?' Delicate readers would be offended – why not 'Unfortunate Women' instead? Anna Jameson though comforting over the *National* – 'everyone who breaks a new path has this to undergo' – similarly counselled caution over terminology. 'It is quite possible to write forcibly without using coarse language.'[70] As Bessie was 'one of the chief contributors' the net result was that 'earlier numbers were almost entirely occupied by questions as to the employment of women, and philanthropy. Women's Suffrage is not mentioned.'[71]

Differences of view as to how far the *Journal* should emulate the established general reviews in order to attract readers and subscriptions continually surfaced. Despite Barbara's financial support and Bessie's ebullient optimism the *EWJ* was in a precarious state. When in 1862 the clear-sighted Emily Davies agreed to take over the editorship for two months – in fact, she did so for about 6 – she was shocked by the confusion that reigned. In a series of letters to Barbara (now married and abroad) she expressed concern on several counts. Naturally there were editorial worries over the quality of contributions, especially since they were dependent upon material given *gratis*, but these were compounded by Bessie's interference particularly on anything to do with religion. They would not get good writers under such 'fettering conditions'. As the hoard of stocked manuscripts diminished Emily was anxious to obtain someone other than a 'half worn out hack' and wondering if Miss Thackeray, fresh from the success of her *Story of Elizabeth*, might be approached.

The major difficulty was money. Her brother citing *Macmillan*'s shift from its original aim to pleasing the public, had said 'Propagandist things never pay'. That didn't 'signify' if they all agreed that their aim was not profit but 'to spread our ideas'. Emily thought that the position needed clarifying.[72] There were problems over printing costs. Bessie's costing-cutting scheme having died the death, and other estimates been obtained, Miss Faithfull's bills, she reported, were still considerably lower than other printers. But she continually noted that they were losing subscribers, on which they depended for running costs. The plan had been to get subscriptions paid in advance with any deficiencies made up by friends. In Cranford such methods might have worked; unfortunately the *EWJ* belonged to the real world of Victorian publishing where with all their advantages the smart young men who had set up the *Reader* were not, with all their connections and masculine advantages, proving particularly successful.

An exceptionally lengthy missive, even for the times, sent on 28 December carried transcripts of the opinions of various interested people whom Emily had consulted. They were, she told Barbara's sister, 'confused and confusing'. There was much support for a 'good story'. Unfortunately Miss Thackeray, like so many other 'names' they knew, George Eliot being the spectacular example, were unable to oblige. Some thought the *Journal* could scarcely justify itself in an overstretched market; others that since 'social questions' always demand attention it was a question of sorting out a proper business basis for it.[73] By early January Emily had come reluctantly to the conclusion that the *Journal* was not viable. They were not holding on to their readership. Old subscriptions which had been constantly dropping off were now doing so at a 'dreadful rate'. The accounts showed that 624 subscribers bringing in £374 did little more than cover the printing costs (£360). The advertisements covered their own advertising, office stationery and the secretary's salary. Once rent and book-keeping had been paid for they were left with £40 for contributors without paying the editorial staff anything.[74] Barbara, often abroad, was losing interest. The *EWJ* was absorbed into the *Alexandra*, which lasted a year. 'The efficient organization of work' was, Bessie wrote in 1864 in her *Alexandra Magazine*, 'immensely more difficult than I once believed'. The *Journal* was relaunched by Jessie Boucherett initially as a quarterly, the *Englishwoman's Review of Social and Industrial Questions* in 1866 and, in the hands of committed female editors, remained a valuable voice on women's issues until it finally ceased publication in 1910.[75]

Emily Davies suffered a baptism of fire in her brief spell editing the *English Woman's Journal* and, during this fractious period, Emily Faithfull discussed starting a 'first-class magazine of Fraser or Macmillan type' using her own printing press, to save costs, with Miss Davies as a *salaried* editor. She was to receive £100 in quarterly instalments, and editor's articles an additional 5s per page. The *Victoria Magazine* was launched in 1863 with Mr Gunning as partner. On its launch an Agreement provided that the editor was to read all manuscripts, deal with correspondence 'connected with the literary working of the Magazine', and should report societies and provide reviews 'except such as may be given to special Reviewers'. The job entailed a considerable amount of interviewing and negotiation by correspondence with important contributors like Arnold. In the case of disputes over editorial contents a majority view of the editor and two partners would prevail – an interesting concept, perhaps intended to avoid the corrosive debates experienced with Bessie. Both Emilys were aware that any new venture would be precarious, but they were trying to put it on a sensible business-like basis. Their agreement was reviewed after six months, and in the event the editor 'was paid only one quarters' salary, & nothing for anything I wrote for the Magazine'.[76] Emily Davies abandoned her experiments with journalism and turned her energies to the founding of a university women's college. Emily Faithfull became publisher/editor of what was to prove a valuable platform for women's causes.

Although aiming at a general market, *Victoria* was inspired by the motives that established the *EWJ*, as that journal noted. It too 'pegged away' at women's issues. Modern critics equally see it as an 'important venture in female publishing'.[77] Feminist activism was for many of these women, like their brothers' professions, the major focus of their adult lives. Journalism was subsumed within the causes for which they fought. Indeed their domestic lives – even among those who married – were often shaped to accommodate them; childlessness or very small families was a common pattern.[78] Some were destined to disappointment in their expectations of the 'practical power' of writing. As Frances Cobbe sadly reflected she once 'fancied ... that I was really given the great privilege of moving many hearts' but 'by degrees ... felt the sorrowful limitation of literary influence'.[79]

Yet with hindsight more recent writers have charted the success of women who 'knew the importance of the press in arousing public interest and in building support for a new cause'.[80] In retrospect the 'special periodical' can be seen to have influenced the political climate. Its ideas, when well written, infiltrated even those journals which opposed them; gradually the 'unmentionable' became common currency for debate. As Fanny Kortright's paper, no supporter of female suffrage, explained in a notice of the *Englishwoman's Review*:

> Whether we agree with the opinions of the writers on social and political subjects or not, we must in all fairness confess that this Review contains an extraordinary mass of talent, shown by good argumentative power, force of language, and excellent composition. The contributors are in earnest, and their work is well done.[81]

Twenty years later Margaret Oliphant saw the heroine of the 'New Woman' novel as

> an example of the new sentiment ... the singular and scarcely recognized revolution which has taken place in the position and aspirations of women during this generation... In Parliament ... men still ... talk as if there was no important difference in the life or sentiments of the women by whom they are surrounded; but if we look back, we will find that the difference is immense, almost uncalculable ...[82]

Feminist journalism had taken a major part in changing this climate. Compared with the 1860s, by the final decade periodicals were awash with articles on employment opportunities for women. *The Englishwoman* series included lady dentists, lady gardeners, lady bookbinders, domestic science and kindergarten teachers, tea-tasting and tea rooms, dairy teachers and dairy farmers; *Sala's Journal's* 'Women and their Work' – the lady doctor, the military embroideress, the photographic maid-of-all-work. The *Englishwoman's Review* now thought 'Far to be preferred over special papers for women is the healthy admixture of news concerning their interests and doings in the columns of the general press'.[83] The 'special periodicals' had by no means run their course; indeed they were to be exceptionally vigorous as the suffrage campaign continued into the following century.[84] But the advent of greater employment opportunities for women and the increasing perception of the general press as offering a platform for women as well as men encouraged the shift which the *ER* remarked. Periodicals were still dominated by men but it was becoming easier for women like Eliza Orme and Frances Low to debate social issues without recourse to a dedicated press with a purpose.

10
Jill of all Trades: Journalism and the Professional Writer

Margaret Oliphant (1828–97); Eliza Lynn Linton (1822–98)

For many nineteenth-century women, as indeed for many men, journalism was a profession in which they were involved for a period of their lives or in which they participated sporadically. For some, however, it was one of the mainsprings of their lives, engaging their physical and intellectual energies, and providing a significant part of their incomes. This was true of both Mrs Oliphant and Mrs Lynn Linton whose writing careers spanned much the same period, the second half of the century. Both wrote in other genres. Margaret Oliphant produced 98 novels, short stories and substantial non-fiction works including her still very readable cultural histories of Italian cities. She was at work on a three volume history of Blackwood's publishing house when she died. Eliza Linton's forays into fiction were less frequent and in critical terms less successful, but like Margaret Oliphant she was an astonishingly prolific periodical contributor. Their careers, running almost in parallel, though Mrs Oliphant was the younger by six years and predeceased Mrs Lynn Linton by a year, illustrate how independently-minded Victorian women could find in the developing profession of journalism at once a release and a curse. It opened a door from the private confines of domesticity on to a public platform where their voices could be heard; it provided a valued source of financial support. But once in the public arena their views were open to attack; at times they felt personally vulnerable; and once embarked on a course of financial independence derived from writing they would inevitably find in it elements of drudgery.

Their first novels were published within three years of each other, Eliza Lynn Linton's *Azeth the Egyptian* in 1846 and Margaret Oliphant's

Passages in the Life of Mrs Margaret Maitland in 1849, and their lifelong involvement in journalism began in the 1850s. Though writing came to provide a cathartic release for the personal anguish in their lives it was essentially the necessary means of earning a living. In many ways they were successful, achieving fame, social standing and acknowledged status as women of letters, but this public image concealed professional disappointment as well as private sufferings. It was after all for their *fiction* that Victorian women were chiefly honoured[1] and neither ever achieved the status and success as novelist that she desired. In her diary Mrs Oliphant, recalling a year that seemed almost unremitting struggle to get work which paid enough, revealed her envy of the financial rewards which the public appetite for their fiction brought George Eliot, Dinah Craik and Mary Braddon.[2] Two years earlier when reviewing Cross's life of George Eliot she wondered how much better a novelist she might have become if she had not been forced to churn out the books and articles to keep the roof over her family's head. Anticipating Eliza Linton's reference to 'her nature ... of that hot-house kind ... dependent upon circumstance for its own condition' she reflected 'How have I been handicapped in life! Should I have done better if I had been kept like her, in a mental greenhouse and taken care of?'[3]

Mrs Lynn Linton herself according to the publisher Tinsley tried desperately hard to be a popular, successful novelist.[4] In old age she stressed the occupational hazards of journalistic life, isolation and bitterness. Confiding to a new acquaintance, the American stunt girl Elizabeth Banks, something of 'her lonely life ... unhappy marriage ... the many things that made her life a not too happy one', she advised her to 'guard against bitterness and cynicism'. It must have been a remarkable encounter – the young American representative of the aggressive 'new' journalism confronting the profession's elder stateswoman, who having branded her brassy and brazen, was astonished to find her a gentlewoman.[5] 'Old, grey-headed, alone ... [her] passions tamed ... [and] energy subdued' she may have felt herself, yet by this final decade of her life Eliza Lynn Linton was established as a doyenne of literary life, taking part in published debates and symposia,[6] the sharpness of her opinions on the New Woman continuing to provoke angry rebuttals from her sister writers.[7] She was noticed as a major journalist and author in articles highlighting men and women of the day[8] and one of the first women members elected to the governing council of the Society of Authors. For her part Margaret Oliphant had enjoyed nearly half a century of critical power. *Blackwood*'s obituary compared her versatility and genius to that of Goldsmith.[9] Like

Eliza Linton she had been invited to contribute to the Hurst and Blackett celebratory book on women authors.[10] She had been the family breadwinner most of her adult life, sending her sons to Eton on the proceeds of her writing, supporting not only her own, but following his bankruptcy, her brother's family. She achieved what many of her compatriots would regard as the ultimate social accolade. She was invited by Queen Victoria to Windsor and the Queen 'as a true Scotchwoman' sent her a copy of her highland Journals.[11] It was to their involvement in journalism as much as to their fiction that Mrs Oliphant and Mrs Linton owed their success, professionally and financially.

Critics have remarked that Mrs Oliphant became a novelist almost by default; she preferred writing biography and criticism.[12] Even by Victorian standards she was astonishingly prolific and her literary reputation has suffered from that 'marvellous industry' which Mrs Gerald Porter so admired in her character.[13] A journalist recognized as a specialist, like Amelia Blandford Edwards, the Egyptologist, might be admired as reaching scholarly heights. But there's a faint whiff of Grub Street in Margaret Oliphant's self-deprecating description of herself as a 'sort of general utility woman' for *Blackwood's*.[14] In her lifetime Eliza Linton was recognized as the first woman staff journalist employed by a major daily newspaper.[15] Her friend and biographer George Somes Layard considered her 'novel-writing' 'but a side issue and subordinate'. He summed up his own admiration for her thus: 'She was great as a journalist, and in journalism she found her highest achievement'.[16]

The desire to be a writer came early to many Victorian women authors. For Eliza Linton the initial impetus was seeking fame and independence, and in the early days of her first successes she gloried in them. She had precocious tastes in literature, and was only ten or eleven when she decided to train herself as a writer.[17] From childhood into old age she was a voracious, eclectic and extraordinarily rapid reader, fascinated by titbits of 'Knowledge'. When, at fifteen she made her first attempts to get into print, enquiring secretly of Richard Bentley if she might contribute to *Bentley's Miscellany* she responded to his encouragement, in highly charged emotional style. If her story were to cast 'the shadow of a shade' over his splendid periodical he was to *burn* it. But if she had talent enough for his journal she would be one of 'the happiest, the *proudest* of mortals'. He held her fate in his hands – to remain 'a purse-knitting, embroidering, flirting young Lady' or grown older and wiser hope she might one day '*dare* to rank with the highest!' Writing was, however, she admitted much more difficult than she had anticipated.[18] A few years more of emotional turmoil, and rebellion against the harsh domestic regime under her father were to pass before she achieved any real success[19] and in her extraordinary fictional *Autobiography of Christopher Kirkland*,[20] she was later to articulate the complex motives which drove her struggle to escape to London. But when success *did* come her response to the reception of her ponderously researched first novel eclipsed even the paroxysms of joy she had experienced in 1844 when *Ainsworth*'s accepted two of her poems.[21] Even though she had had to borrow the £50 to pay Newby for publishing *Azeth,* the favourable reviews left her feeling as if she 'seemed to tread on air, to walk in a cloud of light, to bear on me a sign of strange and glorious significance' – yesterday unknown, today 'flashed into the world of letters'.[22]

Margaret Oliphant's girlhood was, though in a different manner, also 'singularly secluded'. Books, newspapers and magazines formed the 'staple' of family intercourse and amusement. Whilst nursing her sick mother, and having no taste for needlework[23] she turned to writing to while away the long watching hours. Less flamboyant in displaying her emotions than the youthful Eliza Lynn, years later she still recalled 'walking along the street with delightful elation, thinking that, after all, I was worth something – and not to be hustled aside' when Colburn sent her £150 for a new edition of *Margaret Maitland.*[24] The sudden awareness of mattering in the world, counting for something in the public eye, were sensations authorship enabled young women to share with their male peers. Margaret Oliphant was thus already a published writer when her remarkably lengthy association with *Blackwood's* began. Her mother renewed acquaintance with a doctor and *Maga* contributor who introduced her to the editor's brother. Shortly afterwards she submitted her story 'Katie Stewart', 'a little romance of my mother's family, gleaned from her recollections and descriptions'.[25] Yet it was not long before both Eliza Linton and Margaret Oliphant found the need to turn what originated as a creative, intellectual outlet into a bread-winning job. They were to discover that writing was a somewhat perilous way of earning a living[26] but then what work open to women was not? The young Miss Lynn, when Marian Evans knew her in their early London days, struggled to get paid literary work, despite having published fiction. There were dramatic differences between the sums which the most popular novelists could command at their peak, if they were shrewd at business, and the run-of-the-mill earnings. Dickens may have earned £10 000 from *Our Mutual Friend* and George Eliot been offered a similar sum for *Romola* by Smith Elder, but even Mrs Henry Wood, one of the sharpest of contract negotiators, found her average thousand guineas for a three-decker dropping to half that by the end of the 1860s.[27] In 1865 Smith Elder gave Mrs Linton a mere £100, with half-profits for a year after if a second edition were published, for *her* three-volume *Grasp Your Nettle*.[28]

The differences in earnings of journalists may not have been quite so dramatic but there were still huge gaps between those at the top of the profession and the hacks of new Grub Street. Even so when compared to other work available to gentlewomen, it was attractive. Isola, in Eliza Linton's novel *Sowing the Wind* when she had to fill 'the gaping void of the family purse' faced a choice of being a somewhat inadequate daily governess or working 'embroidery and bead pomegranates' at which she excelled but which paid badly.[29] Journalism was a lottery but there was always the chance of making a good living, which was more than one could say for being a governess.

Isabella Fyvie's experiences in the 1860s provide a salutary insight into the alternatives. She tried practically everything available to an impoverished but well-educated and enterprising young woman living in London. She began with hand embroidery and reckoned that if she and her sister sewed their scalloped strips in every spare moment they could net 1s. 6d. a week. She looked into machine-sewing (8s a week). With Mrs Samuel Carter Hall's influence she obtained work at the Electric Telegraph Company but could not stand the noise. She obtained secretarial work, initially through the Langham Place Office for Employment of Women, everything from envelope addressing to making fair manuscript copy for Sir Edwin Arnold to the relatively lucrative law-writing. Throughout, she was trying to develop her own 'literary work'. In her first year with all these efforts, long hours, and often walking long distances to her different engagements, she made £30, gradually increasing this until in 1866 she earned almost £100 to which her 'tiny literary earnings' had contributed. No wonder the offer of £300 for a serial 'for an important magazine' seemed a 'miracle' even though she recognized that her 'swallow' might not 'be the herald of a long summer', and her nine-year 'life-and-death fight for bread and independence' temporarily wrecked her health and nerves. Then with great relief she retreated into the arms of a young solicitor to become Mrs John Mayo.[30]

Neither Mrs Oliphant nor Mrs Linton however found financial stability through marriage. Their husbands were artists not businessmen.

Francis Oliphant, a stained-glass designer who had worked under Pugin, died in 1859 leaving his widow with three young children and little money. She later took responsibility for a nephew's education too.

> I have four people, an entire family, three of them requiring education, absolutely on my hands to provide for... For the next three years ... I can look forward to nothing but a fight *à outrance* for money: however it is to be honestly come by. I don't care how much or how hard I work.[31]

When Eliza Lynn married William James Linton, the engraver, he had been twice-married and was ten years older than she.[32] The organization of his household at Brantwood was feckless. Although she eagerly supported his somewhat disorganized republican activities[33] she was by nature almost obsessively fond of order and cleanliness. (Years later in Italian hotel rooms she used to get up at six in the morning to spring-clean her bedroom).[34] The shambolic domestic arrangements and constant financial crises which Eliza often had to resolve from her own resources, were major elements in the breakdown of the marriage. Ironically, not until he went to America when their marriage was effectively over, did he achieve commercial success. For both Mrs Oliphant and Mrs Lynn Linton financial matters loomed large and were to necessitate constant productivity.

The most financially secure journalistic posts were the salaried ones, the editorships of the established titles and the newspaper staff jobs. An annual salary of several hundred pounds would have been a valuable addition to *any* household finances. Might Margaret Oliphant have had a fairer chance of obtaining the periodical editorship she sought so unsuccessfully had she been a man? It certainly seems likely that a man with Eliza Linton's talents and persistence would have secured more permanent newspaper work; salaried openings in the 1860s and 1870s were largely the province of men. At the very least, had Eliza Lynn really been Kirkland 'he' would not have had to contend as she did with a 'career break' on marriage. Moreover gentlemen journalists of good family had the benefit of school and often university education which was advantageous in terms of the social network it provided as well as the intrinsic value of the formal education. The *Saturday Review,* of which Mrs Linton eventually became one of the more notorious contributors, prided itself in its preliminary announcement on having writers most of whom were known to each other and had been 'thrown together by affinities naturally arising from common habits of thought, education, reflection, and social views',[35] an instance being a major early *Saturday* reviewer, Vernon Harcourt, who was Sir HS Maine's pupil at Trinity Hall and gained introductions through him.[36] Almost certainly a boy with her appetite for learning – she taught herself to read French, Italian, German, Spanish, and 'a little Latin and less Greek' but not to speak them or understand the grammar[37] – would have had schooling, and most probably a university education. Eliza Lynn felt hampered throughout her life by its absence and her sense of inadequacy in this respect must have fuelled the envy she felt for the later generation of 'Girton girls' whom she bitterly satirized.[38] While it may be true she lost nothing by her father's refusal to send her to school because of the limitations of girls' education at the time,[39] had she enjoyed the intellectual training which school and university offered boys of her class, she might have avoided the irritating habit of parading her scholarship which vitiated her literary style, she would probably have risen in hierarchy of a newspaper staff had she wished, and possibly been less bitter. Once she had proved herself, however, her father provided a modest annual allowance. The publication of her second novel was valuable in three ways.

> First it roused the enthusiasm of Walter Savage Landor. ... Secondly, it brought her in touch with Mr. George Bentley, with whom a life-long personal and business friendship ensued. Thirdly ... it greatly impressed an editor who was second to none but Delane in his gift for recognizing journalistic talent.

It provided her with three influential male patrons at a crucial time. She had by now discovered that novel-writing, at least at the stage she had reached, produced modest returns in terms of the hours of research and writing it entailed. She had to find a way of 'turning her literary powers to remunerative account. Newspaper work was the first calling to suggest itself ... The outcome was a social essay (no doubt founded on second-hand information obtained at the British Museum) on the wrongs of all savage aborigines.'[40] She sent it to the *Morning Chronicle* asking for a job. Thus began her important relationship with Douglas Cook, firstly on his staff at the *Morning Chronicle* and later in 1866 as a contributor to the *Saturday Review*, the turning-point of her journalistic career, lifting her at the age of 44 from being 'one of the great nameless band of literary hacks ...[to] a household word in every English-speaking country'.[41] Her staff job on the *Chronicle* provided a comfortable regular income to cushion the vagaries of freelancing.

Without the security of a salaried post there were bound to be times when even successful professional writers suffered financial crises. Both Mrs Oliphant and Mrs Linton were fortunate in their publishers and editors who often advanced money against work to be completed. There seems little doubt that despite her claims never to have had expensive tastes Margaret Oliphant's strained circumstances were caused not only by her generosity to her family but by her extravagant nature.[42] The state pension of £100 granted to her in 1868, the year she visited the Queen at Windsor, earned her gratitude[43] though the practice had its critics.[44] Blackwood was generous in advancing sums when necessary, and Mrs Oliphant's correspondence with him suggests that his encouragement too was a crucial support.[45] Indeed he became in Elisabeth Jay's phrase her 'banker, reviewer, literary adviser, and friend'.[46] When times were hard Eliza Linton also benefited from several advances of between £50 and £100 'which she was to work off by articles and stories as occasion offered'.[47]

Both women perforce learnt the art of haggling. In Eliza Lynn's early negotiations she relied on male support. Loaden acted as a kind of literary agent but when, displeased with Newby, she asked him to contact Bentley and he could not agree terms she made the proposition to Bentley herself.[48] It was with her *Christopher Kirkland* that Bentley first used a royalty payment system, though despite substantial advertising he made a loss.[49] She was never afraid to push for the best deal she could get. When the editor of *The Globe* contacted her she replied, 'Tell me like a good Samaritan what you do pay, and if I am taken on at all, try to get me a permanent engagement on a yearly salary, paid quarterly. It puts a backbone into one's income!'[50] Even at the end of her career she defended her corner, fighting for a good price for work done to what she regarded as demanding professional standards.[51] In 1890 she joined the Author's Syndicate founded by William Colles, a lawyer who set up as a literary agent.

Mrs Oliphant's life seemed a constant battle to pay the bills. As early as 1854 she sought to become a reviewer for *Maga* to obtain a steadier income.[52] In her autobiography she claimed she had always 'a lightly flowing stream of magazine articles' but that this was insufficient and 'a large sum was wanted at brief intervals to clear the way'. An unexpected approach from the *Graphic* provided one such windfall, £1300 obtained 'after a little talk and negotiation'.[53] She was always conscious of disparity. She once pointed out to Craik that 'men have such a huge advantage over us, that they have generally something besides their writing to fall back upon for mere bread and butter'. She constantly compared herself, as Elisabeth Jay has noted 'to the best-paid literary men of her generation'.[54] Ironically noting that Trollope's 'systematic way' in which he 'grinds out his work' nevertheless keeps him 'extremely comfortable; keeps a homely brougham, rides in the Park &c.', she wondered enviously 'if daily bread is all I shall ever be able to manage, and whether I shall have to go on in the same treadmill all my life – I suppose so'.[55] But to reach even this level of financial independence, given that their novels were never runaway bestsellers, both Mrs Oliphant and Mrs Linton had to develop professional reputations which editors and publishers alike respected. It required a remarkable level of self-discipline and was achieved at some cost.

When she was feeling particularly despondent Mrs Oliphant transmuted the drudgery of her work into her story of the disappointed painter 'Mr Sandford', what her cousin called the 'very extraordinary foreshadowing' of her own last years mirrored too in her remarks on real artists condemned to endless repetition. But she also reflected that 'Sickness, incapacity, want of health or ability to work' didn't occur to her'.[56] The 'underlying truth' of Mrs Linton's life' may have been 'sorrow, suffering, trial and determination not to be beaten'[57], but her fighting spirit was as prevalent as the tribulations. As she told Bentley 'my work is *the* point to me'; its rewards brought back 'all the old flow of my long past youth'.[58]

The early chapters of *Kirkland* enthusiastically celebrate literature and the press. As she grew older and more disillusioned with life she tended to emphasize the strains which journalism imposed: 'loneliness and loss' the 'unfortunate investments' – whereby one 'stands to lose all round'. 'Independence of judgment' brings on virulent attacks from journals for which you once worked; lively writing is misinterpreted, and beneath your 'controversial armour' you suffer 'acutely when the lash falls.'[59] The image of Jane Osborn, the newspaper woman, at the end of *Sowing the Wind* is a bleak one. Rejected by the man she loved and dedicated to her work, her physical appearance, 'gaunt and old', the skin 'dark and brown' mirrors her emotional deprivation. She becomes physically more masculine as she grows more careless and indifferent to her dress. Her manners become 'more angular' and her 'bony frame grew leaner'. In terms of Victorian gender constructs this masculinization is not a triumphant one. 'As she went daily to office-work like a man, and blew up compositors and readers like a man too', 'old Johnny Osborn' may have become 'a standing institution' to the office boys at the *Comet*, but at a time when corsets and crinolines were the staple images of femininity 'her frayed black gown trailing about her feet ... her general air of dilapidation and pitchforked apparel'[60] would indicate to much of the outside world merely wretchedness and poverty.

Jane's experiences and attitude seem strongly autobiographical.[61] *Sowing the Wind* was written during Eliza Linton's last summer at Brantwood when it was clear that her marriage with Linton could not be sustained. Its two contrasting female heroines reflect her own confused ideas of ideal womanhood. Though Jane's personal carelessness is an image of Linton rather than Eliza[62] her attitude to an independent career and to her fellow-women is Eliza's own. 'She did not mind what was said of her. So long as she could make a sufficient income ... do her work well and manfully... make women generally understand that they were slaves and idiots, she was content.' She accepted her choice of life 'ungainly and unlovely boy-woman that she was' because though she could not 'play pretty' neither could other women 'work and toil with her'.[63] This sense that the course she herself had chosen was for most women not a viable option is perhaps at the root of Mrs Linton's conflicting views on women's emancipation.

Though she believed in education for girls she saw an irreconcilable opposition between the responsibilities of a profession and those of motherhood. The girl who wants to enter the competitive intellectual world should dedicate herself to 'the Vestal of Knowledge'. 'We cannot combine opposites nor reconcile conflicting conditions.'[64] Her own marriage affected her burgeoning journalistic career adversely, causing a dramatic drop in her output, and a reduced range of outlets. Between 1861 and 1866 the *Athenæum*, *Literary Gazette*, and *Cornhill* were missing from her workbook; *London Society*, *Watch Tower* and a handful of pieces in *Temple Bar* (11 in all) were scarcely adequate compensation. From 97 articles in 1859 the work dwindled year on year reaching a nadir of a mere nine in 1863, all except one for her staple, *All the Year Round*. By then she had lost contact with all her periodical editors apart from Charles Dickens, to whom she had remained loyal after the controversial demise of *Household Words*, resisting Bradbury & Evans's offer to work for *Once a Week*. Nor was she producing much else in the way of literature. It was a vicious circle. Domestic cares disrupted her writing and the loss of income itself fuelled domestic conflicts.[65] Once freed of the trammells of matrimony she organized her domestic, social and professional lives with almost ruthless efficiency. Travelling in

Italy she worked without interruption from nine to three, and combined it with sight-seeing and going in society 'in the most masterly fashion' according to Beatrice Sichel.[66]

For her part Margaret Oliphant early in her life saw her writing as contributing to the family budget and ignored Mary Howitt's terrifying warning that she had lost her own babies through a defective valve in the heart partially caused by 'too much mental work on the part of the mother'.[67] But the conflict between family and professional responsibilities could be acute. Her letters frequently remark *en passant* the interruptions of domestic cares. A long letter to Blackwood enclosing some fiction and proofs of her article on Pugin, expresses anxiety about her son's accident to his arm. He is 'quite crippled by it'.[68] Years later on a journey to France with her family she sent Blackwood's successor 'a chronicle of misfortune ... to explain why my article is late'. Her son Cyril had became violently ill as they were eating in the restaurant before boarding the train. The journey was hastily abandoned; the luggage unfortunately travelled onwards.[69] Throughout the 1880s her professional life was complicated by the necessity, both for work and her ineffectual sons' health, to travel abroad with all the domestic complications that entailed, and, since she rarely travelled simply, funding these trips was itself problematic.[70]

The circumstances painted in her charming domestic picture of Sunday evening at home – her son Tiddy on the arm of her easy-chair 'driving it for a cab' as she wrote her letters, the table heaped with picture-books, and her daughter 'rather sentimental with a bad cold' reading Mrs Jameson – would not have been conducive to serious work. No wonder she envied Ruskin his power to demand uninterrupted peace, and once teasingly asked her friend Mrs Tulloch 'to come and be my wife' as her time was so broken up.[71] She acquired, as Eliza Linton did, the survival instinct. She ignored her own illnesses and disapproved of feminine invalidism.[72] Unlike *North and South*'s Mrs Shaw, widowhood had not bestowed the leisure to settle on her health as a source of anxiety.

Both Mrs Oliphant and Mrs Lynn Linton, however, were happy to cultivate the image of the domesticated lady. When Helen Black visited her in Queen Anne's Mansions, what Mrs Linton called the 'workroom' was a writing table in the 'cosy' library

> placed slantways to catch the best light commanding a beautiful view ... full south over the Surrey Hills.... Papers, reviews, and books of reference are tidily heaped up; the table is full, but in perfect

order... She is altogether a believer in method, regularity, and punctuality.

Despite the collection of books and the precision, authorship is domesticated by references to family photographs, graceful lamp and silk embroideries – cushions, chair seats and handsome fire screen not only worked by Mrs Linton's fingers but to her own designs (no painstaking copies of patterns from ladies' magazines here!).[73]

Domestication is more overt still in Mrs Oliphant's account of her own workplace. Here family life is enacted in the main arena with her own professional work existing in the wings as it were. She compares her own early experience of writing at a corner of the family table 'as if I had been making a shirt instead of writing a book' with Jane Austen's, whose 'family were half ashamed to have it known that she was not just a young lady like the others, doing her embroidery'. Her own, though proud enough of her, never thought to give her any special facilities, and even as an established professional 'all the study I have ever attained to, is the little second drawing-room of my house, with a wide opening into the other drawing-room'. A picture shows her working alcove separated only by a curtain (drawn back) and despite the substantial bookcase the furnishings and ornaments suggest a lady's sitting-room rather than a workplace.[74]

These cosy even elegant images contrast sharply with the dirt and noise of the 'masculine' newspaper office, a place dedicated to its business, yet they also imply an environment where professional work may be constantly interrupted by social and family life. Helen Black tries to fuse the two worlds for her readers. As she settles down to 'a good talk' with her hostess she is assured 'there is no immediate fear of her being disturbed by an emissary from the printers'. Mrs Tweedie's account a year later literally separates 'the feminine side', the drawing-room with its hangings and knick-knacks, from the 'masculine severity' of Mrs Linton's 'writing-room'.[75] The reality of the balancing act needed to maintain professionalism and remain a lady could be stressful. On one point Eliza Lynn and the 'brazen' Elizabeth Banks would have agreed: a good woman journalist should be prepared to take on any editor when her case was good. Eliza Linton knew

that not all are pleasant to deal with. Some bully you, even when you do your best and your article has the place of honour. They think it due to their own dignity, and a useful check on your vanity ... to cut down your presumptuous imagining that you are necessary to the paper; to make you understand that they could find a dozen as good as you, and half-a-dozen better, to take your place.[76]

In her dealings with editors she vacillated between the effusive and the forthright, according to circumstances. Even early in her career she was prepared to take risks. When Bentley delayed replying to her offer of a satire for the *Miscellany* she demanded publication or return, claiming it made a pair with a piece for another magazine.[77] She eventually placed it in the *New Monthly*, although its partner seems not to have been published. But she recognized that editors had their own share of troubles, the 'ungrammatical folk' who believe in private influence and the 'crowd of incapables' who 'think that a publisher's office is like a charitable kitchen'.[78]

Mrs Oliphant too had her battles,[79] even on occasion with John Blackwood who has been described as one whose 'methods of conveying suggestions and criticism are models in a difficult art'.[80] In 1862 she complained that his report of Lewes's criticism on an article struck her

as mighty impertinent. I don't take offence, but I think I have as much right to the due consideration of my standing and *age* in literature as if I were asserting myself in society, ... I have done as much honest work in my day as most people of my years; and patronizing approbation of the kind you told me of does not quite suit me.

She objected to being asked to alter her articles to accord with her editor's views. 'I cannot stultify myself and deny my judgment, you know, with my own hand ... Of course the final excision of it, even of the entire paper, remains always in your hands.'[81]

As established journalists they may not have had to traipse up and down the stairs of editors' offices[82] like their young sisters of the 1890s clutching their portfolios of bright ideas, in search of commissions, but they had to be constantly proactive in their correspondence with editors. The idea for Mrs Oliphant's 'Old Saloon' series was her own. She wrote to William Blackwood in 1886 suggesting

a standing article upon literature, a review of all the books of the month worth reviewing, with admixture of speculation and general comment, as would be natural, ... a regular [article], for which people would look. There is nothing of the kind anywhere ... I think the series I propose would be a popular one.

In December she pursued the idea, stressing the importance of 'a good name'. In 1894 she had a new plan 'The Looker-on', 'a sort of review of … the season, the autumn, the winter season, &c., – with a reflection of the Society and lighter morals, politics, art, and literature of the time'.[83] Journalists, particularly freelances, had to be adept at managing several things at once. Whilst on the staff of the *Morning Chronicle* Eliza Linton produced her third novel and contributed to Chambers' publications. In Paris, as *The Leader*'s correspondent, she wrote regularly for *Household Words*. *Sowing the Wind* was written while she was working for the *Saturday Review*. Mrs Oliphant was planning an article on Turner whilst under 'the most dreadful pressure of work' finishing her biography of Irving and 'snowed up with proofs'.[84] In one letter (1883) to William Blackwood she discusses the series of books she was editing for him, proposing herself as author of the last, and suggesting an essay on American books.[85] Even on their frequent journeys abroad, when research material might need to be sent by post from home, book-length projects and articles were worked on simultaneously.

Although deeply-felt personal trauma surfaced more readily in their fiction than journalism, in other respects they continually mined their experience. Mrs Oliphant wrote sketches of Nettuno, one of the places they stayed during her husband's final illness, and of Capri which she visited soon after her daughter's death.[86] 'Rome in 1877' for the *Queen* was one outcome of Mrs Linton's stay in Rome; during this European trip she was also working on a novel for serialization in the *Gentleman's Magazine*.[87] When renting a house in unfashionable Biella to promote a hotelier friend's business scheme she produced an article on the town's history (*Gentleman's Magazine* Jan/Feb 1884). Throughout her wanderings in the late 1880s 'the stream of *Queen* articles, coloured by her varying surroundings', was in full flow; 'the interruptions of travel and the discomforts of temporary lodgings were never regarded as excuses for any lapse'.[88]

When Mrs Oliphant returned to Florence in 1874 to 'revive [her] impressions of the place' for her book *The Makers of Florence* commissioned by Macmillan, she offered Blackwood articles on the subjects she was researching as 'I should not like to lose any of my material'. They duly appeared.[89] Productivity depended upon economical utilization of material, and their livelihoods depended upon their productivity. Both women were models of the Victorian work ethic. Annie Coghill considered her relative's visit to the Potteries remarkable largely because for 'a whole week she laid aside her work! Never before, and never afterwards until the illnesses of her last year forced it upon her, did she take such a spell of idleness.'[90] The number of her appear-ances in the major periodicals listed in the *Wellesley Index* easily out-classes that of other women.[91] Eliza Linton however wrote for a much greater range. When she finished writing for the *Saturday Review* – she published in 33 of the 52 numbers in 1868 – she contributed weekly to *The Queen* from the mid-1870s until her death in 1898. She learnt to write fluently, with little need for time-consuming changes. Her surviv-ing manuscripts indicate that she made only one draft of an article and alterations and additions were rare[92] but this did not imply a casual attitude to her job. She believed that

> True Success comes only by hard work, great courage in self-correction, and the most earnest and intense determination to succeed ... [a] willingness to see [one's] own short-comings and [the] wish to do well rather than to have praise. It is the whole difference between playing at work and *real* work.[93]

She told an editor 'I know that no man in the press is more "reliable" than I am for punctuality and the best work I can give. I never "scamped" a paper in my life' echoing her description of Jane Osborn who 'never "scamped her work" as she called it'.[94] Even in her last decade the predominant sense of her correspondence is constant activ-ity, whether carrying on her journalism, battling over her controversial novel *The One Too Many*, encouraging young writers, carrying out engagements as a public figure, or simply writing letters – Layard counted 2124 for 1897.

Not surprisingly such constant intellectual and physical activity caused them exhaustion. 'I am often tired to death of work and care – always work, work, whether one likes or not.' Mrs Oliphant wrote to Tulloch when commiserating on his own illness! She once claimed that spinning a novel was a great deal less stressful than researching a non-fiction book and complained of overwork, 'a whirring and whizzing in my head which has compelled me to lay it back upon a cushion and do nothing for a whole day'.[95]

Both she and Eliza Linton worked to the bitter end. Mrs Oliphant's last journey abroad, in April 1897, was to Siena to collect material for a book; on Good Friday she wrote to Blackwood promising an article on Siena and its saint, St Catherine. On her return to Windsor she fell ill this time fatally. Eliza Linton worked even when, in 1880 while she was abroad, blindness threatened. She continued her travels producing a novel *My Love!* serialized in the *Bolton Evening News*. One paper, eventually published posthumously and anonymously in *Temple Bar*, was written while '... my head is swimming, and I am almost blind'. She had been working from 9.30 until 4.30 with only twenty minutes break for luncheon.[96] When she was younger ten or eleven hours a day was not unknown.

She regarded herself as a thorough professional to the very end of her life. When in 1897 the editor of *St James Budget* reduced her weekly essays to two a month because the readership was beginning to find her repetitive, she was so annoyed that she discontinued their association forthwith. She prided herself on her ability to vary her material and style according to the journal, telling one editor that she found 'almost invariably' a paper written for one magazine was unsuited to another; each had 'a certain keynote'. Despite her powerful opinions she generally had the facility to temper them to the medium, adapting to the particular 'key'. *Punch* was one of her rare failures.[97]

Although Margaret Oliphant was less of a chameleon, she took a similar pride in professional adaptability. Writing to William Blackwood (31 October 1882) about her article for December she proposed a short story based on the legend of Glamis. Should it approach 'too nearly the supposed story' or risk offending the Strathmores 'would you prefer a New Books article, or what? Give me my orders, and I will carry them out.'[98]

As writers they had a sense of gendered persona. Eliza Linton objected to the prefix 'Miss' in advertisements for her novel; it projected an image of 'a pink faced young lady who sighs and writes sonnets, and reads novels all her life'. Margaret Oliphant discussing her ideas for 'The Words of a Believer', asked Blackwood's advice on whether the Believer should be a man or a woman, and she once sheltered behind her 'womanish style' to console her '*amour propre*' against a rejection.[99] The public images they projected were very different but they had in common that they were both personae, at variance with the perceptions of those who knew them best. The self-effacing, shy, retiring character of Mrs Oliphant's autobiography was 'markedly at odds with other people's assessments'.[100] There was at times an astringency and an hauteur in her manner to which her friends testified. Mrs Linton's public persona on the contrary seemed harsh, abrasive and cutting, while her friends invariably commented on her personal kindness and generosity.

Mrs Oliphant provides a remarkable instance of a Victorian 'Jill-of-all-trades' who was an accomplished mistress of several. Eliza Lynn Linton is a striking examplar of the conflict imposed on a woman journalist by contesting notions of a woman's rôle in Victorian society. Women who aspired to journalism needed some level of education to have any chance at all against men who in addition to good schooling had often university education and access to the world of gentlemen's clubs. But women with reasonable education came from the middle and upper classes and were therefore conditioned to be 'ladylike'. Periodicals themselves were not only the seat of the debate surrounding women's employment, its acceptable limits, and definitions of femininity, but at times exemplified it – most notably in the women's magazines. If women themselves as reviewers of novels by women sometimes found the limits of femininity unacceptably breached, how much more endangered must be the woman who sought to be a staff journalist. She had to enter, even work in, an office surrounded by men; traipse around the city on assignments in clothes that were either unsuitable for a lady or unsuitable for her job. At the beginning of her career Eliza Linton breached the boundaries of the ladylike, even shocking Dickens. By the end she was uncertain of the effects of that breach, critical of female higher education, horrified to learn to what lengths the lady journalist of the 1890s might go to pay her rent.

11
Journalism and the Novelist

George Eliot, Mrs Gaskell and others

Through the previous chapters run various threads linking nineteenth century fiction to journalism. Although a Mrs Oliphant, combining the two genres throughout her working life, was something of a rarity, many journalists tried their hands at fiction and many novelists dabbled in journalism. Fiction is not a major concern of this book. Yet the influence of periodicals upon the predominant literary genre of the century, prose fiction, was so great that this interrelationship deserves a little space in which these threads can be drawn together. It seems appropriate to close my overview of women journalists by summarizing the effects of the periodical press upon the careers of women novelists. In practical ways it operated as an outlet for the publication of fiction and the launching of novelists; in aesthetic terms it exercised pressures upon the structure, style and content of the novel. Against the background of other female novelists who contributed to periodicals, my focus here is upon the ways in which journalism affected the writing careers of two canonical writers, George Eliot and Mrs Gaskell.

Disraeli, in his Preface to the fifth edition of *Coningsby* (1850, first published 1844) noted an important cultural shift in the dissemination of ideas. Explaining that the aim of his novel was political, he confessed that he had not originally intended to 'scatter his suggestions' in fictional form, but after 'due reflection' chose that 'method which in the temper of the times, offered the best chance of influencing opinion'.[1] Fiction had established a niche for itself as a channel for argument and reform. Although the 1840s was *the* decade of the social-problem novel,[2] the popularity of the genre continued throughout the century to attract those who chose to 'scatter their suggestions' on all manner of political, economic and social issues in novels rather than pamphlets or essays. With varying levels of dexterity and flair writers like Dickens, Martineau and Caird glided between fiction, essay and leader article in pushing their causes.

The novel itself was by no means insulated from other cultural influences. By the mid-nineteenth century periodicals were a pivotal force in the literary world. They published fiction; they reviewed fiction; they debated fiction. They developed a vital rôle in the advertising and dissemination of fiction, at once creating a readership and satisfying its desire. Thus they played a key part in the professional lives of novelists, providing a major market and platform, affording publicity through their reviews, and offering a forum for critical debate in which novelists themselves participated. Finally, as we have seen, even if the job proved not quite the sinecure expected, some writers achieved a measure of power or steady income through editorships gained on the back of success in fiction.[3]

There was an interdependent if sometimes uneasy relationship between the nineteenth-century novelist and the periodical. Gissing's *New Grub Street* reveals his hatred of the worst effects of the proliferation of magazines and of would-be journalists upon literature. On the other hand Mary Braddon not only edited *Belgravia* for a decade, mobilizing it to defend her kind of fiction, but her novel *The Doctor's Wife* gives, in Sigismund Smith, a relatively sympathetic portrait of a journeyman sensation novelist, still cherishing his ambition to write a great novel whilst churning out his fiction in 'penny slices', as happy a hack as any moderately successful journalist.[4]

There were writers of more scholarly inclination than Mary Braddon, of whom Mrs Humphry Ward will stand as an example, who under financial pressure, cheerfully blended fiction-writing with essays and reviewing. By concentrating on the 'higher' journalism Mary Ward reconciled her ambitious artistic aims with the necessity to provide for the elegant lifestyle she and her spendthrift[5] husband expected, though there was always something of a conflict between her Arnoldian standards and her need for a best-seller's income. Despite her formidable record in negotiating terms at the zenith of her popularity, she was horrified on one occasion to find her agent Curtis Brown arranged for her novel to run in the States in the *Ladies' Home Journal*. This dynamic, gaudy type of popular journalism was not the kind of company in which she cared to appear.[6]

A friend criticized her first novel *Miss Bretherton* for being too intellectual, the work of 'a critic not .... a creator'.[7] Certainly by the time she turned her attention to fiction she was steeped in intellectual and critical work. Her offer to the *Manchester Guardian* of a weekly 'Foreign Table Talk' article drawing on the French, German, Spanish and Italian press had been accepted; she used her husband's influence to get more such work on the *Times;* she wrote on politics for the *Oxford Chronicle*; she contributed sporadically to other journals. John Morley thought so highly of her that when he took over the reins at *Macmillan's* in 1883 she was offered a monthly literary article – a lively, readable 'causerie' – which he predicted would become 'as marked a feature in our world, as Ste Beuve was to France'.[8] Although feeling unable to undertake this additional commitment, she nevertheless, in the space of two years, wrote for him well over a dozen such pieces on European literature.

The one thing few nineteenth-century novelists could afford to do with the periodical press was to ignore it. In the initial stages of their career most, far from despising it, were desperately keen to obtain the entrée. Many a female novelist had her first published efforts within the pages of magazines and newspapers. Isabella Banks was only 16 when the *Manchester Guardian* took her poem 'A Dying Girl to her Mother', Pearl Craigie at nine even younger when a Congregationalist magazine *Fountain* accepted her stories. Mrs Annie Hector began with sketches for the *Family Herald*, George Eliot with reviews for the *Coventry Herald* (though by the time her first fiction appeared in *Blackwood's* she had translated important German works and effectively edited the *Westminster*). Bertha Leith-Adams, as an admirer of Dickens, took her first tale to *All the Year Round*, so launching both her long association with that journal and her career in fiction. EE Nesbit's first story was printed in the *Sunday Magazine*; Mrs Henry Wood's early fiction in the likes of *Bentley's* and *Ainsworth's;* Braddon's in Maxwell's serial publications. Mrs Gaskell's apprentice work, a poetic sketch, saw the light of day in *Blackwood's* and her early prose fiction in *Howitt's Journal*. One could go on.

First attempts were often sent in anonymously; luckier girls could draw on family connections. Periodicals aided the process of patronage as well as that of writing in multiple genres. Carefully manipulated, anonymity and pseudonymity provided decent cover for the dominance of one writer within a number, and for authorial experimentation. Mrs Wood kept secret her authorship of *Argosy*'s Johnny Ludlow stories over many years. Marian Evans, the intellectual assistant editor of the *Westminster*, when she turned to fiction, revelled in the protection which the George Eliot persona afforded. It was also undoubtedly easier for influential relatives to slip an untried protegée alongside existing well-known 'names' within the pages of a monthly than to persuade a publisher to shoulder the risk of volume publication. Thackeray, Anne Ritchie's father, obtained his publisher's consent to print her *Story of Elizabeth* in the *Cornhill* which he was editing; Rhoda Broughton did not even need an outsider's permission when her uncle Sheridan Le Fanu serialized *her* first novel *Not Wisely but Too Well* in his *Dublin University Magazine*.

Such were indeed blest. The heroine of Charlotte Riddell's novel *The Rich Husband* represents a more depressing, and one suspects more common, experience. Judith's first of many rejections comes from the editor of *The British Lion* a man who went about the world 'lacerating the hearts of tender young authors, with an indescribable show of kindness and painful adherence to truth. ... If an author succeeded, Mr. Kearn's "hints" were, of course, the basis of his success. If an author failed, he had either neglected Mr Kearn's timely counsels, or else forgotten Mr Kearn's advice to him to abandon literature altogether.' While Judith, after reading every word of the two-and-a-half page letter, throws the missive scornfully on the fire to savour the day when, with two published works to her credit, she can beard him in his grubby den,[9] in the real world not all brutal rejections were so discarded. Isabella Mayo kept for years the long letter 'blotted by the tears with which I read it' which her 'kind critic' Tom Hood junior, sent to the aspiring nineteen-year-old. In refusing the poetry which she hoped would earn some money, he too claimed to 'state his candid opinion'; he too urged her to abandon any idea of a literary career as a livelihood. It must have been scant comfort at the time that he noted the 'great natural merit' of her writing, suggesting that with the leisure to develop her skills – 'Is there no more hopeful way of making money to be found?' – 'in ten years' time .... I should not be astonished to see your poems making a mark'. Fortunately she had the encouragement of Mrs Hall – 'Why, editors don't write long letters like that to everybody!' – who proposed a more practicable three years' writing only for her own 'pleasure and improvement'. During this time Miss Fyvie widened her experience of life and turned her energies to fiction.[10]

Periodicals offered more than an opening to beginners; they provided an increasingly important outlet for fiction which even popular authors needed to exploit. In the earlier decades Catherine Gore's work appeared in such magazines as *Bentley's* and *Tait's*; Julia Pardoe in the *Ladies' Cabinet*.[11] The prolific Mrs Craik turned out fiction and nonfiction for a raft of titles – *Bentley's, Cornhill, Dublin University Magazine, Fraser's, Longman's, Nineteenth Century, Saint Paul's, Macmillan's,*

Chambers', Good Words, Harper's Bazaar. Blackwoods and Bentley had established journals in the early decades but during the 1860s practically every important publisher of fiction set up an associated magazine. They could tie in the serial payment to authors with the volume publication, and moreover could market the book publication on the back of the magazine. John Sutherland argues convincingly that magazines actually increased the authors' market. Despite George Eliot's fears that her library borrowings would haemorrhage in the wake of magazine serialization the reality was 'that readers were swept up rather than away'.[12]

Children's and girl's magazines offered further openings. The *Girl's Own Paper* for instance carried stories by Isabella Fyvie Mayo and articles by the blind novelist, Alice King.[13] Rosa Nouchette Carey who served on its staff emulated the pattern of the adult magazines by publishing several works in six month serial form in that paper prior to the volume issue.[14] By the end of the century newspapers commonly published fiction. Like the penny women's papers which the highly productive journalist LT Meade never scorned[15] such a market attracted woman keen to earn their bread and butter in something more appealing than teaching. But it was not the place for anyone who aspired to be the next George Eliot. Frances Low, advising would-be writers, quotes a woman earning between £300 and £400 a year producing stories, novelettes and fiction for newspapers: One should aim at the intellectual level of 'the average fairly intelligent shop girl' though – encouraging thought! – 'many other women might read it'. Ella Hepworth Dixon's novel points up the paradox of the public's enjoyment of strong meat and hearty appetite for scandal in its *news* with its insistence upon 'wholesome' happy-ending fiction. As an editor explains to the puzzled heroine 'Novels are -er-well-novels. The British public doesn't expect them to be life'.[16]

Women reliant upon writing to support their families could find it a constant, unequal, battle. Though fiction *could* pay well even popular novelists were often grateful for a Civil List pension or Literary Fund grant.[17] So tough had been Charlotte Riddell's life that the ever-optimistic Helen Black in her interview found it quite impossible to ignore the 'early struggles, heavy burdens, severe trials' she suffered. For a Charlotte Riddell 'looking about me for every five-pound note I could get' anything a secondary market could offer would have been a valuable supplement to a precarious income.[18] For a novelist like Mrs Smythies, 'neither strikingly talented like George Eliot, nor fortunately married like Mrs Gaskell', as she poured out serial fiction for

Cassell's, The London Journal and the *Ladies' Treasury* the opportunity to sell on the book copyright after serialization in the *Journal* must have been irresistible.[19] Mary Ward and Marian Evans travelled from journalism to fiction. The journey could be reversed. The close connection between periodical and book publishing of fiction, by providing the novelist with experience of tailoring her work to the magazine market, opened up the possibility of selling other wares, like Mayo's 'reviews and strictly journalistic articles'.[20] The best-selling novelist Marie de la Ramée ('Ouida') having begun with fiction in Harrison Ainsworth's journals became a special contributor to the *Whitehall Review* in the 1880s. When her style of three-decker novel lost favour she could continue to earn something by essay-writing[21] for journals like the *Fortnightly* and *Nineteenth Century*. To someone as desperate as Mrs Smythies, the commission of a series of papers on conduct and etiquette for the *Ladies' Treasury* would have been a god-send.[22]

Novel-writing for periodicals was certainly not an unmixed blessing. It could be grinding work. The image of Isabella Banks, toiling to pay off debts by scribbling night after night into the early hours as she kept a weekly and a monthly supplied simultaneously with separate serials, is scarcely more enticing a picture than Mrs Riddell's other Grub Street in *A Struggle for Fame*.[23] Moreover there were always financial and other risks. Isabella Mayo was to regret staying loyal to Strahan by turning down Cassell's liberal offer for her next serial. Disregarding the advice of experienced friends, until Strahan actually left the firm, from the moment he accepted her *Occupations of a Retired Life* with a promise to take whatever else she chose to send, she worked exclusively for his magazines. She learnt the hard way that such tight arrangements were unwise. 'They tend to set a writer into a groove. Further, they put the writer at great practical disadvantage when they come to an end.'[24]

The conditions of the copyright vested in journal publishers could cause all kinds of complications. Mrs Gaskell, who had become astutely business-like in dealings with her book publishers,[25] nevertheless found pitfalls when attempting to negotiate to her own advantage between the two forms of publication. She was very disconcerted by Dickens's (not unreasonable) refusal to let *North and South* go to America for volume publication while it still ran in *Household Words*, lest the story resurface in England before the serial version finished. The same possibility returned to haunt her with *Lois the Witch*. She was partway through when she was caught up in the tangle of Dickens's quarrel with Bradbury and Evans. *Household Words* had already paid her £40 for three stories; two had been published; *Lois* was to have been the third. But *Lois* was going to be too long for one number and she didn't think it would stand weekly splitting; she preferred to publish it 'entire' in America. Disturbed by the news of the impending launch of *All The Year Round* with its attendant uncertainties she wanted to return the advance but to whom? Might Wills who had moved to Dickens's new magazine insist on publishing it somehow and spoil her plans? He did.[26]

There were other ways in which magazine publication might conflict with one's plans. Mrs Oliphant found herself battling with the *Graphic* over republication rights of her life of Queen Victoria. She intended to re-use it in a book for Cassell's and rescued it just in the nick of time (with Craik's assistance) from the paper's publishers who had it already in type for 'a small octavo volume'. They kept the right for one reprint as a *Graphic* number. Luckily the Victoria material was to be only a small part of her new book so 'the matter is cleared up – rather to my disadvantage but not so much as I at first thought'.[27] The unhappy Mrs Smythies suffered much more harshly following the bankruptcy of Stiff, publisher of the *London Journal*. Having enjoyed success with one of her serials he valued her next one so much that rather than let the new owners inherit it he destroyed the block and stole her manuscript. With two-thirds gone missing the new proprietor was unable to honour the commitment. She lost both her eight guineas a week and her potential volume copyright payment.[28]

The effect of reviews upon book sales either directly or through boosting the demand at libraries was well recognized by novelists and their friends. Some under cover of anonymity shamelessly puffed work, sometimes on a reciprocal basis, with little regard for the critical objectivity which *Blackwood's* claimed for the policy of anonymity. From her perspective as a newly-emerging novelist in the late 1850s, George Eliot thought current reviewing in the monthlies and weeklies 'nauseating' and castigated their writers for incompetence and unscrupulous assessments.[29] Thirty years earlier Mary Howitt wondered how as 'unknowns' she and William had ever gained a favourable notice. 'In many instances a book is reviewed which has never been read or even seen externally.'[30] There was, as we have seen, overt opposition to such unprofessionalism notably by Charles Dilke who campaigned openly through the columns of his *Athenæum* against the pernicious practice of puffing.[31] Nor was the power of the reviewer always left unchallenged by his victims. Mary Braddon was not alone in refusing to ignore what she believed to be unfair criticism of her work; 'The Wild Irish Girl' Lady Morgan had long before used periodicals to counter attacks on her fiction in the Tory reviews.

Serialization in periodicals affected the novel genre even more than the reviews and critical debates they generated. One could go so far as to say that the nineteenth-century novel would not have developed as it did without the intervention of the numerous journals which disseminated it. Specifically the practice of serial publication in weeklies and monthlies created its own artistic and commercial criteria for success and its own constraints upon the genre, bringing about a different kind of relationship with readers, one much more interactive than volume publication invited. The influence of readers was more powerful than one might imagine. They could, and did, flex their collective muscles by dropping a paper if the serial bored them. As Braddon and Dickens had discovered they let editors and authors know what they liked. Correspondence columns even afforded a small input into critical discussion.[32]

As serialization established itself as fundamental to a journal's commercial success so it subtly affected the novel's structure. Earlier magazines had sometimes run fiction in parts. By the 1850s improvements in printing technology and – courtesy of the railways – in distribution, neatly dovetailing into a market burgeoning as literacy spread, were together about to result in an explosion of novel serialization in the weeklies and monthlies. Dickens, whose fictional art grew from his journalistic experience, was a major mover in this field. The *Publishers' Circular* of 1860, remarking that readers now demanded serialized fiction 'as an indispensable feature of their weekly literary entertainments', commented on his innovatory contribution to the fashion.[33] By the mid-1880s even literary monthlies liked their sensation and illustrated journals wanted fiction that provided subjects for dramatic illustration.[34]

The crowd-puller in *All the Year Round* was its serialized novel, and Dickens understood the requirements of weekly parts as well as Braddon understood her monthly. For 'that specially trying mode of publication' he told a would-be contributor, the plan of the chapters, the way in which characters were introduced, the principal settings and 'the progress of the interest' all needed particular care since 'the thing has to be planned for presentation in fragments, and yet for afterwards fusing together as an uninterrupted whole'.[35] Mrs Brookfield, was advised to study *A Tale of Two Cities* or *The Woman in White* as exemplars. Collins's novel, the archetype of the emergent sub-genre of sensation fiction, was ideally suited to fragmentation. Mrs Oliphant's review reflects the connection between the novel's artistry and its form of publication. Its merits, a plot 'astute and deeply-laid' yet free of the 'machinery of miracle', the power Fosco exercises over the reader, Collins's reticent handling of dramatic events, are those that made it such an effective weekly serial, but Oliphant warned that less skilful imitators would coarsen the genre. The aesthetic and moral dangers of sensation fiction were the direct consequence of the 'violent stimulant of ... *weekly* publication, with its necessity for frequent and rapid recurrence of piquant situation and startling incident'.[36]

In Collins's hands the task of serial-writing seemed as deceptively smooth as Count Fosco himself. But it was not easy. In particular the need to keep within the wordage allocated to each portion could as Dickens said of writing *Hard Times* be 'CRUSHING'. More expansive writers like Mrs Gaskell found it intolerable. With *North and South* 'Every page was grudged me', she complained to Mrs Jameson, so that the end was 'huddled & hurried up, especially in the rapidity with which the sudden death of Mr Bell, succeeds to the sudden death of Mr Hale. But what could I do?' Her answer was to overwrite for Dickens – to his annoyance – then, having weighed the merits of modest alterations or going for more substantive rewriting, to insert two extra chapters and expand others for the volume. This spaced out the deaths and allowed other improvements to the narrative.[37]

Her strengths as a novelist did not lend themselves easily to the serial format. She could manage high drama on a small scale. Her novella *Lois the Witch*, despite her own depreciation of it as too melodramatic,[38] builds its sense of physical claustrophobia and screws its psychological tension towards a powerful climax with great economy. In her novels she preferred a leisured pace at which to establish realistic settings within which characters emerged through a myriad little social details. It was not just the compression she disliked. The practicalities inherent in magazine publication irritated. With *Wives and Daughters* she had to write to Smith for help as she had neither manuscript nor the *Cornhill* and 'had forgotten all the names'.[39] When she came to write *Cranford* she had already disposed of a character she now wanted to develop. The original idea was just *one* paper for *Household Words* so Captain Brown was killed off 'very much against my will'.[40] Had he survived, the kingdom of the Amazons would have been rather different. Having accepted Dickens's offer to contribute to its first issue, she followed with other contributions, and subsequently published in major British and American journals, but ultimately she disliked journalism. Though a useful outlet for potboilers it was not her publishing métier. She once declined to write essays for a new periodical on the grounds that what she had done before was as a mark of respect to Mr Dickens, and she refused Dickens's own generous offer for another serial.[41]

Yet these despised forays into Grub Street contributed to the work of her maturity. In pieces such as 'Company Manners', 'French Life' and 'Cumberland Sheep-shearers' she writes as the sharp-eyed reporter observing different customs and nuances of social behaviour; in others ('An Accursed Race') as an amateur social historian. Although far removed from the women interviewers of the 1890s, her sympathetic manner drew people out, and she was quite capable of engineering an interview with a Parisian *lionne* ('French Life'). Her observations then surfaced in her fiction. Mrs Gibson's social pretensions, the small proofs of her emphasis on elegance not ease, like the contrasting manifestations of hospitality in *North and South*, had been foreshadowed in the advice to hostesses in 'Company Manners'. 'The Last Generation in England' anticipated much of the material in the early chapters of *Cranford*.[42] At a superficial level *Cranford* seems to spring from a similar real-life source. Early commentators assiduously identified Cranford streets and dwellings with actual Knutsford locations and matched characters with their 'originals'.[43] She herself admitted to Ruskin that she had seen the cow in the grey flannel jacket and knew the cat that swallowed the cream. Yet she considered a real-life anecdote she recounted to amuse Ruskin's mother 'too ridiculous' to be believed, and dared not put it into *Cranford*. *Cranford* is not social history but essentially an imaginative and selective recreation. Unlike history it must *appear* credible. As Mary Mitford drew on her personal letters for the material of *Our Village* and George Eliot cannibalized her *Westminster* essays and *Coventry Herald* reviews,[44] so Elizabeth Gaskell reworked her observations and anecdotes into her mature fiction.[45] Periodicals at least provided the artist with her preliminary sketchpad.

They played a much more significant part in shaping George Eliot's career. In some ways, once she had escaped the claustrophobic world of her immediate family into the intellectual circles opened to her by the Brays, her entry into the literary world was not untypical in its pattern of introductions and networking. Translations led to articles, and articles to London and the *Westminster*. With Chapman's purchase of the journal she became his assistant. Under her guiding hand the review won notice and praise, but Chapman's financial position was precarious.[46] Outside contributors were comparatively well-rewarded; authors' payments in 1853 were running at £250 each issue despite a small print-run, and articles were sometimes subsidized by well-wishers.[47] Marian, however, was virtually working for nothing.[48] Fiction was to prove much more lucrative.

Her art may have flourished in a mental greenhouse but the earth had been tilled on the drearier wastes of the editor's table. Spending a Saturday afternoon reading a bundle of material on taxation, with the interruption of a request for a quick opinion on a thick German tome, or undertaking what even Chapman termed the 'laborious and difficult' task of reducing a 100-page article on prison discipline to a third of its length[49] was hardly congenial. But judicious cutting and pruning exercised her linguistic skills, and her heavy eclectic reading programme formed the intellectual groundwork of her novels. Unlike Mrs Gaskell, Marian Evans knew firsthand something of the realities of publishing. The *Westminster* was aimed at a very different audience from that of *Household Words*, but the editor's responsibility was still to please. Her letters reveal her concerns. A 'rich number' would provide a 'fortnight's reading and thought'; another will be 'stunning' superior to its predecessor 'in variety and general interest'; then she is 'ready to tear her hair with disappointment' at a third. Lewes's review of *Villette* and *Ruth* disappointed, one article was 50 per cent over-written, a third had been paid for but had had to be burnt. In the event it turned out not quite as bad as she feared.[50] One senses the enormous relief as, tactfully deflecting Bessie's request for something for the *English Woman's Journal*, she confided that she had altogether done with writing articles. She had discovered her true vocation lay elsewhere.[51]

Yet her substantial journalistic background on the reviews did affect the way in which she approached her new career as a novelist. She was sure of her ground as to what her readers deserved. She set the pattern for her editorship with her first issue. She could argue with Chapman over what she considered inept commissioning.[52] With her experience of copy-editing and proof-reading and understanding of the technical side of publishing she could never have replied as Mary Ward did to Jane Courtney. It was from Eliot's own confidence as an editor, able to see her stories 'in some degree from your point of view as well as my own', that as an apprentice novelist she could face John Blackwood and defend the darker touches in her work.[53] Artistically she was to move far from those early days when she and Eliza Lynn were journalists together, but she had already set her mark on the English world of letters, and her experience at its coal-face had marked her too.

Afterword

As I read their memoirs, letters and self-revelatory articles I identified with my subjects – the thrill of one's words in print, the sense of the audience, scuttling behind a pseudonym, organizing domestic life, agonizing over managing a career. I wish I had known more of my illustrious predecessors when I began in journalism years ago; they would have inspired me.

My original idea of a closing word was a brief consideration of how these women's influence has been felt in the twentieth century upon those who followed in their footsteps. I intended drawing on twentieth century sources like the professional associations and the training institutions. My own Oxford college produced an impressive stream of print and broadcasting female journalists, whose arms might be twisted for opinions. There are modern academic studies of the press. Older generations of women have left their recollections. Mary Stott for one, whom I met when I was a rookie journalist, and who impressed me by her sceptical, probing questions at a dishwasher demonstration, has written a thought-provoking retrospective.[1] In the end I followed none of these tracks. No time, no space.

So this is just an off-the-cuff personal memory of journalism as I found it in the late 1950s. Certain journalistic jobs were still not generally considered suitable for women. The editor who eventually appointed me as a graduate trainee told me at a 'speculative' interview he would not want his own daughter to be a newspaper journalist. His provincial evening paper was in other respects nearer to the newspaper world of 1900 than of 2000. The hot-metal press was still in use. The world of the compositors, printers and packers was an essentially masculine one. There were male journalists who began as copy-boys. Indeed copy-boys were still very much in evidence, though copy was also shuttled mechanically around the building – shades of those pneumatic tubes! We talked of 'flimsies' and dreaded seeing our work quite literally 'spiked'.

There were only three other women journalists on that paper when I joined, two of whom for quite different reasons were unusual, one because she was regarded as a first-class reporter sent out to cover dockyard disputes and court cases, the other because she actually *had* started her newspaper career as the editor's secretary. I never saw a woman sub. For women the 'clothes question' was still fraught. My expensive new coat and high-heeled shoes might have to take me from a slum-dwelling interview to a cocktail party all in a day. There were occasions when a hat was *de rigeur*. In one respect we were certainly worse off than the occupants of the new *Times* building of the 1880s where each man had the luxury of his own cloakroom compartment and coat-peg. The dirty mackintosh and my mohair coat jostled for space on communal stands. Computers were an esoteric joke. We may have telephoned rather than telegraphed our copy, though my husband, who worked in the same building, recalls in the mid-1950s sending his race reports word by word on telegram forms from the course and actually subbing telegrams in the office.

Feminists might question how far women journalists have advanced the narrower feminist agenda, yet clearly some things have changed. In my book proposal I said that the profession in the twentieth century was 'open to women'. This was queried. I suppose it depends on one's interpretation of 'open'. But women enter journalism today in substantial numbers and over the past half century have been increasingly evident – particularly perhaps in magazine and broadcasting journalism at fairly senior levels. The 'glass ceiling' no doubt operates, but where are the professions – academia is no exception! – where it does not? I recall in connection with this noting from my daily paper at the end of August 1995 that a certain Amanda Platell, Mirror Group's director of marketing, had been appointed managing director of the *Independent* and its sister Sunday paper. As I write this she is no longer a power on the press but managing publicity for the leader of our parliamentary opposition. What does that prove? That things change swiftly in the press, for women as for men, in this century as in the last.

Geraldine Jewsbury exemplifies in her response to Carlyle's criticism of one of her articles the pragmatic approach of so many nineteenth-century women journalists. 'All things in this world are done like Mosaic work, by pin-points of endeavour – each looks of no use in itself' adding that 'an individual attempt at a conclusion, however honestly meant, always does look impotent to one always dwelling in large, broad, general principles'.[2] My work for this book has proceeded very much along these lines, mosaic-fashion, collecting scattered slips of information, sorting and sifting, drawing like colours together. There will no doubt be pieces missing, and parts of the picture remain more shadowy than others. As with all mosaics the pieces might have been arranged differently. As with what are, in my view at least, the best archaeological reconstructions the picture is still left incomplete. Yet it will be I hope of use to others, whether like Carlyle they are mapping out in 'large, broad, general principles' or, like Mrs Lankester, peering down the microscope at that scarlet drop of life.

Select Biographical Appendix

This contains brief biographical information, drawn from a variety of sources, on 100 women mentioned in this book. The intention is to provide a handy quick reference. It makes no claim to be comprehensive but includes the major figures dealt with, apart from novelists whose involvement in journalism was relatively insignificant, and others selected to give coverage across the century and across the range of journalistic activities. I have deliberately included a few figures, even when I have so far very limited information on them, because of their distinctive journalistic contribution and because they rarely appear in standard reference works. The distinguishing feature of my listing is that it foregrounds involvement in journalism.

Allingham, Helen (Paterson) 1848–1926 Illustrator In 1870 began 'drawing on wood' for *Once a Week, Cornhill, Aunt Judy's* and other magazines. Joined staff of *The Graphic* where according to an 1880s biographical directory 'her vigorous drawing and excellent composition soon attracted attention'. Mentioned in Hatton and Fox Bourne in connection with this paper.

Other work: Watercolorist particularly rural scenes, featuring cottages, children and gardens. Portrait painter. Persuaded Tennyson and Carlyle to sit for her. 'Your wife is the *only* person who has made a successful portrait of me' Carlyle told her husband. Her work was admired by Ruskin.

Of Unitarian stock, she numbered several ministers among her relatives. Educated Unitarian school for girls (founded by her maternal grandmother Sarah Smith Herford), School of Design, Birmingham, Female School of Art and Royal Academy, London. Married William Allingham, the poet and diarist, in 1874, the year he became editor of *Fraser's Magazine*. In the late 1880s she worked alongside Kate Greenaway for a period.

Aria Mrs. *Fin de siècle*, early twentieth-century highly successful fashion writer and columnist. Wrote for *Queen, Lady's Pictorial, Gentlewoman, Hearth and Home, Englishwoman, Daily Chronicle* and others. From all accounts she was a witty and lively hostess.

Austin, Sarah (Taylor) 1793–1867, b Norwich d Surrey, Weybridge. Periodical contributor and reviewer. One of the small number of women of her time to contribute to the *Edinburgh, British and Foreign, Foreign Quarterly* reviews. Began writing for the *Athenæum*, in 1834, contributing intermittently over many years, particularly on French and German literature, on which she wrote with authority. Lived for some time in Germany and was one of Dilke's foreign correspondents.

Other work: Translator.

Her husband John was a well-known jurist, her daughter later Lady Lucie Duff Gordon, a travel writer.

Baron-Wilson Margaret, Mrs Cornwell (Harries) fl 1834–50, Editor women's magazines. She was an energetic and enterprising editor who successfully ran the *New Monthly Belle Assemblée* after editing its predecessors the *Penny Belle Assemblée* (1833), the *Weekly BA* (1834) *La Ninon* (1832–3)

Other work: Poet

Her husband was a wealthy and well-known London solicitor.

Becker, Lydia Ernestine 1827–90 Founder-editor of the *Woman's Suffrage Journal* (published by Society for Women's Suffrage) from 1870 until her death in 1890. Active in the Manchester suffrage movement, but also became attached to the Langham Place group.

Beer, Rachel (Mrs Frederick) fl 1890s Only woman to edit two major nationals concurrently (*Observer, Sunday Times*). Her husband had a proprietary interest in the *Observer*. Her leaders in the *Sunday Times* called 'The World's Work' were described as 'a platform for her thoughts and ideals'. Member of Institute of Journalists. Subscribing member of the Society of Women Journalists, where she was listed as 'of the *Sunday Times*'.

Beeton, Isabella Mary (Mayson) 1836–65 b London d Greenhithe, Kent. Women's magazine editor, journalist. Married publisher Samuel Orchart Beeton in 1856. Shortly afterwards began writing for his innovative *Englishwoman's Domestic Magazine*, eventually becoming editor. Worked also on his *Queen* and helped plan *Young Englishwoman* launched in 1864, the year before her death from puerperal fever following the birth of her fourth son, Mayson. As fashion editor she, with Sam, launched the first paper patterns published in Britain.

Other work: Cookery writer. Her cookery and domestic columns for *EDM* led to her best-selling *Household Management*, the bible of the Victorian kitchen.

Following the death of her father, Rev John Mayson, her mother married Henry Dorling, widower and clerk of the course at Epsom, where Isabella helped her grandmother look after the extended family of Dorling and Mayson siblings in the Grand Stand. Two of Isabella's children died very young. Mayson became a journalist, special correspondent for Northcliffe's *Daily Mail*.

Belloc, Bessie Raynor (Parkes) 1829–1925. Founder editor of pioneer feminist journal, the *English Woman's Journal* (1858–64). Briefly edited its forerunner, the *Waverley*, and another short-lived periodical the *Alexandra Magazine* which absorbed *EWJ*. Began journalistic career writing for local newspapers and radical journals. Also published in *Good Words* and *The Month*.

Other Work: Poet. With Barbara Bodichon, her great childhood friend, was a founder of the women's activist group based in Langham Place, but in later years withdrew from active involvement in the suffrage campaigns etc.

Born into a family of reforming sympathies, her father being a Unitarian Birmingham solicitor and friend of Mill and Bentham, and her maternal grandfather, Joseph Priestley. Converted to Catholicism, partly because of her interest in the social work of Catholic nuns. Married Louis Belloc who died suddenly after only five years of marriage. Their children were the writers Hilaire and Marie Belloc-Lowndes.

Belloc-Lowndes, Marie Adelaide (Belloc) 1868–1947 b France d Eversley Cross. For a period *Review of Reviews'* office manager. Between 1889 and 1895 wrote for *Pall Mall Gazette*. WT Stead gave her her first major writing job in 1888 helping with guide to Paris Exhibition of 1889. During the 1890s travelled unchaperoned over England and France interviewing for *PMG* and others. In the 1890s ran training courses for members of Society of Women Journalists.

Other work: Fiction

Daughter of Bessie Parkes, sister of Hilaire Belloc.

Besant, Annie (Wood) 1847–1933 b London d India in Adyar near Madras. From 1874–85 co-editor and proprietor with Charles Bradlaugh of the *National Reformer* for which she wrote a weekly column under the pseudonym 'Ajax'. She subsequently founded the Law and Liberty League and with WT Stead, whom she addressed in correspondence as 'Dear Sir Galahad', edited its journal *Link*. Contributor to the *Westminster* and *Pall Mall Gazette*.

Other work: Writer on religious issues. Social and political activist. Helped organize the 1888 match-girls strike. Active in local government, serving on the London School Board. She had wide interests. President of the Theosophical Society from 1901–33. Advocate of Indian independence.

Her parents were of Irish extraction but her father died when she was a small child. Her marriage in 1867 to a brother of writer Walter Besant, the Rev. Frank Besant, was an unhappy one. They separated in 1873 and she eventually lost custody of her children through her free-thinking views and association with Bradlaugh. She was tried and convicted for publishing a pamphlet advocating birth control. Despite her religious views Cardinal Manning apparently admired her.

Betham-Edwards, Matilda Barbara 1836–1919 b Westerfield, Suffolk d Hastings, Sussex. Periodical Essayist. Specialized in articles on French life. Published in *Good Words*, *Fraser's* etc.

Other work: Travel writer. Novelist.

Childhood was spent on her parents' farm in the country and she attended school for only a short period. She had however access to her father's library and came from a family with literary and scholarly interests. Her aunt was the poet Mary Matilda Betham, and Amelia Blandford Edwards her cousin. Lived in Germany for a period. Travelled in France, Spain and Algeria with Barbara Bodichon, and attributed to Eugene Bodichon her abiding interest in France. She avoided political and feminist issues in her writings, though she was apparently a republican and Home Ruler. She was honoured by the French government in 1891 in recognition of her writings on France.

Billington Mary F. fl Turn-of century twentieth-century reporter. Also worked as a descriptive writer for the *Daily Telegraph*, covering major public events of the period. Career began in the provinces. Contributor to *Pearson's Magazine*, *Merry England*. Staff correspondent on both *Daily Graphic* and *Echo*. With Frances Low trained female journalists.

Black, Clementina (Patten) 1853–1922 Contributor particularly on women's issues to *Fortnightly R Woman, Young Woman, Contemporary, Nineteenth Century; National, New Athenæum, Bookman, Common Cause, Economic Journal, Englishwoman, English Illustrated Magazine, Illustrated London News, Longman's Magazine, Monthly Packet, Spectator, Temple Bar, Women's Industrial News, Woman's World, Daily Record*.

Other Work: Novelist. Activist: founder Women's Trade Union Association; co-organizer match-girls' strike with Annie Besant; founder member Labour Party.

Father supported her aspirations. She took early responsibility for the family because her mother spent much time nursing her chronically ill father. On mother's death she tried teaching but, dissatisfied, moved to London with sisters to earn a living writing.

Blackburn, Helen 1842–1903 b County Kerry d Westminster. Sole editor of the *Englishwoman's Review* 1881–1890, then assisted by Antoinette Mackenzie until 1903.

Other work: Actively involved in the Suffrage movement and its societies. Author of *A Handbook for Women engaged in Social and Political Work* (1881).

Her father was a civil engineer. She came to London in 1859.

Blessington, Countess of (Marguerite Power) 1789–1849 b Clonmel Tipperary, d Paris. In early 1830s briefly she contributed lively gossip column to *Daily News*. Editor from 1834 *The Book of Beauty*, from 1841 *Keepsake*. Contributed to, among other papers, *New Monthly Magazine* which published 'Conversations with Lord Byron'.

Other Work: Novelist; important salon hostess.

Her father was a small Irish landowner and spendthrift, among whose ill-starred ventures was a newspaper. She and the Earl of Blessington, her second husband, lived so extravagantly that despite his great wealth he died in relatively poor circumstances. She then lived with Count d'Orsay (who had been married to her stepdaughter) re-establishing her salon at Gore House, London. On her eventual bankruptcy they fled to Paris, where she died shortly afterwards.

Bodichon, Barbara (Leigh Smith) 1827–91 b Wathington, Sussex d Scalands Gate, Sussex. Founder of the early feminist *English Woman's Journal*, for which she put up the capital and to which she contributed articles on issues such as women's property rights, education and employment. Began her journalistic work writing articles for newspapers.

Other Work: Artist. Feminist activist. Founded the innovative Portman Hall School. Founder of the Langham Place group. Pamphleteer on women's issues. Early campaigner for the Married Women's Property Act and a major mover in the establishment of the Women's Suffrage Committee. With Emily Davies helped establish Girton College, Cambridge, to which she left the proceeds of the sale of her paintings.

She was the illegitimate daughter of the radical Norwich MP Benjamin Smith and a milliner Anne Longden, who died when she was a child. Florence Nightingale was a cousin. From her father she had an annual income of £300 settled on her when she came of age. Studied at the newly-founded Bedford Square Ladies' College. She considered a permanent relationship with the publisher Chapman, but following her father's disapproval ended it. In 1857 married Eugene Bodichon whom she met in Algiers, after which she divided her time between England, where she had a beautiful country home, Scalands, and Algeria. Her wide circle of friends included Anna Jameson, Mary Howitt and George Eliot apart from other feminists of her own generation.

Boucherett, Emilia Jessie 1825–1905 b Market Rasen. Editor the *Englishwoman's Review* 1866–70. She revived its forerunner the *English Woman's Journal* in 1865 changing its name and helping to finance the relaunch. She came into contact with the Langham Place Group after being inspired by an article by Harriet Martineau in the *Edinburgh* and having seen the *EWJ*. Contributor to the *Edinburgh* and *Contemporary* reviews particularly on women's issues.

Other work: Writer on issues of women and employment. Founded Society for Promoting the Employment of Women. Drafted with Emily Davies and Barbara Bodichon the suffrage petition presented to Parliament in 1865.

Her father was High Sheriff of Lincolnshire. She was educated at a Ladies' School and subsequently, until she went to London, helped run a dispensary and cottage hospital in her home town.

Braddon, Mary Elizabeth (later Maxwell) 1835–1915 b London d Richmond, Surrey. Editor of *Belgravia*, 1867–1876. She gained editorial experience as assistant to Mrs Samuel Carter Hall on *St. James's Magazine*, worked with Sala on *Temple Bar*, and edited the Christmas annual *The Mistletoe Bough*, all of which were owned by her lover (later husband) John Maxwell. Her sensation fiction was the staple of *Belgravia* and her work also appeared in *Punch*, the *World*, *Figaro* etc.

Other work: Actress. Fiction. One of the great exponents of the sensation novel genre, which she defended in *Belgravia* and in her portrait of Sigismund Smith in *The Doctor's Wife* (1864). Pseudonyms: Babington White, Ada Buisson.

Father a solicitor who abandoned his family whilst Mary was a child. For a while she worked as an actress. She was able to marry publisher John Maxwell only after she had borne him five children while his wife was living, though confined to a lunatic asylum.

Browne, Matilda fl. 1860s onwards. Fashion writer, eventually editor of the *Englishwoman's Domestic Magazine*. Her Silkworm's 'Spinnings in Town' was a lively column in *EDM* of which she became fashion editor after Isabella's death. She had been a friend of both Beetons and went with Sam to Ward Lock when they took over his company because of debts 18 months later. In later years was editor of *Myra's Journal* and *Sylvia's Journal*.

Busk Mary Margaret (Blair) 1779–1863. Translator and essayist. Regular contributor through 1830s to *Foreign Quarterly Review*. Also wrote for *Blackwood's Magazine, London, Westminster Review, Athenæum*. Her main subjects were European literature, history and art.

Other work: wrote for Society for Diffusion of Useful Knowledge; edited the Child's Library.

She learned French, Italian, Latin and Dutch. Her brother Alex was a great friend of John Wilson 'Christopher North'. Her husband William Busk, was MP for Barnstaple, Devon. When he lost the seat he had spent £10 000 on the campaign. His finances never recovered and his wife's earnings were essential to the family income.

Caird, Alice Mona, (Alison) 1858 ?–1932 b Isle of Wight d Hampstead. A 'writer of trenchant essays'. This phrase in her obituary notes the dramatic effect of her controversial articles on marriage in the *Westminster Review* in 1888 and her riposte to Eliza Linton in the *Fortnightly* and *Nineteenth Century* in the 'Wild Women' debate of the 1890s. Her *Westminster* articles led to further pieces in the *Daily Telegraph*, sparking off a heated correspondence in that paper's Letters to the Editor. Her essays were later collected in *The Morality of Marriage*, 1891.

Other work: Novelist (pen-name G. Noel Hatton); anti-vivisectionist; women's activist.

Her father was an inventor. Relatively little is known of her early life – (her d.o.b is variously given as 1854 and 1858) – although she apparently spent part of her childhood in Australia. She married A Henryson-Caird in 1877.

Campbell, Lady Colin (Gertrude Elizabeth Blood) 1861–1911 b Ireland. Journalist, critic. Worked under Stead on the *Pall Mall Gazette*. She was art critic of the *World*. Subscribing member Society of Women Journalists by 1900.

Other work: Fiction. *Darell Blake: a Study* draws on her journalistic experience. Pseudonym GE Brunefille.

Educated in Italy and France. Obtained legal separation from her husband, the younger son of Duke of Argyll, on grounds of cruelty.

Carpenter, Susan, fl turn of the century. Believed to be the first woman to work for the Press Association. First journalistic assignment a series of letters in the *Lady* exposing the real conditions of women emigrants to Australia. Wrote regularly for the *Belfast Northern Whig*, also *Pall Mall Gazette* as 'Mrs. Pepys'.

Other work: Promoted Unionist cause in London.

Of Irish origin she was related to Mary Carpenter, close friend of Frances Cobbe.

Claxton, Adelaide, (Mrs GG Turner) fl 1859-c1908. Illustrator on a regular basis for periodicals. Her work appeared in *Bow Bells, London Society, Illustrated Times* (1859–66). She and her elder sister, Florence, jointly illustrated various series in the *Englishwoman's Domestic Magazine* in the 1860s. Adelaide specialized in ghost subjects according to Hayes and also satirized 'social follies' according to Vizetelly.

Other work: Illustrator of books, figure painter.

Both she and Florence as young girls accompanied their father on travels to Australia, Ceylon and India. Married George Gordon Turner in 1874.

Claxton, Florence (Mrs Farrington) Wood engravings and illustrations on regular basis for weekly and monthly magazines and newspapers including *Churchman's Family Magazine, Illustrated Times, London Society, Aunt Judy's, Good Words, Illustrated Londern News*. Specialized in historical drawings. She provided the illustrations for Charlotte Yonge's *The Clever Woman of the Family*.

Other work: Book illustrator. Painter in oils and water-colours. For the 1858 exhibition of the Society of Female Artists painted *Scenes from the Life of the Female Artist* which appears to have cast a somewhat sardonic eye on the struggles and disappointments of the young aspirant.

Married a physician. See also under Adelaide Claxton.

Clerke, Agnes Mary 1842–1907 b Skibereen, Co. Cork, Ireland d South Kensington. Writer and essayist specializing in astronomy and its history. Published particularly in the *Edinburgh Review* but also in *British Quarterly Review, Contemporary Review, Fraser's, Macmillan's, Quarterly Review* amongst others.

Other work: Popularizer of science and historian of astronomy. Contributor to *DNB* and *Encyclopaedia Britannica*. In 1903 elected honorary member of Royal Astronomical Society.

Her father was a classical scholar who, until the family moved to Dublin managed a bank in Skibereen where he owned land. Astronomy was his recreation and he interested Agnes in it. She lived in Italy from 1867–77 where she was able to study in the libraries of Florence. Her 'Copernicus in Italy' appeared in the *Edinburgh* in '77 and began her long association with that journal.

Clerke, Ellen 1840–1906 b Skibereen, Ireland. Essayist and journalist. For 20 years wrote a weekly letter for the Catholic paper the *Tablet* and on a temporary basis filled in for the editor if required. From 1878–1900 a regular contributor to the *Dublin Review* on geographical and topical political and economic subjects, especially on Africa and India. Also articles of Roman Catholic interest. Wrote also in *Westminster Review*.

Other work: Poet. Member of Manchester Geographical Society to whose journal she contributed.

She was a considerable linguist, fluent in Italian. Sister of Agnes Clerke whose companion she was throughout her life.

Cobbe Frances Power 1822–1904 b Dublin Ireland d Hengwrt, North Wales. Leader writer and essayist. One of the most prominent women journalists of her day. She gave her first journalistic income, £14 for sketches in *Macmillan's*, to a charitable mission for workhouse girls. Had spell as Italian Correspondent for *London Daily News*. On staff of *Echo* 1868–75 for which she was a regular leader writer. Her first leader appeared on 10 December 1868 two days after its launch. In the late 1870s she was leader writer for the *Standard* and for a time special correspondent for the *Daily Mail*. Edited *Zoophilist*. Among other periodicals to which she contributed were the *Contemporary, Cornhill, Fortnightly, Fraser's, Macmillan's, Modern Review, National Quarterly, Quarterly, Temple Bar, Theological Review, Spectator, Reader, Examiner*.

Other work: Anti-vivisectionist. Philanthropist. Reformer. Writer on religious subjects.

Knew many of the women activists of the day including members of the Langham Place group. Amongst her close friends were Mary Somerville and Mary Carpenter. Daughter of Charles and Frances Cobbe, she was educated at home on the family estate in Ireland, though she spent two years at a school in Brighton.

Coke Mrs Talbot fl 1886–90s. One of the more professional of the 'Society Women Journalists'. Began writing for *Queen* in 1886, a post she resigned when her husband as commander of a regiment was ordered to Egypt at short notice. She also wrote for *Hearth and Home*, of which she was part-proprietor, and cheaper women's periodicals such as *Woman's Life*, and *Home Chat*. She was described as the 'leading authority on art furniture and home decoration' (Billington) and Evelyn March-Phillips thought highly of her gardening and needlework articles. It was said that many thousands of pounds were spent yearly on her advice. She was a subscribing member of the Society of Women Journalists. Her husband was Deputy Adjutant-General to the Duke of Connaught.

Cook Eliza 1817/8–1889 b Southwark, London d Wimbledon, Surrey. Editor *Eliza Cook's Journal* 1849–1854. She also wrote much of its contents which included poetry and social essays with a feminist slant. One of her particular concerns was women's poor working conditions. She gave up the journal only because of ailing health. Her writings for it were republished as *Jottings from My Journal*, and her popular 'Diamond Dust' feature was also reissued in volume form.

Other work: Poet. Published in *Metropolitan Magazine; New Monthly Magazine; Weekly Dispatch*.

Entirely self-educated. She was the youngest of eleven children of a brazier/tinman. She had at one time a 'romantic friendship' with the actress Charlotte Cushman and was known for her masculine style of dressing.

Costello, Louisa 1799–1870 b Ireland d Boulogne. Periodical contributor of travel, historical and biographical sketches, particularly on French and Swiss topics. Notably for *Bentley's Miscellany*, 1840–54, also for *Household Words, Fraser's, Literary Gazette, New Monthly, Ladies' Companion, Dublin University Magazine*. Reviewer of French literature for *Athenæum*.

Other work: Novelist. Poet. Painter of miniatures.

When she was 15, on the death of her father, an Irish officer in British army, the family moved to Paris. She supported her mother and brother Dudley seeing him through Sandhurst by work as a governess and painting miniatures. Rewarded by French government for her work – co-operatively with Dudley – on illuminated MSS.

Courtney, Janet Elizabeth (Hogarth) 1865–1954 b Lincolnshire Reader and sub-editor on *Fortnightly Review*. 1928–9 had spell as acting editor. Occasional contributor. She was closely associated with the direction of that review during her husband's editorship. Assisted with *Anti-Suffrage Review*.

Other work: Helped start Times Book Club and with editing of *Encyclopaedia Britannica*. Author of *Making of an Editor* (1930) and several books of recollections. In 1894 became first superintendent of women clerks at the Bank of England.

One of fourteen children of Rev. George and Jane Hogarth. Educated at school in Grantham and Oxford. Her husband, WL Courtney, was her tutor at Oxford. He became editor of the *Fortnightly* in 1895. At the time of her marriage she was his reader. His dying words to his wife were of the paper, 'Do you think you can carry on?'

Couvreur, Jessie Catherine (Huybers) 1849–97 d Brussels. Belgian correspondent of the *Times*, following the death of her second husband, the Belgian journalist and *Times* correspondent. Her brief included Holland and she thus provided the Dutch view of the Jameson raid.

Other work: novelist under the pseudonym 'Tasma'; lecturer.

Of Belgian parentage she spent her early years in Tasmania later travelling extensively in Australia and Europe. One of the few women of her day who claimed to have rounded Cape Horn in a small sailing ship. She divorced her first husband the Tasmanian Charles Forbes Fraser in 1883, and married Couvreur two years later.

Cowden Clarke, Mary Victoria (Novello) 1809–1898 b London d Genoa. Editor of *Musical Times* 1853–56. Contributor to *Table Book, National Magazine, Ladies' Cabinet*. Periodical contributor throughout her long life.

Other work: Critic and Shakespearean editor and popularizer; fiction mainly for children; editions of Shakespeare. With her husband she wrote recollections of the literary figures they had known.

She came from a musical family. Her father was a musician and composer and musical publisher. Amongst her parents' circle were Charles and Mary Lamb, Keats and the scholar and critic Charles Cowden Clarke whom she married in 1828 despite the great difference in their ages. After their marriage they moved to Italy.

Cowslade See under **Smart**

Craigie, Pearl Mary Teresa (Richards) 1867–1906 b Chelsea, near Boston Massachusetts d London. Essayist and critic. She wrote drama and art criticism for periodicals during early years of her marriage. For *Life* she also contributed 'Notebook of a Diner-out' by 'Diogenes Pessimus'. Contributor to the *Pall Mall Gazette* and the *Academy*, for which she wrote a series of reflective essays. Amongst her many other essays and sketches were her letters on the Delhi Durbar of 1903, when she was a guest of the Curzons, published in the *Daily Graphic* and *Collier's Weekly*. Was a President of the Society of Women Journalists.

Other work: Novelist, dramatist under the pseudonym 'John Oliver Hobbes'. Her verse tragedy was serialized in *Anglo-Saxon Review* and other work in the *Pall Mall Budget*. Anti-Suffragist.

American by birth, a fact of which she was proud. Her father John Morgan Richards's work took him to London when she was only a few months old. Pearl and her mother, Laura, followed the following year. The Congregationalist magazine *Fountain* published her stories when she was only nine. Educated at a boarding school in Newbury and day school in London. Married in 1887 Richard Walpole Craigie, but the marriage was unhappy. They divorced in 1895. She converted to Catholicism in 1892. She was an inveterate traveller and socializer and her prolific writings drew on these experiences.

Crawford Emily Johnstone 1831/2–1915 b Dublin, Ireland d France. One of the best known and ablest of women foreign correspondents. Became Paris correspondent for *Daily News* on the death of her husband George Crawford, barrister and journalist, in 1885, writing regularly until 1907. One of the longest-serving contributors to *Truth*, her letter from Paris ran from 1877 until her death. She wrote also for *Contemporary Review, National Review, Macmillan's, National Review II, Fortnightly Review, New York Tribune* and *Woman's World*.

She knew all the major figures in the Paris of her day, including Victor Hugo, Gambetta, and Clemenceau. Although she lived in Paris she was elected President Society of Women Journalists.

D'Arcy Ella 1851–c 1937* b London d Kent. Sub-editor on *Yellow Book*. Her letters to John Lane reveal something of the drama when Beardsley's illustrations and cover design were suppressed following the trial of Oscar Wilde. Contributed stories to 10 of the 13 issues of the *YB*.

Other work: Fiction some of which appeared in *Blackwood's, All the Year Round* and *Temple Bar*. Acted as secretary to Henry Harland.

Little is known of her life. Her parents were of aristocratic Irish breeding and she was educated in France and Germany. Trained as an artist at the Slade, but her defective eyesight encouraged her to write instead. *Also given as 1839

Davies, Emily 1830–1921 b Southampton Editor of the early feminist *English Woman's Journal* for a brief but crucial period when it was foundering for lack of financial backing and clear direction. She advised that it was unviable. She was also the first editor, again for a short period only, of Emily Faithfull's *Victoria Magazine*.

Other work: Pioneer campaigner for women's higher education. Founder Girton College. Active suffragist once she had secured her objectives on university education. In 1919 was one of the few early campaigners able to record her vote.

Daughter of the rector of Gateshead, Rev. John and Mary (Hopkinson) Davies, she had an evangelical upbringing, and was educated largely at home.

Dilke, **Emilia** Francis (Strong) 1840–1904. Art critic, art correspondent, and writer on women's and social issues for key journals such as *Contemporary, Fortnightly* and *New* reviews. She wrote for the *Westminster* and within a few years of contributing to the *Academy* was appointed its art editor.

Other work: Art historian. Trades union activist. President of the Women's Trades Union League.

Her father was a retired Indian Army officer who turned to provincial banking. Married, first the Oxford don and much older Mark Pattison, who encouraged her to choose a subject in which to specialize, and secondly, after

Pattison's death, Sir Charles Dilke the prominent politician embroiled in an infamous divorce suit which ruined his political career.

Dilke studied art history with Ruskin at the South Kensington School of Art. One of George Eliot's 'spiritual daughters' she was reputedly the model for Dorothea in *Middlemarch*, an allegation which Sir Charles always refuted.

Dixie, Lady Florence Caroline (Douglas) 1857–1905 b London d Annan, Dumfriesshire. War correspondent, periodical contributor. She was probably the first female war correspondent, sending dispatches to the *Morning Post* during the Zulu War and Boer War peace negotiations, where, glass of whisky in hand, she could apparently hold her own in any mess tent. She was one of the few women who contributed (anonymously) to *Vanity Fair*. Turned down the offer of an editorship of a proposed women's paper because she disagreed with the proprietor over the stance on 'women's affairs'.

Other Work: Explorer. Novelist. Poet. Travel writer. Supporter of Home Rule for Ireland, and various sex equality causes. Supported cause of the Zulu king.

Youngest of the children of the seventh Marquess of Queensberry. Married 1875 Sir Beaumont Dixie. Despite having two sons she travelled widely. Was a brilliant horsewoman and a good shot. One of the earliest women to pursue big game hunting, she later denounced blood sports.

Dixon, Ella Nora Hepworth 1855–1932. Editor *The Englishwoman* 1895–6 Wrote for *Lady's Pictorial, Woman's World, St James's Gazette, Woman, Daily Mail, Daily Telegraph*. Art critic for five years on *Westminster Gazette*.

Other work: Fiction. *The Story of a Modern Woman* (1894) drew on her journalistic experiences. Pseudonym Margaret Wynam.

Daughter of William Hepworth Dixon editor *Athenæum*. Educated partly in Heidelberg. Studied art in Paris.

Drew, Catherine fl 1890s. London-based journalist. First woman vice-president of Institute of Journalists in 1895. Representative at 1st International Conference of the Press, July 1894.

Irish by birth.

Eastlake, Lady (Elizabeth née Rigby) 1809–1893 b Norwich d London Periodical essayist and critic. Published in *Edinburgh, Foreign Quarterly, Fraser's, London* and *Murray's* reviews and magazines. Her most sustained commitment, however, was to the *Quarterly Review*, to which Lockhart invited her to contribute reviews and articles of interest to women. Her journalistic career spanned half a century, her final article appearing in *Longman's* in January 1893. She wrote authoritatively on art, literature and travel, and was a most influential reviewer.

Other work: Translation.

She was the fourth daughter of Dr Edward Rigby's large family. From 1827 for two years the family lived in Heidelberg. Her extended journey through the Baltic provinces to Russia to visit her married sister provided the basis of her early travel writings. Married Sir Charles Locke Eastlake, Keeper National Gallery, in 1849 and from this social position was to continue her travels and involvement in the world of art.

Edwards, Mary Ellen (firstly Mrs Freer, secondly Mrs Staples) 1839–1910 b Kingston on Thames. A prolific illustrator, one of the small group of women artists who was salaried or employed as a regular contributor to magazines. On the staff of *Graphic* from its launch. Highly successful and popular illustrator of fiction. The sheer variety of the magazines in which her work appeared suggests the versatility of her appeal *Belgravia, Dark Blue, Aunt Judy's, Cassell's, Illustrated*

Times, London Society, Cornhill, Churchman, Good Words, Illustrated London News, Golden Hours, Illustrated Times, Girls Own Paper, Little Wide-Awake. She was the chief illustrator of Mrs Wood's *Argosy.*

Edwards, Amelia Blandford 1831–1892 b London d Weston-super-Mare. Essayist, reviewer, specialist in Egyptology. Her early experiments in writing began with juvenile stories; her journalistic career proper with articles and criticism (music, drama, and art) for papers such as the *Saturday Review* and *Morning Post* of which she became a staff member. For the *Academy* alone she wrote over 100 articles on Egypt on which topic she also contributed to the *Times.* Among other papers in which her work appeared were *All The Year Round, Graphic, Illustrated London News, Argosy.*

Other work: Novelist. Egyptologist. History and travel books. Lectured in USA 1889–90.

Eliot, George (pseudonym of Mary Ann (Marianne) Evans, later Mrs Cross) 1819–1880 b Warwickshire d London. Reviewer and editor. Though nominally assistant editor for Chapman's *Westminster Review* she was effectively its (unpaid) editor from 1852–54. During this period she also reviewed for it fiction, philosophy, foreign literature. Early journalism appeared in the *Coventry Herald and Observer*, whose editor, Charles Bray, became a friend. Her articles, translations and fiction appeared in *Blackwood's, Contemporary, Fortnightly* and *Fraser's.*

Other work: Novelist, translator.

She had a rural upbringing in the midlands, her father being a land agent. Educated in various local schools but also arranged lessons in German and classical languages from local masters. She lost her evangelical faith to her father's distress, and later became much influenced by Comtism. Following her father's death she went to London where she met George Henry Lewes, who was married but unable to procure a divorce, and with whom she eventually lived as his wife. After his death she married a young friend John Walter Cross. She was a patron and friend to many young women, including Edith Simcox, Barbara Bodichon, Bessie Parkes and Emilia Dilke.

Ewing, Juliana Horatia (Gatty) 1841–1885 b Ecclesfield, Yorkshire d Bath. Children's magazine editor/contributor and illustrator. Co-ran with her sister *Aunt Judy's* immediately after the death of their mother Margaret Gatty. Her stories remained a mainstay of the paper. Her early fiction appeared in *Monthly Packet* and *London Society.*

Other work: Prolific writer of children's books.

Enjoyed a somewhat desultory education but it provided encouragement for writing. Married Major Alexander Ewing in 1867 and travelled with him to New Brunswick.

Faithfull, Emily 1836(?5)–1895 b Headley rectory nr. Epsom, Surrey d Manchester. Editor. Pioneer of women's printing. Her main achievements in journalism/publishing were the foundation of the Victoria Press (1860) and the *Victoria Magazine*, which she also edited for many years. This was launched, in partnership with Mr Gunning in 1863/4 and ran until 1880. Though a general interest magazine, it played an important rôle in publicizing positively the work of the women's movement. Her press was staffed by women and provided training. For this initiative she was appointed Printer and Publisher in Ordinary to Her Majesty. In 1877 helped found the *West London Express* and during 1870s was on the staff of the *Ladies' Pictorial* for which she was still producing a 'careful Women's Column' (Green) in the early 1890s.

Other work: Feminist. Member of the Langham Place Group. Lectured in America 1872–3.

Farrington See **Claxton** (Florence)

Fenwick-Miller, Florence (Mrs Ford) b 1854 d 1935 Editor, columnist, leader writer. Her energetic journalistic career spanned forty years. Took over the *Woman's Signal* in 1895 as proprietor/editor (unpaid) and popularized it whilst maintaining its support for suffrage and women's issues generally. Closed in 1899 when she could no longer afford the time, energy and financial subsidy. Edited *Outward Bound* a monthly circulating in the colonies. From 1886–1918 wrote a lively Ladies' Column for *Illustrated London News*. Her syndicated letter as 'Filomena' ran for 'many years' in provincial papers. Wrote leaders on a weekly basis for two provincial dailies. As a freelance contributed to many magazines including *Lady's Pictorial, Young Woman, Echo, Woman's World, Fraser's, National Review, Modern Review*, as well as to feminist papers.

Other work: Suffragist. Elected first treasurer of International Woman's Suffrage Committee. Member of London School Board. Lecturer. Miscellaneous writer. Wrote biography of Harriet Martineau.

Married Frederick Alford Ford in 1877 but unusually retained her own surname after marriage and was known as Mrs Fenwick-Miller (sometimes hyphenated, sometimes not.)

Friederichs Hulda fl 1880s onwards Newspaperwoman. Interviewer, editor. In 1882 she was appointed by Stead as chief interviewer on *Pall Mall Gazette* and established a formidable reputation in this field. Probably the best known woman interviewer of her day, she was a generalist, and avoided women's topics. She was one of the few national women newspaper journalists who were not fashion/social correspondents. When Astor purchased the *PMG* she was amongst the staff who left with Cook, the editor. Worked with him on Newnes's new *Westminster Gazette*. Newnes later appointed her to assist Spender on the *Saturday Westminster*. She also edited the *Budget* for him.

Other work: Biographical and historical books. Wrote *The Life of Sir George Newnes* and books on Gladstone and the Salvation Army. German by birth but fluent in English. She became a friend of both the Newnes and Gladstones. She believed that professional women should just get on with their jobs and not be regarded as particular phenomena.

Gatty, Margaret (Scott) 1809–1873 b Burnham, Essex d Ecclesfield, Yorkshire Founder and editor 1866–73 *Aunt Judy's Magazine,* one of the best-known children's magazines of the period. She encouraged her family to contribute and was a major contributor herself – her 'Emblems' being a distinctive feature. Her daughter, Horatia Katherine Frances **Gatty**, edited it from 1873–85, initially with Juliana (see Ewing). Horatia closed the magazine on Juliana's death.

Other work: Botanist, and popularizer of science. She illustrated her *Parables from Nature* and her *History of British Seaweeds* remained an authority until long after her death. A sea serpent and a seaweed were named after her.

Youngest daughter of Rev. Dr Alexander John Scott who had been Nelson's chaplain. Her mother died when she was two. Married Rev. Alfred Gatty, vicar of Ecclesfield where she brought up her family of ten children, and remained all her life.

Gordon-Cumming, Constance Frederica 1837–1924. Periodical essayist. Contributed particularly on travel subjects to the literary reviews and magazines including *Blackwood's, British Quarterly, Contemporary, Cornhill, London Quarterly, Macmillan's, National Review II, New Review, Nineteenth Century*, and *Temple Bar*.

Other work: Travelled widely in India, the East and California. She was known as the 'Scottish Traveller'.

Gow, Mary L (Mrs Hall) 1851–1929 b London. Illustrator. Contributed to *Argosy*, the *Quiver, Graphic* and *Cassell's Family Magazine*.

Other work: Figure subjects in oil and watercolour.

Studied Queen's Square School of Art and at Heatherley's. Her father, James Gow, and brother Andrew Carrick were both history and genre painters and Mary worked in the family business contributing figure subjects until her father's death in 1885. Married Sydney P Hall, painter and illustrator. She was listed in 1897 as suffrage supporter.

Graves, Clotilde Inez Mary 1863–1932 b Cork, Ireland. A journalist for over thirty years working at one time under Sir Sidney Low on the *St James's Gazette*. Wrote also for the *World, Punch*, and *Hood's*. She adopted men's clothes as more convenient for her profession.

Other work: Novelist, dramatist.

The third daughter of Major WHG and Antoinette Graves, she was born in the Buttevant Barracks. Largely self-taught though she studied art at Royal Female School of Art, Bloomsbury and later illustrated some of her work. Became Catholic in 1896. Retired to a convent following ill-health in 1928.

Greenaway, Kate 1846–1901 b London. Magazine Illustrator for *Graphic, Cassell's, Illustrated London News, People's Magazine, Girl's Own Paper, Little Wide-Awake*. Occasional illustrator in the mid 1880's.

Other work: Watercolourist; Book illustrator.

Her father John Greenaway was a wood engraver for the *Illustrated London News*. She studied at Islington school, Heatherley's and the Slade. Began exhibiting at the Royal Academy in 1877.

Greville, Lady (Violet Beatrice -sometimes given as Beatrice Violet) fl 1880–90s. Society and gossip columnist, writer on women's sports and pastimes. One of Edmund Yates's 'discoveries', she was an early contributor of society articles and paragraphs to the *World*. Best known for her 'Place aux Dames' column in the *Graphic*; she also contributed a society column to the more down-market *Home Chat*. Said to have edited a couple of papers.

Other work: Novelist

Daughter of James, fourth Duke of Montrose. Married in 1863 the heir to the first Lord Greville. Billington attributed her professional success, 'daring, brilliancy, and romance ... united', partly to hereditary influence. She may have had in mind the history of the Montroses, but equally, as a journalist, she was hardly unaware that Lady Greville's mother was the redoubtable Caroline, Duchess of Montrose ('Carrie Red' – *nom de course* 'Mr Manton') whose passion in life was the turf, and who was the first woman to be expert in both the racing form and breeding of horses, even if a capricious owner with a turn of phrase colourful enough to equal any bookmaker's.

Hall, Anna Maria Carter (Fielding) 1800–1881 b Dublin, Ireland d East Molesey, Surrey. Editor of annuals and magazines. Contributor to periodicals including her husband's journals. Edited *Sharpe's London Magazine* in 1852 and 1862–63 was the first editor of Maxwell's *St James's Magazine*. Both arrangements were short-lived though her editorships seem to have been effective and energetic. A dispute with the new proprietor of *Sharpe's* led to her refusal to complete her serial for that paper. Edited several annuals, amongst them *Finden's Tableaux*, *Juvenile Forget-Me-Not* and *Juvenile Budget*.

Other work: Novelist. Kortright called her 'the Christianized Edgeworth of our day'. Philanthropist – she helped amongst other causes in the foundation of Brompton Consumption Hospital, the Governesses Institute, and the Nightingale Fund. Temperance movement supporter. Salon hostess.

Her mother was widowed when she was young and she spent much of her childhood in her step-grandfather's house in Wexford. She came with her mother to England in 1815. Married the editor Samuel Carter Hall in 1824 and was generally known in literary circles as Mrs SC Hall or Mrs Samuel Carter Hall. The Carter Halls were noted for their 'at homes' and evening parties attended by many of the literary and publishing figures of their day, including LEL, the Howitts, Mary Russell Mitford. Mrs Hall received a civil list pension in 1868.

Hasell, Elizabeth Julia 1830–1887 Essayist, critic, specialist in the literature of southern Europe. From 1859 for nearly twenty years she contributed to *Blackwood's*; also *Saint Paul's* in the 1870s, mainly on literature and poetry, especially classical and European literature. Reviewed for the *Athenæum*.

Other work: Wrote volumes on Calderon and Tasso for the Foreign Classics series and edited/wrote on the Bible.

A remarkable scholar, she taught herself Latin, Greek, Spanish and Portuguese. She lived in Penrith where she took a particular interest in developing education within the district and would walk long distances over the hills to teach in the village school.

Hoey, Frances Sarah (Johnston) 1830–1908 b near Dublin, Ireland d Beccles, Suffolk. Journalist. She had a long and varied career. From 1853 she reviewed and contributed articles on art for Irish press, *Freeman's Journal* and the *Nation;* in the mid-1850s began writing for the *Morning Post*. Her 30-year association with *Chambers's Journal* started in 1865. She helped found *World* in 1874. As a journalist her most famous exploit was her 'scoop' when on one of her frequent visits to Paris she was able to report on the Commune of 1871, the first English journalist to do so. She wrote it up for the *Spectator* as 'Red Paris' thus initiating an association with that paper. For over 20 years she produced a 'Ladies Letter' for an Australian paper. Frances Hayes's *Women of the Day* described her as 'one of the most accomplished writers of our time'.

Other work: Novelist. Translator from French and Italian.

Married at 16 Adam Murray Stewart who died in 1855. In London she met and married secondly John Cashel Hoey, a journalist associated with Young Ireland movement. Known as Mrs Cashel Hoey. She converted to husband's Catholicism.

Holdsworth, Annie E (Mrs Lee-Hamilton) c1857–c1910 b Kingston, Jamaica. Worked on Stead's *Review of Reviews* in the 1890s. Co-edited with Lady Henry Somerset the feminist magazine *Woman's Signal*.

Other work: Active feminist, novelist, poet. Mr Boas, the reformer in her novel *Joanna Traill, Spinster* is believed to be a portrait of WT Stead.

Her father was a Yorkshire minister who worked with emancipated slaves. She was educated in London and Scotland. Married Eugene Jacob Lee-Hamilton, a writer.

Howitt, Mary (Botham) 1799–1888 b Coleford, Gloucestershire d Rome. Periodical contributor. Editor *Fisher's Drawing Room Scrap-Book* for three years following the death of Letitia Landon, co-editor with William of their ambitious but ill-fated venture, a popular progressive magazine aimed at the working classes, *Howitt's Journal*. Her work appeared in *Athenæum, Household Words, All The Year Round*, and *Sharpe's* amongst others.

Other work: Poet. Translator (from German, Swedish and Danish including Hans Anderson and Frederika Bremer). Miscellaneous writer of books. Children's writer. Novelist. It is estimated that she wrote, translated or edited over 100 books.

Her parents were prosperous Quakers and she was educated at home and at Quaker schools. Married fellow Quaker and writer William Howitt (1792–1879) in 1821. They had five children and she and William collaborated on various publications throughout their lives. She had a wide circle of friends across the generations, including Keats, LEL, Barbara Bodichon, Mrs Gaskell, Frederika Bremer, Octavia Hill, Ellen Wood, the Pre-Raphaelites. Mary Howitt received a civil list pension 1879. She converted to Catholicism towards the end of her life.

Humphry Mrs CE (Lloyd) d 1925 when resident in Maidenhead. Columnist on dress, fashion and etiquette. Best known as 'Madge' of *Truth* for which gossipy 'letter' she was reputedly paid £500 pa. and which was much imitated. She wrote also for the *Globe* and *Daily News*. Charles Williams, the war correspondent, is said to have encouraged her journalism. She was a President of the Society of Women Journalists.

Other work: Books on etiquette and cookery.

Daughter of Rev. James Graham, Londonderry Cathedral. Educated Dublin. Married in 1881. Described her interests as reading, gardening and 'the play'. Her sister Ethel Lloyd contributed on fashion to the *Daily Telegraph* and worked on the *Lady's Pictorial*.

Jewsbury, Geraldine Endsor 1812–1880 b Measham, Derbyshire d London. Reviewer and periodical contributor. One of the most prolific fiction reviewers of the century particularly for the *Athenæum* between 1849 and 1880. In the 1840s she wrote on social issues for *Douglas Jerrold's Shilling Magazine*. Her articles often had a feminist slant. Also contributed to various journals including *Household Words, Westminster Review* and *Ladies Companion* and Mrs Hall's *Juvenile Budget*.

Other work: Novelist. Publisher's reader for Bentley and Sons 1858–80. The combination of her coverage of so many novels in the *Athenæum* and her lengthy service in advising Bentley gave her considerable influence in the market for fiction.

Her father Thomas Jewsbury was a Manchester cotton merchant. Her mother died when she was six and she was brought up by her sister Maria who was her rôle model professionally. The family moved to Manchester in 1818. She became a close friend of the Carlyles particularly Jane. She regarded Carlyle's comments on her early work as vital training in writing. She moved to London to be near the Carlyles in 1854.

Jewsbury, Maria Jane (later Fletcher) 1800–1833 b Measham, Derbyshire d Poona, India. Periodical contributor. Encouraged to write by Alaric Watts, editor of the *Manchester Courier* who saw a poem she had published in another paper. She contributed to various annuals and notably forcefully written articles for the *Athenæum* between 1830–32.

Other work: Poetry. Fiction, and her popular *Letters to the Young* based on advice to her younger sister.

Became a friend of the Wordsworths. Like her sister, Geraldine she suffered bouts of ill health. In 1832 married Rev. William Kew Fletcher, a chaplain with the East India Company, but died of cholera the following year. She did not live to see Wordsworth's 'Liberty' dedicated to her.

Johnstone (Mrs Christian) 1781–1857 b Fifeshire, Scotland. Magazine and newspaper proprietor and editor. Her ventures were influential in terms of their cultural impact and progressive views. With her second husband she was joint editor of the *Inverness Courier* 1817–24. Her *Schoolmaster & Edinburgh Weekly* launched 1832 changed its title to *Johnstone's Edinburgh* in 1833. When *Johnstone's* merged with *Tait's Edinburgh* she took a half share in the merged paper and became principal editor from 1834–46 and was responsible for most of the book reviews.

Other work: Cookery book under 'Meg Dodds', fiction.

She shunned publicity, possibly because of her anomalous position as a divorced woman. She married first Mr M'Leish and second John Johnstone.

Knox Isa (Craig) 1831–1903 b Edinburgh. Journalist on *Scotsman* 1853–57. Her poems published in that paper attracted enough attention for her to be offered a post on the staff. Briefly edited *Argosy* for Strahan.

Other work: Poetry, fiction. Secretary and literary assistant to National Association for the Promotion of Social Science. Member of Langham Place Group.

Daughter of a hosier, she was orphaned in childhood. Largely self-educated. Married her cousin John Knox in 1866.

Kortright, Fanny (Frances) Aikin 1821–1900 b London. Journalist, editor. Her journalistic career began at age of 17 when she joined the staff of a country newspaper as leader writer. Edited and wrote most of the *Court Suburb Magazine* 1868–70.

Other work: Fiction. Several serials published in the *Family Herald*. Her novels were popular in Canada. Wrote pamphlet against Women's Rights Movement.

Her father, Nicholas Berkley Aiken Kortright, was American by birth but for 50 years a British naval officer.

Lawrance, Hannah 1795–1885. Reviewer and periodical contributor. Occasional contributor to *Tait's*, *Blackwood's*, *Fraser's* and *Household Words*. Staff writer for Dilke's *Athenæum* specializing in reviewing historical and antiquarian books. Wrote regularly for *British Quarterly Review* from 1847–70 on art and literary topics.

Other work: author of *Historical Memoirs of the Queens of England* and *The History of Woman, and Her Influence on Society and Literature.*

Linton Eliza (Lynn) 1822–1898 b Keswick, Cumberland d London. Leader writer, reviewer and periodical essayist. First woman staff journalist on a national daily paper. One of the most prolific and best-known women periodical contributors of her day. For John Douglas Cook's *Morning Chronicle* between 1849–51 she was 'office handyman' reviewer and leader-writer. She left after a major disagreement. For a spell in Paris was correspondent for the *Leader*, also contributing to Dickens's *Household Words* on which she became a 'regular'. Her most notorious journalistic achievement was her 'Girl of Period' sketches attacking the modern young woman in Cook's *Saturday Review*. She developed this success by becoming the standard-bearer of those opposed to the radical feminist wing. She was active in journalism until her death. She wrote for so many different magazines and papers that there is no room to list them. Amongst them were *Universal Review, Ainsworth's, Cornhill, Fortnightly, Dark Blue, Macmillan's, Belgravia, Good Words, All The year Round, Athenæum, Daily News, Tinsley's Magazine,* and *Chambers'.* In 1896 she was among the first women elected to the Society of Authors and the first to serve on its committee.

Other work: Novelist

Born in Keswick, Cumberland, youngest of twelve children of the Rev. James Lynn William and his wife Charlotte, daughter of the Bishop of Carlisle. Her mother died whilst she was still young and she had no formal education and a bleak childhood. Her father, however, was persuaded to allow her to go to London to try her luck as a writer where she studied in the British Museum and vindicated his trust by successfully publishing her first novel. Ainsworth was her 'first literary godfather' and she found in Walter Savage Landor a literary mentor and substitute father. As a young journalist she knew George Eliot. Married the widower William James Linton, the engraver and political reformer, who in 1850 helped Lewes and Thornton Hunt found the radical *Leader,* and whose family she had helped care for during his first wife's fatal illness. The couple were incompatible and they separated. She was not a believer in divorce and throughout her life personally and professionally liked to be known as Mrs (or Eliza) Lynn Linton.

Low*, Frances fl late 1880s onwards. Editor of *Queen.* In the early 1890s Fanny Green said she was one of the only two women then editing a woman's paper. Contributed to *Nineteenth Century* and *Fortnightly* on social issues. Took initiatives in the training of women journalism. With Mary Billington taught journalism to young women and published a textbook on the subject.

Other work: Books, including one on Queen Victoria's dolls.

Her sister Florence was also a journalist and writer on religious topics. Her brothers (both later knighted) Sidney and Maurice Low were well-known journalists too. *Billington's article in *Pearson's* (1896) spells her name 'Lowe'.

Lugard see **Shaw**

Martineau, Harriet 1802–1876 b Norwich d Birmingham. Leader writer, reviewer and periodical essayist, one of the most distinguished and best-known journalists of her century. Specialist in economics and sociological issues, contributing to many journals including *Cornhill, Dublin University Magazine, Edinburgh Review, London Westminster, Macmillan's, New Monthly, Quarterly, Tait's, Westminster, Household Words.* Her most sustained journalistic commitment was her work as leader-writer/reviewer for the *Daily News* between 1852 and 1866 when she was writing for the paper almost daily, even though then living in Ambleside in the lake district. She did not avoid political subjects and was a powerful supporter of the abolitionist cause. Also wrote some leaders for Arthur Arnold's *Echo.* Her early journalism was as an unpaid contributor to the religious journal the *Monthly Repository.* She had a lucid, direct and vigorous style eminently suited to newspaper journalism.

Other work: Fiction. Treatises and sociological studies. Her *Illustrations of Political Economy* (1832–4) using a narrative format were particularly popular.

Her *Society in America* (1837) written after her tour of north America was critical of many aspects of that society.

Of Huguenot descent, her father Thomas was a manufacturer of 'bombazines and camlets' and mother, Elizabeth Rankin, daughter of a Newcastle sugar-refiner. The family were Unitarians. She was early afflicted by partial deafness which contributed to her childhood sense of isolation. After her father's death when the family business collapsed she had to earn her own living. Her period of sustained journalism came when she was a well-established writer and debilitated by a serious heart condition. Martineau was one of the most formidable intellectual women of the century, and whilst making no claim to being an original thinker, her popularization of the ideas of others made her a highly influential figure.

Mayo, Isabella (Fyvie) 1843–1914 b London. Reviewer, periodical essay writer for papers such as *Sunday at Home, Good Words*. Her first commission was to supply verses to accompany woodcuts.

Other work: Poetry, fiction (pseudonym 'Edward Garrett'). For a period she worked as secretary/receptionist at Langham Place.

Her parents were Scottish by birth. After her father's death the family business collapsed and she determined not only to maintain herself but to repay outstanding debts. Her early attempts at writing were encouraged by Jean Ingelow. Mrs S Carter Hall was a helpful patron.

Meade, LT (Elizabeth Thomasina later Mrs Toulmin Smith) 1844*–1914 b Bandon, Co. Cork d Oxford. Periodical contributor. Editor *Atalanta*, a magazine for girls 1887–98. Edited this lively, innovative and successful journal, initially with Alicia Leith, then on her own, then in collaboration with John Staples and AJ Symington. She gave it up only because of the pressure of her writing and domestic responsibilities. Alongside her prolific fiction she contributed articles on her own profession, travel, charitable ventures and art to magazines like the *Sunday Magazine* and the *Strand*.

Other work: Stories and novels, particularly for girls. She promoted women's education and employment through her writings and was active in women's clubs. She was, along with women like Mary Ward, Mary Braddon and Rhoda Broughton, on the committee that set up the employment information bureau at the Lyceum Club, and a Committee member of the pro-suffrage The Pioneer. She argued for the establishment of a school to teach fiction writing.

Born the first child of a Church of Ireland clergyman, Rev. Richard Thomas Meade and his wife Sarah. Educated at home by a strict governess, she began writing in childhood. Later, in London, she researched at the British Museum under the guidance of Dr Richard Garnett, Superintendent of the Reading Room. After her mother's death in 1874 and her father's remarriage the following year she moved to England on a permanent basis. Married Alfred Toulmin Smith, a London solicitor in 1879. She had four children, one of whom died as a baby. Her daughter, Hope, trained as an artist and illustrated some of her mother's books. *Garriock gives this date from her tombstone in Wolvercote cemetery, Oxford, rather than the usual 1855.

Meteyard, Elizabeth 1816–1879 b Liverpool. Periodical essayist, journalist. She wrote the leading article for the first issue of *Douglas Jerrold's Weekly Newspaper*;

the editor signed it 'Silverpen' and her pseudonym was born. Contributed also to *Sharpe's London Magazine*; and *Eliza Cook's Journal*.

Other work: Fiction, books for children.

Daughter of Mary and William Meteyard. Her father was an army surgeon. After his death she settled in London and her writing helped support her brothers. She was a friend of Mary Howitt's.

Meynell Alice Christina Gertrude (Thompson) 1847–1922, b Barnes, Surrey d London. Essayist, critic. Reviewer from 1876. Her work appeared in the *Observer, Daily Chronicle, Spectator, Saturday Review, Scots Observer, Tablet* and the *Pall Mall Gazette* 'Wares of Autolycus' column to which she was one of the longest-serving and most popular contributors. Art critic for *PMG* from 1901. Jointly with her husband edited and wrote for the *Weekly Register*; and *Merry England* (founded in 1893) which Wilfred owned. They also jointly edited the shortlived *Pen: A Journal of Literature* (1880). Elected President of the Society of Women Journalists at the suggestion of Lady Colin Campbell.

Other work: Poet; supporter of women's suffrage and other social issues. She and her husband ran an informal literary salon. Amongst their friends were Meredith, Patmore, Francis Thompson and Wilfrid Blunt.

Daughter of Christiana and Thomas James Thompson. Most of her childhood was spent in Italy and Switzerland within a highly cultured family. Her sister was Lady Butler, the artist. Converted to Catholicism in 1868. Married Wilfrid Meynell 1877 and her journalism was carried out within an informal domestic environment raising seven children.

Mitford, Mary Russell 1781–1855 b Alresford, Hampshire d Swallowfield, Berkshire. Reviewer, sketch writer, annual editor. Her most famous work, *Our Village*, which inaugurated the sub-genre of the rural village sketch, was originally published in the *Lady's Magazine* and was an instant success. Her early reviews, dramatic sketches and articles were written for magazines in order to support her parents. Her work in various genres appeared in many magazines and annuals. She edited several volumes of *Finden's Tableaux* to which she persuaded Elizabeth Barrett Browning to contribute.

Other work: Dramatist. Poet. Fiction and letter-writer – several volumes were published during the nineteenth century.

Daughter of George Mitford, a medical man who never practised and Mary Russell, the wealthy daughter of a Hampshire clergyman. Educated at Hans Place, she was a voracious reader throughout her life. Her father, though charming, was a spendthrift and an inveterate gambler. Mary's £20 000 win in a lottery as a child was spent on an extravagant country house. By the time her father was bankrupt all that remained to her was a crested dinner-service. The family moved to a tiny cottage in Three Mile Cross, near Reading, which was the basis of her most famous work. Her wide circle of friends included Samuel and Anna Maria Hall, Felicia Hemans, Harriet Martineau, Amelia Opie, Elizabeth Barrett Browning, the Hoflands, Haydon, the painter, and Henry Chorley.

Morgan, Lady (Sydney Owenson) 1783?–1859 b Dublin Ireland d London. Reviewer for *Athenæum* of books in Italian and French and on French history and politics. Contributed also to *New Monthly Magazine*. She responded with spirit in various periodicals to attacks on her fiction.

Other work: Novelist; also wrote some verse. Best known for her novel *The Wild Irish Girl*.

The first woman to receive a pension for 'services to the world of letters'. Her date of birth is uncertain and has been given as early as 1775/6. Her father Robert MacOwen, an Irish actor, changed his surname to Owenson. Married the surgeon to the Marquis and Marchioness of Abercorn. Geraldine Jewsbury worked with her in her last years on her autobiography.

Mozley, Anne 1809–1891 b Gainsborough Lincs. Essayist and editor. In the late 1850s began contributing to *Bentley's Quarterly*, to *Blackwood's* in the 1860s–1870s. She contributed short, distinctive essays to the *Saturday Review*. She specialized in subjects of interest to women including dress, social manners and women's rights. As a reviewer she was one of those who recognized *Adam Bede* as the work of a woman. She started the *Magazine for the Young* in 1842 and was its editor. She kept knowledge of her journalistic career within the family. She was one of eleven children of Mozley, a bookseller and religious publisher.

Müller Henrietta B d 1906. Feminist editor. Founder and editor of the *Woman's Penny Paper* in 1880 which became in 1888 the *Women's Herald* and had an all-women staff. She edited and wrote under the name of Helena Temple (also HB Temple) and it was as 'Miss Temple' that she fought an unsuccessful campaign for her journalists to be admitted to the Press Gallery in the House of Commons. Founder member of the Women's Printing Society which printed *WPP*.

Other work: Suffragist and activist in local government. An outspoken member of the School Board. Member of Moral Reform Union.

She was a Girton graduate. Her sister Eva (later McLaren) before her marriage worked with Octavia Hill and Josephine Butler.

Norton Hon Mrs Caroline (Sheridan) 1808–1877 b London d London. Editor *Court Magazine* (which had been relaunched from the *Belle Assemblée* by Bell) 1832–4 for which she wrote much of the contents. For a time she was on the editorial staff of Colburn who owned several newspapers and magazines. One of the early women reviewers for the *Times*.

Other work: Poetry. Best known for her influential pamphlets arising from her battles with her husband who brought a notorious action against Lord Melbourne for adultery with his wife. Though Melbourne was acquitted his wife was ruined socially. She fought for custody of her children and against her estranged husband's claim upon her earnings. She was an early inspiration to women journalists.

One of the three beautiful daughters of Thomas Sheridan, and grand-daughter of Richard Brinsley Sheridan, the dramatist.

O'Conor Eccles, Charlotte 1863–1911 b Roscommon, Ireland. Journalist. Began on provincial English paper where she ran a ladies' column. Described her struggle as a woman journalist seeking work in Fleet Street in an article in *Blackwood's*. Worked in London for the *New York Herald*. Writer and interviewer for *Windsor Magazine*, *Sketch* and many other magazines.

Other work: Fiction (pseudonym Hal Godfrey). Lectured in Ireland for the Board of Agriculture and Technical Instruction. Interested in housing for the poor.

Educated Upton Hall, Birkenhead, and convents in France and Germany. Fellow of the Institute of Journalists. She listed her interests as 'reading, travel, conversation'.

Oliphant, Margaret (Oliphant Wilson) 1828–1897 b Wallyford, Midlothian d Wimbledon, London. Critic and essayist. One of the most influential reviewers of her century. Her writing career spanned half a century. She published essays and fiction in a wide range of high-class journals including *Cornhill, Contemporary, Edinburgh, Fraser's, Longman's, Macmillan's, New Review* and *St Paul's*. Her most important connection was with *Blackwood's* for whom she was the major literary reviewer from 1854 until almost the end of her life, covering a wide range of subjects and reviewing most of the important fiction of her time. Her sketches are lively and late in life she was still experimenting. Her 'Looker-On' column published in her final decade was considered by Charlotte Yonge to be her best periodical writing. She never, however, achieved the magazine editorship she sought.

Other work: Novelist. Biographer. Miscellaneous writer. On the conservative side of the suffrage debate.

Daughter of Francis Wilson and Margaret Oliphant, the family moved in Scotland and later to Liverpool with her father's work. Married her cousin Francis Oliphant who suffered from poor health and died leaving her an impoverished young widow. Her writing not only provided for her own family, including sending two sons to Eton, but also for her brother and his children. The great tragedy of her life was to endure the deaths of all her six children including the two sons who survived to adulthood.

Orme, Eliza fl from mid-1880s. Leader writer for the *Weekly Dispatch* during the 1880/90s. Listed alongside Mrs Crawford, the only other woman, by Fox Bourne amongst the leader-writers of the day.

Other work: Suffrage committee member in 1866. Was a patron of 'Hertha' Marks the Jewish girl, one of Girton's first students, whom Barbara Bodichon took under her wing. Eliza managed Hertha's 'Girton fund'.

She studied law at Hitchin.

Pfeiffer, Emily Jane (Davis) 1827–1890 b Montgomeryshire, Wales d Putney. Periodical contributor on women's issues, including education suffrage, trades unionism etc. in *Cornhill Magazine, Contemporary Review* during the 1880s. Many collected in *Women and Work* (1887).

Other work: Poet. Painter.

Daughter of R Davis, army officer. Her father's financial problems precluded any systematic education. Her happy marriage to a successful German businessman who had settled in England, however, brought her the leisure to develop her poetic talents. A bequest in her will for higher education for women was used to erect a hall of residence for women at University College, Cardiff.

Power, Marguerite 1813–1867. Annual editor and periodical contributor. Edited *Keepsake* 1851–7 following the death of her aunt the Countess of Blessington. Also contributed to *Household Words, All the Year Round, Illustrated London News, Once a Week, Forget-me-not*.

Other work: Novelist. Wrote memoir of Lady Blessington.

Daughter of Colonel Power. Stayed with her aunt at Gore House and went with her to Paris. She dedicated one of her novels to Dickens, who contributed a story to *Keepsake* during her editorship. Dickens, Thackeray and Forster raised £200 for her.

Riddell, Charlotte Eliza Lawson (Cowan) 1832–1906, b Antrim Ireland d Hounslow. Co-proprietor and editor of *St James's Magazine* in succession to Mrs Hall though the exact dates have not been established. Also founded and edited a magazine *Home* (though no known copies are in existence). Wrote for the *Lady of the House*, a Dublin magazine.

Other work: Novelist specializing in business/commercial themes. Her works immensely popular at one time, later fell from favour. *A Rich Husband* and *A Struggle for Fame* deal with Grub Street and fiction-writing. Pseudonym FG Trafford.

Her father was High Sherriff of Co. Antrim, but when his health broke down the family's circumstances were precarious. Moved to London in 1855. Her husband, Joseph Hadley Riddell, a civil engineer, provided technical information for her books but his own career was something of a disaster financially, and the income from her writing was vital.

Rye, Maria Susan (1829–1903) b London d. Hemel Hempstead. Periodical journalist. Promoter of women's issues. She joined Beeton's *Englishwoman's Domestic Magazine* as a regular contributor after winning an essay competition, writing on social issues and historical subjects of interest to women. Her article on the proposed married women's property act in this mainstream women's paper attracted the attention of the Langham Place group. She became a shareholder/contributor to the *EWJ*, and helped Emily Faithfull with the Victoria Press.

Other work: She was active in promoting expanded employment opportunities for women. Established a law-copying office. An advocate of female emigration she established the Female Middle Class Emigration Society. This involved her in travel to Australia, New Zealand and Canada. Having visited a children's home in New York in 1867 she founded a home for pauper children in London. Her final active years were much taken up by work with the Church of England Waifs and Strays Society (est. 1891).

She came from an intellectual and cultured family. Her father, Edward Rye, was a solicitor and noted bibliophile to whose extensive library she had access. One brother became a well-known antiquarian, librarian to Royal Geographical Society.

Sale-Barker, Lucy Elizabeth (Drummond Davies) 1841–1892. Children's magazine editor. Founded *Little Wide-Awake* in 1875 and for over 25 years edited this illustrated magazine aimed at young children. She wrote many of the stories herself. Its title was the pet name for her little boy.

Other work: Prolific children's story-writer. Philanthropic enterprises.

She married John Sale-Barker as her second husband in 1865.

Shaw, Flora Louisa (later Lady Lugard) 1851–1929 b Dublin, Ireland. Foreign correspondent, specialist in colonial affairs. Head of Colonial Dept. at the *Times*. She also wrote on other current affairs and reviewed. An enterprising interview with the exiled Zebehr Pasha was published by the *Pall Mall Gazette*; leading to further commissions. She became an accredited correspondent to CP Scott's *Manchester Guardian* and the *PMG* in Egypt where she met Moberly Bell who eventually brought her on to the *Times* though initially he had to hide the sex of his new correspondent from his proprietor. Had she been a man she would almost certainly have been offered a departmental headship much earlier. Her dispatches were much admired, always well-researched and drew upon her connections and friendships with diplomats, foreign office staff and men such as Cecil Rhodes.

The third of fourteen children of General Shaw and his wife Marie (de Fontaine) she was educated mainly at home and spent much of her childhood at her grandfather's house in Kimmage, Ireland, though she also enjoyed a period with French relatives. Flora came from a military and political background. Her grandfather, Sir Frederick Shaw, had represented Dublin University for 20 years, and was on the point of taking up the Secretaryship of Ireland, when a crippling attack of rheumatic fever put an end to his political career. With her parents' move to Woolwich and her mother's illness and eventual death in 1870, Flora took on the burden of nursing and household management. Ruskin was an early mentor. In the 1880s feeling the need for a home of her own she took a small cottage at Abinger in Surrey, where George Meredith, her neighbour, became a close friend. It was he who introduced her to Stead. She married relatively late in life.

Simcox, Edith Jemima 1844–1901. Critic, periodical essayist. She was perhaps the most perceptive and sympathetic of George Eliot's reviewers. Contributor to the highbrow *Academy* from the outset (1869) for over 25 years, reviewing foreign literature, novels, poetry, biography and general subjects. She contributed essays on art, social and women's issues to a range of reviews including *Contemporary, Fortnightly, Nineteenth Century, Fraser's, Longmans', Macmillan's, North British, Saint Paul's*. Her early work in particular appeared under the pseudonym 'H. Lawrenny'. For the *Manchester Guardian* she wrote several reports of International Trades Congresses.

Other work: Activist and social reformer. A major venture was the shirt-making co-operative which she ran with Mary Hamilton from 1875–84.

Her father was a merchant. She lived most of her life with her mother. Her review of *Middlemarch* brought her into contact with George Eliot to whom she formed a romantic attachment, transmuted into adoring friendship but expressed in her *Autobiography of a Shirtmaker* unpublished until recently.

Skene, Felicia Mary Frances 1821–1899 b Aix en Provence, France. Religious editor. Edited *Churchman's Companion* 1862–80.

Other work: Novelist, poet. Philanthropist. Organized band of nurses during outbreak of cholera in Oxford 1854. The proceeds from her novels were devoted to charity, and she tackled subjects such as prostitution in her fiction.

Daughter of James Skene, friend of Sir Walter Scott, she was an important early influence on young Mary Arnold. She had herself been much influenced by the Tractarians and wrote a memoir of her cousin Alexander Penrose Forbes the friend of Pusey censured for promulgating the doctrine of the real presence.

Smart, Anna Maria (Carnan) 1732–1809 b Reading, Berkshire d Reading. Newspaper editor. Long-serving editor (1762–1809) of one of the country's oldest provincial newspapers, the *Reading Mercury* founded 1723, and covering Berkshire/Oxfordshire. Her stepfather arranged that after his death she and her brother should have control of her family's business for her own and her children's benefit. John Carnan managed the printing side whilst she managed the

newspaper, eventually in partnership with her son-in-law. Under her management the paper expanded, increased in size and brought forward its country
edition times. After her son-in-law's unexpected suicide she carried on alone,
although well into her seventies, until her own death. Her daughters Marianne
Cowslade and Elizabeth Anne le Noir ran the business until 1811 and Marianne
seems to have continued as editor at least into the mid-twenties.

Other work: She was a devout Catholic who assisted French émigrés.

Daughter of William and Mary Carnan, stepdaughter of John Newbery.
Married in 1852 Christopher Smart, the poet, from whom she separated as his
bouts of madness increased.

Stannard, Mrs Henrietta Eliza (Palmer) 1856–1911 b York d Putney. Editor of
Golden Gates (later *Winter's Weekly*) said by Black to be the first penny weekly
ever entirely owned and published by a popular novelist. Founded in 1891 it
ran until 1895. Active in the professionalization of writing. Was first president
of the Writers Club in 1892 and President of Society of Women Journalists
(1901–3). Practical measures were sorely needed. Whilst one journalist criticized
the dining-room of her women's club as 'miniature' and badly-staffed, Charlotte
O'Conor Eccles found the Writer's Club her professional life-line.

Other work: Fiction particularly novels of army life. Her first stories were published in the *Family Herald* and for ten years from 1874 she contributed short
fiction and serials to that paper. Her early pseudonym was 'Violet Whyte' but
she was better known as 'John Strange Winter'.

Daughter of Emily and Henry Vaughan Palmer, rector of St Margaret's York,
and former army officer. Educated at Bootham House School, York. Married
Arthur Stannard 1884.

Swanwick, Helena (Sickert) 1864–1939 b Munich d Maidenhead. Reviewer,
essayist and columnist. For 18 years reviewed for the *Manchester Guardian*.
Wrote on gardening and domestic subjects and said to have been paid a huge
sum for an article about economics for Wilde's *Woman's World*. Edited *Common
Cause* in the early twentieth century.

Other work: Prominent twentieth-century feminist. Lecturer in Psychology,
Westfield College, London.

Her father was a painter and illustrator of Danish origin, her mother the ille-
gitimate daughter of a Cambridge don. Her brother was the artist Walter Sickert.
The family moved to England in 1868. She was educated at a French boarding
school and Notting Hill High and was an early Girtonian taking the Moral
Sciences Tripos, though she had to struggle against her mother's opposition,
and whilst at school was expected to carry out domestic chores for her brothers.
Friend of CP and Rachel Scott. Committed suicide after the outbreak of World
War II.

Taylor, Frances Margaret. Editor Catholic journals. She was the founding editor
of the *Month* though she ran it for one year only in 1864. Proprietor and editor
of the *Lamp* 1862–71. The *Lamp* had been launched in 1846 as a popular penny
paper promoting Catholic principles. Frances Taylor successfully reorganized it.
Among her contributors was her friend Lady Georgiana Fullerton.

Other work: Author, editor or translator of over 20 books. Founded with
Georgiana Fullerton an order of nuns, the Poor Servants of the Mother of God,
originally to work among London's poor. She became the first superior general.

The London convent was near the Jesuit Church in Farm Street and the sisters taught in parochial schools, nursed and ran refuge and rescue homes for women.

Daughter of a Church of England clergyman, she converted to Catholicism after her experiences as a nurse with Florence Nightingale.

Tonna, Charlotte Elizabeth (Browne) 1790–1846 b Norwich d Ramsgate. Editor religious magazines. Evangelical Protestant. She edited the *Protestant Annual, Christian Lady's Magazine* and *Protestant Magazine*. She was associated with the *CLM* from its inception in 1834, initially as part of a small team, until 1846 when her fatal illness forced her to give up. Her use of the magazine to provide a space for Christian women to discuss ethical questions caused her to be dubbed 'a muslin divine' by the *Quarterly*.

Other work: Social-problem novelist. Wrote anti-catholic tracts and Orange songs.

Her father was rector of St Giles' in Norwich. Used her sobriquet 'Charlotte Elizabeth' to avoid the surname of her first husband, Capt. Phelan, from whom she was separated. Married Lewis Hippolytus Joseph Tonna, ultra-protestant author, after Phelan's death.

Toulmin, Camilla (Mrs Newton-Crosland) 1812–95 b London. Editor, periodical contributor. Worked as sub-editor to Leitch Ritchie on *Friendship's Offering*, though she was the effective editor. Also assisted Marguerite Power in editing the *Keepsake*. Edited *Ladies' Companion*. Contributed to *Chambers'* for more than 50 years in various genres, also to *Bentley's, People's Journal, Old Monthly Magazine, London Journal, Ainsworth's, Douglas Jerrold's* and to the annuals.

Other work: Poet, novelist. Children's stories. Pseudonyms: Emma Grey, Mrs Macarthy, Helena Herbert.

Her father a solicitor died when she was only eight.

Turner See **Claxton**

Ward, Mary Augusta (Arnold) 1851–1920 b Hobart, Tasmania d London. Reviewer and periodical contributor particularly during the 1870s and 1880s for a wide range of literary reviews including: *Cornhill Magazine, Fortnightly Review, Macmillan's, New Review, Quarterly, Pall Mall Gazette* and *Saturday*. She also reviewed for the *Times*.

Other work: Novelist. Active philanthropist. Set up nurseries for working women. Supported higher education for women. Anti-suffragist.

Her father was the son of Dr Thomas Arnold of Rugby. Matthew Arnold was her uncle, and Mary was always conscious of being an Arnold. Her early education was disorganized but when the family moved to Oxford with the help of Mark Pattison she was able to undertake an ambitious programme of study. She knew French, German, Italian and Spanish and became an acknowledged expert on early Spanish history and literature. The Pattisons and Felicia Skene were important early influences. She married a young Oxford don, T Humphry Ward, in 1872. The marriage was happy but his career was a disappointment and Mary's earnings from her immensely popular novels were vital to the family's standard of living, and her punishing workload undermined her health. Awarded CBE. Appointed one of the first women magistrates 1920, though by then she was in very poor health.

White, Jessie Meriton (later Mario) 1832–1906 b near Portsmouth d Florence. Foreign correspondent for *Daily News*, based in Genoa. Also wrote on Italian affairs for periodicals, notably the *Nation*.

Other work: Italian liberationist. Field nurse with Garibaldi's campaigns. Daughter of Jane and Thomas White. Her father was a shipyard owner. Educated by governesses, various schools, and the Sorbonne. Married Alberto Mario, a Garibaldian officer.

Winter, John Strange See **Stannard**

Wood Ellen (Price)1814–1887 b Worcester d London. Editor *Argosy* 1867–87 purchased from Strahan as a vehicle for her fiction for which she is best-known. She wrote much of *Argosy*'s contents, some like her popular *Johnny Ludlow* stories anonymously, and left sufficient material for the magazine, under her son's editorship, to continue publishing her work until long after her death.

Other Work: Novelist. Her sensation novel *East Lynne* established her reputation and was attacked by Margaret Oliphant. Her early work appeared in *Ainsworth's*, *Bentley's Miscellany*, and Colburn's *New Monthly Magazine*, her later fiction in such journals as *Good Words* and *St. James's*.

The daughter of Thomas Price, a Worcester glove manufacturer, and his wife Elizabeth, she had a somewhat lonely, bookish childhood in the prosperous household of her grand-parents. She suffered from a curvature of the spine, being virtually bedridden from thirteen to fifteen. Much of her writing was done from a reclining chair. She married in 1836 Henry Wood, a banker, and the family lived in France for many years. Financial problems resulted in a return to England and her income from writing then became a valuable family asset.

Worboise, Emma Jane (later Guyton) 1825–1887 b Birmingham. Religious editor. She edited James Clarke's monthly *Christian World Magazine* from its inception in 1866 until shortly before her death. It was intended to complement Clarke's immensely popular weekly. Within the constraints of a religious magazine aimed at a family readership Worboise encouraged women to participate more fully as Christian daughters, wives and mothers in church and public affairs.

Other work: Novelist. Her first novel was published when she was only 21. Her later work was published by Clarke and her serialized fiction appeared in his various periodicals.

She was the eldest child of an Anglican clergyman George Baddeley Worboise. Married Etherington Guyton.

Yonge Charlotte Mary 1823–1901 b Otterbourne, Hampshire d Otterbourne. Editor/contributor. One of the longest-serving Victorian editors, she began the *Monthly Packet* in 1851 and reluctantly gave up the editorship in 1899. Her strong Anglican moral and religious principles influenced the nature of this magazine for girls and young women. Also edited *Monthly Paper of Sunday Teaching* (1860–75) and *Mothers in Council* (1890–1900). Her work appeared in other journals including *Macmillan's* and *Magazine for the Young*.

Other work: Novelist. Sunday School teacher for over 70 years.

Charlotte's religion was integral to her life and work. Her mother was a vicar's daughter. Charlotte was educated at home by her father, William Crawley Yonge, strictly but, on an intellectual level, she enjoyed a liberal education, studying maths, Greek, science and history as well as religion. Later Keble was a powerful influence on her.

Notes

Preface

1. For a dinner à deux 'Olla Podrida' suggested this recipe as the third of six (inc. the salad) courses. For those who wish to try it: skewer your pigeon with bacon, roast and serve on croûtons with a purée of mushrooms and potato ribbons.
2. (Crawford 1897 526)
3. (Courtney 1934 169, 36 ref also to p 38)

1   Introduction

1. Much more recently a study of journalists who shaped the twentieth-century press echoed this masculine stress in its title.(Andrews and Taylor 1970)
2. (Hatton 1882 49–52)
3. Patrick Leary has rescued her, in this context, from oblivion. (Leary 1994 119)
4. (Cross 1985 167) John Gross's *The Rise and Fall of the Man of Letters* finds room for James Hannay yet Frances Cobbe's seven lines are mainly devoted to one article of hers which he was **not** tempted to read.
5. (Spender 1986)
6. (Cobbe 1996)
7. (Onslow 1998 56–7)
8. (Porritt c 1901 19); (Escott 1911; Krishnamurti 1991) Perry edited the *Morning Chronicle* (Koss 1973 91)
9. (Gross 1991 (revised ed. first pub. 1969) 48)
10. (Scott 1952 58)
11. (Blowitz 1893 41)
12. *Seventh Annual Report of the SWJ 1900–1*
13. Bradbury & Evans's *Ladies' Companion at Home and Abroad*
14. (Caine 1992 on Cobbe 111)
15. Robert L Patten, 'What Do Editors Do?', unpublished Plenary Address to RSVP, Simon Fraser University, Vancouver, July 21–2, 1998. On memoirs see (Brown 1985)
16. Neither she nor 'Golden Bee' appears in Lohrli's index; (Betham-Edwards 1898 204–5) See also (Lohrli 1973 43)
17. (Black 1893 17–8)
18. Some contemporary reviewers read it as a 'Revolting Daughter' book, as the title and structure invite. The heroine may strike a late twentieth-century reader as more tragic and sympathetic. (Duncan 1895 (first pub 1894))
19. (Dixon 1894 178, 114, 183) (Dixon 1930 31)

20. e g (Altick 1957; Boyce, Curran *et al.* 1978; Shattock and Wolff 1982; Brown 1985)
21. (Houghton 1982 21)
22. (Scott 1952 78)
23. (Hatton 1882 91–2)
24. See (Brown 1985 114); (Billington 1896 104)
25. (Fox Bourne 1887 371–2)
26. (Hatton 1882 37–41, 58)
27. See (Altick 1957; Williams 1961)
28. (Fox-Bourne c 1901 17) (Friederichs 1911 51)
29. (Johnstone 1832); (Johnstone 1834) On circulation/price-cutting see also (Marchand 1971 44–5)
30. *Household Words*, 21 August 1858 'The Unknown Public'
31. ([Times] 1935–52) Vol. I 163, 243; Vol III 118
32. See e.g. (Beetham 1990 9–13) on women's magazines
33. (Escott 1911 234)
34. (Linton 1894 (first pub 1867) 264); (Scott 1952 391)
35. (Hatton 1882 116)
36. (Pennell 1897)
37. (Fenwick Miller 1884 222)
38. (Parkes 1865 120–1)
39. This was Christian Johnstone, (Bodichon 1987)
40. (Baron-Wilson 1851)
41. (See Stokes 1989)
42. (O'Connor 1889 428, 431, 423)
43. (See Stokes 1989); (Beetham 1996 16–7)
44. (Friederichs 1911 51–3)
45. (anon 1897)
46. (Friederichs 1911 83ff)
47. Some credit Stead with inventing 'New Journalism'. (Scott 1952 238)
48. (Linton 1890 525–31)
49. (Ross 1936 400–3; 16–7)
50. (Crawford 1893);
51. (anon 1894 246–7)
52. *Womanhood* Vol III, 255–6. Hers was not a stereotypical 'servant problem' complaint. She advised typists affected by falling rates to combine to protect their interests.
53. (G.H.P. 1891 395)

2   Obstacles and Opportunities

1. (Madden 1855 233)
2. (Sutherland 1991 82ff) (Leary 1994 119–20)
3. Mrs Purcell seems to have been genuinely kind, even prescribing a special glass of wine with meals to build up her strength. (Cowden-Clarke 1896 31)
4. (Cook) 1849); (Beale 1879 107–8) (anon 1896) They mentioned 500 and 600 sitting the exam for a handful of posts.
5. Girton BRP 37/2 Letter to her father in 1850. See Chapter 5

6. (Low 1904 83)
7. (Mayo 1910 96, 127)
8. Girton Bodichon Papers B303
9. (Hatton 1882 28)
10. (Sanders 1986 183)
11. (Ireland 1892 xii)
12. (Madden 1855 229–30)
13. (Martineau 1877 (new ed. 1983) 357); (Cowden Clarke *et al.* 1969 115 (memoir prefaced 1878))
14. (See McKenzie 1961)
15. (Billington 1896 102)
16. (Simcox 1887 398); (Martineau 1877 433–4)
17. (Howitt 1889 42)
18. (Billington 1896)103
19. When the Spanish-American war ended Margaret Sullivan of the *Chicago Chronicle* was apparently the oldest editorial writer in the city. (Ross 1936 551); (Crawford 1893 370–1)
20. As opposed to domestic service which she considered often demeaning. (Mayo 1910 360)
21. (Cowden-Clarke 1896 101)
22. (Madden 1855 241–3); (Meynell 1965 10–11) See (Sanders 1986 168) on contemporary views of Martineau's masculinity, and (Martineau 1877 (new ed. 1983) 204ff) for other *Quarterly* attacks.
23. (Clarke 1990 97)
24. (Haight 1968 83); (Mayo 1910 143)
25. (Eccles 1893 831)
26. See (Ross 1936 6, 562–4)
27. (Ross 1936 332, 483–4); (Banks 1902 51)
28. (Brown 1985 81)
29. (Altick 1948 184, 202)
30. (Hatton 1882 41)
31. (Linton 1894 (First pub 1867) 173)
32. (Hatton 1882 115)
33. (Fenwick Miller 1884 15–7)
34. Girton BRP I 'My Childhood'; Diary 1849 4/5, 11, 12
35. (Tweedie 1894 356–7); (Linton 1897)
36. Art schools at least provided some opportunity for mixed classes, though women suffered from various cultural and institutional discriminatory practices. See (Cherry 1993)
37. (Broomfield 1997 10, 3)
38. (Black 1893 128) (Dilke 1905 18)
39. Less than a third of nearly 100 respondents were experienced journalists; many others clearly attracted by the requirement to 'dress well'. Another optimist advertised herself in *The Englishwoman* 's columns of governesses, companions and secretaries anxiously seeking work.
40. (Bennett 1898 75–7); (Banks 1902 63)
41. (Duncan 1895 (first pub 1894) 71–3)
42. (Eccles 1893 831)
43. (Crowquill 1845 360) Writer/caricaturist Alfred Forrestier

44. *Monthly Packet* Vol XV, 1858, 224; Felicia Skene's *Churchman's Companion* accepted a story. (Sutherland 1991 38–9, 31ff)
45. (Mayo 1910 96)
46. (Martineau 1877 (new ed 1983) 118–9); (Fenwick Miller 1884 38–9)
47. cited (Anderson 1987 24–5)
48. (Cowden-Clarke 1896 44–5)
49. (Mayo 1910 120–4)
50. (Coleridge 1903 200–2)
51. (Beetham 1996 185)
52. (Bennett 1898 24) Was Bennett the first with this unfortunate suggestion which occasionally works but meanwhile creates many frustrated secretaries?
53. Girton BRPV 27/1. John Frederick Feeny purchased the *Birmingham Journal* in 1844 and founded the *Birmingham Post* in 1857
54. (Lochhead 1961 23–4); (Mayo 1910 126)
55. (Anderson 1987 137); (Black 1893 62); (Black 1893 9) Black's phraseology implies it was after his *death* she wrote *The Wooing o't* for *Temple Bar*
56. (See Cherry 1993)
57. (Betham-Edwards 1898 121–2)
58. (Howitt 1889 195)
59. See discussion by (Levine 1990 26–8) of Barbara Bodichon, Frances Cobbe, Henrietta Müller, Emily Sherriff.
60. Girton Emily Davies 'Family Chronicle' 262–3; (Edwin Pratt cited Levine 1990 63–4); On female friendships/networks generally see Levine and (Clarke 1990)
61. (Macpherson 1878 294)
62. Girton BRP VI
63. (Erskine 1915 256)
64. (Dilke 1869 597)
65. (Dixon 1894 53)
66. D'Orsay married her step-daughter, abandoning her 'almost at the church door' (Madden 1855 369), obituary of D'Orsay in *La Presse* cited 354
67. (Madden 1855 228–9). Patrick Leary first pointed out to me that Mrs Hall was indeed running a literary salon, whose relative informality was greatly appreciated by Mrs Newton Crosland (Crosland 1893 1278).
68. Greenwood was Sara Jane Lippincott, noted for her European travel sketches. She exploited those she dined with, including Dickens, Thackeray, the Brownings. Mrs Oliphant, another victim, presumably included among the 'great' Rosa Bonheur, and among the 'small' the Chinese mandarin whose rendering of a sentimental ballad sounded to her like the howl of a dog. (Ross 1936; Jay 1990 41) (Lee 1955 82–3)
69. (Mayo 1910 128–9); (Crossland 1893)
70. It may be judged how far women felt club society had changed that one of its 'most drastic rules' was that no married couple could be members, although spouses could be invited as guests. The dinners were held at the Pall Mall restaurant. (Dixon 1894 109)
71. (Humphry 1979 (first pub 1897) 119, 123); (Eccles 1893 836)
72. (anon 1894 245–6); (Green 1891 498–9); (anon 1895)
73. *Seventh Annual Report of the SWJ 1900–1*

74. (Bonham-Carter 1978 87)
75. (Cobbe 1996 259)
76. (Simcox 1996 593)
77. (Stead 1892 13)
78. (Bennett 1898 16–20) Despite the patronizing tone, his practical advice e.g. on approaching editors and studying a paper's form was sound.
79. (Ireland 1892 204); (Stead 1892 13)
80. (Green 1891 499 504); (Blowitz 1893 38–9)
81. A point Mrs Cotes made (Duncan 1895 61)
82. (Crawford 1893 368)
83. (Ross 1936 578); (Banks 1902)
84. (Stead 1892 14); (Mayo 1910 104)
85. (G.H.P. 1891 395)
86. (Lochhead 1961 31); (Cobbe 1996 252–3) 'Angelical' refers to the painter Angelica Kauffman (reprinted in Lacey 1986 354–77)
87. (David 1987 x)
88. A greater cause sometimes subsumed personal interests as with those Conservative women serving on provincial School Boards for whom 'The service ethic of education was often stronger ... than formal party loyalties.' (Hollis 1987 137)
89. (EWJ Dec 1859 Parkes 1986 161)
90. (anon 1863 209)
91. (Fenwick Miller 1884 164–5)

3   A Fifth Estate

1. (Stead 1892 14)
2. (Cobbe 1894 Vol 2 [67])
3. See Chapter 9. (See Caine 1992 119) for Cobbe's financial circumstances.
4. Somerville Papers, Bodleian Library, MSFP 18. (September 6 1871) I am grateful to Sally Mitchell for providing a transcript of this letter and confirming the year, omitted from the letter.
5. (Cobbe 1894 75, 77); (Crawford 1893 370)
6. (Melnyk 1996 140–1); (anon 1894 247–8); (Fox Bourne 1887 160); (Low 1904 91)
7. (Hatton 1882 58)
8. (Eccles, 1893 831)
9. (Billington 1896 101)
10. (Autolycus) 1893) (anon, October 1894) quotes weekly rates of 30s – £3. 10s for reporting; £2. 10s – for sub-editing.
11. (Hubbard 1875 75) The reporting discussed is note-taking and shorthand reporting for Parliamentary committees etc.
12. (Hogarth 1897 928)
13. (Crawford 1893 367)
14. (Allingham and Radford 1990 (first pub. 1907) 273)
15. (Brown 1985 7–25)
16. (anon 1897 579); See also (Fox Bourne, 1887 367ff)
17. (Hatton 1882 180–1)

18. *Pall Mall Gazette* April 7, 1893
19. (Hatton 1882 168); (Tweedie 1894 361)
20. (Bennett 1898 96)
21. (Shand 1879)
22. (Linton 1885 Vol I 265–6)
23. (Times 1939)
24. (Martineau 1853)
25. (cited Brown 1985 80–1)
26. (Porritt c 1901 20); (Hunter 1992)
27. (Jones 1993 44)
28. (Brown 1985 82)
29. (Fox Bourne 1887 381–2)
30. (Koss 1973 20)
31. (anon 1894 248)
32. (Black 1893 4)
33. (Tweedie 1894 359); (Layard 1901 59)
34. (Fox Bourne 1887 152–5) Though it, like other dailies, was certainly not in the circulation league of the *Times*.
35. (Linton 1885 Vol I 266–9) Layard mentions 20gns for 6 (long) articles a month with reviews paid additionally and estimated at 'certainly not less than £250 per year'. Mrs Tweedie's information is at variance – leaders three days a week paid at £20 for six. Mrs Linton's memory may have failed her.
36. (Linton 1885 270–1)
37. (Fox Bourne 1887 155) The term 'political' is used quite strictly. Questions of social conditions and economic issues are excluded.
38. (Tweedie 1894 359)
39. (Escott 1911 232)
40. (Linton 1894 10)
41. (Black 1893 5)
42. (Anderson 1987 67)
43. (Linton 1890 524–5)
44. (Linton 1894 223)
45. (Escott 1911 230); (Reid 1897 61)
46. (Green 1891 500–1)
47. (Green 1891 505)
48. (Johnson 1925 193)
49. (Escott 1911 214)
50. (Fenwick Miller 1884)194 For summaries of these leaders see (Webb 1960; Pichanick 1980; Arbuckle 1994)
51. (Hoecker-Drysdale 1992 129) For her journalism 129ff.
52. (Hatton 1882 52); (Haight 1956–1978 257); (Fenwick Miller 1884 79–80, 135–6, 178, 187, 164–5)
53. She used this method for one of her early *Repository* pieces. 'Prison Discipline' 1832 drew on the 8th *Report of the Committee of the Society for the Improvement of Prison Discipline* and a series of *Punishment of Death* articles.
54. (Cobbe 1894 68–9)
55. She did so because leaders based solely on reports resulted in readers' letters enclosing money for surviving relatives. (Cobbe 1894 69)
56. (All republished in Cobbe 1876)

57. (Cobbe 1894 69); Letter, 17 May [1874] to Sarah Wister, Historical Society of Pennsylvania.
58. (Green 1891)
59. (Billington 1896 111); (G.H.P. 1891)
60. (Billington 1896 102); (Crawford 1893 371)
61. (Cobbe 1894 72–3)
62. (Crawford 1893 371) (Autolycus) 1893) She would hardly have been successful if she ever did as she claimed and recommended the same product for both the complexion and cleaning boots.
63. (Eccles 1895 352)
64. (Bennett 1898 82)
65. (anon 1895 January)
66. (Hunter 688); (Billington 1896 105)
67. (1939 455ff); (Green 1891 505) Correspondents based in other cities earned considerably less, depending upon the amount of work involved.
68. (Crawford 1893 369); (anon nd (1913))
69. (Fox Bourne 1887 311)
70. (Hatton 1882 96)
71. (Fox Bourne 1887 350)
72. (Green 1891 505–6); (Crawford 1893 367)
73. (Hogarth 1897 928)
74. (cited anon 1893) 'Record of Events'
75. (anon 1893) 'Record of Events'
76. (Kitchin 1925)
77. See (Bell 1927 156; Bell 1947 50ff, 92)
78. (*History of the Times* Vol III 1947 220–47) For her handling of the Committee see e g 229, 231, 235, 237
79. (Crawford 1893 362–3)
80. (Banks 1902 235–6, 283)
81. (Green 1891 502–3)
82. (Scott 1952 271–2); (Friederichs 1911 119–21)
83. (Billington 1896 111)
84. (Ross 1936 17–8)
85. (Banks 1902 273, 108–9)
86. (Banks 1902 211–2); (Ross 1936 17)
87. (Scott 1952 364–5, 374)
88. (Meynell 1965 vii-xi); (Scott 1952 374)
89. (Meynell 1929 124ff); (Meynell 1965 xff)
90. (Madden 1855 272)
91. (Wiener 1985 260); (Green, 1891)
92. (Low 1904 39, 12); (O'Connor, 1889 429–30); (anon 1897–8 248)

4 At Our Library Table: Reviewers and Critics

1. (Spender 1986) Chapter 9 (Parrinder 1991 327)
2. Although they often had family connections to this milieu. Consider Mary Ward, Anne Mozley. (Tuchman and Fortin 1989) argues a similar marginalization of women from high-culture fiction.

3. (Gross 1991 (revised ed. first pub. 1969) 81) The first three chapters, notwithstanding, provide a highly readable overview of nineteenth-century reviews.
4. (Clarke 1990 94)
5. (Trela 1996 89) (Mermin 1993) Ch.6 may be usefully read alongside Parrinder.
6. (Curran 1998 19–22)
7. Reading Mitford collection 424 27 Nov 1830
8. Proliferation of magazines benefited authors' payments. (Leary 1994 108), (Escott 1911 230)
9. cited (Pykett 1990 12)
10. (Marchand 1971) especially 18, 24, chapter 3, 328–35
11. (Low 1904 12–3)
12. (Reid 1897 61); (Times/1939 437ff; 467; 486, 472–3). The authors, if grudgingly, also acknowledge absurdity in Broome's response to Josephine Butler's *Women's Work*. 476
13. (Showalter 1978 228)
14. (Duncan 1895)
15. (Dixon 1894 147, 143–4)
16. (Gross 1991 88), (Linton 1890 522–3); (Coleridge 1903 340)
17. (Hutton 1989 39) Subleader on John Grote's A Few Words on Criticism' (Haight 1956–78 318, 437)
18. cited (Hutton 1989, 40–3) *Spectator* 29 June 1861
19. (Oliphant 1856 351–2) She contrasts the author throwing himself into a work which then becomes a separate entity.
20. (Gross 1991 11)
21. (Busk 1835 376)
22. (Haight 1956–1978 224–5), (Coleridge 1903 340) Eliot seemingly avoided even favourable press coverage.
23. Reading, Mitford Collection 454 Elford/June, 1822; (Sutherland 1991 89)
24. See (Showalter 1978 88–95)
25. Cited (Mansfield 1998 81)
26. The shift to signature began in the mid-1860s, although weeklies maintained anonymity and Fox Bourne thought the *Athenæum* gained by it. (Shand 1897 237); (Fox Bourne 1887 317); (Oliphant 1887 January 145)
27. (Oliphant 1887 May 735) (Lobban and William Blackwood 1897 162); (Curran 1998 10–11, 16)
28. (Marchand 1971) Chapter 2, 161
29. (Linton 1885 III, 96–9)
30. (Fryckstedt 1983 30–1)
31. Cited (Fryckstedt 1983 24–5)
32. (Cobbe 1894 77)
33. (Eliot 1855) reprinted (Pinney 1963 138)
34. *Athenæum*, 27 January 1866 31(*Treason at Home*, Mrs Greenhough); 28 July 1866, 110–1(Charlotte Hardcastle)
35. (Oliphant 1895 645)
36. (Linton 1996 364, 366) first pub. *Temple Bar* April, 1885; Others questioned Eliot's originality. Charlotte Yonge considered she 'could represent but not create.' (Coleridge 1903 340) Papin's Digester – a kind of early pressure cooker.

37. (Coghill 1899 217); (Linton 1899 57); (Anderson 1987 46)
38. (Eastlake 1848 173; Oliphant 1896; Sadleir 1944) Sadleir's quotation from Broughton's letter is picked up by both (Showalter, 1982 177) and (Fryckstedt 1983 85) who also discuss the Grimstone fictionalization in *A Beginner*.
39. (Haight 1968 81–2); (Showalter 1978 25); (Oliphant 1855 561)
40. (Flint 1993) ch.7 and 8 discusses influences/prohibitions on the young woman reader.
41. Girton 'Family Chronicle' 290–1; (Shand 1886 25)
42. My information on de Mattos comes from Marysa Demoor's paper 'Anonymous Women Reviewers and the *Athenæum*' given at RSVP Conference Manchester 1992. She identified fewer than ten women contributing between 1828 and 1850 but some 40 during 1880–1910.
43. (Fryckstedt 1983 87–8) *Athenæum*, 12 June 1897
44. See (Carney 1996), (Fryckstedt 1985)
45. (Clarke 1990 91–2)
46. *Athenæum* 19 May 1866, 667, *Plain John Orpington* (John Harwood)
47. e.g. Mrs Newby's 'hazy notion that a foundry is a large blacksmith's shop' *Athenæum* 20 January 1866; Miss March Phillips's impracticable proposals 24 November 1860, 702–3
48. *Athenæum* 15 July 1865, 79–80
49. *Athenæum* 10 March 1866, 329
50. *Athenæum* 2 June 1866 733. See also (Fryckstedt 1983 36–7)
51. (Jay 1990 xvi)
52. (Oliphant 1857; Oliphant 1894; Oliphant 1895)
53. (Kramer 1995); (Trela 1995)
54. (Oliphant 1879 465–7, 475, 481)
55. (Oliphant 1862 574–6); See examples (Onslow 1998 68)
56. (Oliphant 1896)
57. (Showalter 1978 91–3) (Eastlake 1848 163–74)
58. (Oliphant 1855 555–60)
59. *Athenæum* 24 March 1866, 395–6; (Oliphant July 1875 99) She also preferred the grave Antonio to the 'bears'. (Oliphant June 1887)
60. (Allott 1968 (first pub. 1959) 47, 49)
61. *Westminster Review* LXVI October 1856 reprinted (Pinney 1963 318–9, 325) This issue includes her fulsome review of *Dred*.
62. (Pykett 1992 74–6)
63. (Sergeant 1897 181) (Oliphant 1895 646); (Oliphant 1862 567)
64. (anon IV 1862; anon V 1862; Robinson 1995 110–1)
65. (Oliphant 1867; Robinson 1995 114f)
66. (Pinney 1963 263–4)
67. (Pinney 1963 216, 3, 334, 134–5); *Athenæum*, 18 February 1865 232–3
68. (Haight 1966 (first pub. Houghton Mifflin, 1965) 73–80)
69. (McKenzie 1961 76, xi); (Fulmer 1998 113)
70. (Simcox 1883)
71. (Tredrey 1954 131)
72. (Hasell 1875 323); (Hasell 1879 420–1); (Hasell 1875)
73. (Marchand 1971 219–26); (Fulmer 1998 117)
74. (Dilke 1869 591); (Dilke 1905 67)

75. Born Emily Francis Strong, she retained the 'S' of her maiden name in her signature after marriage thus marking her independence. (Dilke 1905 19) She later chose to be known as Emilia. Kali Israel's *Names and Stories* (1999) explores the significance of these changes.
76. In a flattering reference to the influence of her late husband.
77. (Eisler, 1981 18); (Dilke 1905 19); (Cherry, 1993 40). See also (Mansfield, 1998 83) on the motives, professional and financial, which led to her leaving the *Westminster*.
78. (Pattison 1883 353); (Dilke, 1873 534–5) Her comments that the 'most essential structure' the 'scientific facts' of a piece of 'natural' foliage being 'subjectively naturalesque' look towards modernism.
79. (Pattison 1872)
80. (Dilke 1873); (Dilke 1869)
81. (Mansfield, 1998); (Eisler 1981 168, 159)
82. (Johnston 1994)
83. (Low 1904 23)
84. (Pennell 1894 732–4)
85. (Ward 1891 771, 773)
86. (Johnstone, 1834 612–3) Favourably reviewing Martineau's *Illustrations of Political Economy*.
87. (Arbuckle 1994) *Daily News* 27 January 1853
88. (Crawford, 1893 363)
89. *The Ladies' Cabinet* defended Stowe in a half-column reply to a reader. Vol.1 NS (2nd) 1852, 224. See also Chapter 6 (Mrs Hall)
90. (Eliot 1963 325–7)
91. (Arbuckle 1994 249–54)

5 Something to Say, a Living to Earn: Periodical Contributors

1. (Beetham 1996 43); cited (Lohrli 1973 398) Patterson edited several papers, was a contributor to *Blackwood's* and many other periodicals particularly on economic issues.
2. (Lohrli 1973 24–34)
3. (Jay 1995 245)
4. Reading, Mitford Collection Frances Trollope 18 Sept, 1831
5. (Petersen 1998) argues for a carefully-planned launch of Anna in journalism. (Lohrli 1973 280, 324) (Storey *et al.* 1988 417)
6. Best known for her first novel *Comin' thro' the Rye*. (Black 1893 75)
7. See (Diamond 1997)
8. (Fenwick Miller 1884 62)
9. Reading, Mitford Collection 433. Elford/22 March, 1821
10. (Meynell 1929 137–9)
11. e.g. See her on Cowley or the Austen charades and 'conditions of silence'. *PMG* 26 July, 1895 and 18 April, 1897. Some *PMG* literary essays have been reprinted, though with Meynell's subsequent alterations, in (Meynell 1965)
12. (Bennett 1898 79)
13. (Storey *et al.* 1988 790); (Lohrli 1973 338)

14. See (Showalter 1978 79ff)
15. See (Lightman 1997 192ff)
16. (Mozley 1868 426–7)
17. (Cross 1985 200)
18. All are reprinted in (Mozley 1864)
19. (Bennett 1898 86)
20. (Chorley 1872 133); Reading, Mitford Collection, 434. Elford/4 April 1821; Redding/20 April 1832. Writers were paid by the number of pages filled. The paper 'sheets' were printed and folded to make pages of the requisite size, folio, quarto etc.
21. (Leary 1994 108–9)
22. (Chapple and Pollard 1997 No. 70)
23. (Lohrli 1973 105, 21)
24. Information from (Lohrli 1973). The column entries for 7 June were under-estimated in the case of both women. Compare (7 June) Mrs Gaskell unusually on the going rate at £4 for seven-and three-quarter columns of 'Disappearances' and John Capper's £3 for seven-and-a-quarter.
25. (Meynell 1929 100); (Green 1891 505) (Low 1904)
26. (Leary 1994 108–9); (Chorley 1872 132)
27. (Dixon 1930 161); (Hughes 1996 174, 188)
28. (Madden 1855 229); (Mayo 1910 149) Reading, Mitford Collection, Elford/15 June 1822; (Badeni 1981 100)
29. (Linton 1885 Vol III, 101–2)
30. (Trevelyan 1932 37, 42); (Sutherland 1991 90) Between 1881 and 1885 Mrs Ward wrote fifty long and 200 short articles (Badeni 1981 73)
31. (Ireland 1892 350)
32. (Ireland 1892 200–1) See (Fryckstedt 1985) on her work for Jerrold
33. (Layard 1901 137) quoting her autobiographical novel (Linton 1885 Vol.III, 95)
34. (Chorley 1872 221) (1846)
35. (Watson nd 141, 160) Just over a decade later it had run to fourteen separate editions.
36. (Coleridge 1903 341); (Hall 1883 note 177–8, 175)
37. (Watson 162)
38. (Mitford 1848? 183–4, 191)
39. (Mitford 1893 61, 67–8)
40. (Mitford 1893 11, 161); (Lohrli 1973 303)
41. (Ritchie 1893 xxxix–xl)
42. (Mitford 1893 3)
43. Reading, Mitford Collection Elford/403, 8 April 1820; 433, 22 March 1821
44. (Mitford 1835 273) 'Belford Races' (Mitford 1848? 241)
45. (Oliphant 1855 555) This also contained her *Jane Eyre* remarks.
46. (Mitford 1910 287)
47. Royal Military College for Officers.
48. (Lohrli 1973 241–2)
49. (Costello 1845 275),
50. (Thomson 1845 182, 185, 190)
51. (Ritchie 1893 xxvi) (Meynell 1965 83–4)
52. (Lochhead 1961 31, 103)
53. (Eastlake 1865 287)

54. (Eastlake 1857 460–4, 443–4, 467)
55. (Lobban and William Blackwood 1897 162)
56. (Oliphant 1861 671); (Coghill 1899 156–8) She knew something of Pugin as her husband trained under him.
57. 'The Pictures of the Year', *Blackwood's,* June 1888, 813–26, Discussed more fully in (Onslow 1998)
58. (Oliphant 1873; Oliphant 1875; Oliphant 1885; Oliphant 1886)
59. (Coleridge 1903) 340–2
60. (Oliphant 1894)
61. (Ward 1885); (Betham-Edwards 1878)
62. (Betham-Edwards 1898 126–7)
63. (Jay 1995 cited 241)
64. (Lawrance 1854) Dickens's editing may deserve some credit (Diamond 1997 9–10)
65. (Lightman 1997 65, 70)
66. (Lightman 1997)
67. (Lightman 1997 71–3)
68. 'Letter to the Deaf' is reprinted in (Martineau 1996); (Martineau 1854) 137
69. Bodleian, Somerville Papers MSFP-18 Mary Somerville/Sept. 6 [1871]
70. Some are reprinted in (Broomfield and Mitchell 1996) and (Lacey 1986)
71. (Freeman 1977 258–9)
72. (Anderson 1987 168)
73. (Linton 1996 356)
74. (Layard 1901 136–50)
75. (unsigned 1868)
76. (Linton 1899 82–6)
77. (Anderson 1987 71)
78. 'Laws concerning Women' 1856, 'The Condition of Women' 1858, 'The Great Unrepresented' 1866
79. (Oliphant 1879 206)
80. (Linton 1854, 1 April 159); (Linton 1854, 29 April)
81. (Layard 1901)140; (Linton 1897)
82. In the back of the copy of her *Literary Life* held at Lancaster University.
83. (Linton 1891 79–80)
84. Notably in her *Westminster* article (1888) resulting in an avalanche of letters to the *Telegraph*, but more immediately in papers by Caird and Clementina Black in the *Fortnightly*.
85. (Caird 1892 322, 328)
86. (Linton 1899 31, 21)
87. (Oliphant 1895 904)
88. (Grand 1996); (Grand 1996 668)
89. (Betham-Edwards 1919 223–4)

6　In the Editor's Chair

1. (Scott 1952 103)
2. (Sala 1895 426, 429–30) Sala globe-trotting for the*Telegraph* enjoyed 'the wages of an ambassador and the treatment of a gentleman'. (Hatton 1882 132)

3. (Schmidt 1983 6, 10). Stephen took over in 1871. After Thackeray's retirement the magazine was run by an editorial committee. (Schmidt 1983 9–10)

4. (*Times* 1939 529) In 1845 after an outstandingly successful year. In tougher times he offered to relinquish it. (1939 12, 16) The £1000 pa left to John Walter II as manager was also to be reduced if profits fell below £5000 (Vol III, 431)

5. (Green 1891 505), (Griffiths 1991 51)

6. (Hall 1883 306–7) He received no salary and minimal profits.

7. By 1880 it was £400. (Scott 1952 95, 114)

8. (Freeman 1977 134)

9. (Gissing 1891 86, 15) The Jedwoods are based on Maxwell and Braddon.

10. See (Hatton 1882 116–8, 134–6)

11. (Cowden-Clarke 1896 152–3.)

12. See (Hatton 1882 41–3) for changing social position of Fleet Street journalists.

13. (Shattock 19 98, 101)

14. (*Times* 1939 Vol II, 508, 59–60, 520)

15. Cramped quarters compared with their Midlands home. (Campbell 1889 45) He sacrifices his marriage to ambition.

16. (Hall 1883 314). See also Mary Mitford's scathing opinion of Campbell Chapter 5

17. (Dixon 1930 161)

18. See directions on stories by Harriet Parr, Eliza Linton and Emily Jolly and Martineau's article in letters to Wills 22 July 1855 and 14 October 1854 (Storey *et al.* 1993 680–1, 438)

19. (Billington 1896 103)

20. (Scott 1952 22)

21. (Billington 1896 102–3).

22. (Green 1891 501–2)

23. (Bennett 1898 9)

24. (Fox Bourne 1887 371)

25. (Coghill 1899 246); (Clarke 1992)

26. (Banks 1902 153–6)

27. See (Trela 1995 22) (Jay 1995 249–50), (Coghill 1899 219, 221, 249)

28. (Beetham 1996 42–44) For their importance see (Maidment 1984)

29. (Friederichs 1911 229)

30. See (*Times* 1935–52 Vol I 174–83, III 436–44) By 1816 several women were shareholders.

31. (de Saint Victor 1984 21)

32. (Scott 1952 116, 156–7); (Sullivan 1984)

33. (Beetham 1996 43)

34. (Mayo 1910 131)

35. (Hunter 688)

36. (Griffiths 1991 51) Harmsworth's anxiety was not without cause. An initial circulation of well over 250 000* rapidly sank to less than a tenth of that. *Figures quoted variously: 265 217 (Griffiths), 276 000 (Andrews and Taylor 1970 53)

37. (Anon c 1901 12)

38. (Hughes 1996 185–7)
39. Bodichon Papers B 312
40. (anon 1846)
41. (Jerrold 1901 372)
42. *Great Expectations* came to the rescue (Sutherland 1976 175–8) (Srebrnik 1986 59–61, 45)
43. She suggested *Temple Bar, Cornhill* or *St James's*. 'They publish such *trash* ... they must want *poetry*.' (Mayo 1910 132–3)
44. (Ross 1936 323 ff)
45. See (Fox Bourne 1887 276); (Hatton 1882 28–9)
46. (Hatton 1882 29–30) The proprietor of the *Western Daily Press* sat for Plymouth; Joseph Cowen, owner of the *Newcastle Chronicle* for Newcastle.
47. (Campbell 1889 10–20)
48. [Anon, c 1901 129, 99–100)
49. See (Burton 1954 108–13)
50. (Anon c 1901 106)
51. (Grant 1872 549–9)
52. (Ross 1936 481, see also 591–2)
53. (Friednichs 1911); Billington notes the *Sunday Times* earlier period of 'feminine control' under the Australian gold-mining heiress, Alice Cornwell.
54. (Billington 1896 103); (Griffiths 1991 51),
55. (Maidment 1984 89)
56. (Howitt 1889 255, 245); (Johnstone 1834)
57. (Madden 1855 264). He instances a writer being offered – and on this occasion refusing – £600 for 120 lines. *The Keepsake* ceased in 1857. (Shattock 1993 7)
58. (Watson nd 235–6) Reading, Mitford Collection, Letter to D Bogue June 1838; (Chorley 1872 266–8)
59. See (Moring 1993) on Eliot's use of the annual in this incident.
60. (Howitt 1889 205); (Hall 1883 308–9) Another estimate was 400 guineas (Adburgham 1972 241)
61. See (Tillotson 1954)
62. (Madden 1855 266–71)
63. Jerden claimed her literary earnings reached £2000 to £3000 pa; even Miss Power's more modest estimate c£1000 is impressive. (Madden 1855 229 273) Blessington was wealthy but their joint extravagence meant he died heavily in debt.
64. (Hunt 1996)
65. (Howitt 1889 205–6, 221); (Moring 1993 22)
66. (Howitt 1840)
67. (Adburgham 1972 245) (Howitt 1840 6)
68. (Johnstone 1839 812)
69. (Howitt 1889 40–1)
70. (Howitt 1889 43) Also (Maidment 1984 88)
71. (Howitt 1889 214)
72. See (Spatt 1985; Mancoff 1991).
73. The others were LEL, Lady Sidney Morgan, Caroline Norton, Lady Blessington, Mary Mitford, Jane Porter and Harriet Martineau. (Leary 1994 118); (Marks 1986)

74. (Mitchell 1984 393)
75. (Hall 1852)
76. See (Leary 1994 112–5)
77. (Merrifield 1852 68) Tightlacing remained a contentious subject for decades to come. (Beetham 1996 81–8)
78. Her own interests surface – Ireland's problems; philanthropic initiatives; domestic concerns.
79. (anon 1852 61) Bremer praised the book's 'fairness' and 'living truths' but thought Stowe's solution '*first* emancipation, and *then* education' counter-productive.
80. (anon 1852 61)
81. Payne had recently died. The enormously popular song was still going strong in Britain over a century later.
82. (anon 1852 383)
83. (Beetham 1996 80)
84. *Sharpe's* n.s.III, 158
85. (Hall 1883 334)
86. (Hall 1861 (v).)
87. (R. 1861) proposed gentlewomen be housekeepers in wealthy households.
88. (Mayo 1910 129)
89. (Hall 1861 v)
90. After the sale in 1876 came work by Wilkie Collins, Mark Twain, Charles Reade and Hardy's *Return of the Native*.
91. (Wolff 1974 138)
92. (Altick 1957 359) After a dramatic start *Temple Bar* stabilized at c13 000 (Scheuerle 1984 404) Even the astonishingly successful *Cornhill* which reached twice that in 1869 steadily dropped to c12 000 by the early 1880s. (Schmidt 1983 12)
93. Girton Bodichon Papers, B305
94. *The Welcome Guest* (1860) and the aborted *May Fair Magazine* (1864) (Wolff 1979 90)
95. (Wolff 1974 19–20.) The flattering tone is typical.
96. Braddon mentioned £1800 plus retention of copyright. (Sutherland 1976 142–5); (Wolff 1974 26, 138–9)
97. See (Onslow 1995 468–9.)
98. (Wolff 1974 14) (Gettmann 1960 160–3)
99. Reproduced (Flint 1993 279) Wood claimed it was translated into 'Parsee and Hindustanee' and the readers read *East Lynne* to 'Hindoos in their own tongue'. (Wood 1887 440)
100. (Flint 1993 286–91)
101. e.g.'The Physiology of Picnics' (Vol. 2, 427–35) Compare 'Up for the Season' (Vol. 11, 1870, 473–79) and the 'In a Country House' (Vol. 20) series
102. Vol. 5, 244
103. George Augustus Sala was editor 1860–63, purchasing it in 1862. It published several Braddon novels.
104. *Bookseller* 27 October, 1860, 614. Cited (Scheuerle 1984 407)
105. (Wolff 1974 156–8)
106. (Wolff 1974 144)

107. e.g. 'Married for Money' Vol. 2, 98–100; 'Held in Play'
108. See (Robinson 1995 114–9)
109. *Pro Aris et Focis* won the Queen's approval. The hyphenated surname is used by *Court Suburb.*
110. (Kortright 1868)
111. For its launch and reasons for failure see (Srebrnik 1986 85ff)
112. See (Gettmann 1960 111–5) on her dealings with Bentley.
113. (Wood 1887 259)
114. (Wood 1887 260, 340), (Elwin 1934 243–5).
115. (Mayo 1910 165–6)
116. As late as 1891 it was kept by Tindall's Circulating Library at Newmarket, alongside *Chambers' Journal, The Gentleman's, Longman's, Cornhill, Harper's magazines* and *Temple Bar.*
117. (Lang 1980 23)
118. (King 1880) King acknowledged her activism but sought to displace it in favour of quiet sanctity. Contrast Procter's poem 'Now', selected for her obituary in *The English Woman's Journal.* Reprinted (Lacey 1986 19)
119. Sarah Doudney 'In Loving Remembrance. Mrs. Henry Wood' *Argosy* Vol 43 printed, facing Contents in the bound volume January–June 1887, following Mrs. Wood's death in February 1887. Listed in Contents as p 161 it was presumably the final item in the March issue. (Wood 1887 260, 266)
120. (Meynell 1965 12–6)
121. (Badeni 1981 71); (Meynell 1929 89).
122. (Dixon 1930 121)
123. (Meynell 1929 68)
124. (Cowden-Clarke 1896 221)
125. (Saintsbury 1883 14)

7   A Niche in the Market

1. (See Ballaster *et al.* 1991 79)
2. (Billington 1896); (Palmegiano 1976)
3. She wrote children's fiction and tales popularizing Shakespeare.
4. (Altick 1948 176–7) Novello volunteered *Musical Times,* turning it into a fortnightly and cramming it with advertisements (mainly for Novello publications) to render it liable to extortionate taxes.
5. See (Beetham 1996 48–56); (Drotner 1988 49–60 et passim)
6. (Cross 1985 200)
7. (Gissing 1891 8)
8. (Scott 1952 391). See (Drotner 1988) for account of *GOP*
9. Others were Laura Valentine and Elizabeth Day.
10. (Drotner 1988 118–9) The correspondence columns of *AJ* and *GOP* suggest a readership including girls as old as 17 and 18.
11. (Lang 1980 22–4)
12. (Hutton 1989 171)
13. *Aunt Judy's Magazine* Christmas 1866, 2, 123, May Day 1868, 191
14. (Gatty 1868) By the 1890s 'Letterbox' was carrying correspondence from China, Japan and Australia as well as from all over Europe.

15. (Gatty 1868) (Lang 1980 24)
16. (Coleridge 1903 277–8)
17. (Garriock 1997 182–5)
18. 'Riddle-box' and 'Letterbox' were so popular that they were the two departments still going strong a decade later.
19. (Altick 1948 228), (Gatty 1885 763)
20. The *Little Wide-Awake:* storybook by Mrs Sale-Barker (1876) boasted nearly 400 pictures; the coloured annuals and associated book series maintained this emphasis.
21. (Thwaite 1967)
22. These were so markedly English that it surprises to find illustrated poems and tales about a negro family. Routledge's American link may have been responsible.
23. A guinea was £1. 1shilling i.e. £1. 5p
24. (Sale-Barker 1885 32)
25. (Gissing 1891 29, 8–9, 416–20)
26. (March-Phillips 1894 668–9)
27. (Hargrave 1914 294)
28. (Beetham 1996 188–9)
29. (Billington 1896 103).
30. Helena Temple was the pseudonym of Henrietta Müller; (March-Phillips 1894 665); (Palmegiano 1976)
31. (Green 1891 503)
32. (anon 1894 249–50) The context of the address naturally affected the tone of her analysis.
33. (White 1970 38–41); (Beetham 1996 70–3) (Auerbach 1997)
34. *Ladies' Cabinet* Vol X, 1843 443, 63, 135
35. *Ladies' Cabinet* Vol 1 n.s. May, 1844 pp i-ii
36. (Auerbach 1997 123–6, 86–9)
37. (Auerbach 1997 126–7), (Beetham 1996 40)
38. *NMBA* Vols 9, 1838 and 16, 1842
39. (Baron-Wilson 1851); (Sala c 1901 202)
40. (Warren 1858 iii-iv)
41. (Freeman 1977 175)
42. Publisher of *Le Moniteur de la Mode,* an up-market journal with an international market. Its *raison d'être* was David's large beautifully coloured fashion plates and a folding paper pattern. (Freeman 1977 164–5)
43. See (Freeman 1977 164–73); (Beetham 1996 75–9)
44. (Freeman 1977 169–70)
45. (Freeman 1977 230)
46. (Beetham 1996 69–73, 81)
47. (Freeman 1977 134); (Shattock 1993 33); (Beetham 1996 60)
48. (Freeman 1977 163–4, 169)
49. (Beetham 1996 79–81) Though Mrs Mary Bell ran the fashion for *La Belle Assemblée* in conjunction with her dress shop from 1810–20, see (Adburgham 1972 226–7)
50. (Browne 1868)
51. (Browne 1874 (Town); Browne 1874 319 (Seaside))
52. (anon c 1901)

53. (Warren 1858 iv); (anon 1859? 23)
54. (Meynell 1883 390). Compare her moral attitude to good manners (Meynell 1883 109)
55. (anon 1897 55) 'Women of the Month'
56. (Browne 1868)
57. (Green 1891 503)
58. (Dixon 1894 113)
59. (Bennett 1898 89–95)
60. (Hughes 1996 18)
61. (Dixon 1894 180)
62. (March-Phillips 1894 661)
63. (Duncan 1895 (first pub 1894) 101, 163)
64. (March-Phillips 1894 664)
65. (Dixon 1894 114–5)
66. (Duncan 1895 (first pub 1894) 99)
67. In contrast America's Mrs Croly (Jenny June) introduced her fashion column in the mid-1850s, heading up the woman's department of the *World* when her husband became managing director. Her shopping columns were already popular in the early 1870s. (Ross 1936 43–5)
68. (Billington 1896 107)
69. (Aria 1895)
70. (March-Phillips 1894 668)
71. (Altick 1948 136–7) The early Shakespeare articles led to the commission for her popular tales *The Girlhood of Shakespeare's Heroines*.
72. (Mayo 1910 71); (Diamond 1997)

8   Handmaids and Decorators

1. Some of these issues were taken up in R Patten's paper. See Introduction.
2. (Scott 1952 269); (Coghill 1899 158)
3. (Martineau 1853 341–2) The new *Telegraph* of the 1880s had introduced a system of pneumatic tubes connecting editor's, sub-editor's and printer's departments so that copy and proofs could be sent on without the need for messengers (Hatton 1882 117)
4. (Shand 1879 478); (Dixon 1894 104–11)
5. (Hatton 1882 135–6)
6. (MacDonagh 1897 99–100)
7. (Friederichs 1911) 229–31
8. (Adburgham 1972 261)
9. (anon 1894 248); (Green 1891 501)
10. (Haight 1978 110)
11. (Courtney 1934 36)
12. (Haight 1956–78 47–51, 63–4, 57–8)
13. (Wolff 1979 99)
14. See (Wolff 1974 24, 29–33 157–8, 144–5)
15. (Sala 1868 55)
16. (D'Arcy 1990 12, 16–9, 23–4) The suppression followed Wilde's arrest and demands by William Watson that the Beardsley drawings be removed.

17. (Hammond 1934 41–2)
18. (Stead 1892 14); (Eccles 1893 834–5) (Mayo 1910 80–4)
19. (Low 1904 5); (anon 1894 249)
20. (See Faithfull 1860; Faithfull 1861)
21. (Rye 1859 330–6) The messengers were men.
22. (Mayo 1910 72–3)
23. (Levine 1990 150)
24. See (Cherry 1993)
25. See (Maidment 1992)
26. (Hatton 1882 231–9) Possibly Georgina Bowers who worked for *Punch*.
27. See (Cherry 1993 172)
28. Girton Bodichon B308
29. (Elwin 1934 243)
30. (Srebrnik 1986 40)
31. e.g. 'Lusignan' Vol 3, 1867, 'Tyro' Vol 5 1868
32. (anon 1894 247); (March-Phillips 1894 665)
33. (Jay 1995 50); (anon 1894 248); (Pennell 1897 661)

9   A Press for a Purpose

1. (Parkes 1864 258)
2. (Mermin 1993 107–9)
3. (Bennett 1898 84) He excepted the brilliantly edited *British Weekly*.
4. (Scott 1992 159); (Melnyk 1996)
5. quoted (Mermin 1993 85)
6. (Drotner 1988 36, 59) quoting Gorham
7. She later explained that for the first two years she was only one of several assistants, but the consistency of her touch suggests she was even then more than just titular editor.
8. (Tonna 1834 1–2)
9. See (Kovacevic 1975); (Beetham 1996)
10. (Tonna 1834a); (Tonna 1834b).
11. (FCPS 1834; GEM 1834)
12. (Tonna 1834), and p 408
13. (GEM 1834; GEM 1835; JK. 1835)
14. See (Beetham 1996 51–3)
15. (Tonna 1843); (Tonna 1845)
16. (Coleridge 1903 334–5, 343, 345, 278)
17. (Coleridge 1903 201–3, 180)
18. (Yonge 1851) The age-group will seem odd to some modern readers, but it reflects an idea of the 'marriageable young woman' in parental care and protection. See discussions in e.g. (Drotner 1988); (Flint 1993)
19. (Yonge 1851)
20. Mrs Trimmer, also a Sunday School enthusiast, edited the *Family Magazine* 1788–9 and the *Guardian of Education* 1802–6.
21. See eg Vol 15, 1858, Vol 22, 1861.
22. (Yonge 1851)
23. (Coleridge 1903 344) referring to a review of *Red Pottage*, 278

24. (Melnyk 1996)
25. cited (Melnyk 1996 133)
26. (Boyce *et al.* 1978 273–7); (Dickens 1850 2)
27. (Beetham 1996)36
28. Maidment raises an interesting question as to why this genre proved so congenial to women at this period. (Maidment 1984 93)
29. (Cook 1849) and Editorial
30. (Cook 1849); (Cook 1850)
31. (Cook 1852); (Cook 1853); (Cook 1854)
32. ('Blackwood' 1849)
33. (Crawford 1897 525)
34. Obituary cited (Krishnamurti 1991)
35. (Courtney 1934 142)
36. I am indebted to Anthea Broomfield for this information from her paper to RSVP Conference Chicago 1997.
37. See (Levine 1990 81–102)
38. See (unsigned 1878 439) and (Doughan and Sanchez 1987) for a fuller list of feminist journals of the period.
39. Her particular cause was getting women onto the local poor-law boards.
40. (unsigned 1878 433–4, 437–8)
41. (Cobbe 1894 217) Julia Ward Howe seems in her old age to have been similarly impressive. (Ross 1936 387)
42. (Coleridge 1903 253)
43. eg (Crawford 1897)
44. (Beetham 1996 176–7)
45. *ER* 17 January 1894 53–4
46. (Green 1891 499)
47. (Billington 1896 106). Joint editors immediately after Müller were Mrs Frank Morrison and Christina Bremner.
48. (Van Arsdel 1982)
49. (Woods 1899–1900); (Lion 1900)
50. (Parkes 1864 258)
51. (Bostick 1980)
52. (unsigned 1878 433)
53. See (Herstein 1985 70–1 and 66–7) for account of Parkes' and Bodichon's association with the *Waverley*.
54. Davies was editor during autumn 1862. Girton Davies Papers 8.1
55. (Parkes 1864 258)
56. Girton Bodichon B303
57. Girton Parkes BRP I
58. Girton Parkes BRP V
59. Girton Bodichon Papers B302
60. (Mayo 1910 97)
61. The initial finance was £1000. Barbara was illegitimate, but enjoyed an exceptionally unfettered upbringing and the kind of education usually offered only to boys.
62. (Cobbe 1894 76)
63. (Hirsch 1998 21ff)
64. (Parkes 1864 364–5)

65. (Haight 1956–78 379) Girton Parkes BRP V1. Transcript by Judy Johnston.
66. Herstein says she was mainly concerned with the literary contents and had little editorial power. (Herstein 1985 67–8)
67. Girton Bodichon B302
68. (Herstein 1985 69); (unsigned 1858 202)
69. Girton Bodichon B312
70. Girton Parkes II 64/1; V 35/1–2 Josephine Butler faced similar attacks over her sexual vocabulary. (Showalter 1978 193)
71. Girton Davies 8.1
72. Girton. Bodichon B302
73. Bodichon Papers B 304, B303
74. Bodichon Papers B305, B306
75. (Parkes 1864 260) On Boucherett's resignation for health reasons Caroline Ashurst Biggs became editor until her death in 1889 when Helen Blackburn assisted by Antoinette Mackenzie took over. It reverted to a monthly in 1875, then a quarterly in 1890. For further information on the interrelationship of the Langham Place publications see (Nestor 1982) and (Hirsch 1998 184–206).
76. Bodichon Papers 2 B305
77. (unsigned 1878 439) (Beetham 1996 176)
78. See Levine's sample of activists revealed only 16% known to have borne children. (Levine 1990 45)
79. (Cobbe 1894 Vol II 76)
80. (Bostick 1980 125) See also Herstein, Levine, Nestor
81. (unsigned 1868) A later review was much more scathing.
82. (Oliphant 1889 207) August
83. *Englishwoman's Review,* 15 January 1895, 54
84. See (Doughan and Sanchez 1987); (Beetham 1996 174–7)

10   Jill of All Trades: Journalism and the Professional Writer

1. (Cross 1985 165–7)
2. (Jay 1990 157)
3. (Jay 1990 15) The entry is for February 1885 (Linton 1996 370) When repeating 'hot-house quality' towards the end of the review it is clear Linton intends Eliot's dependence upon the support and adulation of a man, rather than just a passionate nature.
4. (Anderson 1987 108)
5. (Banks 1902 189–91)
6. (Anderson 1987 189)
7. Among them Millicent Fawcett, Sarah Grand and Mona Caird. See (Anderson 1987 191–2, 212–3); also Chapter 5 this volume.
8. (Anderson 1987 215)
9. (Lobban and William Blackwood 1897)
10. (Oliphant 1897)
11. (Coghill 1899 281)
12. (Colby 1979 92)
13. (Porter 1898 350)

14. (Oliphant 1897 (2nd ed) Vol 2, 475)
15. See for instance (Black 1893 4)
16. (Layard 1901 212–3)
17. Black claims 11 (Black 1893 2), Tweedie 10 (Tweedie 1894)
18. (Anderson 1987 25) citing Bentley Collection.
19. See (Anderson 1987 33)
20. Although she transposes the sexes of several key characters including the narrator she admitted to Rhoda Broughton it was a veiled account of her own life and career with some blurring of fact and fiction. The sexual distortion was a mechanism to enable her to write what she dared not express openly. (Layard 1901 247) Layard relied heavily on this novel to fill gaps in his knowledge. See (Layard 1901 viii); as did Herbert Van Thal (Thal 1979)
21. (Layard 1901 46)
22. (Linton 1885 Vol 1, 258)
23. Here she differed from Mrs Lynn Linton who became noted for her embroideries often of her own design (Black 1893 8)
24. *Passages in the Life of Mrs Margaret Maitland, of Sunnyside, written by Herself* first published 1849
25. (Jay 1990 24, 35, 28–9).
26. See (Cross 1985 164ff); (Showalter 1978 48ff); (Sutherland 1976) for the economics of fiction writing.
27. (Sutherland 1976 42, 189–90)
28. Her first novel after a decade's silence in which she concentrated on journalism, restricting fiction to short stories for periodicals. Her retreat from fiction was induced partly by the adverse reaction to *Realities*.
29. (Linton 1894 (First pub 1867) 228–9)
30. (Mayo 1910 69–116)
31. (Coghill 1899 199–200)
32. (Anderson 1987 74)
33. Linton in 1850 co-founded *The Leader* with Lewes and Thornton Hunt but resigned little more than a year later. At Brantwood, his rambling estate in the Lake District, he published his own periodical, the *English Republic*. A former follower commented on the eccentricity of setting up a printing office 'in a remote quarter of the Lake District, miles away from the nearest railway station'.(Layard 1901 91–2)
34. (Layard 1901 193)
35. (Fox Bourne 1887 247)
36. Douglas Cook, Eliza Lynn's own editor went to Aberdeen University, and trained under Delane on the *Times* (Escott 1911 231–2). Harcourt did some work for the *Chronicle* whilst still an undergraduate. *DNB* see also (Fox Bourne 1887 153)
37. (Linton 1885 70–1)
38. In her journalism and fiction especially *The One Too Many* serialized in the *Lady's Pictorial* 1893. This last provoked the anger of her beloved protegeé Beatrice Harradan, herself a Girton girl, who nevertheless wrote a sympathetic introduction to her *Literary Life*.
39. (Anderson 1987 23)
40. (Layard 1901 56–7)

41. (Layard 1901 136)
42. See (Jay 1990; Jay 1995 117, 214)
43. (Coghill 1899 186–7)
44. Mrs Mayo objecting to pensions seems to refer to Mrs Oliphant 'If she passed her life ... in perpetual financial struggle, it was not through lack of large receipts, but through some mistake in expenditure.' (Mayo 1910 190)
45. e.g. (Coghill 1899 156)
46. (Jay 1995 49)
47. (Layard 1901 132)
48. (Anderson 1987 47–8) quotes Bentley Collection EL to RB 6 April 1848, 21 June, 9 July 1847, 26, 28 Feb 1848
49. As the 5s a copy was payable only after 1000 and it sold only 648 she got only the lump sum of £250. (Gettmann 1960 116 126, 128)
50. (Cited Anderson 1987 140)
51. See (Anderson 1987 188)
52. (Jay 1995 15)
53. (Jay 1990 133–4)
54. (Coghill 1899 247); (Jay 1995 249)
55. (Coghill 1899 218)
56. (Coghill 1897 279); (Jay 1990 117)
57. (Layard 1901 vii)
58. (Anderson 1987 134)
59. (Linton 1885 Vol 3, 313, 309–12)
60. (Linton 1894 (First pub 1867) 314)
61. See (Anderson 1987 106–7)
62. In *Kirkland* 'Esther's clothing is described similarly (Linton 1885 Vol III, 32) but unlike the thoroughly professional Jane she is also characterized by a general lack of organization. 'Nothing could make her punctual nor orderly.' Mrs Linton herself was meticulously punctual and organized. See (Layard 1901 193); (Anderson 1987 22)
63. (Linton 1894 (First pub 1867) 314)
64. (Linton 1897 508)
65. (Layard 1901 125–6, 131)
66. (Layard 1901 193)
67. (Jay 1995 15)
68. (Coghill 1899 155, 157)
69. (Coghill 1899 29, 67)
70. See (Jay 1995 35)
71. (Coghill 1899 154, 185)
72. (Jay 1995 228–9)
73. (Black 1893 5–6, 8)
74. (Jay 1990 30, and opp,149)
75. (Black 1893 2); (Tweedie 1894 363–4) The attempt to smooth over any professional/domestic conflict is typical of Black's approach in this series of sketches of women writers. Helen Mathers had once enjoyed the luxury of a large writing-room but now neither she nor her manuscript has any dedicated space. Her 'authoress look' has ceased to affect her household – account books, her son's airgun and her husband's correspondence all invade the writer's space, but the authorial stress upon Mathers' laughter as she recounts this removes any hint of conflict.

76. (Linton 1885 101)
77. (Anderson 1987 51)
78. (Linton 1885 Vol III,101–3)
79. See (Jay 1995 272–3)
80. (Tredrey 1954 143–6)
81. (Coghill 1899 161, 192)
82. (Banks 1902)
83. (Coghill 1899 284–5, 328)
84. (Coghill 1899 158) The Turner piece appeared in *Maga*, January 1862 (Oliphant 1862)
85. (Coghill 1899 262)
86. *Maga* January 1865, October, 1859. See Oliphant's reference (Jay 1990 110, 76)
87. (Layard 1901 213, 241–2)
88. (Layard 1901 246)
89. (Coghill 1899 205) (Oliphant 1874; Oliphant 1875)
90. (Coghill 1899 243)
91. (Jay 1995 245)
92. (Anderson 1987 139)
93. (Layard 1901 212)
94. (Linton 1894 (First pub 1867) 113); (Anderson 1987 138) citing a letter to Mr Friswell 12 January 1874 UCLA MSS.
95. (Coghill 1899 254, 158)
96. (Anderson 1987 173); (Layard 1901 354); (Tweedie 1894 362)
97. (Anderson 1987 223 71–2 [quoting BC MSS April 8 1894] 139) Despite her longstanding friendship with editor Shirley Brooks he accepted only one piece which appeared heavily sub-edited (Anderson 1987)
98. (Coghill 1899 261–2)
99. (Anderson 1987 48 quoting Bentley Collection); (Oliphant 1895); (Coghill 1899 329, 149)
100. (Jay 1990 xii)

11   Journalism and the Novelist

1. (Disraeli 1850 vi)
2. See (Tillotson 1954)
3. The list of women editors discussed in Chapters 6, 7 and 9 is not exhaustive, e.g. Florence Marryat edited *London Society* for four years. Even Thackeray and Trollope were surprised by the job's complexity. See (Colby 1985)
4. (Braddon 1864 10 ff)
5. He speculated in art. (Sutherland 1991 88)
6. (Sutherland 1991 286–7)
7. (Trevelyan 1932 44)
8. (Trevelyan 1932 42) See also (Sutherland 1991 89–90)
9. (Riddell 127) The incident seems to have been adapted from Mrs Riddell's own experience with Newby who published an early novel under her maiden name and who when she returned years later with a view to republishing was astonished to discover she was the author of *George Geith*.

10. (Mayo 1910 137–40, 130)
11. In 1850 she averaged £270 pa from all sources including periodical writing. (Cross 1985 182)
12. (Sutherland 1976 38)
13. (Drotner 1988 116, 158–60)
14. (Black 1893 153)
15. (Beetham 1996 note 215)
16. (Low 1904 28); (Dixon 1894 182)
17. (Showalter 1978 48–52); See (Cross 1985 198)
18. (Black 1893 12, 24)
19. (Cross 1985 189, 192)
20. (Mayo 1910 168)
21. Like Ward she was an anti-suffragist.
22. (Cross 1985 191)
23. (Cross 1985 194)
24. (Mayo 1910 146–7)
25. (Sutherland 1976 96–8)
26. Letter to Charles Norton 9 March 1859 (Chapple and Pollard 1997 534–5) *Lois* ran in *ATYR* 8–23 October 1859. Volume Reprint in *Right at Last* 1860 For Dickens's quarrel see (Sutherland 1976 166–7).
27. Publishers Archives, University of Reading. Craik (MS 1448) 71
28. (Cross 1985 190)
29. (Haight 1956–78 Vol II 437)
30. (Howitt 1889 Vol I 195)
31. (Marchand 1971 122ff.) Dilke was the grandfather of Emilia Dilke's second husband.
32. Original letters were rarely published but 'Answers to correspondents' indicate their views.
33. Cited (Sutherland 1976 168–9) See 41–3 for commercial impact of serialization.
34. (Shand 1886)
35. (Dickens 1880 249–50)
36. (Shand 1886 566–8)
37. (Chapple and Pollard 1997 328–9) See (Hopkins 1952; Easson 1982) on serialization. For a reading more sympathetic to Gaskell than Dickens on this issue see (Hughes and Lund 1999)
38. (Chapple and Pollard 1997 534–5)
39. (Chapple and Pollard 1997 740)
40. (Chapple and Pollard 1997 748)
41. (Chapple and Pollard 1997 699)
42. For *Sartain's Union Magazine*
43. See Ward's Preface to *Cranford*
44. (McCormick 1986 57, 61)
45. For examples of reworking (Sharps 1970); (Onslow 1973) unpublished
46. (Haight 1956–1978 Vol II 21, 163) Joseph Parkes considered him in 1854 on the verge of bankruptcy. Also (Haight 1968 109)
47. (Haight 1968 109),
48. (Haight 1968 91)
49. (Haight 1956–78 Vol II 68), (Haight 1978 Vol VIII 95)

50. (Haight 1956–78 Vol II 45, 91, 93–4)
51. (Haight 1956–78 Vol II 431)
52. (Haight 1968 96); (Haight 1956–78 Vol V 63–4)
53. (Haight 1968 233–5)

Afterword

1. Well I didn't know then that burnt-on rice-pudding was particularly difficult to remove; at 21 I was duly amazed by the disappearance of gravy stains. Washing-up was done by hand in our house, and I always offered to dry. (Stott 1985)
2. (Ireland 1892 201)

Select Bibliography

Works of Reference

In addition to standard biographical dictionaries I have also drawn on:

Blain, V., P. Clements, and I. Grundy (eds) (1990). *The Feminist Companion to Literature in English: Women Writers from the Middle Ages to the Present*. London, Batsford.

Griffiths, D. (1992). *Encyclopaedia of the British Press 1422–1992*. London, Macmillan.

Houfe, S. (1978). *Dictionary of British Book Illustrators and Caricaturists 1800–1914*. Woodbridge, Antique Collectors' Club.

Pettys, C. (1985). *Dictionary of Women Artists: an international dictionary of women artists born before 1900*. Boston, Mass., GK Hall.

Schlueter, P. and J. Schlueter (eds) (1988). *An Encyclopedia of British Women Writers*. London, St James Press.

Shattock, J. (1993). *The Oxford Guide to British Women Writers*. Oxford, Oxford University Press.

Sutherland, J. (1988) *The Longman Companion to Victorian Fiction*. Harlow, Longman.

Todd, J. (ed) (1989). *Dictionary of British Women Writers*. London, Routledge.

Archives

I have referred to manuscript material in the following archives:

Girton College, Cambridge, the Bodichon, Davies and Parkes papers
The Historical Society of Pennsylvania, the Wister family papers
Reading Borough Libraries, the Mitford collection
Reading University, the Publishers' Archives
Somerville College, Oxford, the Mary Somerville papers

Periodicals

Apart from individual journals cited I have consulted runs or samples of runs of the following nineteenth-century periodicals:

The Alexandra Magazine
The Argosy
Atalanta
The Athenæum
Aunt Judy's Magazine
Belgravia
Blackwood's Magazine
Christian Ladies' Magazine

The Court Suburb Magazine
The Daily News
The Drawing-Room Album and Companion for the Boudoir
The Drawing-Room Scrap Book
The Echo
Eliza Cook's Journal
The Englishwoman
Englishwoman's Domestic Magazine
The Englishwoman's Review
The English Woman's Journal
Finden's Tableaux
Household Words
Howitt's Journal
The Keepsake
The Ladies' Cabinet of Fashion, Music & Romance
Ladies' Companion at Home and Abroad
The Ladies' Treasury
Little Wide-Awake
Merry England
Mrs Ellis's Morning Call: a Table-Book of Literature and Art
The Monthly Packet of Evening Readings
The Morning Chronicle
New Monthly Belle Assemblée
The Pall Mall Gazette
St James's Magazine
St Nicholas: Scribner's Illustrated Magazine for Girls and Boys
Sala's Journal
Sharpe's London Magazine
Tait's Edinburgh Magazine
Temple Bar
Twilight
The Victoria Magazine
Womanhood

Works cited

(1939). *The History of the Times: The Tradition Established*. London, The Times.
(1947). *The History of the Times: The Twentieth Century Test*. London, The Times.
Adburgham, A. (1972). *Women in Print: Writing Women and Women's Magazines from the Restoration to the Accession of Victoria*. London, George Allen & Unwin.
Allingham, H. and D. Radford, (eds) (1990, first pub. 1907). *William Allingham: the Diaries*. London, Folio Society.
Allott, M. (1968, first pub. 1959). *Novelists on the Novel*. London, Routledge & Kegan Paul.
Altick, R. (1948). *The Cowden Clarkes*. London, New York, Oxford University Press.
Altick, R.D. (1957). *The English Common Reader: A Social History of the Mass Reading Public 1800–1900*. Chicago, London, University of Chicago Press, Cambridge University Press.

Anderson, N.F. (1987). *Woman against Women in Victorian England: A Life of Eliza Lynn Linton*, Indiana University Press, Bloomington Ind.

Andrews, L. and H.S. Taylor (1970). *Lords and Laborers of the Press: Men who Fashioned the Modern British Newspaper*. London and Amsterdam, Southern Illinois University Press.

anon (1846). 'Preface'. *Sharpe's London Magazine* 1: unnumbered.

anon (1852). 'Books and Their Authors'. *Sharpe's London Magazine* 1 ns: 60–4.

anon (1862). 'Philosophy of Sensation'. *St James's Magazine* V: 340–6.

anon (1862). 'A Sensation Novel'. *St James's Magazine* IV: 217–25.

anon (1859?). 'How Far Should the Fashions be Followed?' *'The Ladies' Treasury* 2: 23.

anon (1863). 'A Lady and her Marriage Settlement'. *Englishwoman's Domestic Magazine* 7 ns (May): 207–11.

anon (1893). 'Record of Events'. *Englishwoman's Review* (10 April): 112–3.

anon ('Wares of Autolycus') (1893). 'Journalism as a Profession by a Lady Journalist'. *Pall Mall Gazette* (June 26).

anon (1894). 'Ladies with a longing for Journalism'. *Cassell's Saturday Journal* 19 September: 6.

anon (1894) 'Journalists' Pay at Home and Abroad'. *Cassell's Saturday Journal* 24 October: 106.

anon (1894). 'Record of Events'. *Englishwoman's Review* (15 October): 244–51.

anon (1895). 'Passing Notes'. *Englishwoman's Review of Social and Industrial Questions* (15 January): 53–4.

anon (1896). 'Wanted – a Lady Clerk'. *Cassell's Saturday Journal* 19 February: 459.

anon (1897). 'The Old Journalists and the New'. *Saturday Review* LXIII: 578–9.

anon (1897). 'Women of the Month'. *The Englishwoman* 5: 55.

anon (1897–98). 'How to Obtain Journalistic Work'. *Atalanta* 11: 248–9.

anon (c 1901). *Progress of British Newspapers in the 19th Century Illustrated*. London, Simpkin, Marshall, Hamilton, Kent & Co. Ltd.

anon (nd (1913)). *'Truth' 1877–1913: The Story of a Great Journal*. London, Truth.

Arbuckle, E.S., (ed) (1994). *Harriet Martineau in the London Daily News: Selected Contributions, 1852–1866*. New York, Garland Publishing, Inc.

Aria, M. (1895). 'In Fashionland'. *The Englishwoman* 2: 133–8.

Auerbach, J. (1997). 'What They Read: Mid-Nineteenth Century English Women's Magazines and the Emergence of a Consumer Culture'. *Victorian Periodicals Review* 30:2 (Summer): 121–40.

Badeni, J. (1981). *The Slender Tree: A Life of Alice Meynell*. Padstow, Cornwall, Tabb House.

Ballaster, R., M. Beetham, E. Frazer and S. Hebron (1991). *Women's Worlds: Ideology, Femininity and the Woman's Magazine*. London, Macmillan.

Banks, E.L. (1902). *The Autobiography of a 'Newspaper Girl'*. New York, London, Dodd, Mead & Co. Methuen.

Baron-Wilson, M. (1851). 'A Few Words by the Editress'. *New Monthly Belle Assemblée* 35: 39–42.

Beale, A. (1879). 'Our Mission Homes in Paris'. *Argosy* XXXVIII: 106–12.

Beetham, M. (1990). 'Towards a Theory of the Periodical as a Publishing Genre'. in *Investigating Victorian Journalism*. L. Brake, A. Jones and L. Madden. London, Macmillan: 19–32.

Beetham, M. (1996). *A Magazine of Her Own?: Domesticity and Desire in the Woman's Magazine, 1800–1914*. London and New York, Routledge.

Bell, E.H.C.M. (1927). *The Life & Letters of C.F. Moberly Bell*. London, Richards Press.

Bell, E.H.C.M. (1947). *Flora Shaw – Lady Lugard DBE*. London, Constable.

Bennett, E.A. (1898). *Journalism for Women: A Practical Guide*. London, New York, John Lane, The Bodley Head.

Betham-Edwards, M. (1878). 'Social Aspects of the Paris Exhibition'. *Fraser's Magazine of Town and Country* 98 os, 18 ns (August).

Betham-Edwards, M. (1898). *Reminiscences*. London, George Redway.

Billington, M.F. (1896). 'Leading Lady Journalists'. *Pearson's Magazine* (July): 101–11.

Black, H. (1893). *Notable Women Authors of the Day*. London, David Bryce & Son.

'Blackwood' (1849). 'Periodicals'. *Eliza Cook's Journal* I: 182.

Blowitz (1893). 'Journalism as a Profession'. *Contemporary Review* 63 (January): 37–46.

Bodichon, B. (1987). 'Women and Work' (1857) in *Barbara Leigh Smith Bodichon and the Langham Place Group*. C.A. Lacey, Routledge & Kegan Paul: 36–73.

Bonham-Carter, V. (1978). *Authors by Profession*. London, Society of Authors.

Bostick, T. (1980). 'The Press and the Launching of the Women's Suffrage Movement, 1866–1867'. *Victorian Periodicals Review* XIII (4): 125–31.

Boyce, G., J. Curran, P. Wingate, (eds) (1978). *Newspaper History from the Seventeenth Century to the Present Day*. London, Constable.

Braddon, M. (nd, first published 1864). *The Doctor's Wife*. London, Simpkin, Marshall, Hamilton, Kent & Co.

Broomfield, A. (1997). *Undoing What Lady Journalists Do: Clementina Black and The New (Woman) Journalism*. RSVP, Chicago, unpublished.

Broomfield, A. and S. Mitchell, (eds) (1996). *Victorian Prose: An Anthology of Women Writers*, Garland Press.

Brown, L. (1985). *Victorian News and Newspapers*. Oxford, Clarendon Press.

Browne, M. (1868). 'Spinnings in Town'. *Englishwoman's Domestic Magazine* IV ns (February): 96–9.

Browne, M. (1874). 'Spinnings at the Seaside'. *Englishwoman's Domestic Magazine* XVI: 310–11.

Browne, M. (1874). 'Spinnings in Town'. *Englishwoman's Domestic Magazine* XVI (January): 34–9.

Burton, K.G. (1954). *The Early Newspaper Press in Berkshire (1723–1855)*. Reading, privately published

Busk, M. (1835). 'Modern German School of Irony'. *Blackwood's Magazine* 38: 376–87.

Caine, B. (1992). *Victorian Feminists*. Oxford, Oxford University Press.

Caird, M. (1892). 'A Defence of the So-Called "Wild Women". *Nineteenth Century* XXXI: 811–29.

Campbell, L.C. (1889). *Darrell Blake: A Study*. London, Trischler and Company.

Carney, K.M. (1996). 'The Publisher's Reader as Feminist: The Career of Geraldine Endsor Jewsbury'. *Victorian Periodicals Review* 29 (2) Summer: 146–58.

Chapple, J.A.V. and A. Pollard, (eds) (1997). *The Letters of Mrs Gaskell*. Manchester, Mandolin.

Cherry, D. (1993). *Painting Women: Victorian Women Artists*. London, Routledge.

Chorley, H., (ed) (1872). *Letters of Mary Russell Mitford*. Second Series. London, Richard Bentley and Son.

Clarke, J.S. (1992). 'Home, a Lost Victorian Periodical'. *Victorian Periodicals Review* XXV (2) Summer: 85–8.

Clarke, N. (1990). *Ambitious Heights: Writing, Friendship, Love – the Jewsbury Sisters, Felicia Hemans, and Jane Welsh Carlyle*. London, New York, Routledge.

Cobbe, F. (1894). *Life of Frances Power Cobbe by Herself*. London, Richard Bentley & Sons.

Cobbe, F.P. (1894). *Life of Frances Power Cobbe by Herself (Vol 2)*. London, Richard Bentley & Sons.

Cobbe, F.P. (1996). 'What shall we do with our Old Maids?' in *Prose by Victorian Women*. A. Broomfield and S. Mitchell. New York, London, Garland Publishing: 236–61.

Coghill, A.L. (1897). 'Mrs. Oliphant'. *Fortnightly Review* LXII n.s.: 277–85.

Coghill, A.L. (1899). *The Autobiography and Letters of Mrs M.O.W. Oliphant*. Edinburgh and London, William Blackwood and Sons.

Colby, R.A. (1985). 'Goose Quill and Blue Pencil'. in *Innovators and Preachers*. J.H. Wiener. Westport, Greenwood: 203–31.

Colby, R. and V. (1979). 'Mrs. Oliphant's Scotland: the Romance of Reality'. *Nineteenth Century Scottish Fiction*. I. Campbell. Manchester, Carcanet New Press: 89–104.

Coleridge, C. (1903). *Charlotte Mary Yonge: her Life and Letters*. London, Macmillan.

Cook, E. (1849). 'A Word to My Readers'. *Eliza Cook's Journal* (5 May): (i).

Cook, E. (1852). 'The Education of Women'. *Eliza Cook's Journal* VIII (20 Nov.): 57–9.

Cook, E. (1854). 'An Old Question from a New Point of View'. *Eliza Cook's Journal* XI: 62–3.

Cook, E. (unsigned) (1849). 'Governesses'. *Eliza Cook's Journal* I: 305–7.

Cook, E. (unsigned) (1850). 'The Advertisement'. *Eliza Cook's Journal* IV: 282–5.

Cook, E. (unsigned) (1853). 'Work for Stafford House'. *Eliza Cook's Journal* IX (30 April): 1–3.

Costello, L.S. (1845). 'Sketches of Legendary Cities No IV: Monmouth'. *Bentley's Miscellany* XVII: 265–76.

Courtney, J.E. (1934). *The Women of My Time*. London. Lovat Dickson.

Cowden Clarke, C., M. Cowden Clarke, et al. (1969). *Recollections of Writers*. Fontwell, Sussex, Centaur Press.

Cowden-Clarke, M. (1896). *My Long Life: An Autobiographic Sketch*. London, T. Fisher Unwin.

Crawford, E. (1893). 'Journalism as a Profession for Women'. *Contemporary Review* LXIV (September): 362–71.

Crawford, V. (1897). 'Feminism in France'. *Fortnightly Review* LXI n.s. (Jan–June): 524–30.

Crosland, N. (1893). *Landmarks of Literary Life 1820–92*. New York, Charles Scribner's Sons.

Cross, N. (1985). *The Common Writer: Life in Nineteenth Century Grub Street*. London, Cambridge, Cambridge University Press.

Crowquill, C.A. (1845). 'Glimpses and mysteries: The Author'. *Bentley's Miscellany* XVII: 357–60.

Curran, E. (1998). 'Holding on By A Pen: The Story of a Lady/Reviewer, Mary Margaret Busk'. *Victorian Periodicals Review* **31** (1) Spring Special Issue: Victorian Women Editors and Critics: 9–31.

D'Arcy, E. (1990). *Some Letters to John Lane*. Edinburgh, Tragara.

David, D. (1987). *Intellectual Women and Victorian Patriarchy: Harriet Martineau, Elizabeth Barrett Browning, George Eliot*. New York, Cornell University Press, Ithaca.

de Saint Victor, C. (1984). 'Anglo-Saxon Review'. in *British Literary Magazines: The Victorian and Edwardian Age 1837–1913*. A. Sullivan. Westport, Connecticut, Greenwood Press. **III**: 14–22.

Diamond, M. (1997). 'Maria Rye and *The Englishwoman's Domestic Magazine*'. *Victorian Periodicals Review* **30**: (1) Spring: 5–16.

Dickens, C. (1850). 'A Preliminary Word'. *Household Words* **1** (1): 1–2.

Dickens, C. (1880). *The Letters of Charles Dickens*. London, Chapman & Hall.

Dilke, C.W., the Rt Hon Sir (1905). 'Memoir (of Lady Dilke)'. *The Book of Spiritual Life*. C.W. Dilke. London, John Murray.

Dilke, E. (1869). 'Art'. *Westminster Review* **35 ns** (April): 585–98.

Dilke, E. (1869). 'Art and Morality'. *Westminster Review* **35 ns** (January): 148–84.

Dilke, E. (1873). 'The Use of Looking at Pictures'. *Westminster Review* (October): 415–23.

Dilke, E. (1905). The Book of Spiritual Life. *The Book of Spiritual Life*. C.W. Dilke, the Rt Hon Sir. London, John Murray.

Disraeli, B. (1850). *Coningsby; or The New Generation*. Preface to the Fifth Edition. London, Henry Colburn: [v]–viii.

Dixon, E.H. (1894). *The Story of a Modern Woman*. London, W Heinemann.

Dixon, E.H. (1930). *As I Knew Them: Sketches of People I have Met on the Way*. London, Hutchinson.

Doughan, D. and D. Sanchez (1987). *Feminist Periodicals 1855–1984: An Annotated Critical Bibliography*, Harvester.

Drotner, K. (1988). *English Children and their Magazines 1751–1945*. New Haven and London, Yale University Press.

Duncan, J.S. (1895 first pub 1894). *A Daughter of Today*. London, Chatto & Windus.

Easson, A. (1982). Introduction in *North and South*. A. Easson. Oxford, Oxford University Press: [ix]–xviii.

Eastlake, E. (1848). '*Vanity Fair; a Novel without a Hero; Jane Eyre; an Autobiography*'. *Quarterly Review* **84** (December): 153–85.

Eastlake, E. (1865). 'Galleries of the Louvre'. *Quarterly Review* **117**: 287–323.

Eccles, C.O'C. (1893). 'Experiences of a Woman Journalist'. *Blackwoods* **153**: 830–8.

Eisler, C. (1979) Lady Dilke: 'The Six Lives of an Art Historian'. in *Interpreters of the Visual Arts* (eds) C.R. Sherman and A.M. Holcomb: 147–80.

Eliot, G. (1855). 'Lord Brougham's Literature'. *Leader* **VI** (7 July): 652–3.

Eliot, G. (1963). [Three Novels]. *Essays of George Eliot*. T. Pinney. London, Routledge & Kegan Paul: 325–34.

Elwin, M. (1934). *Victorian Wallflowers*. London, Jonathan Cape.

Erskine, M.S., (ed) (1915). *Anna Jameson: Letters and Friendships*. London, T. Fisher Unwin.

Escott, T.H.S. (1911). *Masters of English Journalism: A Study of Personal Forces*. London, T Fisher Unwin.

F.C.P.S (1834). 'Geology'. *Christian Lady's Magazine* **1**: 393–5.

Faithfull, E. (1860). Victoria Press in *Barbara Leigh Smith Bodichon and the Langham Place Group*. C.A. Lacey. London, 1987, Routledge & Kegan Paul: 287–291.

Faithfull, E. (1861). 'Women Compositors' in *Barbara Leigh Smith Bodichon and the Langham Place Group*. C.A. Lacey. London, 1987, Routledge & Kegan Paul: 287–91.

Fenwick Miller, F. (1884). *Harriet Martineau*. London, WH Allen.

Flint, K. (1993). *The Woman Reader 1837–1914*. New York, Oxford, Oxford University Press.

Fox Bourne, J.R. (1887). *English Newspapers: Chapters in The History of Journalism*. London, Chatto & Windus.

Fox-Bourne, J.R. (c 1901). 'London Newspapers'. *Progress of British Newspapers in the 19th Century Illustrated*. London, Simpkin, Marshall, Hamilton, Kent & Co. Ltd: 9–18.

Freeman, S. (1977). *Isabella and Sam: the Story of Mrs. Beeton*. London, Victor Gollancz.

Friederichs, H. (1911). *The Life of Sir George Newnes*. London, Hodder and Stoughton.

Fryckstedt, M.C. (1983). *Geraldine Jewsbury's* Athenæum *reviews: Mirror of Mid-Victorian Attitudes to Fiction*. Uppsala, University of Uppsala.

Fryckstedt, M.C. (1985). 'Geraldine Jewsbury and Douglas Jerrold's *Shilling Magazine*'. *English Studies* lxvi: 325–37.

Fulmer, C. (1998). *A Monument to the Memory of George Eliot: Edith J Simcox's Autobiography of a Shirtmaker*, Garland.

Fulmer, C.M. (1998). 'Edith Simcox: Feminist Critic and Reformer'. *Victorian Periodicals Review* **31** (1) Spring Special Issue: Victorian Women Editors and Critics: 9–31.

G.E.M (1834). 'Geology'. *Christian Lady's Magazine* **1** (March): 198–204.

G.E.M (1834). 'On the Use of Music'. *Christian Lady's Magazine* **2**: 241–56 (inc. editorial commentary).

G.E.M (1835). 'On the Use of Dancing'. *Christian Lady's Magazine* **2**: 228–38 (inc editorial commentary).

G.H.P. (1891). 'Young Women as Journalists'. *Girl's Own Paper*: 395–6.

Garriock, J.B. (1997). 'Late Victorian and Edwardian Images of Women and their Education in the Popular Periodical Press with particular reference to L.T. Meade'. Liverpool University, Liverpool. (unpublished thesis)

Gaskell, E. 'The Last Generation in England'. *Cranford*. E.P. Watson.

Gatty, H. (1885). 'Farewell'. *Aunt Judy's Magazine*: 763–4.

Gatty, M. (1868). 'Editor's Address'. *Aunt Judy's Magazine* May Day: 1–3.

Gettmann, R.A. (1960). *A Victorian Publisher: A Study of the Bentley Papers*. Cambridge, Cambridge University Press.

Gissing, G. (1891). *New Grub Street*, Smith Elder & Co.

Grand, S. (1996). 'The New Aspect of the Woman Question' in *Prose by Victorian Women: An Anthology*. B. Andrea and S. Mitchell, Garland.

Grand, S. (1996). 'The New Woman and the Old' in *Prose by Victorian Women: An Anthology*. B. Andrea and S. Mitchell, Garland.

Grant, J. (1872). *The History of the Newspaper Press: The Metropolitan Weekly and Provincial Press*. London, Routledge.

Green, F.L. (1891). 'Journalism as a Profession for Women'. *Monthly Packet of Evening Reading* **2 n.s.** (July–December): 498–506.

Griffiths, D. (1991). 'A Woman's Work'. *British Journalism Review* **2** (3, Spring): 50–4.

Gross, J. (1991, revised ed first pub. 1969). *The Rise and Fall of the Man of Letters: Aspects of English Literary Life since 1800*. London, Penguin.

Haight, G.S., (ed) (1956–78). *George Eliot Letters Vol II*. London, Oxford University Press.

Haight, G.S., (ed) (1956–78). *George Eliot Letters Vol V*. London, Oxford University Press.

Haight, G.S., (ed) (1966, first pub. Houghton Mifflin, 1965). *A Century of George Eliot Criticism*. London, Methuen.

Haight, G.S. (1968). *George Eliot: A Biography*. London, Oxford University Press.

Haight, G.S., (ed) (1978). *George Eliot Letters Vol V111*. New Haven, London, Yale University Press.

Hall, A.M. (1852). 'Preface'. *Sharpe's London Magazine* **1 n.s.**

Hall, A.M. (1861). 'Preface'. *St. James's Magazine* **1** (July): v.

Hall, S.C. (1883). *Retrospect of a Long Life: from 1815 to 1883*. London, Richard Bentley.

Hammond, J.L. (1934). *C P Scott of the Manchester Guardian*. New York, Harcourt Brace & Co.

Hargrave, M. (1914). 'Women's Newspapers in the Past'. *The Englishwoman* **21** (Jan/Mar): 292–301.

Hasell, E. (1875). 'Elegies'. *Blackwood's* (September): 345–66.

Hasell, E. (1875). 'Tennyson's *Queen Mary*'. *Blackwood's* (September): 322–35.

Hasell, E. (1879). '*Ion*'. *Blackwood's* **CXXVI** (October): 419–34.

Hatton, J. (1882). *Journalistic London, being a series of sketches of Famous Pens and Papers of the Day*. London, Sampson Low, Marston, Searle & Rivington.

Herstein, S.R. (1985). 'The *English Woman's Journal* and the Langham Place Circle: A Feminist Forum and Its Women Editors' in *Innovators and Preachers*. J.H. Wiener: 61–76.

Hirsch, P. (1998). *Barbara Leigh Smith Bodichon, 1827–1891, Feminist, Artist and Rebel*. London, Chatto & Windus.

Hogarth, J.E. (1897). 'The Monstrous Regiment of Women'. *Fortnightly Review* **LXII** (**42**) **n.s.**: 926–36.

Hollis, P. (1987). *Ladies Elect: Women in English Local Government 1865–1914*. Oxford: Clarenion.

Hopkins, A.B. (1952). *Elizabeth Gaskell: Her Life and Work*. London, John Lehmann.

Houghton, W. (1982). 'Periodical Literature and the Articulate Classes' in *The Victorian Periodical Press: Samplings and Soundings*. J. Shattock and M. Woolf. Leicester, Leicester University Press: 3–28.

Howitt, M. (1840). 'Preface' in *Fisher's Drawing Room Scrap Book*. M. Howitt. London, Fisher, Son & Co: 3.

Howitt, M., (ed) (1889). *Mary Howitt: An Autobiography*. London, Wm. Isbister Ltd.

Howitt, M. (1889). 'Preface' in *Mary Howitt: An Autobiography*. M. Howitt. London, Wm. Isbister Ltd. **1**: v–xiii.

Howitt, W. (1840). 'L.E.L.' in *Fisher's Drawing Room Scrap Book*. M. Howitt. London, Fisher, Son & Co: 5–8.

Hubbard, L.M. (1875). *The Year-book of Women's Work*. London, Labour News Publishing Office.

Hughes, L.K. (1996). 'A female aesthete at the helm: *Sylvia's Journal* and "Graham R. Tomson", 1893–94'. *Victorian Periodicals Review* 29 (2) Summer: 173–92.

Hughes, L.K and M. Lund (1999). *Victorian Publishing and Mrs. Gaskell's Work*. Charlottesville, London, Univerisity Press of Virginia.

Humphry, M. (1979, first pub 1897). *Manners for Women*. Exeter, Webb & Bower.

Hunt, T.L. (1996). 'Louisa Henrietta Sheridan's *Comic Offering* and the Critics: Gender and Humor in the Early Victorian Era'. *Victorian Periodicals Review* 29 (2) Summer: 95–115.

Hunter, F. (1992). 'Women in British journalism' in *Encyclopaedia of the British Press 1422–1992*. D. Griffiths. London: 686–90.

Hunter, F. (1992). *Women Reporters: Entry, Training, Career and Networking in Late Victorian England*. RSVP, Manchester, unpublished paper.

Hutton, R.H. (1989). 'Mr Grote on the Abuses of Newspaper Criticism (1861)' in *A Victorian Spectator: Uncollected Writings*. R.H. Tener and M. Woodfield. Bristol, Bristol Press: 39–43.

Ireland, M.A., (ed) (1892). *Selections from the Letters of Geraldine Endsor Jewsbury to Jane Welsh Carlyle*. London, Longmans, Green & Co.

Israel, K. (1999). *Names and Stories: Emilia Dilke and Victorian Culture*. Oxford, Oxford University Press.

J.K. (1835). To G.E.M. *Christian Lady's Magazine*. 3: 124–7 (inc editorial commentary).

Jay, E., (ed) (1990). *The Autobiography of Margaret Oliphant*. Oxford, New York, Oxford Universtiy Press.

Jay, E. (1995). *Mrs. Oliphant: 'A Fiction to Herself'*. Oxford, Clarendon Press.

Jerrold, W. (1901). *Thomas Hood: His Life and Times*, New York.

Johnson, R.B., (ed) (1925). *The Letters of Mary Russell Mitford*. London, John Lane, The Bodley Head.

Johnston, J. (1994). 'Invading the House of Titian: The Colonization of Italian Art. Anna Jameson, John Ruskin and the *Penny Magazine*'. *Victorian Periodicals Review* 27 (2): 127–43.

Johnstone, C. (1832). 'Cheap Periodicals'. *Tait's Edinburgh Magazine* 1 (September): 721–4.

Johnstone, C. (1834). 'Johnstone's Edinburgh Magazine: The Cheap and Dear Periodicals'. *Tait's Edinburgh Magazine* 4 (January): 490–500.

Johnstone, C. (1839). 'The Annuals for 1840'. *Tait's Edinburgh Magazine* 6: 812–3.

Jones, A.G. (1993). *Press, Politics and Society: A History of Journalism in Wales*. Cardiff, University of Wales Press.

Kanner, B.S. (1980). 'The Women of England in a Century of Social Change: A Select Bibliography' in *Suffer and Be Still: Women in the Victorian Age*. M. Vicinus. London, Methuen University Paperbacks.

King, A. (1880). 'Adelaide Procter' *Argosy* XXX: 149–153.

Kitchin, H. (1925). *Moberly Bell and His Times*. London, Phillip & Co.

Kortright, F.A. (1868). 'Introduction'. *The Court Suburb Magazine* 1 (1): 1.

Koss, S. (1973). *Fleet Street Radical: A G Gardiner and the* Daily News. London, Allen Lane.

Kovacevic, I. (1975). *Fact into Fiction: English Literature and the Industrial Scene, 1750–1850.* Leicester, Leicester University Press.

Kramer, D. (1995). 'The Cry that Binds: Oliphant's Theory of Domestic Tragedy' in *Margaret Oliphant: Critical Essays on a Gentle Subversive.* D.J. Trela. Selinsgrove, London, Susquehanna UP, Associated University Presses: 147–64.

Krishnamurti, G., (ed.) (1991). *Women Writers of the 1890's (exhibition catalogue).* London, Henry Souteran.

Lacey, C.A., (ed.) (1986). *Barbara Leigh Smith Bodichon and the Langham Place Group.* London, Routledge & Kegan Paul.

Lang, M. (1980). 'Childhood's Champions: Mid-Victorian Children's Periodicals and the Critics'. *Victorian Periodicals Review* 13 (1/2): 17–29.

Lawrance, H. (1854). 'Flying Coaches'. *Household Words* IX: 608–13.

Lawrance, H. (1854). 'John Dunton Was a Citizen'. *Household Words* IX: 338–44.

Layard, G.S. (1901). *Mrs. Lynn Linton: her life, letters and opinions.* London, Methuen.

Leary, P. (1994). '*Fraser's Magazine* and the Literary Life, 1830–47'. *Victorian Periodicals Review* 27: (2) Summer: 105–27.

Lee, A. (1955). *Laurels and Rosemary: The Life of William and Mary Howitt.* London, Oxford University Press.

L'Estrange, A.G. (ed.) (1870). *Life of Mary Russell Mitford, Authoress of "Our Village", etc. Related in A Selection from her Letters to Her Friends.* London, Richard Bentley and Son.

Levine, P. (1990). *Feminist Lives in Victorian England: Private Roles and Public Commitment.* Oxford, Basil Blackwell.

Lightman, B. (1997). 'Constructing Victorian Heavens: Agnes Clerke and the "New Astronomy"' in *Natural Eloquence: Women Reinscribe Science.* B.T. Gates and A.B. Shteir. Wisconsin, University of Wisconsin Press: 61–75.

Lightman, B. (1997). '"The Voices of Nature": Popularizing Victorian Science' in *Victorian Science in Context.* B. Lightman. Chicago, London, University of Chicago Press: 187–211.

Linton, E.L. (1854). 'One of Our Legal Fictions'. *Household Words* IX (29 April): 257–60.

Linton, E.L. (1854). 'Rights and Wrongs of Women'. *Household Words* IX (1 April): 158–61.

Linton, E.L. (1885). *The Autobiography of Christopher Kirkland.* London, Richard Bentley & Son, facsimile (ed.) Garland Publishing, USA.

Linton, E.L. (1890). 'Literature: Then and Now'. *Fortnightly Review* XLVII n.s.: 517–31.

Linton, E.L. (1891). 'The Wild Women: As Politician'. *Nineteenth Century* (July): 79–88.

Linton, E.L. (1894, first pub 1867). *Sowing the Wind.* London, Chatto & Windus (first pub. Tinsley).

Linton, E.L. (1897). 'The Higher Education of Women'. *Fortnightly Review* LXII n.s. (Jul–Dec.): 498–510.

Linton, E.L. (1899). *My Literary Life.* London, Hodder and Stoughton.

Linton, E.L. (1996). 'George Eliot' (1885) in *Prose by Victorian Women.* A. Broomfield and S. Mitchell. New York, Garland Publishing: 361–76.

Linton, E.L. (1996). 'The Girl of the Period' in *Prose by Victorian Women*. A. Broomfield and S. Mitchell. New York, Garland Publishing: 356–60.

Lion, E. (1900). 'Successful Business Women'. *Womanhood* IV: 54–5.

Lobban, J.H. and I. William Blackwood (1897). 'Mrs. Oliphant'. *Blackwood's Magazine* (July): pp 161–64.

Lochhead, M. (1961). *Elizabeth Rigby, Lady Eastlake*. London, John Murray.

Lohrli, A., (ed.) (1973). *Household Words*. Toronto, University of Toronto Press.

Low, F.H. (1904). *Press Work for Women: A Text book for the Young Woman Journalist*. London; New York, L Upcott Gill; Charles Scribner's Sons.

MacDonagh, M. (1897). 'In The Sub-Editor's Room'. *Nineteenth Century* 42 (XLII) (December): 999–1008.

Macpherson, G. (1878). *Memoirs of the Life of Anna Jameson*. London, Longmans Green & Co.

Madden, R.R. (1855). *The Literary Life and Correspondence of The Countess of Blessington*. London, T C Newby.

Maidment, B. (1992). *Into the 1830's: Some origins of Victorian Illustrated Journalism*. Manchester, Manchester Polytechnic Library.

Maidment, B.E. (1984). 'Magazines of Popular Progress & the Artisans'. *Victorian Periodicals Review* XVII: 83–93.

Mancoff, D.N. (1991). 'Samuel Carter Hall: Publisher as Promoter of the High Arts'. *Victorian Periodicals Review* 24: (1) Spring: 11–21.

Mansfield, E. (1998). 'Articulating Authority: Emilia Dilke's Early Essays and Reviews'. *Victorian Periodicals Review* 31 (1) Spring Special Issue: Victorian Women Editors and Critics: 75–86.

March-Phillips, E. (1894). 'Women's Newspapers'. *Fortnightly Review* n.s. LVI: 661–9.

Marchand, L.A. (1971). *The Athenæum: A Mirror of Victorian Culture*. New York, Octagon Books.

Marks, P. (1986). 'Harriet Martineau: Fraser's "Maid of [Dis]Honour"'. *Victorian Periodicals Review*: 28–34.

Martineau, H. (1853). 'Mr Wiseman in Print'. *Household Words* VIII (3 December): 339–42.

Martineau, H. (1854). 'Deaf Mutes'. *Household Words* IX: 134–8.

Martineau, H. (1859). 'Female Industry'. *Edinburgh Review* CIX: 144–67.

Martineau, H. (1877, new ed. 1983). *Autobiography*. London, Smith Elder & Co (new ed. Virago).

Martineau, H. (1996). 'Letter to the Deaf' in *Prose by Victorian Women: An Anthology*. B. Andrea and S. Mitchell, Garland.

Mayo, I.F. (1910). *Recollections – of what I saw, what I lived through, and what I learned, during more than fifty years of social and literary experience*. London, John Murray.

McCormick, K. (1986). 'George Eliot's Earliest Prose: The Coventry *Herald* and the Coventry Fiction'. *Victorian Periodical Review* XIX, (2) Summer: 57–62.

McKenzie, K.A. (1961). *Edith Simcox and George Eliot*. Oxford, Oxford University Press.

Melnyk, J. (1996). 'Emma Jane Worboise and *The Christian World Magazine*: Christian Publishing and Women's Empowerment'. *Victorian Periodicals Review* 29 (2) Summer: 131–45.

Mermin, D. (1993). *Godiva's Ride: Women of Letters in England, 1830–1880*. Bloomington and Indianapolis, Indiana University Press.

Merrifield, M. (1852). 'Some Thoughts on Children's Dress'. *Sharpe's London Magazine* **2 n.s.**: 65–70.

Meynell, A. (1883). 'Bogeys of Provincial Life: Inelegance'. *Merry England* **1**: 385–90.

Meynell, A. (1883). 'Lovely and Pleasant in their Lives'. *Merry England* **1**: 108–13.

Meynell, A. (1965). 'Miss Mitford' in *The Wares of Autolycus: Selected Literary Essays of Alice Meynell*. London, Oxford University Press: 82–5.

Meynell, A. (1965). *The Wares of Autolycus: Selected Literary Essays of Alice Meynell*. London, Oxford University Press.

Meynell, V. (1929). *Alice Meynell: a Memoir*. London, Jonathan Cape.

Mitchell, S. (1984). 'Sharpe's London Magazine' in *British Literary Magazines: The Victorian and Edwardian Age 1837–1913*. A. Sullivan. Westport, Connecticut, The Greenwood Press. **III**: 393–7.

Mitford, M.R. (1835). *Belford Regis or Sketches of a Country Town*. London, Richard Bentley.

Mitford, M.R. (1848?). *Our Village*. London, Henry G Bohn.

Mitford, M.R. (1893). *Our Village*. London, Macmillan and Co.

Mitford, M.R. (1893). 'Violeting' in *Our Village*. London, Macmillan and Co.: [59]–68.

Moring, M. (1993). 'George Eliot's Scrupulous Research'. *Victorian Periodicals Review* **XXVI** (Spring): 19–23.

Mozley, A. (1864). *Essays on Social Subjects*. London, Blackwoods.

Mozley, A. (1868). 'Clever Women'. *Blackwood's Magazine* **CIV** (**104**) October: 420–7.

Nestor, P. (1982). 'A new departure in women's publishing: *The English Woman's Journal* and the *Victoria Magazine*'. *Victorian Periodicals Review* **15** (3): 93–106.

O'Connor, T.P. (1889). 'The new journalism'. *New Review* **I**: 423–34.

Oliphant, M. (1855). 'Modern Novelists – Great and Small'. *Blackwood's Magazine* (May): 554–68.

Oliphant, M. (1856). 'Sidney Smith'. *Blackwood's Magazine* **LXXIX** (March): 350–61.

Oliphant, M. (1857). 'Modern Light Literature – Society'. *Blackwood's Magazine* (October): 423–8.

Oliphant, M. (1861). 'Augustus Welby Pugin'. *Blackwood's Magazine* (December): 670–98.

Oliphant, M. (1862). 'J.M.W. Turner, R.A'. *Blackwood's Magazine* (Jan): 17–34.

Oliphant, M. (1862). 'Sensation Novels'. *Blackwood's Magazine* **91** (May): 564–84.

Oliphant, M. (1867). 'Novels'. *Blackwood's Magazine* **102** (September): 257–80.

Oliphant, M. (1873). 'In London'. *Blackwood's Magazine* (February): 222–34.

Oliphant, M. (1874). 'Two Cities – two books'. *Blackwood's Magazine* **116** (July): 72–91.

Oliphant, M. (1875). 'Art in May'. *Blackwood's Magazine* (June): 747–64.

Oliphant, M. (1875). 'Michael Angelo'. *Blackwood's Magazine* (October): 461–82.

Oliphant, M. (1875). 'New Books'. *Blackwood's Magazine* **XVIII** (July): 83–99.

Oliphant, M. (1879). 'Hamlet'. *Blackwood's Magazine* (April): 462–81.

Oliphant, M. (1879). 'Two Ladies'. *Blackwood's Magazine* (February): 206–19.

Oliphant, M. (1885). 'London in May'. *Blackwood's Magazine*: 684–705.

Oliphant, M. (1886). 'London in January'. *Blackwood's Magazine* (February): 245–66.

Oliphant, M. (1887). 'In Maga's Library: The Old Saloon'. *Blackwood's Magazine* **141** (January): 126–53.

Oliphant, M. (1887). 'The Rev.W. Lucas Collins'. *Blackwood's Magazine* (May): 734–6.

Oliphant, M. (1887). 'The Old Saloon: The Literature of the Last Fifty Years'. *Blackwood's Magazine* (June): 737–61.

Oliphant, M. (1889). 'The Old Saloon'. *Blackwood's Magazine* **146** (August): 254–75.

Oliphant, M. (1894). 'The Looker-on'. *Blackwood's Magazine* **156** (August): 285–308.

Oliphant, M. (1895). 'Fancies of a Believer'. *Blackwood's Magazine* **157** (February): 135–49.

Oliphant, M. (1895). 'The Looker-on'. *Blackwood's Magazine* **157** (June): 902–29.

Oliphant, M. (1895). 'Men and Women'. *Blackwood's Magazine* **157** (April): 621–50.

Oliphant, M. (1896). 'The Anti-Marriage League'. *Blackwood's Magazine* **159**: 135–49.

Oliphant, M. (1897, 2nd ed.). *Annals of a Publishing House: William Blackwood and His Sons*. Edinburgh, London, William Blackwood and Sons.

Oliphant, M. (1897). 'The Sisters Brontë'. *Women Novelists of Queen Victoria's Reign: A Book of Appreciations*. A. Sergeant. London, Hurst & Blackett: 174–92.

Onslow, B. (1973). 'Environment and the Social Scene in the Works of Mrs. Gaskell, with some comparison with the Novels of Jane Austen and George Eliot'. University of Manchester, Manchester (unpublished thesis).

Onslow, B. (1995). 'Deceiving Images, Revealing Images: The Portrait in Victorian Women's Writing'. *Victorian Poetry* **33** (3–4), Autumn/Winter: 449–73.

Onslow, B. (1998). '"Humble Comments for the Ignorant": Margaret Oliphant's Criticism of Art and Society'. *Victorian Periodicals Review* **31** (1) Spring Special Issue: Victorian Women Editors and Critics: 9–31.

Palmegiano, E.M. (1976). *Women and British Periodicals, 1832–1876*. Toronto, Victorian Periodicals Newsletter, University of Toronto.

Parkes, B. (1986). 'What Can Educated Women Do?' in *Barbara Leigh Smith Bodichon and the Langham Place Group*. C.A. Lacey. London, Routledge & Kegan Paul: 150–62.

Parkes, B.R. (1864). 'The Use of a Special Periodical'. *Alexandra Magazine* **1** (September): 257–63.

Parkes, B.R. (1865). *Essays on Women's Work*. London, Alexander Strahan.

Parkes, B.R. (signed B.R.P.) (1864). 'A Review of the Last Six Years'. *English Woman's Journal* **12** (February): 361–8.

Parrinder, P. (1991). *Authors and Authority: English and American Criticism 1750–1990*. London, Macmillan.

Pattison, E.F.S. (Lady Dilke) (1872). 'The Exhibition of the Royal Academy of Arts'. *The Academy* (May 15th): 184–5.

Pattison, E.F.S. (1883). 'The Royal Academy II'. *The Academy* (19 May): 353–4.

Pennell, E.R. (1894). 'The Two Salons'. *Fortnightly Review* **n.s. LV**: 731–7.

Pennell, J. (1897). 'Art and the Daily Paper'. *Nineteenth Century* **42** (XLII): 653–62.

Petersen, L.H. (1998). 'Mother–Daughter Productions: Mary Howitt and Anna Mary Howitt in "Howitt's Journal", "Household Words", and Other Mid-Victorian Publications'. *Victorian Periodicals Review* **31** (1) Spring Special Issue: Victorian Women Editors and Critics: 9–31.

Pichanick, V.K. (1980). *Harriet Martineau: The Woman and Her Work, 1803–76*. Ann Arbor, University of Michigan Press.

Pinney, T., (ed.) (1963). *Essays of George Eliot*. London, Routledge and Kegan Paul.

Porritt, E. (c 1901). 'Newspaper Work when the Century was Young'. *Progress of British Newspapers in the 19th Century Illustrated*. London, Simpkin, Marshall, Hamilton, Kent & Co. Ltd: 19–21.

Porter, M.G. (1898). *Annals of a Publishing House: William Blackwood and His Sons*. Edinburgh, London, William Blackwood and Sons.

Pykett, L. (1990). 'Reading the Periodical Press: Text and Context' in *Investigating Victorian Journalism*. L. Brake, A. Jones and L. Madden. London, Macmillan: 1–18.

Pykett, L. (1992). *The 'Improper Feminine': The Women's Sensation Novel and the New Woman Writing*. London, New York, Routledge.

R., E. (1861). 'The Domestic Grievance'. *St James's Magazine* **2**: 228–34.

Reid, W. (1897). 'Some Reminscences of English Journalism'. *Nineteenth Century* **42** (**XLII**) July: 55–66.

Riddell, M.J.H. (nd). *The Rich Husband*. Philadelphia, T B Peterson & Brothers.

Ritchie, A.T. (1893). 'Introduction' in *Our Village*. London, Macmillan and Co.: (vii–liii).

Robinson, S.C. (1995). 'Editing *Belgravia*: M E Braddon's Defense of "Light Literature"'. *Victorian Periodicals Review* **28**: (2) Summer: 109–22.

Robson, A. (1987). 'The noble sphere of feminism'. *Victorian Periodicals Review* **XX**: 102–7.

Ross, I. (1936). *Ladies of the Press: The Story of Women in Journalism by an Insider*. New York, London, Harper & Brothers.

Rye, M.S. (1859). The Rise and Progress of Telegraphs. *Barbara Leigh Smith Bodichon and the Langham Place Group*. C.A. Lacey. London, 1987, Routledge & Kegan Paul: 287–91.

Sadleir, M. (1944). *Things Past*. London, Constable.

Saintsbury, G. (1883). 'The Young England Movement'. *Merry England* **1**.

Sala, G.A. (1868). 'The Cant of Modern Criticism'. *Belgravia* **4** (February): 44–55.

Sale-Barker, L. (1885). 'The Editor's Corner'. *Little Wide-Awake* (January): 31–2.

Sanders, V. (1986). *Reason over Passion: Harriet Martineau and the Victorian Novel*. Sussex, Harvester Press.

Scheuerle, W.H. (1984). 'Temple Bar' in *British Literary Magazines: The Victorian and Edwardian Age 1837–1913*. A. Sullivan. Westport, Connecticut, The Greenwood Press. **III**: 403–7.

Schmidt, B.Q. (1983). 'The Patron as Businessman: George Murray Smith (1824–1901)'. *Victorian Periodicals Review* **16**: 3–14.

Scott, J.W.R. (1950). *The Story of the Pall Mall Gazette*. London, OUP.

Scott, J.W.R. (1952). *The Life and Death of Newspaper*. London, Methuen & Co.

Scott, R. (1992). 'The Sunday Periodical: *Sunday at Home*'. *Victorian Periodicals Review* **XXV** (4) Winter: 158–62.

Sergeant, A. (1897). *Women Novelists of Queen Victoria's Reign: A Book of Appreciations*. London, Hurst & Blackett: 174–92.

Shand, A.I. (1879). 'Contemporary Literature: VIII Newspaper Offices'. *Blackwood's Magazine* (October): 641–62.

Shand, A.I. (1886). 'The Novelists and their Patrons'. *Fortnightly Review* XL **n.s.** (July–Dec): 25–35.

Shand, A.I. (1897). 'Contemporary Literature: III Magazine Writers'. *Blackwood's Magazine* (February): 225–47.

Sharps, J.G. (1970). *Mrs Gaskell's Observation and Invention. A Study of her Non-Biographic Works*. Sussex, Fontwell Linden Press.

Shattock, J. (19). 'Showman, Lion-Hunter, or Hack: The Quarterly Editor at Mid-Century'. *Victorian Periodicals Review* **16**: (**3/4**): 89–103.

Shattock, J. (1993). *The Oxford Guide to British Women Writers*. Oxford, Oxford University Press.

Shattock, J. and M. Wolff, (eds) (1982). *The Victorian Periodical Press: Samplings and Soundings*.

Showalter, E. (1978). *A Literature of Their Own: British Women Novelists from Bronte to Lessing*. London, Virago.

Simcox, E. (1883). '*Groundwork of Economics* (review)'. *The Academy* (October 27): 275–6.

Simcox, E. (1887). 'The Capacity of Women'. *The Nineteenth Century* **XXII**: 391–402. Reprinted in *Prose by Victorian Women: an anthology*. B. Andrea and S. Mitchell, Garland: 584–97.

Spatt, H.S. (1985). 'The Aesthetics of Editorship: Creating Taste in the Victorian Art World' in *Innovators and Preachers*. J.H. Wiener: 43–60.

Spender, D. (1986). *Mothers of the Novel: A Hundred Good Women Writers before Jane Austen*. London, New York, Pandora Press.

Srebrnik, P.T. (1986). *Alexander Strahan: Victorian Publisher*. Michigan, University of Michigan.

Stead, W.T. (1892). 'Young Women and Journalism'. *The Young Woman* **1** (Oct 1892–Sept 1893): 12–14.

Stokes, J. (1989). *In the Nineties*. London, Harvester.

Storey, G., K. Tillotson and N. Burgis (eds) (1988). *Letters of Charles Dickens* (10 vols) Vol 6. Oxford, Clarendon.

Storey, G., K. Tillotson and A. Easson (eds) (1993). *Letters of Charles Dickens* Vol 7. Oxford, Clarendon.

Stott, M. (1985). *Before I go: reflections on my life and times*. London, Virago.

Sullivan, A., (ed.) (1984). *British Literary Magazines: The Victorian and Edwardian Age 1837–1913*. Westport, Connecticut, The Greenwood Press.

Sutherland, J. (1976). *Victorian Novelists and Publishers*. Chicago, London, University of Chicago Press, Athlone Press.

Sutherland, J. (1991). *Mrs. Humphry Ward: Eminent Victorian, Pre-Eminent Edwardian*. Oxford, New York, Oxford University Press.

Thal, H.V. (1979). *Eliza Lynn Linton: The Girl of the Period*. London, Boston, Sydney, George Allen & Unwin.

Thomson, K. (1845). 'Memorials of the Departed Great'. *Bentley's Miscellany* **XVII**: 182–90.

Thwaite, M.F. (1967). Introduction. *Little Wide-Awake: an Anthology from Victorian Children's and Periodicals*. L. De Vries. London, Arthur Barker: 7–11.

Tillotson, K. (1954). *Novels of the Eighteen-Forties*. Oxford, Oxford University Press.

Tonna, C.E. (1834). 'Introduction'. *Christian Lady's Magazine* 1 (January): 1–6.

Tonna, C.E. (1834). 'Preface'. *Christian Lady's Magazine* 1 (Jan–June): i–iii.

Tonna, C.E. (1834). 'Unguarded Hours (Editorial Response)'. *Christian Lady's Magazine* 1: 330–5.

Tonna, C.E. (1843). 'Preface'. *Christian Lady's Magazine* XIX: i–iii.

Tonna, C.E. (1845). 'Preface'. *Christian Lady's Magazine* XXIII: i–ii.

Tredrey, F.D. (1954). *The House of Blackwood 1804–1954*. Edinburgh, London, William Blackwood and Sons.

Trela, D.J. (1995). 'Introduction: Discovering the Gentle Subversive'. *Margaret Oliphant: Critical Essays on a Gentle Subversive*. D.J. Trela. Selinsgrove, London, Susquehanna UP, Associated University Presses: pp 11–27.

Trela, D.J. (1996). 'Introduction: Nineteenth Century Women and Periodicals'. *Victorian Periodicals Review* 29 (2) Summer: 89–94.

Trevelyan, J.P. (1932). *The Life of Mrs. Humphry Ward*. London, Constable.

Tuchman, G. and N. Fortin (1989). *Edging Women Out: Victorian Novelists, Publishers and Social Change*. New Haven, Yale University Press.

Tweedie, M.A. (1894). 'A Chat with Mrs. Lynn Linton'. *Temple Bar* (July): 355–64.

unsigned (1858). 'The "Saturday Review" and the "English Woman's Journal": The Reviewer Reviewed'. *The English Woman's Journal* I (3 May): 201–4.

unsigned (1868). 'The Father of the/The Girl of the Period'. *The Court Suburb Magazine* I (1): 40–1.

unsigned (1868). 'Literary Notices'. *The Court Suburb Magazine* I: 286.

unsigned (1878). 'Women's Newspapers: A Sketch of the Periodical Literature Devoted to the Woman Question'. *Englishwoman's Review* LXVI (15 October): 433–40.

Van Arsdel, R.T. (1982). 'Mrs. Florence Fenwick-Miller and the *Woman's Signal,* 1895–1899'. *Victorian Periodicals Review* XV: 107–18.

Ward, M. (1891). 'Noticeable Books – Philomythus'. *Nineteenth Century* XXIX (May): 68–74.

Ward, M.H. (1885). 'The New National Gallery at Amsterdam'. *Macmillan's Magazine* 52 (September): 383–91.

Warren, M. (1858). 'Preface'. *The Ladies' Treasury* 1: iii–iv.

Watson, V. (nd). *Mary Russell Mitford*. London, Evans Brothers.

Webb, R.K. (1960). *Harriet Martineau: A Radical Victorian*. London, Heinemann.

White, C. (1970). *Women's Magazines 1693–1968*. London, Michael Joseph.

Wiener, J.H. (1985). 'Edmund Yates: The Gossip as Editor' in *Innovators and Preachers*. J.H. Wiener. Westport: 259–74.

Williams, R. (1961). *The Long Revolution*. London, Chatto & Windus.

Wolff, R.L. (1974). 'Devoted Disciple: The Letters of Mary Elizabeth Braddon to Sir Edward Bulwer-Lytton, 1862–1873'. *Harvard Library Bulletin* XXII (January, April): 5–35, 129–61.

Wolff, R.L. (1979). *Sensational Victorian: The Life and Fiction of Mary Elizabeth Braddon*. New York, London, Garland.

Wood, C. (1887). 'Mrs. Henry Wood. In Memoriam'. *The Argosy* XLIII (April, May, June): 251–70, 334–53, 422–42.

Woods, H.E. (1899–1900). 'Should Clever Women Marry?' *Womanhood* IV: 375.

Yonge, C. (1851). 'Hints on Reading'. *The Monthly Packet* 2: 478–80.

Yonge, C. (1851). 'Preface'. *The Monthly Packet* 1 (Jan–June): i–iv.

Index

For ease of reference the definite article has been omitted from the titles of periodicals. References in **bold** are entries in the Biographical Appendix.